Network Analysis, Architecture, and Design

THIRD EDITION

The Morgan Kaufmann Series in Networking
Series Editor, David Clark, M.I.T.

For further information on these books and for a list of forthcoming titles, please visit our Web site at http://www.mkp.com.

Network Analysis, Architecture, and Design

THIRD EDITION

James D. McCabe

ELSEVIER

Amsterdam • Boston • Heidelberg • London
New York • Oxford • Paris • San Diego
San Francisco • Singapore • Sydney • Tokyo

Morgan Kaufmann Publishers is an imprint of Elsevier

MORGAN KAUFMANN PUBLISHERS

Acquisitions Editor	Rick Adams
Publishing Services Manager	George Morrison
Editorial Assistant	Kimberlee Honjo
Composition	Integra Software Services
Copyeditor	Carol Leyba
Proofreader	Phyllis Coyne et al. Proofreading Service
Indexer	Michael Ferreira
Interior printer	The Maple-Vail Book Group
Cover printer	Phoenix Color Corporation
Cover Design	Dick Hannus
Cover Image	Havi Hoffman "Teaching Space to Curve" (Sundial Bridge)

Morgan Kaufmann Publishers is an imprint of Elsevier.
30 Corporate Drive, Suite 400, Burlington, MA 01803, USA

This book is printed on acid-free paper.

Library of Congress Cataloging-in-Publication Data
(Application submitted)

ISBN: 978-0-12-370480-1

For information on all Morgan Kaufmann publications, visit our Web site at www.mkp.com or www.books.elsevier.com

Printed in the United States of America
07 08 09 10 11   10 9 8 7 6 5 4 3 2 1

Dedication

For Jean and Ruth, Ron and Pam, Seana and Riley. This is also for Shelby, whose artistic skill I endeavor to replicate in my writings.

Foreword

Jim McCabe's third edition of *Network Analysis, Architecture, and Design* defines a disciplined approach to network architecture and design. Jim's approach addresses the critical elements required to successfully design and deploy networks in an increasingly complex environment. There is constant pressure to deploy new features and services while increasing the quality of existing services and network security. In addition, market forces are pressing network operators to closely manage investment in new infrastructure and decrease operations and maintenance costs. In the three years since Jim released the second edition the landscape has fundamentally changed. It is no longer possible to overbuild the network and hope to "grow" into it. Converged services, Voice over IP, and emerging IPv6 deployments are forcing network architects to return to the fundamentals of engineering best practices.

Jim's focus on requirements analysis, design traceability, and design metrics is right on target. Jim has developed a mature, repeatable methodology, that when followed properly, produces well-engineered and scalable networks. This is not a book on the theory of network architecture and design, it is a practical guide based on Jim's wealth of experience. The concepts have been proven in the successful deployment of numerous networks.

The timing of this edition could not be better. We are at the start of a major transition, deploying the next generation of networks. Jim provides the guidance to successfully architect and deploy them.

John McManus, US Department of Commerce

Contents

1   Introduction

5 Network Architecture

8   Performance Architecture

9   Security and Privacy Architecture

10   Network Design

Preface

Network Analysis, Architecture, and Design, Third Edition is about making intelligent, informed network engineering decisions. This includes processes to develop and validate requirements for your project, and applying them in making architecture and design decisions. These processes have been adopted by corporations, universities, and government agencies around the world.

Although this book focuses on networking, the decision-making processes can be applied to any IT engineering project, from developing a national network to a small enterprise LAN, from an overall network upgrade to focusing on particular capabilities such as VPNs, QoS, or MPLS. For example, the processes in this book have recently been applied to projects to develop an external security perimeter (as part of a defense-in-depth strategy) and an IPv6 addressing architecture.

During the ten years that span the publications of the first and second editions of *Network Analysis, Architecture, and Design*, several concepts in this book have entered the mainstream of network engineering. Traffic flow analysis, and the coupling of requirements to traffic flows, is increasingly important in providing security and performance across the network. Developing and validating requirements to formally prepare for the network design are essential to ensure accuracy and consistency within the design.

Network Analysis, Architecture, and Design, Third Edition provides an updated design section that includes how to evaluate and select vendors, vendor products, and service providers, as well as diagramming the design. The analysis sections have also been updated to couple requirements to the architecture and design, including requirements validation and traceability.

Approach

Network Analysis, Architecture, and Design, Third Edition will help you to understand and define your network architecture and design. It examines the entire system, from users and their applications, to the devices and networks that support them.

This book is designed to be applied to undergraduate and graduate programs in network engineering, architecture, and design, as well as for professional study for IT engineers and management (including CTOs and CIOs). It is structured to follow the logical progression of analyzing, developing, and validating requirements, which form the basis for making decisions regarding the network architecture, which in turn forms the basis for making network design decisions. When I teach network analysis, architecture, and design at universities, corporations, or conferences, I find that students readily adapt the material in this book as part of their engineering process.

In this book, I provide you with step-by-step procedures for doing network analysis, architecture, and design. I have refined this process through years of architecting and designing large-scale networks for government agencies, universities, and corporations, and have incorporated the ideas and experiences of expert designers throughout the book. Like an open standard for a technology or protocol, the procedures in this book are the result of several contributions, and offer you the cumulative experience of many network architects and designers.

I tackle some of the hard problems in network analysis, architecture, and design, and address real architecture and design challenges, including how to:

- Gather, derive, define, and validate real requirements for your network
- Determine how and where addressing and routing, security, network management, and performance are implemented in the network, and how they interact with each other
- Evaluate and select vendors, vendor products, and service providers for your project
- Developing traceability between requirements, architecture decisions, and design decisions
- Determine where to apply routing protocols (RIP/RIPv2, OSPF, BGP-4, MPLS), as well as classful and classless IP addressing mechanisms
- Determine where to apply performance mechanisms, including quality of service, service-level agreements, and policies in your network

In addressing challenges such as these, I provide guidelines, examples, and general principles to help you in making the tough decisions. You may find some or all of them to be useful, and I encourage you to modify them to fit your architecture and design needs.

For those using this book in a class or for self-study, there are a number of exercises at the end of each chapter. In addition, the Web page for this book at the publisher's Web site (www.mkp.com) contains additional material useful in your progress through the book, as well as a password-protected solutions manual to the exercises available to instructors.

Roadmap

The first four chapters are based on the systems approach, requirements analysis, and flow analysis from the first edition. They have been updated to include changes and improvements in network analysis since the release of the second edition. Chapter 1 introduces network analysis, including the systems approach, and provides definitions and concepts that will be used throughout the book. Chapters 2 and 3 focus on the concepts and process of determining requirements for your network, and Chapter 4 discusses how traffic flow analysis can be used to couple performance requirements to various traffic flows.

Chapters 5 through 9 cover the network architecture process. Chapter 5 provides an introduction to network architecture, developing internal and external relationships within and between major functions (addressing and routing, security, network management, and performance) in the network. Chapters 6 through 9 detail each of these major functions, developing component and reference architectures that describe their internal and external relationships.

Chapter 10 discusses the design process. This takes the results of the previous chapters and applies them toward making design decisions, including how to evaluate and select vendors, vendor products, and service providers, and diagramming the design.

For appropriate chapters, I have provided a list of recommended reading that will be useful to you in understanding the concepts of that chapter. Since this book introduces a fair number of new concepts, I also provide an extensive glossary of acronyms and terms that are used throughout the book.

Acknowledgments

First of all, many thanks to Pat Dunnington (NASA) and John McManus (Department of Commerce) for giving me the opportunity to refine the latest design concepts during my time at NASA. I would also like to thank Havi Hoffman for use of her photo "Teaching Space to Curve" as the front cover of this book.

Also, thanks to Tony Arviola and Bessie Whitaker of NASA for their help in adopting the concepts of this book and applying them to several engineering projects across NASA.

The material presented in this book is based on a compilation of my own professional experiences and those of other members of the networking community. As always, I am solely responsible for any errors in this book. The analysis, architecture, and design processes are continually evolving, and any feedback from you on how to improve these processes is most welcome. Questions, comments, and suggestions can be sent to me at doowah_1@yahoo.com or through Morgan Kaufmann Publishing.

The people at Morgan Kaufmann Publishing have been a wonderful influence on the development of this edition. Many thanks to Dr. David Clark (Series Editor), Rick Adams (Senior Acquisitions Editor), Rachel Roumeliotis (Associate Editor), and Kathryn Liston (Project Manager).

The chapters on requirements and flow analyses are based on early work on data flow analysis done while I was at the Numerical Aerodynamic Simulation (NAS) facility at NASA Ames Research Center in Mountain View, CA. I owe much thanks to Bruce Blaylock, who had the foresight to encourage this work, as well as the tenacity to help me through the process.

CHAPTER CONTENTS

1

Introduction

I begin this book with a description of the analysis, architecture, and design processes. Many of the concepts and terms used throughout this book are introduced and defined in this chapter. Some of these concepts may be new to you, while others are presented in a different light. Glossaries of terms and acronyms are presented at the end of this book for easy reference.

1.1 Objectives

In this chapter I will introduce the fundamental concepts of this book: that the network is part of a system that provides services to its end users; that there are processes for developing an analysis, an architecture, and a design for a network; and that there are ways to characterize a network.

1.2 Preparation

In order to understand and apply the concepts in this chapter, you should be familiar with basic networking concepts. This includes the functions and features of the TCP/IP protocol suite, technologies such as the variants of Ethernet, synchronous optical network (SONET), and wave division multiplexing (WDM), and the basics of network routing, security, performance, and management.

1.3 Background

Network analysis, architecture, and design have traditionally been considered art, combining an individual's particular rules on evaluating and choosing network technologies; knowledge about how technologies, services, and protocols can be meaningfully combined; experience in what works and what doesn't; along with (often arbitrary) selections of network architectures. However, as with other types of art, success of a particular network design often depends primarily on who is doing the work, with results that are rarely reproducible. This may have been acceptable in the early days of networking, when networks were more of a hobby than a critical resource and did not directly support revenue generation. Today, however, networks are embedded within our work, home, and outside environments. They are considered "mission-critical"[1] to corporate success and provide near real-time access to information throughout the world. As such, the design of a network must be logical, reproducible, and defensible. This premise is the foundation for this book.

Traditionally, network analysis, architecture, and design have been based on developing and applying a set of rules for the network. In developing a set of rules, an individual may draw from personal experience as well as from general rules such as the 80/20 rule (where 80% of a network's traffic is local and 20% is remote) or the adage "bridge when you can, route when you must" (bridging being simpler, easier, and cheaper at the time). As we see later in this book, although both of these rules are ancient from the perspective of networking history, they still apply today, albeit in modified form. Such rules were useful when there weren't many choices in network technologies and services, and when the differences between choices were clearly understood. But times have changed, and our notion of designing networks must adapt to the variety of options now available to us, the variety of services that networks can offer to end users, and the subtle nuances brought about by combining network technologies, techniques, and services.

Example 1.1.

Consider the subtleties in network behavior introduced through the use of virtual private networks, intranets, or VPNs. VPNs are quite useful; however, care must be taken to understand their potential impact on network security, routing, and management. Since VPNs tunnel (encapsulate) and can encrypt traffic flowing across a network, they often require more effort to secure, monitor, and manage. How VPNs impact security, routing, and management will be considered during the architecture process.

Network analysis, architecture, and design have traditionally focused on *capacity planning*, which is over-engineering a network to provide an amount of capacity (also known as *bandwidth*) estimated to accommodate most short- and long-term traffic fluctuations over the life cycle of the design. The result is a bandwidth

---

[1] Ambiguous terms such as these will be defined in this chapter.

"buffer" that can handle these fluctuations. As network traffic grows over time, this bandwidth buffer is reduced, and users experience problems related to traffic congestion. This is an inefficient use of network resources, wasting money up front in resources that are not used while failing to provide the flexibility needed to adapt to users' changing traffic requirements. Network bandwidth is only one component of network resources that we must consider. We also need to consider how delay through the network, as well as network reliability, maintainability, and availability (RMA), can be optimized. In today's evolving networks, delay and reliability can be more important than capacity.

In this book we explore how the analysis, architecture, and design processes have changed and how they continue to change. We discuss how these processes work together in engineering a new or existing network. We approach networks from a different perspective—as a system providing services to its users—and we discuss how networks can be designed to provide many different types of services to users. In taking this approach we emphasize network analysis, which helps us understand what is required of a network in supporting its customers and their applications and devices. As we will see, these processes require an investment in time and effort, but the return on investment is significant. These are powerful tools that can help you build better networks, improving the ability of your organization to get its work done.

This book begins by applying a systems methodology to networking. This methodology is relatively new, and you will learn a number of useful definitions in regard to network analysis, architecture, and design. The rest of this book is logically divided into three sections. The first section covers the analysis process: specifically, how to develop requirements, understand traffic flows, and conduct a risk analysis. The analysis process prepares you for dealing with network architecture, discussed in the second section. Here I describe how to make technology and topology choices for your network, how to understand the relationships among the various functions within your network, and how to use this information to develop an architecture. In the final section the network architecture is used as input for the design process, where location information, equipment, and vendor selections are used to detail the design. Information flows between analysis, architecture, and design processes are presented in Figure 1.1.

Network analysis, architecture, and design will help you identify and apply network services and performance levels needed to satisfy your users. Through these processes you will be able to understand the problems you are trying to address with the new network; determine the service and performance objectives

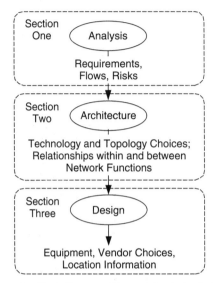

FIGURE 1.1   Information Flows Between Network Analysis, Architecture, and Design

needed to tackle these problems; and architect and design the network to provide the desired services and performance levels.

1.4   Overview of Analysis, Architecture, and Design Processes

Network analysis, architecture, and design are processes used to produce designs that are logical, reproducible, and defensible. These processes are interconnected, in that the output of one process is used directly as input to the next, thus creating flows of information from analysis to architecture, and from architecture to design.

Network analysis entails learning what users, their applications, and devices need from the network (Figure 1.2). It is also about understanding network behavior under various situations. Network analysis also defines, determines, and describes relationships among users, applications, devices, and networks. In the process, network analysis provides the foundation for all the architecture and design decisions to follow. The purpose of network analysis is twofold: first, to listen to users and understand their needs; and second, to understand the system.

In analyzing a network we examine the state of the existing network, including whatever problems it may be having. We develop sets of problem statements

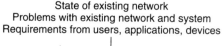

Descriptions of problem statements for network
Descriptions of requirements for network
Descriptions of traffic flows
Mappings of applications and devices to network
Descriptions of potential risks

FIGURE 1.2   Inputs To and Outputs From the Network Analysis Process

and objectives that describe what our target network will be addressing. And we develop requirements and traffic flows, as well as mappings of users, applications, and devices, in support of our problem statements and objectives. As such, network analysis helps us understand what problems we are trying to solve, and in the process we compile information that will be used in developing the architecture and design.

Example 1.2.

The analysis, architecture, and design processes can be applied to any network project, regardless of size or scope. Since we are developing sets of problem statements, objectives, and requirements as input to the analysis process, we can scale the architecture and design to meet the scope of the project. Consider the use of VPNs from Example 1.1. We can develop problem statements, objectives, and requirements for VPNs in an existing network, and develop an analysis, architecture, and design solely around a VPN deployment.

Network architecture uses the information from the analysis process to develop a conceptual, high-level, end-to-end structure for the network. In developing the network architecture we make technology and topology choices for the network. We also determine the relationships among the functions of the network (addressing/routing, network management, performance, and security), and how to optimize the architecture across these relationships. There usually is not a single "right" architecture or design for a network; instead there are several that will work, some better than others. The architecture and design processes focus on finding those best candidates for architecture and design (optimized across several parameters) for your conditions.

The network architecture process determines sets of technology and topology choices; the classes of equipment needed; and the relationships among network functions (Figure 1.3).

Network design provides *physical* detail to the architecture. It is the target of our work, the culmination of analysis and architecture processes. Physical detail includes blueprints and drawings of the network; selections of vendors and service providers; and selections of equipment (including equipment types and configurations) (Figure 1.4).

Descriptions of problem statements for network
Descriptions of requirements for network
Descriptions of traffic flows
Mappings of applications and devices to network
Descriptions of potential risks

Technology choices for network
Topology choices for network
Relationships between network functions
Equipment classes

FIGURE 1.3   Inputs To and Outputs From the Network Architecture Process

Technology selections for network
Topology selections for network
Relationships between network functions
Equipment classes

Vendor selections for network
Service Provider selections for network
Equipment selections for network
Blueprints and drawings of network

FIGURE 1.4   Inputs To and Outputs From the Network Design Process

During network design we use an evaluation process to make vendor, service provider, and equipment selections, based on input from the network analysis and architecture. You will learn how to set design goals, such as minimizing network costs or maximizing performance, as well as how to achieve these goals, through mapping network performance and function to your design goals and evaluating your design against its goals to recognize when the design varies significantly from these goals. Network design is also about applying the trade-offs, dependencies, and constraints developed as part of the network architecture. Trade-offs, such as cost versus performance or simplicity versus function, occur throughout the design process, and a large part of network design concerns recognizing such trade-offs (as well as interactions, dependencies, and constraints) and optimizing the design among them. As part of the design process you will also learn how to develop evaluation criteria for your designs.

As we show throughout the remainder of this book, network analysis, architecture, and design combine several things—requirements, traffic flows, architectural and design goals, interactions, trade-offs, dependencies, constraints, and evaluation criteria—to optimize a network's architecture and design across several parameters. These parameters are chosen and analyzed during the analysis process and prioritized and evaluated during the architecture and design processes. On completion of these processes you should have a thorough understanding of the network and plenty of documentation to take you forward to implementation, testing, and integration.

Example 1.3.

A network's architecture and design are analogous to the architecture and design of a home. Both the network and home architecture describe the major functional components of each (for the network: network management, addressing and routing, security and privacy, and performance; for the home: plumbing, electrical, HVAC [heating, vacuum, air conditioning], framing) and the relationships among them (for the network: interactions, dependencies, trade-offs, and constraints; for the home: where each component is placed relative to the others). The network and home designs are also similar in that they both provide physical detail to the architecture. For the network this means where major network devices are located; and, for the home, where ducts, outlets, faucets, drains, and so forth are located.

1.4.1 Process Components

We now add detail to the analysis, architecture, and design processes. Each of these processes has actions that will be taken by project personnel and results or products of each action. There is also input to begin the process. Thus, the processes are expanded in Figure 1.5.

Each of the processes and products has components that describe specific actions or results. The full set of process components is shown in Figure 1.6.

This set of process components represents a complete implementation of network analysis, architecture, and design, and forms the basis for the remainder of this book. Some components, however, may be reduced in importance or removed

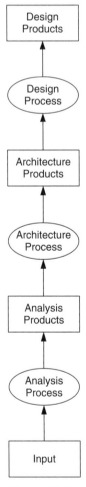

FIGURE 1.5   Processes Shown with Associated Input and Products

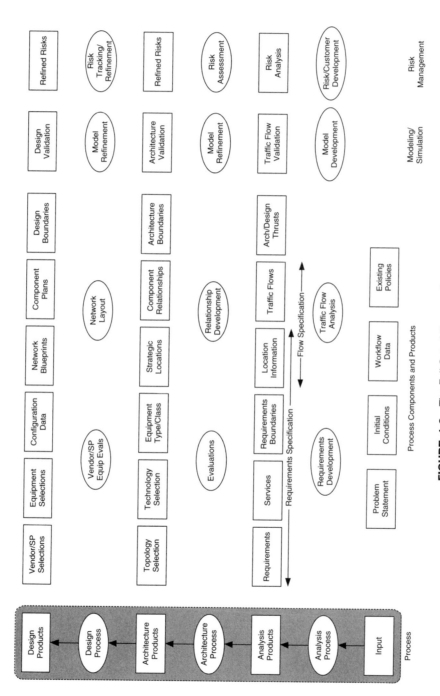

FIGURE 1.6   The Full Set of Process Components

on a per-project basis. Throughout this book we discuss which components are necessary, and which may be reduced in importance.

1.4.2 Tactical and Strategic Significance

Network analysis, architecture, and design are part of the engineering process that forms the basis of networking projects. Such projects have immediate, tactical (near-term), and strategic (long-term) significance, and networking projects should consider all of these areas. I recommend that network projects have a plan that includes current, near-term, and long-term targets. While the current target will be a network design, the near-term and long-term targets can be proposed enhancements to the current target, lists of problem statements, objectives, and requirements for near-term and long-term, or all of these. For example, Figure 1.7 shows a one-year/three-year/five-year project plan.

The idea behind this plan is to develop a network design that will be implemented within one year, will prepare us for any changes we might need to make to the network within three years, and will keep us in the direction of what is planned for five years in the future. The long-term (five-year) target is a rough estimate. We will likely not know what new networking technologies, services, or levels of performance will be available five years out, nor will we know how our customers' business plans will change, nor what network problems will arise during that time. But we should have an idea of where we want to be, with the understanding that we may have to make significant changes to the long-term target during those five years. Thus the long-term target is variable.

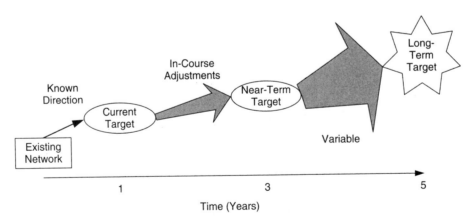

FIGURE 1.7   A One-/Three-/Five-Year Project Plan

The current (one-year) target should be well understood and is the focus of our analysis, architecture, and design effort. In between the one-year and five-year targets, the near-term (three-year) target is intended to be somewhat flexible, yet better understood than the long-term target. A significant change in the long-term target (e.g., the result of a planned merger, outsourcing, or major change in a company's business) can be mediated by course corrections in the near-term plan.

Although a one-/three-/five-year plan is shown here, the important concept is to have both tactical and strategic approaches to your plan. Experience shows that one-/three-/five-year plans are very good starting points, but depending on your customers, you may rapidly evolve your network with a six-month/one-year/two-year plan, or take a longer-term view with a one-year/five-year/ten-year plan. I have seen all of these plans work to meet the needs of their customers.

Example 1.4.

Voice over IP (VoIP) is of interest to many organizations and is an example of a network project that would benefit from tactical and strategic plans. If we apply the one-/three-/five-year plan discussed earlier, the current target (one-year plan) would include the network design for VoIP, based on what is achievable within one year, and the problem statements, objectives, and requirements that result from the requirements analysis process. For example, the current target may be a design that only prepares for VoIP by improving the overall reliability of the network. The near-term target (three-year plan) would conceivably build on the current target to add or expand VoIP to those areas that can support it. The long-term target (five-year plan) would address any major changes that occurred over the previous four years, including advancements in VoIP technology and an assessment whether to continue with VoIP or evolve to new or different technologies.

These plans are intended to be iterative and should be regularly reviewed, on the order of twice yearly, once per year, or every two years, depending on your plan. At each iteration the current, near-term, and long-term targets are reviewed and checked against the ongoing sets of problem statements, objectives, and requirements developed during the analysis, architecture, and design processes. One iteration of the cycle (including network implementation, test, and acceptance) is shown in Figure 1.8.

Each iteration is an incremental step toward the near-term and long-term targets, as shown in Figure 1.9. The steps 1, 2, 3, and 4 correspond to the steps in the process shown in Figure 1.8. Thus each iteration is a full cycle as shown above.

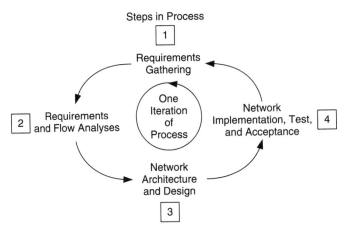

FIGURE 1.8   The Cyclic and Iterative Nature of Processes

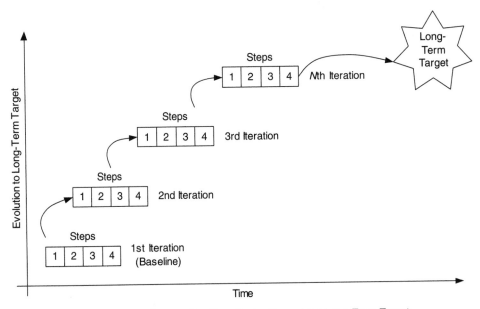

FIGURE 1.9   Process Iterations Evolve Toward the Long-Term Target

1.4.3 **Hierarchy and Diversity**

All of these processes center around two important characteristics of networks: their levels of hierarchy and diversity. *Hierarchy* is the degree of concentration of networks or traffic flows at interconnection points within the network, as well as the number of tiers of interconnection points within the network. In general, as networks grow in size and numbers of users, applications, and devices increase, hierarchies provide separation and structure within the network. Hierarchies are important because they help us in determining the sizes of networks, including routing and addressing configurations, and the scaling of network technologies, performance, and service levels. A key concept of this book is understanding these hierarchies, learning how and where they will occur, and learning how to take advantage of them.

Along with hierarchy, there must be some consideration for the degree of *diversity* (a.k.a. redundancy or interconnectivity) in the network design. As hierarchy provides structure in the network, diversity balances this structure by interconnecting the network at different levels in the design to provide greater performance through parts of the network. Diversity is important in that it provides a mechanism to achieve performance within a hierarchical structure. The dynamic between hierarchy and diversity is perhaps one of the most fundamental trade-offs in network architecture and design, and it shows up several times in the analysis, architecture, and design processes.

Hierarchy and diversity may be a bit confusing at this point, but this concept will become clearer as we progress through the book. Hierarchy is fundamental to networking (as it is throughout nature) because it provides a separation of the network into segments. These segments may be separate, smaller networks (subnets) or broadcast domains. Hierarchy is necessary when the amount of traffic on the network grows beyond the capacity of the network or when interactions between devices on the network result in congestion (e.g., broadcast storms).

Figure 1.10 illustrates levels of hierarchy and diversity in a network. This is a typical tree structure for a network, with circles representing networks or routers and lines representing the communications links between networks and/or routers. In this figure there are four levels of hierarchy, from core (or backbone) networks to access networks closest to users. Note that the end points of this tree (commonly referred to as *leaves*; they represent the end networks, devices, or users) all occur at the same level of hierarchy. This does not have to be the case; indeed, in most networks there are leaves at most levels of hierarchy.

An example of adding hierarchy to a network is changing from a flat (bridged or layer 2 switched) structure to a routed structure. This may be done to reduce the size of the broadcast domain or the number of devices reached by a broadcast message. Adding routing to the network breaks a broadcast domain into a number of smaller broadcast domains, and traffic flows are concentrated at routers. Figure 1.11 shows this scenario. Hierarchy is also added to networks when evolving from

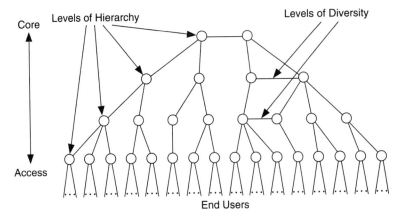

FIGURE 1.10   Hierarchy and Diversity in a Network

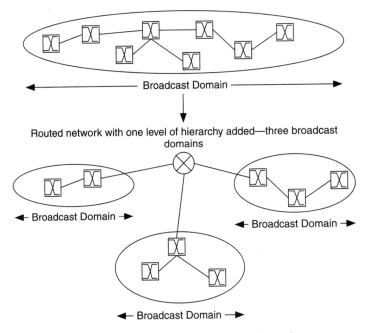

FIGURE 1.11   Hierarchy Added to a Network

a single autonomous system (AS) to connecting multiple ASs, as well as when migrating from Interior Gateway Protocols (IGPs) to Exterior Gateway Protocols (EGPs) and to policy-based routing.

A content delivery network (CDN) is an example of adding diversity to a network. A CDN bypasses the core of a network, where congestion is most likely to occur, and directly connects devices or networks lower in the hierarchy (Figure 1.12). This provides better, more predictable performance but can also affect the network hierarchy by modifying its routing behavior.

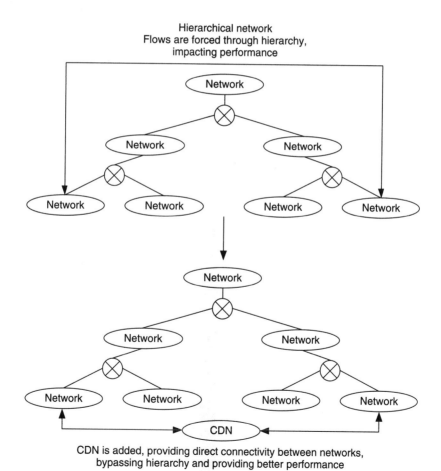

FIGURE 1.12   Diversity Added to a Network

1.4.4   Importance of Network Analysis

The importance of network analysis is emphasized in this book because experience has shown that networking personnel find it extremely valuable—once they are convinced of its importance. Analysis takes work, and when you know that there will be a payoff, you are more likely to do that work.

In this book you will learn how to gather and analyze network requirements and traffic flows. *Network requirements* are requests for capabilities in the network, usually in terms of performance and function, which are necessary for the success of that network. Network requirements can be gathered and/or derived from customers, applications, and devices. Such requirements are fundamental to a network's architecture and design because they form the basis for customer expectations and satisfaction. Requirements, in conjunction with measurements on the existing network (if there is one), are used to derive traffic flows (sets of network traffic that have some common attributes, such as source/destination address, information type, routing, or other end-to-end information). Analysis of these flows imparts location and directional information onto requirements. This is where performance requirements and architecture start to converge and is often the point in these processes where one can begin to see where "hot spots"—focal points for network performance—will appear in the network. As we will see, evaluating security risks is also part of the analysis process.

Results of the analysis process, the requirements and flow specifications, are then used as input for both network architecture and design. In developing the network architecture, a number of component architectures, targeting particular functions of the network, are evaluated. Desired component architectures are then combined into the reference architecture, which provides a high-level view of your network. This high-level view is then physically detailed during the network design process.

Network analysis is important in that it helps us understand the complexity and nuances of each network and the systems they support. Analysis also provides data upon which various decisions are made, and these data can and should be documented as part of an audit trail for the architecture and design processes. Such data help ensure that the resulting architecture and design are defensible.

Understanding Network and System Complexity

In general, networks and the systems they support are becoming increasingly complex. Part of this complexity lies in the sophistication of the capabilities provided by that network. Consider, for example, how services can be incorporated into a current state-of-the-art network. Infrastructure capacity planning, which often includes traffic over-engineering, may now be expanded to include support for delay-constrained applications and may contain a variety of capacity and delay control mechanisms, such as traffic shaping, quality of service at multiple levels in the network, service-level agreements to couple services to customers, and policies to govern and implement service throughout the network. (Note that *quality of service* refers to determining, setting, and acting on priority levels for traffic flows. A *service-level agreement* is an informal or formal contract between a provider and user that defines the terms of the provider's responsibility to the user and the type and extent of accountability if those responsibilities are not met. Finally, *policies* are high-level statements about how network resources are to be allocated among users.) Analysis of these mechanisms—how they work and interoperate—is covered in detail later in this book.

Network and system complexity is nonlinear. Network optimization must consider competing and often conflicting needs. In addition, multiple groups with differing ideas and desires (e.g., users, corporate management, network staff) influence the network design. The network is either designed by committee or through a systematic approach that the groups can agree on.

Networks have evolved to incorporate more sophisticated capabilities. Early (first-generation) networks focused on supporting basic connectivity between devices and on how to scale networks to support growing numbers of users (e.g., segmenting networks using bridges or routers). Second-generation networks focused on interoperability to expand the scope and scale of networks to allow connections among multiple disparate networks. We are currently at the stage in network evolution where service delivery is important to the success of users and their applications. This stage can be considered the third generation of networking. Figure 1.13 illustrates the various generations of networking and their interactions.

We are beginning to see steps toward next-generation capabilities, such as rudimentary decision making within the network. It may be expected that components of the network will evolve to become self-configurable and manageable, especially for those networks that must be configured or administered by end users (e.g., telecommuters, users of mobility/portability services). Indeed, this will become necessary as the complexity and performance of networks increase and as services offered by networks become more sophisticated. Grid networks are a clear step in this direction.

Users, applications, and devices are also evolving more sophisticated capabilities. An example of this is the dynamic between hierarchy and diversity that can be seen in the current Internet. As application and device traffic flows evolve to incorporate information regarding quality, performance, and cost (e.g., real-time

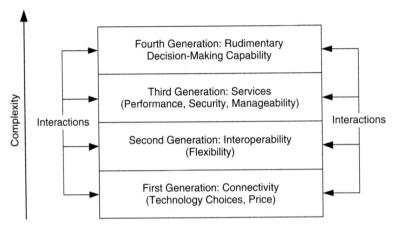

FIGURE 1.13   Generations of Networking

streaming media), it is expected that these characteristics can be used to ensure paths through the Internet that will support high-performance or high-quality delivery of such traffic. Hierarchy in the Internet often forces traffic flows through nonoptimal paths, crossing several ASs with differing performance and service characteristics, hindering high-performance, high-quality delivery. Figure 1.14 shows a hierarchy of multiple levels of networks from core (or backbone) network providers to access network providers. Traffic flows between end users may travel across several levels of this hierarchy.

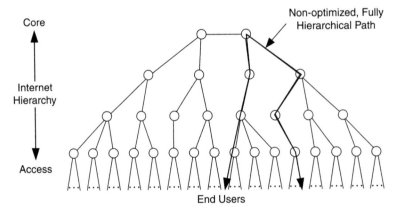

FIGURE 1.14   Hierarchy and Traffic Flow

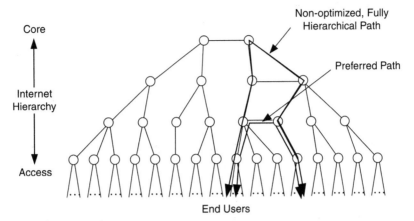

FIGURE 1.15 Diversity Added to Improve Performance of Select Traffic Flows

To counteract the impact of hierarchy, diversity can be introduced into the Internet at strategic points, providing shortcuts that bypass parts of the Internet. The result is that, for some select flows, paths are optimized for high-performance, high-quality delivery (Figure 1.15). The dynamic between hierarchy and diversity exists in all networks to some degree, and part of the analysis process is determining where and how to apply it. In Figure 1.15 connections are added between networks at the same level of hierarchy, in essence providing a "shortcut" or "bypass" around part of the Internet, resulting in better performance characteristics. This concept of adding diversity to improve performance along select paths can be readily applied to enterprise networks.

Analysis helps us understand how technologies influence networks, users, applications, and devices (and vice versa). This is important for gauging how users of the network will adapt to the network, which affects the overall life cycle of the network. Consider, for example, the evolution of routing protocols, shown in Figure 1.16. Although the Routing Information Protocol (RIP), an Interior Gateway Protocol (IGP) deployed as part of early TCP/IP releases, was simple and easy to use, its limitations were stressed as networks expanded to accommodate larger groups of users (workgroups) and even groups of networks (autonomous systems [ASs]). Routing technology adapted by adding hierarchy to routing, in terms of new IGPs such as Open Shortest Path First (OSPF), as well as in development of Exterior Gateway Protocols (EGPs) such as Border Gateway Protocol (BGP), which can accommodate hierarchy in groups of networks (AS hierarchy). This process continues today as high-level policies are being introduced to control

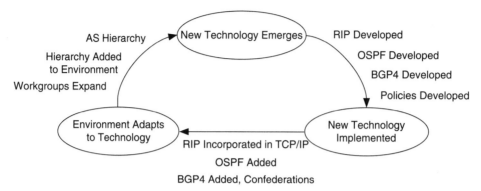

FIGURE 1.16   Routing Evolution

routing at a level above IGPs or EGPs, and BGP4 introduces hierarchy through grouping BGP4 routers into confederations. We discuss routing protocols in detail in the addressing and routing architecture (see Chapter 6).

Similarly, users, applications, and devices also influence their environment. As new, upgraded, or different users, applications, and devices are added to a network, the requirements on that network may change. The analysis process must examine how high-end computer and applications servers, data storage, analysis and archival systems, and specialized environment-specific devices such as PDAs, video cameras, or medical equipment impact the network.

Finally, the analysis process helps us understand the forces and changes at work within the system (network and its users, applications, and devices). Networks are highly dynamic, changing the rest of the system and being changed by the system. Some of the factors leading to change in the system include usage behavior and patterns; what, how, where, and when each user impacts the system; the emergence of new capabilities—for example, optical switching, faster central processing units (CPUs), and cheaper memory; and changes in scope and scale of the environment, including consolidation and outsourcing.

Architecture and Design Defensibility

An important (and often overlooked) part of network analysis is the documentation that provides information about decision making in the network architecture and design processes. During the analysis process we are gathering data that can be used to determine which architectural and design decisions need to be made, details regarding each decision (including reasons for each decision), dependencies between decisions, and any background material used to arrive at these decisions.

Data from network analysis, along with any decisions made during the process, can be documented to form an *audit trail*, that is, the set of documents, data, and decisions, for the architecture and design. Audit trails are useful for describing and defending a particular network architecture or design. An audit trail helps address questions such as "Why did you choose that technology?" "Why doesn't this new network perform as expected?" or "Why did this network cost so much?" Having documented your analysis of the existing network, the problems to be addressed, requirements for the new network, and all decisions made regarding that network, you will be able to answer questions at any time about your new network.

Decisions made regarding the network architecture and design need to be defensible from several perspectives: technical, in order to be able to address any technical challenges made against your architecture and design; budgetary, to ensure that network costs are within budget or to justify why a budget has been exceeded; schedule, to ensure that time frames for development, installation, testing, and operations are being met; and resources, such as personnel or equipment, to ensure that the customer has everything necessary to build and operate this network.

An audit trail is also useful as a historical document about the network. Over time, after the network is made operational, new network personnel can review this document to understand the logic behind the way the network was designed. Ideally, this document should be periodically reviewed, with new information added regarding changes to the network. Thus, an audit trail becomes a history for that network.

Experience shows that the set of documents, data, and decisions in an audit trail can be vital in making day-to-day tactical design decisions throughout the project. The investment in time at this phase of the project can save large amounts of time and resources later in the project.

The Web is a great tool to use in building an audit trail. Because an audit trail contains information about the old network, the new network, and decisions made about the new network, having this information easily accessible by those who use the network makes a lot of sense. Putting such information on internal Web pages allows easy access by everyone, and changes or additions to the audit trail can be seen immediately. Although there may be some information that your customer might not want everyone to view, such as the results of a risk analysis, most information usually can be accessible to everyone. For information that is restricted (need-to-know), hidden and password-protected Web pages can be used. Of course, when putting sensitive information at a common location, such as a Web site, sufficient security from outside attacks (hackers) should be provided.

An audit trail can be developed using standard word processing and spreadsheet software tools, and software tools specialized for this purpose are available. Problem statements, objectives, requirements, decisions, and all background data are entered into the audit trail, and all information is time stamped. Examples of audit trail information are presented later in this book.

1.4.5   Model for Network Analysis, Architecture, and Design

Networking traditionally has had little or no basis in analysis or architectural development, with designers often relying on technologies that are either most familiar to them or that are new, popular, or suggested by vendors and/or consultants. There are serious problems with this traditional approach. In particular, decisions may be made without the due diligence of analysis or architectural development, and such decisions, especially those made during the early phases of the project, are uninformed.

As a result, there may not be an audit trail for the architecture and design; and therefore, the architecture and design may not be defensible. In addition, such an architecture/design may lack consistency in its technological approach. Lacking data from analysis and architecture, we may not have a basis for making technology comparisons and trade-offs. And most importantly, without the proper requirements gathering and analysis, we cannot be sure if our network will meet the needs of its users. Therefore, network analysis, architecture, and design are fundamental to the development of a network.

Network analysis, architecture, and design are similar to other engineering processes in that they address the following areas:

- Defining the problems to be addressed
- Establishing and managing customer expectations
- Monitoring the existing network, system, and its environment
- Analyzing data
- Developing a set of options to solve problems
- Evaluating and optimizing options based on various trade-offs
- Selecting one or more options
- Planning the implementation

Defining the problems to be addressed should entail a quick evaluation of the environment and project—in essence performing a sanity check on the task at hand, as well as determining the size and scope of the problems, determining that you are working on the right problems, and checking the levels of difficulty anticipated in the technologies, potential architectures and designs, administration, management, and politics in that environment. As you size up the problems faced in this project, you should begin to estimate the level of resources needed (e.g., budget, schedule, personnel). You should also develop your own view of the problems affecting that environment. You may find that, from your analysis of the situation, your definition of the problems may differ from the customer's definition. Depending on how far apart your definitions are, you may need to adjust your customer's expectations about the project.

Example 1.5.

Once, in performing an analysis on a customer's metropolitan-area network (MAN), I realized that the problem was not what the customers thought. They thought that the technology chosen at that time, switched multimegabit data service (SMDS), and the routing protocol (OSPF) were not working properly together. However, the problem actually was that the network personnel had forgotten to connect any of their LANs to the MAN. Of course, when they ran tests from one LAN to another, no data were being passed. It was an easy problem to fix, but a lot of work was spent changing the customer's view on the problem and expectations of what needed to be done. The customer originally wanted to change vendors for the routing equipment and replace the SMDS service. Eventually, they were convinced that the equipment and service were fine and that the problem was internal to the organization.

Although SMDS is not widely available anymore, its behavior as a non-broadcast multiple-access (NBMA) technology is similar to other currently available technologies.

An early part of every project is determining what your customer's expectations are and adjusting these expectations accordingly. The idea here is not to give customers false expectations or to let them have unrealistic expectations, because this will lead to difficulties later in the project. Instead, the goal is to provide an accurate and realistic view of the technical problems in the network and what it will take to solve them. Customers' expectations will likely focus on budget, schedule, and personnel but may also include their opinions about technologies and methodologies. And, at times, politics become embedded within the project and must be dealt with. The key here is to separate technical from nontechnical issues and to focus on technical and resource issues.

Part of determining customers' expectations means understanding what customers want to do with their network. This may involve understanding the customer's business model and operations. In addition, the customer may expect to have significant input into the development of the network. As you set the customer's expectations, you may need to establish the lines of communication between the network architecture/design group, management, users, and network staff.

Having established what the customer's expectations are, you may need to adjust and manage these expectations. This can be done by identifying trade-offs and options for resources, technologies, architectures, and designs and then presenting and discussing trade-offs and options with your customer. Bringing customers into the process and working with them to make critical decisions about the network will help them become comfortable with the process.

If an existing network is part of this project, monitoring this network, as well as other parts of the system and its environment, can provide valuable information about the current behavior of users, applications, and devices and their requirements for the new network. Monitoring can also validate your and your customer's definitions of the problems with the existing network. When it is possible to monitor the network, you will need to determine what data you want to collect (based on what you want to accomplish with the data), any strategic places in the network where you want to collect this data, and the frequency and duration of data collection.

At this point in the process you should have several sets of information with which you can begin your network analysis. You may have historical data from network management; data captured during monitoring; requirements gathered from users, staff, and management; the customer's definition of the problem; and your definition. All of these data are used in the network analysis, of which there are three parts: requirements or needs analysis, flow analysis, and a risk (security) analysis. Information in these analyses can be placed on the customer's internal Web page, as mentioned earlier, although some information (e.g., the results of the risk analysis) may have to be kept private.

Results of the network analysis are used in the architecture and design processes, where sets of options are developed, including potential architectures, designs, topologies, technologies, hardware, software, protocols, and services.

These sets of options are then evaluated to determine the optimal solutions for the problems. Criteria need to be developed throughout the analysis, architecture, and design processes in order to evaluate these options. Along with these criteria, you will use the results of the network analysis, including requirements, trade-offs, and dependencies between options.

Having selected one or more options, you can complete the network architecture and design and prepare for implementation. At this point you may consider developing a project plan to determine schedule, budget, and resources, as well as major and minor milestones, checkpoints, and reviews.

1.5   A Systems Methodology

We begin the network analysis process with a discussion of the systems methodology approach to networking. Applying a systems methodology to network analysis, architecture, and design is a relatively new approach, particularly in the Internet Protocol (IP) world. *Systems methodology* (as applied to networking) means viewing the network that you are architecting and designing, along with a subset of its environment (everything that the network interacts with or impacts), as a system. Associated with this system are sets of services (levels of performance and function) that are offered by the network to the rest of the system. This approach considers the network as part of a larger system, with interactions and dependencies between the network and its users, applications, and devices. As you will see, the systems methodology reveals interesting concepts which are used throughout this book.

One of the fundamental concepts of the systems methodology is that network architectures and designs take into account the services that each network will provide and support. This reflects the growing sophistication of networks, which have evolved from providing basic connectivity and packet-forwarding performance to being a platform for various services. As discussed earlier, we are currently at the stage in network evolution where services are important to the success of many networks (third-generation networks). Some examples of third-generation networks are service-provider networks that support multiple levels of performance and pricing to their customers, content-distribution networks that specialize in high-performance transport, and enterprise networks that incorporate and apply billing and usage models to their customers.

When a network is viewed as part of a system that provides services, the systems methodology works quite well for a variety of networks, from small and simple to large, complex networks. It helps in determining, defining, and describing the important characteristics and capabilities of your network.

1.6   System Description

A *system* is a set of components that work together to support or provide connectivity, communications, and services to users of the system. Generically speaking,

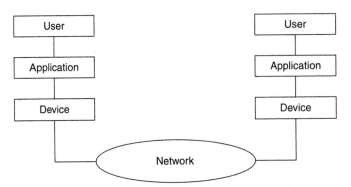

FIGURE 1.17   Generic Components of a System

components of the system include users, applications, devices, and networks. Although users of the system can be considered to be outside the system, they also have requirements that include them as part of the system. Throughout this book we include users as part of the system. Figure 1.17 shows how these components are connected within the system.

Figure 1.17 shows the generic components of a system. These components can be subdivided, if necessary, to focus on a particular part of the system. For example, users in a corporate network could be further described as network and computer support personnel, as well as developers and customers of that corporation's product. In a similar sense, applications may be specific to a particular user, customer or group, generic to a customer base, or generic across the entire network.

If we were to compare this view of a system with the open system interconnect (OSI) protocol model, it would look like Figure 1.18. Note that, in this comparison, some of the OSI layers are modified. This is to show that there may be multiple protocol layers operating at one of the system levels. For example, the OSI physical, data link, and network layers may be present at the device level and may also be present multiple times at the network level (e.g., at switches and routers throughout the network).

Figure 1.19 shows that devices can be subdivided by class to show specialized functions, such as storage, computing, or application servers, or an individual device may be subdivided to show its operating system (OS), device drivers, peripheral hardware, or application programming interface (API).

All of these components work together to provide connectivity and communications across the network, among users, applications, and devices. The connectivity and communications can be tailored to meet the specific needs of users and

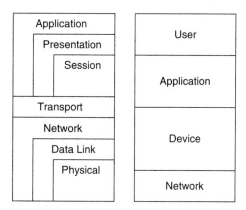

FIGURE 1.18   Comparison of OSI Layers to System Levels

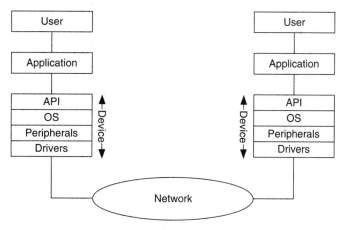

FIGURE 1.19   Device Component Separated into Constituents

applications, such as real-time delivery of voice or streaming media, best-effort delivery of noninteractive data, or reliable delivery of mission-critical data.

The degree of granularity used to describe system components is a trade-off between the amount of detail and accuracy you want in the description and how much time and effort you are willing to put into it. If you are the network architect responsible for a corporate network, you may be able to invest time and resources into developing a detailed description of your system's components, whereas a consultant or vendor's design engineer may have little time and resources to spend on such a description. It is important to note, however, that even a small amount of time invested here will pay dividends later in the analysis process.

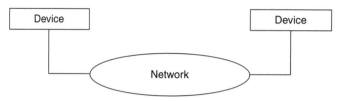

FIGURE 1.20   Traditional View of a System

The traditional view of a system focused on the network providing connectivity between devices (Figure 1.20) and typically did not consider the users or applications.

This traditional view of a system is not complete enough for today's networks. In particular, we need to include users and their applications in the system description. Experience shows that this degree of descriptiveness in the set (users, applications, devices, and networks) is usually sufficient to provide a complete and accurate description of most general-access systems, yet not so large as to be overwhelming to the network architect. (*General-access* is a term to describe common access of users to applications, computing, and storage resources across a network.) Within this set, users represent the end users, or customers, of the system. These end users are the final recipients of the network services supported by the system.

One reason for identifying components of the system is to understand how these components interface with one another across component boundaries. By defining what the components of the system are, we are also setting what is to be expected across each interface. For example, using the standard set (users, applications, devices, and networks), Figure 1.21 shows potential interfaces.

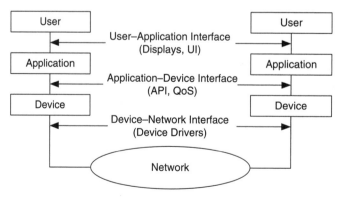

FIGURE 1.21   A Generic System with Interfaces Added

Although the description of the system given in Figure 1.21 is usually satisfactory for the start of most network architectures, there may be times when you want to describe more components or have more defined interfaces. For example, the device-network interface may be simple or complex, depending on what you are trying to accomplish. For a network that will be providing simple connectivity, the network-device interface may be a standard LAN interface (e.g., 100BaseT Ethernet) without any prioritization or virtual LAN (VLAN 802.1p/q) tagging. For a network that provides more than simple connectivity, such as quality of service, the device-network interface may be more closely coupled with the device or application. This may be accomplished by using drivers that bypass portions of the protocol stack and APIs that can interpret application performance requirements.

Although the system description is an attempt to identify components across the entire system, we need to recognize that most systems are not completely homogeneous and that components may change in various parts of the system. This usually occurs in parts of the system that perform specific functions, such as a device-specific network (e.g., a video distribution network) or a storage-area network (SAN). For example, although an SAN may be described as the set (users, applications, devices, and networks), users may be other devices in the system, and the only application may be for system storage and archival.

1.7 Service Description

The concept of network services in this book builds upon the services work from the Internet Engineering Task Force (IETF). This organization has been developing service descriptions for IP networks. In general, they see network services as sets of network capabilities that can be configured and managed within the network and between networks. We apply this concept to network analysis, architecture, and design, integrating services throughout the entire system. This will help you take advantage of the services concept by analyzing, architecting, and designing based on services, and it will also prepare you for the near future, when services will be configurable and manageable within the network.

Network services, or services, are defined here as levels of performance and function in the network. We can look at this from two perspectives: as services being offered by the network to the rest of the system (the devices, applications, and users) or as sets of requirements from the network that are expected by the users, applications, or devices. Levels of performance are described by the performance characteristics capacity, delay, and RMA (reliability, maintainability, and availability), whereas functions are described as security, accounting, billing, scheduling, and management (and others). This is described in more detail in the next section.

It is important to note that the concept of services used in this book is based on what networks can deliver to the system. Thus, it is not to be confused with services that other parts of the system (e.g., applications) can deliver to each other (e.g., graphics rendering services). When the term *service* is used in this book, it is in reference to network service.

Network services in most of today's networks are based on best-effort (unpredictable and unreliable) delivery. In addition to best-effort delivery, we examine some new types of services, including high-performance, predictable (stochastic or probabilistic), and guaranteed services. These new services require some different ways of looking at networks, and you will see how to incorporate such services into your architecture and design. We also look at single-tier and multiple-tier performance in the network, and show how to distinguish between them and how they relate to best-effort, predictable, and guaranteed services.

Network services are hierarchical, and individual service characteristics can be grouped together to form higher-level descriptions of a service, as shown in Figure 1.22.

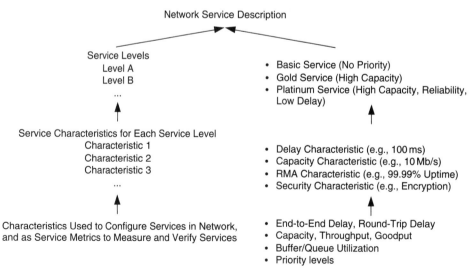

FIGURE 1.22   Grouping Characteristics into Service Levels and Descriptions

1.8   Service Characteristics

One of the goals of network analysis is to be able to characterize services so that they can be designed into the network and purchased from vendors and service providers (e.g., via requests for information [RFI], quote [RFQ], or proposal [RFP], documents used in the procurement process). *Service characteristics* are individual network performance and functional parameters that are used to describe services. These services are offered by the network to the system (the *service offering*) or are requested from the network by users, applications, or devices (the *service request*). Characteristics of services that are requested from the network can also be considered requirements for that network.

Examples of service characteristics range from estimates of capacity requirements based on anecdotal or qualitative information about the network to elaborate listings of various capacity, delay, and RMA requirements, per user, application, and/or device, along with requirements for security, manageability, usability, flexibility, and others.

Example 1.6.

Examples of service characteristics are:

- Defining a security or privacy level for a group of users or an organization
- Providing 1.5 Mb/s peak capacity to a remote user
- Guaranteeing a maximum round-trip delay of 100 ms to servers in a server farm

---

Such requirements are useful in determining the need of the system for services, in providing input to the network architecture and design, and in configuring services in network devices (e.g., routers, switches, device operating systems). Measurements of these characteristics in the network to monitor, verify, and manage services are called *service metrics*. In this book we focus on developing service requirements for the network and using those characteristics to configure, monitor, and verify services within the network.

For services to be useful and effective, they must be described and provisioned end-to-end at all network components between well-defined demarcation points. "End-to-end" does not necessarily mean only from one user's device to another user's device. It may be defined between networks, from users to servers, or between specialized devices (Figure 1.23). When services are not provisioned end-to-end, some components may not be capable of supporting them, and thus the services

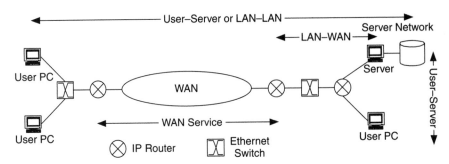

FIGURE 1.23 Example Demarcations Points to Describe End-to-End within a Network

will fail. The demarcation points determine where end-to-end is in the network. Determining these demarcation points is an important part of describing a service.

Services also need to be configurable, measurable, and verifiable within the system. This is necessary to ensure that end users, applications, and devices are getting the services they have requested (and possibly have been paying for), and this leads to accounting and billing for system (including network) resources. You will see how service metrics can be used to measure and verify services and their characteristics.

Services are also likely to be hierarchical within the system, with different service types and mechanisms applied at each layer in the hierarchy. For example, Figure 1.24 shows a quality-of-service (QoS) hierarchy that focuses on bulk traffic

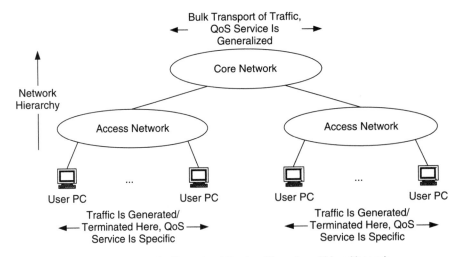

FIGURE 1.24 An Example of Service Hierarchy within a Network

transport in the core of the network while placing specific services at the access network close to the end users, applications, and devices.

1.8.1 Service Levels

Service characteristics can be grouped together to form one or more *service levels* for the network. This is done to make service provisioning easier in that you can configure, manage, account, and bill for a group of service characteristics (service level) instead of a number of individual characteristics. For example, a service level (e.g., premium) may combine capacity (e.g., 1.5 Mb/s) and reliability (as 99.99% uptime). Service levels are also helpful in billing and accounting. This is a service-provider view of the network, where services are offered to customers (users) for a fee. This view of networking is becoming more popular in enterprise networks, displacing the view of networks as purely the infrastructure of cost centers.

There are many ways to describe service levels, including frame relay committed information rates (CIRs), which are levels of capacity; classes of service (CoSs), which combine delay and capacity characteristics; and IP types of service (ToSs) and qualities of service (QoSs), which prioritize traffic for traffic conditioning functions, which are described in the performance architecture (see Chapter 8). There can also be combinations of the aforementioned mechanisms, as well as custom service levels, based on groups of individual service characteristics. These combinations depend on which network technology, protocol, mechanism, or combination is providing the service.

In Figure 1.25 service offerings, requests, and metrics are shown applied to the system. In this example a demarcation of services is shown between the device and network components. Depending on the service requirement or characteristic, however, demarcation may also be between the device and application components.

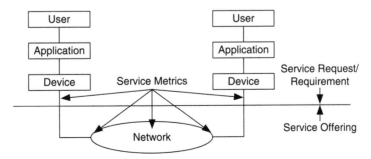

FIGURE 1.25   Service Requests, Offerings, and Metrics

Example 1.7.

A request came from a customer that each building should have Fast Ethernet (FE) capacity to the rest of the network. As part of the requirements analysis, this request became a requirement for 100 Mb/s peak capacity from the users in each building. This *service request* was then matched in the requirements and design processes by a technology choice that could meet or exceed the request. In this case FE was chosen as the technology, and the service offering was 100 Mb/s to each building. *Service metrics* were then added, consisting of measuring the FE connections from the IP switch or router at each building to the backbone.

Services and service levels can be distinguished by their degrees of predictability or determinism. In the next section we discuss best-effort delivery, which is not predictable or deterministic, as well as predictable and guaranteed services. Services and service levels are also distinguished by their degrees of performance. You will see how the service performance characteristics capacity, delay, and RMA are used to describe services and service levels.

1.8.2 System Components and Network Services

Network services are derived from requirements at each of the components in the system. They are end-to-end (between end points that you define) within the system, describing what is expected at each component. Service requirements for the network we are building are derived from each component. There can be user requirements, application requirements, device requirements, and (existing) network requirements. Because we are building the network component, any requirements from the network component come from existing networks that the new network will incorporate or connect to.

Component requirements are added one to another, being refined and expanded as the network comes closer to being realized. User requirements, which are the most subjective and general, are refined and expanded by requirements from the application component, which are in turn refined and expanded by the device and network components. Thus, requirements filter down from user to application to device to network, resulting in a set of specific requirements that can be configured and managed in the network devices themselves. This results in a service offering that is end-to-end, consisting of service characteristics that are configured in each network device in the path (e.g., routers, switches, hubs). As in Figure 1.26, service characteristics are configured and managed within each

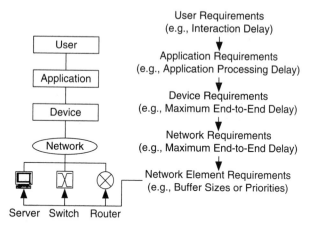

FIGURE 1.26   Requirements Flow Down Components, from User to Network

element and at interfaces between elements. These services are the most specific of all and have the smallest scope (typically a single network device).

Defining network services and service metrics helps keep the system functioning and can provide extra value or convenience to users and their applications. By defining service metrics we are determining what we will be measuring in the network, which will help us in network monitoring and management.

Recall that network services are sets of performance and function, so requirements may also include functions of one of the components. Examples of functions include network monitoring and management, security, and accounting. Services such as these must be considered an integral part of the network architecture and design. In this book, security (and privacy) and network management each have their own architectures. This may seem obvious, but traditionally, services such as security and network management have been afterthoughts in architecture and design, often completely forgotten in the architecture until problems arise.

Example 1.8.

The network path shown in Figure 1.27 was designed to optimize performance between users and their servers. The graph at the bottom of the figure is an estimate of the expected aggregate capacity at each segment of the path. In this network a packet over SONET (POS) link at the OC–48 level (2.544 Gb/s) connects two routers, which then connect to Gigabit Ethernet (GigE) switches.

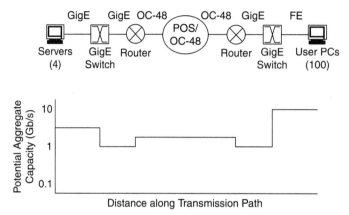

FIGURE 1.27   The Capacity at Each Point in the Transmission Path before the Addition of a Security Firewall

After it was implemented, a security firewall was added at the users' LAN (with FE interfaces), without it being considered part of the original analysis, architecture, or design. The result was that the firewall changed the capacity characteristics across the path by reducing throughput between the user PCs and the GigE switch, as shown in Figure 1.28.

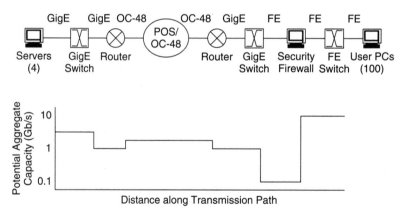

FIGURE 1.28   The Capacity at Each Point in the Transmission Path after the Addition of a Security Firewall

One of our architectural and design goals is to identify such performance bottlenecks before the network is implemented. By considering security, network management, services, and routing and addressing in the analysis process, we are much more likely to understand their behavior and effect on each other and the network. We are therefore able to architect the network to accommodate their requirements and interoperability.

When service characteristics apply to individual network devices, such as routers, switches, data service units (DSUs), and so on, some of these characteristics may be vendor specific. In this book we focus on those characteristics that are part of public standards and not vendor specific.

It is important to note that although standards-based characteristics are "standardized" on the basis of having their descriptions publicly available (e.g., via an IETF RFC), sanctioned by an organization recognized by the networking community, or generally accepted and used as a *de facto standard*, the implementation of characteristics is open to interpretation and often varies across vendors and vendor platforms.

1.8.3   Service Requests and Requirements

Service requests and requirements are, in part, distinguished by the degree of predictability needed from the service by the user, application, or device making the request. Based on their predictability, service requests are categorized as best effort, predictable, or guaranteed. Service requests and requirements can also be appropriate for single- or multiple-tier performance for a network.

Best-effort service means that there is no control over how the network will satisfy the service request—that there are no guarantees associated with this service. Such requests indicate that the rest of the system (users, applications, and devices) will need to adapt to the state of the network at any given time. Thus, the expected service for such requests will be both unpredictable and unreliable, with variable performance across a range of values (from the network being unavailable to the lowest common denominator of performance across all of the technologies in the end-to-end path). Such service requests either have no specific performance requirements for the network or are based solely on estimates of capacity. When requirements are nonspecific, network performance cannot be tuned to satisfy any particular user, application, or device requirement.

Guaranteed service is the opposite of best-effort service. Where best-effort service is unpredictable and unreliable, guaranteed service must be predictable and reliable to such a degree that, when service is not available, the system is held accountable. A guaranteed service implies a contract between the user and provider. For periods when the contract is broken (e.g., when the service is not available), the provider must account for the loss of service and, possibly, appropriately compensate the user.

With best-effort and guaranteed services at opposite ends of the service spectrum, many services fall somewhere between. These are *predictable services*, which require some degree of predictability (more than best effort) yet do not require the accountability of a guaranteed service.

Predictable and guaranteed service requests are based on some a priori knowledge of and control over the state of the system. Such requests may require that the service either operates predictably or is bounded. Therefore, such services must have a clear set of requirements. For the network to provision resources to support a predictable or guaranteed service, the service requirements of that request must be configurable, measurable, and verifiable. This is where service requests, offerings, and metrics are applied.

Note that there are times when a service can be best effort, predictable, or guaranteed, depending on how it is interpreted. Therefore, it is important to understand the need for a good set of requirements because these will help determine the types of services to plan for. Also, although the term *predictable* lies in a gray area between best effort and guaranteed, it is the type of service most likely to be served by most performance mechanisms, as we see in Chapter 8.

For example, suppose a device requires capacity (bandwidth) between 4 and 10 Mb/s. There must be a way to communicate this request across the network, a way to measure and/or derive the level of resources needed to support this request, a way to determine whether the required resources are available, and a method to control the information flow and network resources to keep this service between 4 and 10 Mb/s.

Capacity (or bandwidth) is a finite resource within a network. For example, the performance of a 100 Mb/s FE connection between two routers is bounded by that technology. If we were to look at the traffic flows across that 100 Mb/s connection, we would see that, for a common best-effort service, capacity would be distributed across all of the traffic flows. As more flows were added to that connection, the resources would be spread out until, at some point, congestion occurs. Congestion would disrupt the traffic flows across that connection, affecting the protocols and applications for each flow. What is key here is that, in terms of resource allocation, all traffic flows have some access to resources.

This is shown in Figure 1.29. In this figure available capacity (dashed curve) decreases as the number of traffic flows increases. Correspondingly, the loading on the network (solid curve) from all of the traffic flows increases. However, at some point congestion affects the amount of user traffic being carried by the connection, and throughput of the connection (heavy curve) drops. As congestion interferes with the end-to-end transport of traffic, some protocols (e.g., TCP) will retransmit

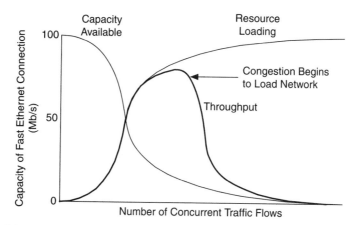

FIGURE 1.29 The Performance of a Fast Ethernet Connection under Best-Effort Conditions

traffic. The difference between the loading and the throughput curves is due to retransmissions. This is undesirable, for while the connection is being loaded, only a percentage of that loading are successfully delivered to destinations. At some point all of the traffic on that connection could be due to retransmissions and throughput would approach zero. This approach is used in best-effort networks.

In contrast, consider a traditional telephony network. Calls are made on this network, and resources are allocated to each call. As more calls are added to the network, at the point where all of the resources have been allocated, additional calls are refused. The exiting calls on the network may suffer no performance degradation, but no new calls are allowed until resources are available. *Call admission control* (CAC) is a mechanism to limit the number of calls on a network, thereby controlling the allocation of resources.

This is shown in Figure 1.30. Individual calls are shown in this figure, and each call is 10 Mb/s for simplicity. As each call is accepted, resources are allocated to it, so the availability drops and loading increases for each call. When the resources are exhausted, no further calls are permitted. Congestion is not a problem for the existing calls, and throughput is maximized. This approach is similar to a guaranteed service.

There is a trade-off between these two approaches to resource allocation in a network. Although a best-effort network allows access to as many traffic flows as possible, performance degradation across all of the traffic flows can occur. Admission control preserves resources for traffic flows that have already been allocated resources but will refuse additional traffic flows when resources are exhausted.

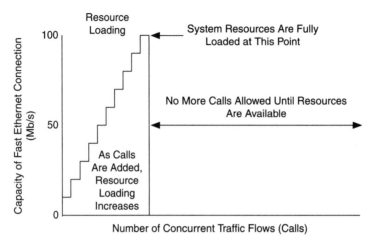

FIGURE 1.30   The Performance of a Fast Ethernet Connection under CAC

In many networks both approaches (or a hybrid between them) are desired. For example, a voice over IP (VoIP) service, which provides a telephony service across a data network, requires some of the characteristics of CAC while operating over a best-effort network. Such hybrid approaches are discussed in detail in Chapter 8.

Service requests and requirements can also be low or high performance in terms of capacity, delay, and RMA. Low- and high-performance requirements depend on each particular network. A requirement is low or high performance relative to other requirements for that network. *Low performance* is an indicator that the service request or requirement's performance characteristics are less than a performance threshold determined for that network. Likewise, *high performance* is an indicator that the service request or requirement's performance characteristics are greater than a performance threshold determined for that network. Thus, in determining low and high performance for a network, we will develop one or more performance thresholds for that network. Multiple-tier performance indicates that there are multiple tiers of performance for that network. Single-tier performance requirements are roughly equivalent within a network.

Note that low and high performances are not described in terms of best-effort, predictable, or guaranteed service because they are independent of each other. *Best-effort, predictable,* and *guaranteed service* refer to the degree of predictability of a request or requirement, whereas *low* and *high performances* refer to a relative performance level for that request or requirement. For example, a network can be entirely best effort (most current networks are), yet we can often distinguish low- and high-performance requirements for such a network. And when a network has low- and high-performance regions for capacity, delay, and RMA, there may be predictable or guaranteed requirements in either region.

By their nature, each service has its associated set of requirements. These requirements are based on the levels of performance and function desired by the user, application, or device requesting service. Performance requirements are described in terms of capacity, delay, and RMA, whereas functional requirements describe specific functions needed in the service, such as multicast, security, management, or accounting. We use requests for performance and function in developing the network architecture and design—for example, in describing the overall level of performance needed in the network.

As mentioned earlier, service performance requirements (capacity, delay, and RMA) can be grouped together, forming one or more service levels. For example, a service request may couple a specific capacity (e.g., 1.5 Mb/s) with a bound on end-to-end delay (e.g., 40 ms). At times, such service levels can be mapped to well-known service mechanisms such as frame relay CIR or IP ToS or QoS. Thus, service levels are a way to map performance and functional requirements to a well-known or standard network service offering. A properly specified service provides insight into which performance characteristics should be measured in the network to verify service delivery.

1.8.4 Service Offerings

Service requests that are generated by users, applications, or devices are supported by services offered by the network. These service offerings (e.g., via frame relay CIR or IP ToS or QoS, mentioned in the previous section) are the network counterparts to user, application, and device requests for service.

Service offerings map to service requests and thus can also be categorized as best effort, predictable, or guaranteed. Best-effort service offerings are not predictable— they are based on the state of the network at any given time. There is little or no prior knowledge about available performance, and there is no control over the network at any time. Most networks today operate in best-effort mode. A good example of a network that offers best-effort service is the current Internet.

Best-effort service offerings are compatible with best-effort service requests. Neither the service offering nor the request assumes any knowledge about the state of or control over the network. The network offers whatever service is available at that time (typically just available bandwidth), and the rest of the system adapts the flow of information to the available service (e.g., via TCP flow control).

Example 1.9.

An example of a best-effort service request and offering is a file transfer (e.g., using FTP) over the Internet. FTP uses TCP as its transport protocol, which adapts, via a sliding-window flow-control mechanism, to approximate the current state of the network it is operating across. Thus, the service requirement from FTP over TCP is best effort, and the corresponding service offering from the Internet is best effort. The result is that, when the FTP session is active, the performance characteristics of the network (Internet) and flow control (TCP windows) are constantly interacting and adapting, as well as contending with other application sessions for network resources. In addition, as part of TCP's service to the applications it supports, it provides error-free, reliable data transmission.

On the other hand, predictable and guaranteed service offerings have some degree of predictability or are bounded. To achieve this, there has to be some knowledge of the network, along with control over the network, in order to meet performance bounds or guarantees. Such services must be measurable and verifiable.

Just because a service is predictable or guaranteed does not necessarily imply that it is also high performance. Take, for example, the telephone network. It offers predictable service but low performance (in terms of capacity). To support voice conversations, this network must be able to support fairly strict delay and delay variation tolerances, even though the capacity per user session (telephone call) is relatively small, or low performance. What is well known from a telephony perspective is somewhat new in the current world of data networking. Support for strict delay and delay variation is one of the more challenging aspects of data network architecture and design.

Predictable and guaranteed service offerings should be compatible with their corresponding service requests. In each case, service performance requirements (capacity, delay, and RMA) in a service request are translated into the corresponding performance characteristics in the service offering.

Example 1.10.

An example of a predictable service request and offering can be seen in a network designed to support real-time streams of telemetry data. An architectural/design goal for a network supporting real-time telemetry is the ability to specify end-to-end delay and have the network satisfy this delay request. A real-time telemetry stream should have an end-to-end delay requirement, and this requirement would form the basis for the service request. For example, this service request may be for an end-to-end delay of 25 ms, with a delay variation of ± 400 μs. This would form the request and the service level (i.e., a QoS level) that needs to be supported by the network. The network would then be architected and designed to support a QoS level of 25 ms end-to-end delay and a delay variation of ± 400 μs. Delay and delay variation would then be measured and verified with service metrics in the system, perhaps by using common utilities, such as ping (a common utility for measuring round-trip delay) or TCPdump (a utility for capturing TCP information), or by using a custom application.

We use various methods to describe service performance requirements and characteristics within a network, including thresholds, bounds, and guarantees. We also show how to distinguish between high and low performance for each network project.

This approach does not mean that best-effort service is inherently low performance or that predictable or guaranteed services are high performance. Rather, it signifies that predictability in services is an important characteristic and is separate from performance. There are times when a network is best architected for best-effort service, and other times when best-effort, predictable, and guaranteed services are needed. We will see that when predictable or guaranteed services are required in the network, consideration for those requirements tends to drive the architecture and design in one direction, while consideration for best-effort service drives them in another direction. It is the combination of all services that helps make the architecture and design complete.

1.8.5 Service Metrics

For service performance requirements and characteristics to be useful, they must be configurable, measurable, and verifiable within the system. Therefore, we will describe performance requirements and characteristics in terms of *service metrics*, which are intended to be configurable and measurable.

Because service metrics are meant to be measurable quantities, they can be used to measure thresholds and limits of service. Thresholds and limits are used to distinguish whether performance is in conformance (adheres to) or nonconformance (exceeds) with a service requirement. A *threshold* is a value for a performance characteristic that is a boundary between two regions of conformance and, when crossed in one or both directions, will generate an action. A *limit* is a boundary between conforming and nonconforming regions and is taken as an upper or lower limit for a performance characteristic. Crossing a limit is more serious than crossing a threshold, and the resulting action is usually more serious (e.g., dropping of packets to bring performance back to conformance).

For example, a threshold can be defined to distinguish between low and high performance for a particular service. Both low- and high-performance levels are conforming to the service, and the threshold is used to indicate when the boundary is crossed. This threshold can be measured and monitored in the network, triggering some action (e.g., a flashing red light on an administrator's console) when this threshold is crossed. An example of this might be in measuring the round-trip delay of a path. A threshold of N ms is applied to this measurement. If the round-trip times exceed N ms, an alert is generated at a network management station. We discuss this in greater detail in the chapter on network management architecture (Chapter 7).

In a similar fashion, limits can be created with service metrics to provide upper and lower boundaries on a measured quantity. When a limit is crossed, traffic is considered nonconforming (it exceeds the performance requirement), and action is taken to bring the traffic back into conformance (e.g., by delaying or dropping packets). Figure 1.31 shows how limits and thresholds may be applied in the system. In this figure, a threshold of 6 Mb/s is the boundary between low and high performance for a service requirement, and an upper limit of 8 Mb/s is the boundary between conformance and nonconformance for that service. When traffic crosses the 6 Mb/s threshold, a warning is sent to network management (with a color change from green to yellow). These notices can be used to do trend analysis on the network—for example, to determine when capacity needs to be

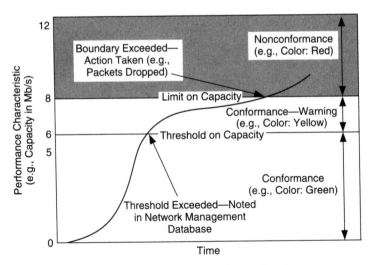

FIGURE 1.31   Performance Limits and Thresholds

upgraded. When traffic crosses the 8 Mb/s limit, the network takes action to reduce the capacity used by that traffic flow and an alert is sent to network management (with a color change from yellow to red) until the capacity level drops below 8 Mb/s and is again conforming.

Thresholds and limits are useful applications of service metrics to understand and control performance levels in the network, in support of services.

1.9   Performance Characteristics

Services may include one or more of the performance characteristics we have mentioned so far in this chapter: capacity, delay, and RMA. Each characteristic is actually a label for a class of characteristics of that type. For example, the term *capacity* is used as a label for the class of characteristics that involves moving information from place to place, including bandwidth, throughput, goodput, and so forth. Similarly, delay is a label for the class of characteristics that includes end-to-end delay, round-trip delay, and delay variation. RMA is a label for the class of characteristics that includes reliability, maintainability, and availability. Thus, when the terms *capacity, delay*, and *RMA* are used in this book, you can use other terms from each class, depending on your network.

There are times when it makes more sense to describe capacity in terms of throughput—for example, when developing requirements for applications. Round-trip delay is commonly used as a measure for delay, although at times delay requirements are expressed in terms of one-way delay.

1.9.1   Capacity

Capacity is a measure of the system's ability to transfer information (voice, data, video, or combinations of these). Several terms are associated with capacity, such as *bandwidth, throughput,* or *goodput*. Although we use the generic term *capacity* throughout this book to reference this class of characteristics, you may choose to use another term in place of or along with capacity.

Example 1.11.

The bandwidth of a SONET OC-3c link is 155.52 Mb/s, which is three times the bandwidth of an OC-1 link (51.84 Mb/s). This bandwidth does not include data-link, network, or transport-layer protocol (e.g., SONET, IP, or transport control protocol/user datagram protocol [TCP/UDP]) overhead or, in the case of wide-area networks, the loss in performance due to the bandwidth × delay product in the network. When a network or element is performing at its theoretical capacity, it is said to be performing at *line rate*. When an OC-3c circuit was tested, values of realizable capacity (throughput) ranged from approximately 80 to 128 Mb/s (measurements taken at the transport [TCP] layer of the National Research and Education Network [NREN] and Numerical Aerodynamic Simulation [NAS] networks, NASA Ames Research Center, March 1996).

1.9.2 Delay

Delay is a measure of the time difference in the transmission of information across the system. In its most basic sense, delay is the time difference in transmitting a single unit of information (bit, byte, cell, frame, or packet) from source to destination. As with capacity, there are several ways to describe and measure delay. There are also various sources of delay, such as propagation, transmission, queuing, and processing. Delay may be measured in one direction (end-to-end) and both directions (round-trip). Both end-to-end and round-trip delay measurements are useful; however, only round-trip delays can be measured with the use of the practical and universally available utility *ping*.

Another measure of delay incorporates device and application processing, taking into account the time to complete a task. As the size of a task increases, the application processing times (and thus the response time of the system) also increase. This response time, termed here *latency*, may yield important information about the behavior of the application and the network. Latency can also be used to describe the response time of a network device, such as the latency through a switch or router. In this case the processing time is of that switch or router.

Delay variation, which is the change in delay over time, is an important characteristic for applications and traffic flows that require constant delay. For example, real-time and near-real-time applications often require strict delay variation. Delay variation is also known as *jitter*.

Together, delay (end-to-end and round-trip), latency, and delay variation help describe network behavior.

1.9.3 RMA

RMA refers to reliability, maintainability, and availability. *Reliability* is a statistical indicator of the frequency of failure of the network and its components and represents the unscheduled outages of service. It is important to keep in mind that only failures that prevent the system from performing its mission, or mission-critical failures (more on this in Chapter 2), are generally considered in this analysis. Failures of components that have no effect on the mission, at least when they fail, are not considered in these calculations. Failure of a standby component needs tending to but is not a mission-critical failure.

Reliability also requires some degree of predictable behavior. For a service to be considered reliable, the delivery of information must occur within well-known time boundaries. When delivery times vary greatly, users lose confidence in the timely delivery of information. In this sense the term *reliability* can be coupled with *confidence* in that it describes how users have confidence that the network and system will meet their requirements.

A parallel can be seen with the airline industry. Passengers (users) of the airline system expect accurate delivery of information (in this case the passengers themselves) to the destination. Losing or misplacing passengers is unacceptable. In addition, predictable delivery is also expected. Passengers expect flights to depart and arrive within reasonable time boundaries. When these boundaries are crossed, passengers are likely to use a different airline or not fly at all. Similarly, when an application is being used, the user expects a reasonable response time from the application, which is dependent on the timely delivery of information across the system.

Along with reliability is maintainability. *Maintainability* is a statistical measure of the time to restore the system to fully operational status after it has experienced a fault. This is generally expressed as a mean-time-to-repair (MTTR). Repairing a system failure consists of several stages: detection; isolation of the failure to a component that can be replaced; the time required to deliver the necessary parts to the location of the failed component (logistics time); and the time to actually replace the component, test it, and restore full service. MTTR usually assumes the logistics time is zero; this is an assumption, which is invalid if a component must be replaced to restore service but takes days to obtain.

To fully describe this performance class, we add availability to reliability and maintainability. *Availability* (also known as operational availability) is the relationship between the frequency of mission-critical failures and the time to restore service. This is defined as the mean time between mission-critical failures (or mean time between failures) divided by the sum of mean time to repair and mean time between mission-critical failures or mean time between failures. These relationships are shown in the following equation, where *A* is availability.

$$A = (MTBCF)/(MTBCF + MTTR) \text{ or } A = (MTBF)/(MTBF + MTTR)$$

Capacity, delay, and RMA are dependent on each other. For example, the emphasis of a network design may be to bound delay: A system supporting point-of-sale transactions may need to guarantee delivery of customer information and completion of the transaction within 15 seconds (where the network delay is on the order of 100s of ms); a Web application can have similar requirements. However, in a computation-intensive application we may be able to optimize the system by buffering data during periods of computing. In this case, delay may not be as important as a guarantee of eventual delivery. On the other hand, a system supporting visualization of real-time banking transactions may require a round-trip delay of less than 40 ms, with a delay variation of less than 500 μs. If these delay boundaries are exceeded, the visualization task fails for that application, forcing the system to use other techniques.

1.9.4 Performance Envelopes

Performance requirements can be combined to describe a performance range for the system. A *performance envelope* is a combination of two or more performance requirements, with thresholds and upper and/or lower limits for each. Within this envelope, levels of application, device, and/or network performance requirements are plotted. Figures 1.32 and 1.33 show two such envelopes. The performance

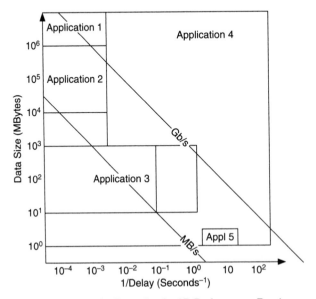

FIGURE 1.32   An Example of a 2D Performance Envelope

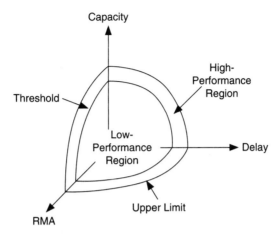

FIGURE 1.33   An Example of a 3D Performance Envelope

envelope in Figure 1.32 consists of capacity, in terms of data sizes transferred across the network, and end-to-end delay. In this figure, delay is shown as 1/delay for consistency.

Figure 1.33 is a 3D performance envelope, showing capacity, delay, and RMA. This envelope also describes two regions of performance, low and high performance, which are functions of the limits and thresholds for capacity, delay, and RMA.

Performance envelopes such as these are useful for visualizing the regions of delay, capacity, and RMA in which the network will be expected to operate based on requirements developed for that network. In Chapter 2 we discuss how requirements are developed for a network.

1.10   Network Supportability

The ability of the customer to sustain the required level of performance (that architected and designed into the network) over the entire life cycle of the network is an area of networking that is often neglected. It is a mistake to assume that a successful network architecture and design meet the requirements only on the day it is delivered to the customer and that future requirements are the responsibility of the customer.

Experience indicates operations and support constitute 80% of the life-cycle costs of a system, whereas development, acquisition, and installation represent only

20%. Good network architects/designers take into account the major factors that affect operability and supportability as they make their decisions. Knowledgeable customers insist that they understand the operations and support implications of a network architecture and design. At times, such issues may be of more concern than the feasibility of a new technology.

The postimplementation phases of a network's life cycle can be broken into three elements: operations, maintenance, and human knowledge. The operations element focuses on ensuring that the network and system are properly operated and managed and that any required maintenance actions are identified. The maintenance element focuses on preventive and corrective maintenance and the parts, tools, plans, and procedures for accomplishing these functions. The human knowledge element is the set of documentation, training, and skilled personnel required to operate and maintain the network and system. Design decisions affect each of these factors and have a direct impact on the ability of the customer to sustain the high level of service originally realized upon implementation of the network.

Failure to consider supportability in the analysis, architecture, and design processes has a number of serious consequences. First, a smart customer, when faced with a network architecture/design that obviously cannot be operated or maintained by his or her organization, will reject the network project or refuse to pay for it. Second, a customer who accepts the architecture/design and subsequent implementation will have inadequate resources to respond to network and system outages, experience unacceptable performance after a period of time, and may suffer adverse effects in his or her operation or business (e.g., a loss of their customers or revenue). Other customers will be highly dissatisfied with their network and either require the architect/designer to return and repair the network by providing adequate materials to sustain its required performance level or will prematurely replace it. None of these cases reflects positively on the network architect/designer or implementation team and can lead to finger pointing that can be more painful than any acceptance test.

Key characteristics of a network architecture and design that affect the postimplementation costs include:

- Network and system reliability
- Network and system maintainability
- Training of the operators to stay within operational constraints
- Quality of the staff required to perform maintenance actions

Some examples of key network architecture/design decisions that affect these characteristics include:

- Degree of diversity of critical-path components in network architecture/design
- Quality of network components selected for installation
- Location and accessibility of components requiring frequent maintenance
- Implementation of built-in test equipment and monitoring techniques

Supportability must be considered throughout the life cycle of the network. An accurate assessment of the requirements for continuous service at full performance level must be included in the requirements analysis process, along with a statement of specific, measurable requirements. During the architecture and design processes, trade-offs must take into account the impact of supportability, and the concept of operations must be formulated. Last, during implementation, two major tasks must be accomplished to ensure supportability:

1. Conformance to the network architecture and design must be validated and nonconformance corrected or (at least) documented to ensure that performance is adequate and that maintenance can be performed.

2. Operations and maintenance personnel must understand and be trained in the technologies that are being deployed, including how to operate the network and system properly, when to perform maintenance, and how to most quickly restore service in the event of a fault.

A detailed discussion of how supportability fits into the overall architecture and design processes is provided in Chapter 2.

1.11 Conclusion

In this chapter you learned definitions of network analysis, architecture, and design; the importance of network analysis in understanding the system and providing a defensible architecture and design; and the model for the network analysis, architecture, and design processes.

You have also learned that networks are not independent entities but rather a part of the system and that the delivery of network services is a goal of the system. Network services consist of performance and function and are offered to users, applications, and devices so that they can accomplish their work on the system. In order to architect and design a network to support services, you need to know what they are, how they work together, and how to characterize them. Once you do this, you will have a broad view of what the network will need to support, which you can take to the next levels of detail as you proceed with the network analysis.

By describing the system as a set of components (e.g., user, application, device, network), you can apply interfaces between these components to help understand the relationships, inputs, and outputs between each of the components.

You have also learned about different types of services, from best-effort, unpredictable, and unreliable service to predictable, bounded, and somewhat predictable service, to guaranteed services with accountability.

To go to a level deeper in the discussion about services, we considered the service performance characteristics capacity, delay, and RMA (reliability, maintainability, and availability). These characteristics are useful only if we can measure and verify their values in the system. We discussed these values, as well as service metrics, thresholds, and boundaries. We learned that performance characteristics can be combined into a performance envelope.

Having thought about systems, services, and their characteristics, we are now ready to quantify what we want from our networks. To do this, we first need to gather, analyze, and understand the requirements from the system. This is *requirements analysis*, the next step in the network analysis process.

1.12 Exercises

1. In Example 1.3, an analogy was drawn between a network's architecture and design and a home's architecture and design. Provide a similar analogy, using a computer's architecture and design.

2. Hierarchy and interconnectivity are a fundamental trade-off in networks. Given the network hierarchy shown in Figure 1.30, with costs assigned to each link, show how interconnectivity would improve the performance of traffic flowing between Joe's computer and Sandy's computer. Costs are shown as numbers but could represent the capacity of each link or the costs incurred by using each link. What is the total cost of traveling the hierarchy between Joe's computer and Sandy's? In this figure, where would you add a link of cost 15 so that the total cost between Joe's computer and Sandy's is less than it is when you travel the entire hierarchy?

3. In Figure 1.9, connections are added between networks in the Internet to provide a better performing path for select traffic flows. An example of this is a content

delivery network (CDN). What is a CDN? Show how a CDN uses interconnectivity to provide better performance characteristics to its users.

4. In defining where services can be applied in a network, end-to-end is determined by where you want a service to start and stop. For example, if your WAN is supplied by a service provider (e.g., an ATM or frame relay service), you may want to define the end points and characteristics of that service. If you use IP routers at each LAN-WAN interface to that service, describe the following: (1) at which network devices would you define the end points of the service, and (2) what characteristics (service metrics) would you use to measure the service?

5. Service requirements flow from user to application to device to network, becoming more specific along the way. If you were given an application requirement for end-to-end delay (e.g., 100 ms) between an application server on one network and users on another network, for example, how might that translate into delay in the network and devices? What types of service metrics could you use to measure it?

6. For Example 1.5, the delay characteristics for the segments (including the processing at the switches) are as follows: for each GigE segment, 100 μs; for the PoS OC-48 segment between routers, 1 ms; for each FE segment, 200 μs; and for the security firewall, 5 ms. Draw graphs showing the end-to-end delay performance (in the direction from user PC to server) before and after the security firewall is added.

7. Which of the following applications require best-effort (unpredictable and unreliable), guaranteed (predictable and reliable, with accountability), or predictable service. Give reasons for your choices.
   - High-quality (phone company-grade) voice calls
   - Voice over IP (VoIP) calls
   - File transfers via FTP
   - Audio file downloads
   - A commercial video-on-demand service
   - User access to servers in a corporation

8. Show how performance boundaries and thresholds could be used in the following scenarios.
   - An application has a service requirement for round-trip delay to be less than 100 ms. If delay is greater than 100 ms, notify the network administrator.
   - A user requires capacity of up to 512 Kb/s but may not exceed 1.5 Mb/s. You want to keep track of how much time the user's capacity is between 512 Kb/s and 1.5 Mb/s.

CHAPTER CONTENTS

2

Requirements Analysis: Concepts

In this chapter you will learn to develop service descriptions for networks and to identify and/or derive network requirements from the system. You will learn that network requirements are coupled to services and will develop a requirements specification to map out requirements and help determine their dependencies. You will learn how to apply the concepts discussed in the last chapter to a variety of user, application, and device requirements and to develop both a requirements specification and an applications map.

2.1 Objectives

In this chapter we expand the concept of requirements for a network. We tune the general systems engineering process, introduced in the last chapter, to the problem of networking. We talk about different types of requirements, from the user, application, device, and network components. And you learn about grouping requirements together, and mapping the locations of applications and devices. The combination of all the requirements and locations is expressed in two documents: a requirements specification and a requirements map.

2.1.1 Preparation

There is little information on the requirements analysis process as it applies to networking. However, there are some excellent preparatory materials that are of a more general systems engineering nature that will provide an overview of the requirements analysis process.

2.2   Background

As you may already have noticed, the network analysis part of this book—consisting of requirements and flow and risk analyses—introduces many new concepts and guidelines and expands upon several existing concepts. Therefore, requirements analysis and flow analysis are separated into three chapters, covering concepts and procedures, respectively, in order to make this material more readable and useful. The chapters on concepts provide background material for each topic, explaining and defining pertinent concepts. The chapters on procedures expand on these concepts to build a process for you to apply to your architectures and designs.

We begin the network analysis process with *requirements analysis*, which is gathering and deriving requirements in order to understand system and network behaviors. This consists of identifying, gathering, deriving, and understanding system requirements and their characteristics; developing thresholds and limits for performance to distinguish between low- and high-performance services; and determining where best-effort, predictable, and guaranteed services may apply in the network.

2.2.1   Requirements and Features

Requirements are descriptions of the network functions and performance needed in order for the network to successfully support its users, applications, and devices (and thus the success of the network project). Using this definition, every requirement for the network must be met for it to be successful. Yet, as we will see, there can be lots of requirements, from a variety of sources, with varying degrees of achievability. If we consider all requirements from all sources as necessary to the success of the network, then we are likely setting expectations that cannot be met. Thus, as part of the requirements analysis process, we must categorize and prioritize requirements, determining those that are truly requirements for the network and those that may be desirable but are not truly requirements.

Requirements that are determined to be necessary for the success of the network project are termed *core* or *fundamental requirements*. Since these requirements are necessary for the success of the project, there must be some way to determine success. Thus, associated with each core/fundamental requirement is one or more *metrics*. Metrics are measurements or demonstrations for each requirement.

Example 2.1. Examples of core requirements and their associated metrics are:

- Performance: The network shall be capable of providing a minimum end-to-end throughput of 100 Mb/s between end devices. Metric: Measurement between select end devices (the set of which TBD), using applications from (Application List), under test conditions (Conditions List).

- Security: The network shall be capable of filtering packets based on an Access Control List (ACL). Metric: Demonstration of filtering unwanted packets, based on the provided ACL, injected into the network.

Network functions and performance that are desired but not necessary for the success of the network project are called *features*. There will be requirements that, as part of the analysis process, are determined to be features for the network. In addition, there will be requirements that may be considered in a later version of the network, those that will be rejected during the analysis process, and requirements that are more informational than required.

As shown in Figure 2.1, requirements are separated into core or fundamental requirements (those that are deemed necessary for that network), features that are desirable for that network, those that may be considered in a later version or upgrade of the network, and requirements that have been rejected (e.g., not really necessary, desirable, realistic, or implementable). Each network should have, as a minimum, a set of core requirements; it will probably also have a set of

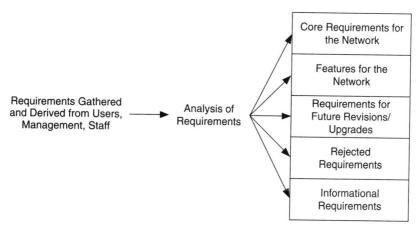

FIGURE 2.1   Requirements Are Separated into Core/Fundamental Requirements, Features, Future, Rejected, and Informational Requirements

informational requirements and may have sets of features, future requirements, and rejected requirements.

Requirements are categorized during the requirements analysis process, through discussions with users, management, and staff, and are approved (signed off) by management. In practice, a first attempt at categorization is done by the analysis group, presented to management to determine whether or not this categorization is on the right track, and then further developed with input from users, management, and staff.

One method to categorize requirements is based on the current practice of the Internet Engineering Task Force (IETF). RFC 2119 identifies key words and phrases that can be used to describe the relative importance of a requirement. These key words and phrases are *Must/Shall/Required, Must Not/Shall Not, Should/ Recommended, Should Not/Not Recommended*, and *May/Optional*:

- *Must/Shall/Required.* These key words indicate an absolute requirement and would be included as core or fundamental requirements for the network.

- *Must Not/Shall Not.* These are also absolute requirements indicating a restriction or prohibition of a function or task. These would also be included as core or fundamental requirements for the network.

- *Should/Recommended.* These key words indicate that a requirement may be valid, but that its implementation is not absolutely necessary for the success of the network. Such requirements would be categorized as features or future requirements for the network.

- *Should Not/Not Recommended.* As with Should/Recommended, these phrases indicate that a requirement may be valid (in this case to prohibit a function or task), but that its implementation is not absolutely necessary for the success of the network. Such requirements would also be categorized as features or future requirements for the network.

- *May/Optional.* When a requirement is truly optional, it may be categorized as a feature or future requirement, or may be rejected.

By using these terms, you help to ensure that there is no confusion regarding requirements and features. We discuss the categorization of requirements in greater detail at the end of the chapter, when we develop the requirements specification.

2.2.2 The Need for Requirements Analysis

Why do requirements analysis? Although requirements analysis is fundamental to the network architecture and design, it is often overlooked or ignored. Why is this the case? A major reason that requirements analysis is not given proper consideration is the degree of difficulty involved. Gathering requirements means talking to users, network personnel, and management, and interpreting the results. Talking to N users may result in $N + 1$ different sets of user requirements. Network personnel and management are often distanced from the users and do not have a clear idea of what users want or need. Additionally, requirements analysis may appear to offer no immediate payoff. Finally, requirements analysis means putting thought and time into preparing for the architecture and design.

Failing to do proper requirements analysis may result in a network architecture and design that are based on factors other than what the users, applications, or devices need. For example, the network may be based on a technology whose primary asset is simply that the designer feels comfortable with it. Or perhaps it is a network based on a particular vendor's equipment, again often one that the designer feels comfortable with. Another obvious example is a project that has a budget constraint or deadline that forces the designer to make do and use familiar, easy-to-apply technologies. Problems with such choices are that they are not objective and that familiar technologies or vendors may not be the right choices for that particular network.

Requirements analysis helps the designer to better understand the probable behavior of the network being built. This results in several payoffs:

- More objective, informed choices of network technologies and services
- The ability to apply technology and topology candidates to networks
- Networks and elements properly sized to users and applications
- A better understanding of where and how to apply services in the network

In addition, trade-offs in the architecture and design need to be performed with the total picture in mind. Sometimes this does not become clear until all users, management, and staff have been consulted and all requirements identified. Many redesign efforts result from an initially incomplete set of requirements.

As you proceed through the rest of this book, you will see that the requirements analysis process forms the foundation upon which the network architecture and design processes are built.

In the requirements analysis process we use requirements to distinguish between low- and high-performance applications for our networks; identify specific services; gather performance requirements for use in flow analysis; and gather other requirements to be used throughout the analysis, architecture, and design processes. We learn that low and high performances are relative to the network we are working on, and we develop and apply performance thresholds and limits to help us distinguish between them.

As mentioned earlier, the requirements analysis results in a requirements specification and a requirements map. A *requirements specification* is a document that lists and prioritizes the requirements gathered for your architecture and design. The *requirements map* shows the location dependencies between applications and devices, which will be used for flow analysis.

Throughout this section (and the others in this book) guidelines are presented on how each process may be implemented. These guidelines are from practical experience and should be used as a starting point for you to develop your own set of guidelines. As we proceed, you are encouraged to think about how each guideline could be implemented, and how you would add to or modify it.

2.3   User Requirements

In the model of system components in our generic system, the user component is at the highest layer. The term *user* represents primarily the end users of the system but can be expanded to include everyone involved in the system, such as network and system administrators and management. *User requirements* comprise the set of requirements that is gathered or derived from user input and represent what is needed by users to successfully accomplish their tasks on the system. Typically, when gathering requirements, everyone involved with that network is considered a potential user. Figure 2.2 shows some example user requirements.

We begin describing requirements at this layer, which will lead to the development of more specific requirements as we work through each of the components.

From the user perspective we can ask, "What does it take to get the job done?" This usually results in a set of qualitative, not quantitative, requirements. Part of our job in gathering and deriving user requirements is to make them quantitative whenever possible.

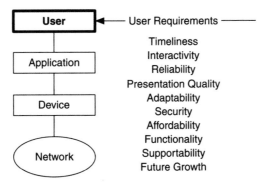

FIGURE 2.2   Types of User Requirements

In general, the system should adapt to users and their environments, provide quick and reliable information access and transfer, and offer quality service to the user. This indicates the following general requirements:

- Timeliness
- Interactivity
- Reliability
- Presentation quality
- Adaptability
- Security
- Affordability
- Functionality
- Supportability
- Future growth

User requirements are the least technical and are also the most subjective. As shown in Figure 2.3, requirements become more technical as they move from users to the network. All of these requirements are developed in more detail as we proceed through the application, device, and network components.

Our intent is to use these basic requirements as a start toward developing more objective and technical requirements in the other components. These example requirements are presented as a guide for you to use in developing requirements for your network, and may change, depending on the user's environment.

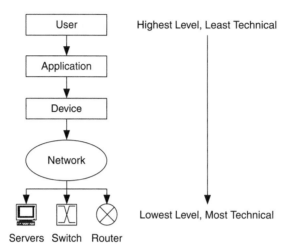

FIGURE 2.3   Requirements Become More Technical as They Move Closer to Network Devices

Timeliness is a requirement that the user be able to access, transfer, or modify information within a tolerable time frame. What a "tolerable" time frame is, of course, depends on the user's perception of delay in the system. It is this perception that we want to quantify. For example, a user may want to download files from a server and complete each transfer within 10 minutes. Or the user may need to receive video frames every 30 ms. Each one of these times indicates a delay that the network will need to provide. For timeliness, end-to-end or round-trip delay can be a useful measurement.

Interactivity is similar to timeliness but focuses on a response time from the system (as well as the network) that is on the order of the response times of users. In the previous example the 10 minutes needed to download the file could be considered as the response time for the system, and we might consider as well that the file transfer is interacting with the user (which it is)—but the degree of interactivity is very low and not of much interest from an architectural or design perspective. What is interesting is when the system and network response times are close to the response times of users, for then changes made in the network architecture and design to optimize response times can have a direct impact on users' perception of interactivity. Therefore, interactivity is a measure of the response times of the system and network when they are required to actively interact with users. Delay—here the round-trip delay,—is a measure of interactivity. Using these descriptions of timeliness and interactivity, then, timeliness is more likely to be associated with bulk file or image transfer, while interactivity is likely to be associated with remote device access (e.g., telnet), Web use, or visualization.

Reliability, that is, availability from the user's perspective, is a requirement for consistently available service. Not only must the user be able to have access to system resources a very high percentage of the time, but the level of service to the user (in terms of application usage or information delivery) must be consistent. Thus, reliability is closely related to the performance characteristic of reliability (discussed in Chapter 1 as part of RMA), but delay and capacity are also important. It is likely that a combination of all performance characteristics would be used to describe reliability.

Presentation quality refers to the quality of the presentation to the user. This may be the user's perception of audio, video, and/or data displays. As examples, consider the current Internet capabilities of videoconferencing, video feeds (live or delayed), and telephony. While it is possible to do all of these on the Internet, there are other mechanisms that currently provide much better presentation quality. It is often not sufficient to provide a capability over a network, but that capability must be *as good as or better than* other mechanisms, or the user will be disappointed. Network architects and designers often miss this concept. Measures of quality will include all of the performance characteristics.

Adaptability is the ability of the system to adapt to users' changing needs. Some examples of this can be found in distance-independence and mobility. As users rely more and more on the network, they are becoming coupled to logical services and decoupled from physical servers. This decoupling means that users do not have to care where servers are located, as long as they can get the services they need. A result of this is distance-independent computing, where the user loses all knowledge of where jobs are being executed, or where data are sourced, stored, or migrated through the network. *Mobility* refers to mobile or nomadic computing, where the user can access services and resources from any location, using portable devices and wireless access to the network. Adaptability to such user needs forces requirements on the system architecture and design.

Security from the user perspective is a requirement to guarantee the confidentiality, integrity, and authenticity of a user's information and physical resources, as well as access to user and system resources. Security is probably closest to the performance characteristic reliability, but it will impact capacity and delay as well.

Affordability is the requirement that purchases fit within a budget. Although this requirement is not technical, it impacts the architecture and design. What we are concerned with in this requirement is what users or management can afford to purchase for the network, so that our architecture and design do not cost too much to implement. As a user requirement, we look at how costs and funding are tied to users, groups of users, and management. We also consider funding as a systemwide requirement, from an overall budget perspective.

Functionality encompasses any functional requirement that the user has for the system. Functions that the system will perform are often tied to applications that are used on the system. Understanding functionality is important in that it leads into application requirements (covered in the next section). Part of understanding functionality is determining which applications users actually want or apply in their daily work. We do not want to analyze applications that no one is planning to use.

Supportability is a set of characteristics that describes how well the customer can keep the network operating at designed performance, through the full range of mission scenarios described by the customer during the requirements analysis process. This includes how users want or need to be supported by their network operations staff, and any interfaces they will have with a network operations center (NOC). For example, will the network need to be reconfigured to meet different or changing user needs? What applications will the network operations staff and/or NOC need to provide support to users and to identify and troubleshoot problems on the network? Information such as this will be used later as input to the network management architecture.

Future growth is determining if and when users are planning to deploy and use new applications and devices on the network.

In addition to these requirements, we want to know how many users are expected on the network, and their locations. If possible, we must estimate the growth in users over the first one to three years after the network becomes operational, or over the expected life cycle of the network.

2.4   Application Requirements

The application component interfaces with the user and device components and is a key part of the requirements analysis. *Application requirements* are requirements that are determined from application information, experience, or testing, and represent what is needed by applications to successfully operate on the system.

Figure 2.4 shows example application requirements. Application requirements are more technical than user requirements but may still be subjective.

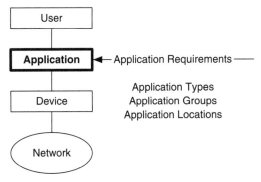

FIGURE 2.4   Types of Application Requirements

2.4.1 Application Types

In the system description (user, application, device, network), the application component is pivotal. This component is often where many requirements for the network are determined, as applications couple users and devices to the network. Applications are often end-to-end, between multiple devices; thus, their requirements span the underlying network.

In the early days of networking, applications required basic connectivity and data transfer across the network. While applications still have these requirements, they are often also required to be high performance or have predictable or guaranteed behavior, to support user requirements for timeliness, interactivity, reliability, quality, adaptability, and security. Thus, user requirements have an impact on application requirements. We can use these service and performance requirements to distinguish between applications that need predictable or guaranteed service and those that can use best-effort service.

Based on service and performance requirements, we type applications as mission-critical, rate-critical, or real-time/interactive, where

- *Mission-critical* applications have predictable, guaranteed, and/or high-performance RMA requirements
- *Rate-critical* applications have predictable, guaranteed, and/or high-performance capacity requirements
- *Real-time* and *interactive* applications have predictable, guaranteed, and/or high-performance delay requirements

These application types are described by their requirements and service metrics.

RMA

Let's first look at RMA, consisting of reliability, maintainability, and availability. Reliability is a statistical measure of the frequency of failure of the network and its components and represents the unscheduled outages of service. Maintainability is a statistical measure of the time to restore the system to fully operational status, once it has experienced a fault. Availability is a measure of the relationship between the frequency of mission-critical failures and the time to restore service. How do these measures relate to the applications that will use the network?

RMA requirements can be subjective. Many users argue that their applications require a high degree of reliability, maintainability, and/or availability from the network, but there are some applications that must maintain high degrees of RMA in order to function. A loss of any part of RMA in such applications may be serious or disastrous, such as:

- Loss of revenue or customers. Examples include applications that handle lots of transactions and money, such as investment banking, airline reservation, or credit card processing applications.

- Unrecoverable information or situation. Telemetry processing and teleconferencing applications are good examples of this type of reliability.

- Loss of sensitive data. Examples include customer ID/billing and intelligence-gathering applications.

- Loss of life. Examples include transportation or health-care monitoring applications.

In these situations either the system is not available to process user/application requests or the system is not available to complete the transactions that are in progress. For applications such as these, a network that offers only best-effort service is not likely to be adequate, owing to its unpredictable and unreliable behavior. These applications require predictable or guaranteed reliability, maintainability, and availability, which may take the form of a predictable or bounded RMA, or a high degree of RMA, or both. Applications that require predictable or high RMA are termed here *mission-critical applications*.

Capacity

In terms of capacity, there are some applications that require a predictable, bounded, or high degree of capacity. Such applications, termed here *rate-critical applications*, include voice, non-buffered video, and some "tele*service" applications

(applications that provide a subset of voice, video, and data together to be delivered concurrently to groups of people at various locations, e.g., teleconferencing, telemedicine, and teleseminars [thus the *tele**]). Rate-critical applications may require thresholds, limits, or guarantees on minimum, peak, and/or sustained capacities.

Note the difference between rate-critical applications and best-effort applications such as traditional file transfer (where the file transfer application is not written to operate only when a predictable or guaranteed service is available). In file transfer (such as in FTP running over TCP, described earlier), the application receives whatever capacity is available from the network, based on the state of the network at that time as well as interactions between TCP and the lower layers. While at times there may be a high degree of capacity, it is inconsistent, and there is no control over the resources in the network to predict or guarantee a specific (usually minimum) capacity in order to function properly. This can often also be tied to the end-to-end delay of the network, as capacity will impact delay.

Delay

Increasing interactivity is arguably the driving force behind the evolution of many applications. Consider the evolutionary path of information access, from telnet and FTP to Gopher (a menu system that simplifies locating resources on the Internet) and Archie (a database that consists of hundreds of file directories) to Mosaic (the precursor to Netscape) and Netscape, made even more interactive with the use of JAVA and virtual reality markup language (VRML). As we saw in the previous section, interactivity relies predominantly on the performance characteristic delay.

Delay is a measure of the time differences in the transfer and processing of information. There are many sources of delay, including propagation, transmission, queuing, processing, and routing. This section focuses on end-to-end and round-trip delays, which encompass all of the delay types mentioned above. From an application service perspective, optimizing the total, end-to-end, or round-trip delay is usually more important than focusing on individual sources of delay. Individual sources of delay become more important as we get into the lower-layer components, as well as in architecture and design optimizations.

Historically, applications used on the Internet did not have strict delay requirements. They relied on best-effort service from the Internet and did not request or expect any service guarantees. Other applications, found primarily on private networks (with proprietary network technologies and protocols), have had more strict delay requirements (as well as capacity and RMA requirements). Some private networks have been effective in providing predictable or guaranteed delay, either by over-engineering the network with substantial spare capacity, or by the trade-off of interoperability with other networks. But we now find that applications with delay requirements are migrating to the Internet, often using VPNs, and applications previously dedicated to a single user or device are now being used across the Internet, forcing a reevaluation of offering services other than best effort on the Internet. This is also forcing a reevaluation of traffic engineering techniques by service providers.

The term *real-time* has been interpreted to mean many different things. Often, real-time means "as fast as possible" by those who do not know, understand, or care about the actual delay relationships between traffic sources and destinations within their network. It is quite difficult to quantify real-time when it is used this way. There are more meaningful ways to describe real-time, as well as non-real-time, interactive, asynchronous, burst, and bulk. These are all described below.

Real-time applications are those that have a strict timing relationship between source and destination, with one or more timers set for the receipt of information at the destination. Information received after the timer(s) expire at the destination is considered worthless and is dropped. Thus, this definition of real-time does not mean that information has to be transferred within a universally known time boundary, but rather that the delay boundary is understood by source and destination, and that the destination does not wait beyond this boundary. Real-time could mean end-to-end delays of 30 ms for some applications and 30 seconds for others. An example of this is non-buffered video playback. If the video stream is delayed beyond the playback timer, the destination will show one or more blank portions of frames (appearing as blips on the screen) and drop the late video. This is done to preserve the time continuity of the video being shown at the playback device. This is what it means to have a strict timing relationship between source and destination—that the information flow is subject to maintaining time continuity.

Real-time is the first of several terms we need to clarify. These terms are often used carelessly, although, as the network architect/designer, we have to take them seriously. Therefore, it is up to us to make sure that ambiguous terms are clarified, as along with requirements based on such terms. This book tries, whenever possible, to provide strict interpretations of such terms to help make them clear.

Given this strict interpretation of real-time, it is safe to say that there are not many real-time applications. But there are some (and their numbers are growing), and it is important to be able to identify them and recognize their strict delay requirements, for they can have a strong impact on the network architecture and design.

Currently, most applications are considered to be non-real-time. *Non-real-time applications* have various end-to-end delay requirements, at times more stringent (in terms of the amount of delay) than real-time applications, but the important factor here is that the destination will wait (within reason) until the information is received. How long the destination will wait is a function of the timers set in the applications, at the devices, and by the protocols used. Non-real-time applications include interactive and asynchronous ones, which account for the vast majority of applications.

Real-time applications are at one extreme of performance; asynchronous applications are at the other. *Asynchronous applications* are relatively insensitive to time, assuming either no timing relationship between source and destination, or a timing relationship outside the bounds of the applications session. A good example of an asynchronous application is email. When email is sent to a recipient, all knowledge of timing (that is, the time when the email is received at any intermediate stop or at the final destination) is lost to the sender. Only if there is an error in the system or recipient information, or if it is requested, is the sender notified. Facsimile is another asynchronous application. When a FAX is sent (when it is buffered in the sending device), the sender loses any knowledge of when the FAX arrives at its destination.

Just as it is important to identify real-time applications, due to their strict timing requirements, it is also important to identify asynchronous applications, due to their lack of timing requirements. Asynchronous applications have little or no impact on the network architecture and design and can usually be ignored.

Just as there are not many real-time applications, there are likewise not many asynchronous applications. Thus, most applications fall in the non-real-time realm, between real-time at one extreme and asynchronous at the other extreme. These applications are called *interactive*. *Interactive applications* assume some timing relationship between source and destination while the application session is active; however, the timing relationship is not as strict as in real-time. Interactive applications are what many people would normally consider real-time, under the connotation of real-time as "as fast as possible." Common interactive applications, such as telnet, FTP, and Web applications, all fall under this type.

Finally, interactive applications may be further subdivided into burst and bulk interactive types. The difference between these types is subtler than with real-time or asynchronous. To distinguish between interactive bulk and burst applications, we need first to understand when the processing times of the system components, particularly the application component, overwhelm the end-to-end or round-trip delay of the network. In other words, we want to distinguish between when an application will frequently and quickly interact with a user and when a user will have to wait substantial periods of time while the application is processing information.

These delay types are summarized in Figure 2.5.

Based on this, *interactive burst applications* are those for which the end-to-end or round-trip network delay is the predominant delay for that application. This type of application is important to identify, as it is sensitive to network delay. Thus, the network architecture and design must accommodate the delay requirements from these applications. An example of an interactive burst application is telnet. During a telnet session, the predominant delay experienced by the user is from the network, not from any processing at the local or remote devices. There are many applications of this type, where users interact with applications and devices across the network and expect responses "as fast as possible."

Interactive bulk applications, by contrast, are those for which processing at the device or application component is the predominant delay. Thus, processing information at either or both end points can overwhelm the end-to-end or round-trip times in the network. This is important to recognize, as the network delay requirement by that application becomes less significant, since it is already eclipsed by application and/or device delays. For example, when an application has high processing delays, say on the order of 100s of ms or seconds, then we have more flexibility in supporting delay in the network than if the processing delay were

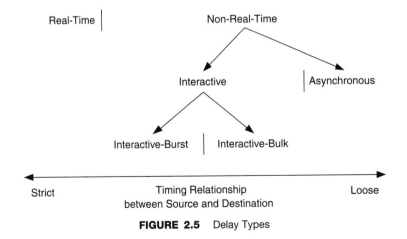

FIGURE 2.5   Delay Types

on the order of microseconds. An example of interactive bulk applications is large file transfer (e.g., FTP). Although FTP has a degree of interaction with the user, there can be times (especially when the file size is large) when the processing of information at the receiving end, as well as the overall time it takes to transfer the entire file, is several orders of magnitude greater than the end-to-end or round-trip network delay.

Why the elaborate breakdown of application types based on delay? As we can see from the above discussion, there are times when an application's requirement for delay is an important consideration in the network architecture and design, and other times when it is not. Whenever we can selectively ignore some applications, and focus on others, the network architecture and design problems become more tractable.

In the next chapter we discuss some of the time parameters associated with interactive burst and bulk applications.

2.4.2 Application Groups

We have so far used various examples of applications to convey application requirements. It is often useful to group applications with similar performance characteristics, as it helps both in the mapping of performance characteristics and in gathering and understanding requirements. It has been useful to me to form groups for applications and keep adding to them as I encounter new applications. When trying to rapidly identify network requirements for a new customer, I have successfully used these groups to help identify requirements, by comparing the new applications to those in groups I have already developed. This process is particularly useful if you have to complete requirements analysis quickly or if you frequently have new customers.

Using the requirements analysis process, the application groups below have been identified. There is some overlap between these groups, and this is not a complete set of groups. It is intended to illustrate how grouping works. You are encouraged to develop your own application groups as you apply the requirements analysis process to your networks.

- *Telemetry/Command-and-Control Applications.* While the title may sound somewhat military, this group actually describes a variety of applications where data and command information is transmitted between remote devices and one or more control stations for command, control, tracking, and determining status of the remote devices. A remote device may be as mundane as an automated teller machine (ATM), sensors in the home, or a remote computer, to esoteric devices such as remotely piloted vehicles (RPVs), spacecraft, or commercial aircraft. Telemetry/command-and-control applications can be characterized as having real-time and/or interactive delay, as well as often being mission-critical.

- *Visualization Applications.* This group ranges from two-dimensional viewing of objects to three-dimensional and virtual reality viewing, immersion, and manipulation of objects. Visualization may be of a numerical simulation or of experimental data. Examples include visualizations of fluid flow fields around various objects (e.g., weather modeling, aeronautics, or medicine), medical, biomedical, and molecular simulations, to commercial and military gaming simulations. Visualization applications can often be characterized as rate-critical and interactive burst.

- *Distributed-Computing Applications.* Applications in this group may range from having the computing devices sharing the same local bus (as in parallel computing), to being co-located at the same LAN (as in a computing cluster), to being distributed across LAN, MAN, and WAN boundaries (as in grid computing). The degree of distribution or parallelism in the computing is also determined by the granularity of the task and the degree of coupling between the computing devices. An example of distributed computing is using desktop computers in the corporate environment late at night, when they are usually idle, by coupling their computing capability to accomplish large tasks normally done on a mainframe. Distributed-computing applications can be characterized as real-time or interactive burst.

- *Web Development, Access, and Use Applications.* Applications in this group are the current interactive equivalents of the traditional remote device and information access utilities telnet and FTP. Web access and use involve accessing remote devices and downloading and/or uploading information. This is done with the aid of graphic interfaces. Typically, Web sessions are interactive, and the amounts of information are small relative to the other application groups (with the possible exception of telemetry/command-and-control). This group of applications is generally considered to be interactive, a mix of interactive burst and interactive bulk.

- *Bulk Data Transport Applications.* When the amounts of information desired are relatively large and the sessions are less interactive (or asynchronous), applications can optimize the data transfer rate at the expense of interactivity. The traditional example of this is FTP; currently, more effective applications such as *mftp* and *arcp* are available. For more information on mftp and arcp, see www.nas.nasa.gov. These applications generally do not have high-performance requirements.

- *Tele*Service Applications*. This group describes the applications that provide a subset of voice, video, and data together to be delivered concurrently to groups of people at various locations. Examples include teleconferencing, telemedicine, and teleseminars (thus the *tele**). The multicast backbone of the Internet is an example of network support for this application group. Tele*service applications can be characterized as having interactive and real-time delay and are often rate-critical and mission-critical.

- *Operations, Administration, Maintenance, and Provisioning (OAM&P) Applications*. System OAM&P applications are required for the proper functioning and operation of the network. Examples include domain name service (DNS), mail services/SMTP, news services/NNTP, address resolution service, network monitoring and management, network security, and systems accounting. These applications are often considered mission-critical and interactive.

- *Client–Server Applications*. These are applications whose traffic flows behave in a client–server fashion, such as enterprise resource planning (ERP), supply chain management (SCM), and customer relationship management (CRM) tools. We discuss traffic flows and client–server flow behavior in detail in Chapter 4. These applications are often mission-critical and interactive.

You may be able to apply more application groups to your networks. If you develop requirements for multiple networks, you will be able to expand upon or modify this list to meet your analysis needs.

2.4.3 Application Locations

Along with typing and grouping applications, it is often useful to determine where an application applies in your (or your customer's) environment. There are usually some applications that apply everywhere, which everyone uses and that reside on almost all devices (e.g., servers, desktops, and laptops). However, often there are applications that apply only to particular users, user groups, servers, floors within a building, or buildings. Whenever possible, you should identify such applications and where they apply, as this will help you in mapping traffic flows during the flow analysis process.

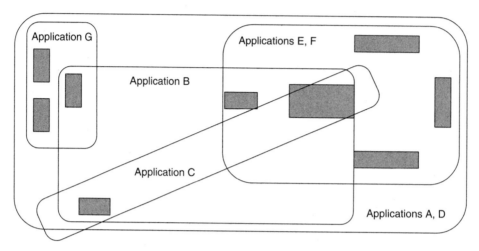

FIGURE 2.6   An Example Applications Map

An example of an applications map, or drawing of where applications apply, is shown in Figure 2.6. In this figure of a campus environment there are three sets of buildings, shown in gray. The location where each application applies is outlined. This is an estimate of the probable locations for applications in an environment, and is the first step toward providing location information in the requirements analysis. In some cases all applications apply everywhere. In other cases we cannot determine where some applications apply. Whenever such information is available, however, mapping that information will help in the requirements and flow analyses.

Application types, their performance requirements, their locations, and application groups form the interface between the application component and the rest of the system.

2.5 Device Requirements

We now turn to the requirements of devices that the network will support, particularly the types of devices, their performance characteristics, and their location information. As you will see, this information builds on the user and application requirements discussed earlier to begin to provide a comprehensive picture of system needs. The relationship of the device component with the rest of the system is shown in Figure 2.7.

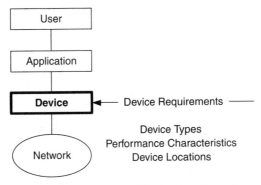

FIGURE 2.7 Types of Device Requirements

2.5.1 Device Types

Devices can be grouped into three categories: generic computing devices, servers, and specialized devices. *Generic computing devices* are the desktop and laptop computers that most users have. This group also includes handheld devices. Popular examples include various forms of Windows-based PCs, laptops and handheld devices, and Mac and LINUX-based workstations and PCs. These are the hosts that form the access points into the network and typically service a single user. Their requirements are important from an end-to-end perspective, as they provide the interface between applications and the network. Their requirements are also important in developing a template for devices from user groups or all users of the network. These end devices also tend to be overlooked, a form of "black box" that networks are connected to and applications run on but are otherwise somewhat ignored.

A lack of understanding of end devices has led to what is known as the "last foot" problem in system performance. This is a modification of the "last mile" problem, which was the difficulty in getting infrastructure, networking, and services into a campus or building. The "last foot" problem is getting services and performance from the device's network interface through the device to its applications and users. This is discussed in detail later in this section.

Typically there are many generic computing devices in a system, and it would be quite difficult to list, describe, and graph each individual device. Therefore, developing a template, or standard description, for one or more "standard" devices in the environment can be useful. Such a description might include device type, network interface, configuration, performance, and applications resident. Figure 2.8 shows an example of a template.

Device Type	NIC Type	Processor	OS	Applications
Low-End PC	10M Ethernet	Pentium I	Win95/98/2000	Word, PP, Finance
High-End PC	10/100M Ethernet	Pentium III/IV	WinPro	Word, PP, DB, Graphics
Generic PC	10/100M Ethernet	Pentium	Win95/98/2000/XP	Word, PP, DB, Graphics
Workstation	10/100M Ethernet	AMD	Linux	DB, Graphic, CAD, SC
Laptop	56 Kb Modem	AMD	Win XP	Word, PP, Others

PP – Powerpoint   CAD – Computer-Aided Drawing
DB – Database   SC – Scientific SW

FIGURE 2.8   An Example Template for Device Descriptions

Servers are computing devices that provide a service to one or more users (i.e., clients). They are typically more powerful, in terms of memory, processing, networking, and peripherals, than users' desktop or laptop devices. Examples of servers include compute servers, storage servers (also known as *mass storage* or *archival* systems), and application servers. Server requirements are important in that they may impact a large number of users. As such, their requirements warrant more attention on a per-device basis than generic computing devices.

Servers also have requirements for "last foot" performance, as well as requirements specific to their server role. A server's functions can often be streamlined to support this server role, which in turn may impact the system. For example, a server may be designed to support high-performance, predictable access to a large number of users. The cumulative effect of users' access to this server on the network needs to be considered. Servers have an impact on the traffic flows within the system; this is examined in the chapters on flow analysis.

Specialized devices are devices that provide specific functions to their users. A parallel computer supporting a large database search engine may be considered either a server or a specialized device, while a video camera on the network would be considered a specialized device. Specialized devices generally do not support direct access to user applications, but rather gather, produce, or process information to be sent to users. Examples of specialized devices include supercomputers, parallel or distributed-computing systems, data gathering and processing systems, medical devices, networked cameras or tools, and handheld devices.

Specialized devices tend to be location dependent. This is significant, for while in most environments generic computing devices and servers are becoming location independent, specialized devices often retain their location dependencies. That said, however, there are times when specialized devices are location independent and servers or generic devices are location dependent. As we will see in gathering requirements, it is important to know and understand the environment we are analyzing, in part to understand any location dependencies of its devices. Specialized devices are often location dependent due to cost. A wind tunnel that provides flow information for car manufacturers is large, stationary, and expensive, making it difficult to replicate. If a network is being built to support this wind tunnel facility, located in Dearborn, Michigan, then the network has to be architected with access to Dearborn in mind, as well as the performance and location requirements of the wind tunnel. Likewise, if a network were being built to provide remote access to medical devices (e.g., CT scanners) for doctors, then the locations of these devices would become access requirements for the system. This is illustrated in Figure 2.9.

While wind tunnels and CT scanners are very specialized (and in the case of wind tunnels, fairly rare) devices, this concept can be expanded to more common devices, such as automated teller machines, traffic sensors, even stoplights. Also

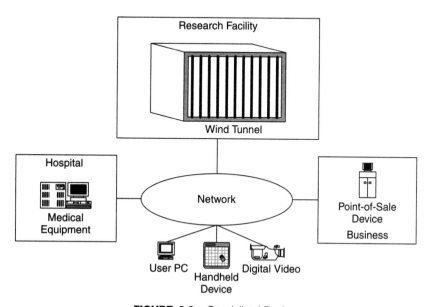

FIGURE 2.9 Specialized Devices

consider location-specific information—from libraries, universities, government centers, or medical centers. Much of this information is also closely tied to its location.

2.5.2 Performance Characteristics

The "last foot" problem introduced earlier focuses on the performance of various components of the device: hardware, firmware, and software that provide the glue between users and applications and the rest of the system. For many environments, it may be difficult to determine or measure the performance characteristics of its devices. Components within a device are proprietary, and performance information about them can be sketchy or unavailable. Software and firmware driving the device, such as the operating system (OS), device drivers, and application programming interface (API), are complex. Therefore, whenever possible, determining this information for a "standard" device and creating a template is a practical solution. Taking the time to research or test one or a few devices, and applying this information in a template, can save a lot of time and still be useful as a first-order approximation of device performance.

Note that device problems frequently are misinterpreted as network problems. Therefore, ignoring device requirements can compromise the network architecture and design. As we will see in the design process, identifying any issues with devices that will be supported by the network can make the design process easier, with more deterministic results.

A simple, general diagram of a device is presented in Figure 2.10. The performance of each of these components impacts the overall performance of the device. As examples, disk-drive seek times, memory access times, and the effectiveness of driver, OS, or API software will all affect the ability of the device to process information to and from the network.

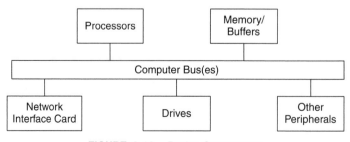

FIGURE 2.10 *Device Components*

By looking at each of these components as integral to the overall performance of the device (and of the system), we are applying the end-to-end perspective within the device—the host in effect becomes a microcosm of the system. What we are looking for in performance characteristics includes

- Storage performance, that is, flash, disk-drive, or tape performance
- Processor (CPU) performance
- Memory performance (access times)
- Bus performance (bus capacity and arbitration efficiency)
- OS performance (effectiveness of the protocol stack and APIs, e.g., the number of memory copies in the protocol stack, or the cost of execution of a given OS on a particular processor)
- Device driver performance

Information about any of these components can be helpful in estimating the overall performance of a device, or in identifying any limiting factors in device performance. For example, testing representative devices may reveal that their network interfaces need to be upgraded (e.g., from 10 Mb/s Ethernet to 10/100 Mb/s Ethernet), or that disk drives need to be replaced, or that an OS upgrade needs to be performed. While it can be time consuming to understand the performance implications of each component of each device type, even a simple and quick attempt at developing device performance requirements can help to ensure that there are no obvious dramatic performance bottlenecks at the device. Understanding at the device component level can help you recognize such bottlenecks early in the analysis process.

2.5.3 Device Locations

Knowing the locations of existing or expected generic computing devices, servers, and specialized devices can be helpful in determining the relationships among users, applications, and networks, as well as the start toward determining traffic flow characteristics for the system.

Location information helps to determine the relationships among components of the system. Coupled with the types and performance requirements of devices, servers, and specialized devices, this information gives us insight on what the relative concentrations of users and devices should be, their placement, and the level of networking needed.

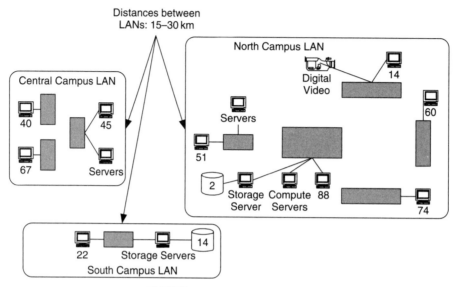

FIGURE 2.11   Device Locations

Figure 2.11 illustrates an environment of three campuses (buildings are shown in gray). Generic computing, servers, and specialized devices are shown for each building. Instead of picturing each user desktop device, a total for each building is noted. The number of each server is shown as well.

Location information also helps to determine the traffic flow characteristics for the system. In Chapter 4 we discuss flow models that describe how traffic flows within the system, based on the relationships between users, applications and devices, are derived partially from location information about these components.

Networks for which location information is particularly important include those whose system components or functions are outsourced; those used in the consolidation of organizations, system components, or functions; and those used in the relocation of system components or functions within an organization.

To see an example of how this information can be used, let's look at an organization that is outsourcing the relocation of its computer resources. The outsourcing agent can either operate, administer, maintain, and provision (OAM&P) the resources at the customer site, or it can remove the resources from the customer site and provide the resources as well as the OAM&P. In the latter case, when the outsourcing agent provides the computing resources, knowing where the resources are to be relocated is important in determining the flow models and level of networking needed. The outsourcing agent may choose a location that is optimized for the administration of the computing resources, yet degrades the overall performance of the system. If a customer's computing resources are accessed via Fast or Gigabit Ethernet, and are then moved away from the customer into a WAN environment, either the access costs to those resources will rise (by requiring high-speed WAN connections) or the performance will degrade. In some cases, moving the resource from a LAN to a WAN environment may result in some applications being rendered unusable.

When the locations of system components change, it is important to evaluate or reevaluate the requirements of the system, to determine if service requirements (both performance and functional) have changed as well. Figure 2.11 illustrates that there are often location dependencies between applications and devices, and that these dependencies need to be identified as part of the device requirements.

For example, if a LAN application that has a requirement for 100 ms round-trip delay is applied to a WAN with a round-trip delay characteristic of 200 ms, the network architecture/design, application(s), or users' expectations will have to be modified to support the new network.

The interface between the device component and the rest of the system consists of the types of devices, their location dependencies, and their performance characteristics.

2.6 Network Requirements

Figure 2.12 shows the relationship of the device component with the rest of the system.

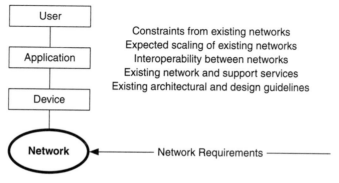

FIGURE 2.12 Types of Network Requirements

For the network component, requirements for a network architecture/design must consider the requirements, services, and characteristics of any existing networks that will be incorporated into, or interface with, the new network.

2.6.1 Existing Networks and Migration

Most network architectures/designs today need to incorporate existing networks. Few networks today are built entirely from scratch. This includes system upgrades, such as adding a new application to the system, migrating to a new or different technology or protocol, or upgrading the network infrastructure, and the expansion or reduction of a system's size or scope. Sometimes the network architecture and design must accommodate any dependencies and constraints imposed by the existing network. Examples include the following:

Scaling dependencies. The existing network can impact how the planned network will scale. For example, how will the addition of the new network to the existing network change the size and scope of the system? Will the change be dramatic, as in growing from a LAN to a WAN, or will the change be within the LAN/MAN/WAN boundaries of the existing network?

Location dependencies. Depending on how the new networks interface with or incorporate the existing network, or how the network modifications are done, the locations and/or concentrations of other components of the system are likely to change. This will show up when we develop flows later in the analysis process.

Performance constraints. The overall performance of the system will be affected by our architecture and design for the expected network (or network modification), how it interacts with the existing network, and its performance levels. Since the performance of the existing network will impact overall system performance, its performance characteristics should be integrated into the performance requirements of the planned network. Since the existing network is already in place, it is usually possible to measure the performance of this network. Thus, while the performance of the expected network is based on a best estimate, the performance of the existing network (and potential performance impacts) can be better understood.

Network, system, and support service dependencies. These include network addressing strategies, security, choices and configurations of routing protocols, and naming strategies, while support services include systemwide security, accounting, and monitoring and management. Current and planned requirements for each of these should be considered.

Interoperability dependencies. Interoperability dependencies between existing and planned networks occur at boundaries between the networks, usually where different technologies or media are used. In addition, by taking an end-to-end perspective on the design, the boundaries between existing and planned networks are points where service information and performance guarantees need to be translated, or they will be lost. Requirements should include the technologies and media of the existing network and any performance and/or functional requirements from the existing network.

Network obsolescence. Even though there may be parts of the existing network that will be integrated into the planned network, these parts, including network devices, protocols, and software, may become obsolete during the life cycle of your new network. Whenever possible, you should note that parts of the network that will be integrated into the planned network, yet are near the end of their usefulness, will need to be transitioned out of the planned network.

In addition, requirements for the users, applications, and devices of the existing network must be considered as part of the system being built, and their requirements analysis done along with the analysis for new parts of the system.

2.6.2 Network Management and Security

Since throughout the architecture and design processes we discuss network management and security, it is useful to briefly outline their requirements here, as a start toward considering them in the architecture and design. It is likely that our analysis of network management and security later in the architecture and design processes will generate new requirements or modify some that we develop here. At this point in the analysis process we want to think in general terms about how we may accomplish network management and security in the new network.

As we will see in the architecture and design processes, there are four categories of network management tasks:

- Monitoring for event notification
- Monitoring for metrics and planning
- Network configuration
- Troubleshooting

Monitoring entails obtaining values for network management parameters from network devices (routers, hubs, switches, etc.) of the system, processing the data, displaying some or all of the data to network operators, and archiving the data. Monitoring for event notification involves taking a frequent snapshot of the network, in order to understand the current state of the network and to help in isolating and solving network problems. If the data are collected for a long-term analysis of network performance, the monitoring is for metrics and capacity, RMA, and/or delay engineering. Network configuration and troubleshooting are more specialized tasks than are modifications of event notification, metrics, and planning.

In monitoring, we want to develop a set of characteristics to use for event monitoring, metrics, and planning. These characteristics may be specific to each type of network device, which will be better understood later in the architecture and design processes. We also need to consider the facilities for accessing these characteristics, which include network management protocols, end-to-end monitoring tools, and direct access methods.

Some architectural issues with network management include determining the paths that the management data will take as well as the hierarchy in management data flows. Management data can be in the path of the users' network traffic (*in-band*) or may take a different path (*out-of-band*). For the pros and cons of in-band versus out-of-band management, see Chapter 7 on network management architecture. Management data flows can be hierarchical, indicating separate components of and locations for the management system, or flat, indicating that the management system is in a single device.

As with the other components of this chapter, the performance characteristics of network management also need to be considered. At this point, we can start to list some potential network management requirements:

- Monitoring methods
- Instrumentation methods. These include the network management protocols (SNMPv3, CMIP, RMON), parameter lists (MIBs), monitoring tools, and access methods
- Sets of characteristics for monitoring
- In-band versus out-of-band monitoring
- Centralized versus distributed monitoring
- Performance requirements

Effect/ Probability	User Devices	Servers	Network Elements	Software	Services	Data
Unauthorized Access	B/A	B/B	C/B	A/B	B/C	A/B
Unauthorized Disclosure	B/C	B/B	C/C	A/B	B/C	A/B
Denial of Service	B/B	B/B	B/B	B/B	B/B	D/D
Theft	A/D	B/D	B/D	A/B	C/C	A/B
Corruption	A/C	B/C	C/C	A/B	D/D	A/B
Viruses	B/B	B/B	B/B	B/B	B/C	D/D
Physical Damage	A/D	B/C	C/C	D/D	D/D	D/D

Effect:
A: Destructive   C: Disruptive
B: Disabling   D: No Impact

Probability:
A: Certain   C: Likely
B: Unlikely   D: Impossible

FIGURE 2.13   Security Risk Assessment

In preparation for developing security requirements for our network, we first need to determine security risks. We will perform a risk analysis for both the existing network and our planned network, to gather information about current security and requirements for new security features. The risk analysis is often structured as a list of questions about the existing network, problems experienced, and network security strengths and weaknesses. It also often contains a risk assessment matrix, which lists potential security problems, system components that need to be protected, and the perceived likelihood and severity of attacks.

Figure 2.13 shows an example of a security risk assessment for a specific organization. In this example a risk analysis was performed as part of the requirements analysis, and the risk matrix shown was completed with the appropriate values.

Security requirements and the results of the risk analysis are used to develop a security plan and define security policies for the network.

2.7   Other Requirements

There are other requirements that apply across all of the components of the system, such as financial and enterprise requirements. There are likely to be other such requirements for your network, and they would be included here.

2.7.1   Supplemental Performance Requirements

In an ideal world, components perform according to specification all the time for the life of the system. Reality is often much less tidy. Couple that with the fact that human beings operate and maintain the systems we build and that their skills, quality, and morale are not always at their maximum means that there are many things that can affect the performance of the network once it is installed. The real world intrudes on the network engineer when he looks beyond the network design and implementation to the initial operational capability (IOC), when the first segments are brought online in a production mode. To satisfy the customers and end users of this creation, the engineer must consider that phase when the network implementation is finally complete and the system is in the hands of the operators. Three characteristics of performance that reflect the customer's impact on our network design are operational suitability, supportability, and confidence. *Operational suitability* is a measure of how well our network design can be configured, monitored, and adjusted by the customer's operators. *Supportability* is a measure of how well the customer can keep the system performing, as designed, over the entire life of the system. *Confidence* is a measure of the ability of the network to deliver data without error or loss at the required throughput.

By identifying, documenting, and validating these constraints with the customer during the requirements analysis phase, the network engineer ensures that the customer understands the trade-offs between cost and performance, acknowledges the time phasing of the total ownership costs, and has a chance to influence these decisions. It also reduces the surprise factor that could hit when the owner has to actually operate the network. In addition, it prepares customers to recognize when their network has exceeded the design capacity and thus to commission an upgrade or service life extension or replacement. Customers who commission a network design to support 1000 connections should be aware that, when their need becomes 20,000 connections, they need an entirely different network; likewise, the need for higher reliability or substantially faster restoration of service during a fault may also warrant a new look at the architecture, components, and operating procedures that comprise the architecture/design.

These three factors must be taken into account when contracting for external services, such as MAN, WAN, or ISP connections, hardware, or maintenance services. The rate at which failures occur and the speed at which service is restored must be included in the specification and must be factors in the selection and award of third-party connectivity services.

These factors are frequently discounted or misunderstood both by network engineers and by the customers themselves. Invariably, when customers are asked for their requirements, these factors are so fundamental to their thinking that they do not think to mention them unless asked. The network engineer must ensure that appropriate questions are asked as part of the requirements process and that the answers are documented so that the design effort will properly factor them into the decisions about architecture, component selection, incorporation of third-party services (e.g., ISP), implementation planning, testing, and initial operational capability.

Operational suitability, supportability, and confidence are described in detail in Chapter 3.

2.7.2 Financial Requirements

A common example of a systemwide requirement is to constrain expenditures to the level of funding available to implement only the network. This requirement serves to limit funding to network devices and services, instead of including other parts of the system (e.g., desktop computers and servers). Funding is often bounded by an overall cost limit, consisting of both one-time and recurring components. One-time costs are based on the actual planning and construction of the network and consist of network architecture, design, procurement, deployment, integration, and testing, and all hardware/software components, as well as the initial installation or establishment of any services from service providers. Recurring costs are for tasks and items that are expected to occur or be replaced/upgraded on a periodic basis. This includes network OAM&P, costs from service providers, and provisions for modifications to the network. Time frames for recurring costs vary, driven by customer/end user, administrative, and management financial cycles and technology life cycles.

The level of funding is usually a constraint to the architecture and design; therefore, it is important to know what this level is as early in the analysis process as possible, in order to avoid creating an architecture and design that are not economically feasible. In knowing funding constraints and the requirements for the network, we should be able to determine when an architecture/design that will meet its requirements will exceed available funding. In determining this early in the process, we can develop arguments for changing the level of funding, the requirements for the network, or both.

The financial requirements gathered during the analysis process will be combined with the users' affordability requirements, to form a complete financial picture of the network. Later in this book we look at funding constraints to the architecture and design and see how these processes work to optimize the architecture and design in order to minimize costs. We will see that it is often beneficial to provide customers with multiple prototype architectures and designs, with well-defined functional and financial differences, so that they can make clear choices about how they want to spend their money.

2.7.3   Enterprise Requirements

There may be times when you have to consider requirements for the network that are commonly considered to be enterprise requirements, such as phone, FAX, voice, and video. The integration of these types of requirements over the same transmission infrastructure as data is becoming common, and such enterprise requirements need to be considered as part of the overall requirements for the network.

2.8   The Requirements Specification and Map

As noted earlier in this chapter, the requirements specification is a document that lists and prioritizes the requirements gathered for your architecture and design, and the requirements map shows the location dependencies between applications and devices. We now discuss these two documents in greater detail.

In going through the requirements analysis process you will be gathering, deriving, and determining requirements from a variety of sources, including users, management, administration, and staff, as well as from documents about the existing network, its applications, and devices. Some requirements will be taken verbatim; others will have to be derived from available information, and still others will have to be estimated.

FIGURE 2.14   Template for the Requirements Specification

When a list of requirements has been developed, you will need to determine which requirements are core or fundamental requirements; which may be considered desirable features for the network; which may be implemented in a future release or upgrade of the network; which are to be rejected; and which actually provide information about the system but may not be actual requirements. You will also need to prioritize requirements to help determine where funds are spent, the order in which functions and features are applied, and where they are applied in the network.

A requirements specification lists all of these requirements and specifies where they were gathered from or how they were derived; reasons why requirements were considered core requirements, features, future requirements, rejected requirements, or informational requirements; and their priority levels.

Figure 2.14 shows a template for this information on a per-requirement basis.

The fields of this template are as follows:

ID/Name. This can be a number identifying the requirement in the order it was gathered or derived, or the name of the requirement.

Date. This indicates the date that this requirement was developed.

Type. This represents the component from which this requirement came (User, Application, Device, Network, Other).

Description. This is a listing of the details, if any, for that requirement. As part of this description, you may indicate whether the requirement is functional or performance in nature.

Gathered/Derived. If the requirement was gathered, this lists where it was gathered. If the requirement was derived, this lists how it was derived.

Locations. This notes where this requirement applies in the environment, if known.

Status. This represents the current state of this requirement (core or fundamental, feature, future requirement, rejected, or informational).

Priority. This is a number representing the priority level of this requirement within its status type.

Requirements may be managed and tracked through common word-processing and spreadsheet software applications. The examples shown here were developed using a popular spreadsheet application. There are also software tools that are optimized for requirements tracking. Experience has shown that most of the common word-processing and spreadsheet applications are sufficient for this task.

Example 2.2. Requirements Analysis for a Company LAN.

A first attempt was made to gather requirements for building a LAN network. The results were as follows:

1. 150 users (60 engineers, 15 HR and Finance, 30 Manufacturing, 10 Management, 30 Sales/Marketing, 5 Other).

2. Each area in the building must support Fast Ethernet connections to the backbone.

3. Database, Visualization, Manufacturing, and Payroll applications are considered mission-critical for this company.

4. Inventory application (INV1) for manufacturing requirements not determined at this time.

5. Database application (DB1) requires a minimum of 150 Kb/s, per session.

6. Engineering users have workstations with GigE NICs.

7. Visualization application (VIS1) for finance requires up to 40 Mb/s capacity and 100 ms round-trip delay.

8. Payroll application (PAY1) requires 100% uptime (while in operation) between finance and outside payroll company.

9. Company must be kept secure from Internet attacks.

10. Company requires a minimum of T1 access to Internet.

11. Current network will be completely replaced, so there are no requirements from existing network.

12. Other general applications: mail, word processing, internal and external Web access.

The first attempt at a requirements specification would look like the one in Figure 2.15. The requirements are simply listed in order, as there are no status or priority levels assigned at this point. There are two exceptions to this: requirements 1 and 11 are shown with a

Requirements Specification							
ID/ Name	Date	Type	Description	Gathered/Derived	Locations	Status	Priority
1	14Jan01	User	User distribution is: 60 engineers, 15 HR and Finance, 30 Manufacturing, 10 Management, 30 Sales/Marketing, 5 Other	Gathered from Management	See Map	Info	TBD
2	12Jan01	Network	Each area of the building must support Fast Ethernet connections to the backbone	Gathered from Management	All Bldgs	TBD	TBD
3	12Jan01	Application	Database, Visualization, Manufacturing, and Payroll applications are considered mission-critical for this company. More information needed.	Gathered from Management	See Map	TBD	TBD
4	20Jan01	Application	Inventory application (INV1) for manufacturing requirements not determined at this time	Gathered from Users (MAN)	See Map	TBD	TBD
5	14Jan01	Application	Database application (DB1) requires a minimum of 150 Kb/s, per session	Gathered from Various Users	TBD	TBD	TBD
6	02Feb01	Device	Engineering users have workstations with GigE NICs	Gathered from Users (ENG)	See Map	TBD	TBD
7	20Jan01	Application	Visualization application (VIS1) for finance requires up to 40 Mb/s capacity and 100 ms round-trip delay	Derived from Application	See Map	TBD	TBD
8	11Feb01	Application	Payroll application (PAY1) requires 100% uptime (while in operation) between Finance and outside payroll company	Gathered from Management	See Map	TBD	TBD
9	12Jan01	Network	Company must be kept secure from Internet attacks	Gathered from Management	TBD	TBD	TBD
10	02Feb01	Network	Company requires a minimum of T1 access to Internet	Gathered from Network Staff	See Map	TBD	TBD
11	02Feb01	Network	Current network will be completely replaced, so there are no requirements from existing network	Gathered from Network Staff	N/A	Info	TBD
12	20Jan01	Application	Other general applications: mail, word processing, internal and external web access. More information needed.	Gathered from Network Staff	TBD	TBD	TBD

FIGURE 2.15   The Beginning of a Requirements Specification

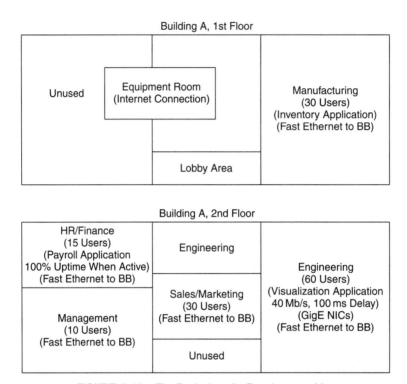

FIGURE 2.16   The Beginning of a Requirements Map

status of informational (info). Also, whenever possible, the locations of these requirements are placed on the corresponding requirements map. The requirements map is shown in Figure 2.16.

2.9   Conclusions

The requirements analysis process is about identifying, collecting, and evaluating requirements for the network. System requirements can be separated into components, where the choice of components is based on your environment and what you want to accomplish with the network architecture and design. In this chapter we considered components based on users, applications, devices, and networks. This is a starting point for grouping requirements. As you develop your own process for requirements analysis, you should determine how you would group requirements.

Requirements form the foundation upon which you develop the network architecture and design. Experience shows that the more effort you put into developing a good set of requirements and understanding the system that will be supported by this network, the better your network architecture and design will be.

By separating system requirements into components, the set of requirements becomes more workable. As we apply the processes, principles, and guidelines of the next chapter to each of these components, you will begin to see how understanding each component helps you to build a picture of the overall system.

Having covered the concepts of requirements analysis, we are now ready to discuss the requirements analysis process. As you work through the next chapter, keep in mind the set of requirements we have identified here for each component of the system, and how they can be combined into a requirements specification and requirements map.

2.10 Exercises

1. Why is requirements analysis important to network architecture and design? Give three reasons.

2. Categorize each of the following requirements as core/fundamental, feature, or informational.
    a. Network must support Fast Ethernet and Gigabit Ethernet interfaces for all devices on the network.
    b. Network backbone should be upgradable in capacity to 10 Gb/s within two years of deployment.
    c. Finance department requires firewall protection to the server.
    d. Existing network consists of 10BaseT Ethernet and FDDI segments.
    e. Network personnel would like to be able to bill users for network service.
    f. Network core must not generate or terminate any user traffic.
    g. Network must support digital video traffic from remote video cameras, and may additionally support sound from these cameras.

3. Categorize each of the following requirements as user, application, device, or network.
    a. Database servers must run brand XYZ software.
    b. Teleconferencing requires at least 350 Kb/s capacity.
    c. Users must be able to submit print jobs of up to 25 MB in size.
    d. Each access network should be able to service 200 corporate users.

4. Give an example of a requirement as it flows from user to application to device to network. Show how it becomes more technical at each component.

5. Which customer requirements below could be categorized as mission-critical? As rate-critical? As real-time? As none of these? Give reasons for each choice.
   a. Processing telemetry data from a space shuttle launch, and providing that data to mission control during launch. (Customer: NASA.)
   b. Processing requests from automated teller machines throughout a city. (Customer: Bank.)
   c. Processing requests for Web pages from your servers. (Customer: Internet service provider.)

6. Give an example of a mission-critical application for each of these three environments: government, military, commercial. Why would each application be considered mission-critical?

7. Section 2.4.1 describes several types of delay (real-time, interactive burst, interactive bulk, and asynchronous). Give examples of applications or traffic types that have each type of delay.

8. Delay performance is increasingly important in support of user and application requirements. Describe why delay is important for the following applications:
   • Voice over IP (VoIP)
   • Non-buffered (real-time) video or audio playback
   • Teleconferencing

9. Based on the following application locations, develop an applications map using the template provided (see Figure 2.17).

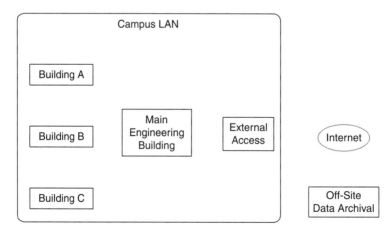

FIGURE 2.17   Template for Exercise 9

a. There is a distributed computing application between all compute servers.
b. There is a data storage/access application between all compute servers and the storage servers in Main Engineering.
c. There is a data migration application between Main Engineering, External Access Building, and Off-Site Data Archival.

10. Which devices below can be considered generic computing devices? Servers? Specialized devices?
a. An ATM machine.
b. Laptops running Linux OS.
c. IBM computing cluster of 128 PCs.
d. Sun Enterprise 450 database server
e. Desktop PC running Windows 2000

11. Add the following devices to the applications map developed in Problem 4.
a. Compute servers are located in Buildings A, B, and C (one server each), and five compute servers are located in Main Engineering.
b. Storage servers are located in Main Engineering (two servers), External Access Building (one server), and at the Off-Site Data Archival location (one server).

12. List the top 10 applications that you expect to use in your (or your customer's) network, or that you currently use in the existing network. List the actual or estimated performance characteristics for each application and try to place them into groups. You can also try to map them to the application groups listed in Section 2.4.2.

CHAPTER CONTENTS

3

Requirements Analysis: Process

The principles, guidelines, and procedures for requirements analysis are all part of the process model. This model, shown in Figure 3.1, outlines the major steps to gather, analyze, and develop requirements for your network.

3.1 Objectives

In this chapter you will learn about gathering and managing user, application, device, and network requirements. This includes setting and managing your customer's expectations about the network. You will learn about determining the variables to measure (service metrics) and how to make measurements. We introduce modeling and simulation, and how they and other approximation techniques can be used to describe user and application behavior. You will learn about developing performance requirements for capacity, delay, and RMA, including developing performance thresholds and limits. These are useful in distinguishing between low- and high-performance requirements for your network. You will learn about general and environment-specific thresholds and limits and how to determine them. Some general thresholds are presented for your use. We also discuss predictable and guaranteed performance requirements and their importance. Along with gathering and developing requirements, you will learn about mapping requirements to geographic locations, in preparation for traffic flow analysis.

3.1.1 Preparation

The material in this chapter builds on what was presented in Chapter 2. Therefore, the recommended sources of information listed in Chapter 2 also apply here.

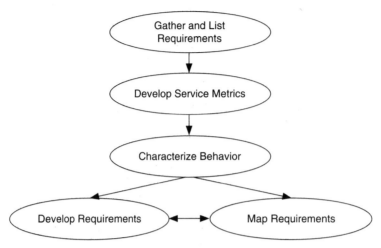

FIGURE 3.1   The Requirements Analysis Process

3.2   Gathering and Listing Requirements

Service requirements are gathered and developed with initial conditions on the architecture and design, with input from users, administration, and management, and then refined by applying our experience and knowledge about the analysis process. Some guidelines for quantifying requirements and developing thresholds and limits are given in this chapter, but first we must communicate with the users to gather their requirements. We begin with a discussion of the initial conditions on the network.

3.2.1   Determining Initial Conditions

Initial conditions are the basis for the start of the analysis process. They help to determine what you are designing toward, as well as the reasons for the architecture and design. *Initial conditions* consist of the type of network project, the scope of the architecture and design, initial architecture/design goals, and any outside forces acting on the network. You need to understand these initial conditions, as they will influence the network architecture and design, and will often act as constraints on the architecture/design. The initial conditions could also be considered to be the current state of the existing network's architecture and design.

Before starting the process of gathering and analyzing requirements, you are likely to have some notion of the initial conditions for the network project you are undertaking. For example, you probably know the type of network project, as well as the scope of the project. Some examples of these are as follows:

Type of Network Project
- New network
- Modification of an existing network
- Analysis of network problems
- Outsourcing
- Consolidation
- Upgrade

Scope of Network Project
- Network size
- Number of sites
- Distance between sites

You may get your initial architecture/design goals from your customer, and part of this process is to validate those goals, possibly adding to, subtracting from, or modifying them during the process. Examples of such goals are:

Initial Architecture/Design Goals
- Upgrade technology/vendor
- Improve performance to part or all of network
- Support new users, applications, or devices
- Solve perceived problems within system
- Increase security
- Support a new capability in system

Initially, you may not even be aware of outside forces, be they political, administrative, or financial, acting on the network unless you are part of the organization requesting the work. Thus, you are likely to have some, but not all, of the initial conditions for the network architecture/design.

Knowing the type and scope of the network project helps you to focus your efforts. For example, replacing an old network with an entirely new one minimizes the number of constraints placed on the architecture/design by the existing network (except for possibly any existing external networks that the new network will have to interface with), allowing you to focus on achieving architectural/design goals for this new network. When the project is a modification or upgrade of an existing network, you have more constraints from the existing network. The existing network provides information about the current behavior of the network and what can be expected from the changes to the network. The existing network constrains the architecture and design from the perspective of how to connect and interoperate with part of or the entire existing network. Thus, the performance and functions of the existing network, along with the reasons for making changes to the network, are important initial conditions.

These conditions also apply when you are doing only the analysis of a network. In this case the network may not be functioning as planned, and you are trying to determine where there are problems in the architecture or design, or where the implementation varies from the architecture/design. If you are building a network to allow for outsourcing of resource OAM&P, then the initial conditions will include where the outsourcing will occur, and the methods used by the outsourcing agent to provide OAM&P functions.

There are likely to be several constraints on the network architecture and design. By examining the initial conditions at the start of the analysis process, you stand a much better chance of understanding, removing, or working with these constraints. Common constraints on a network project include funding limitations; working with various organizations or groups within an organization; organizational rules and regulations; time and schedule limitations; and technical constraints from existing users, applications, devices, networks, and management.

Funding limitations are critical to the network project. As we will see in the architecture and design processes, architecture/design choices are coupled to available funding. Disregarding funding in the analysis process can lead to architecture/design choices that will not be implemented, while considering this limitation up front helps you to make the most intelligent use of funding for the network. In this sense funding limitations can be viewed as positive, in that they force the network architect to develop creative solutions to fit the funding limitations. It is also important to get as good a forecast for future funding as possible.

Organizational constraints, such as whom you will be working with or how groups interact, can become problems during the project. Knowing these constraints in advance allows you to prepare for any organizational problems, usually by buffering yourself and the project from problem groups or individuals. Sometimes, but not always, management can help with this type of constraint.

There are often political constraints to the network project. Sometimes the technical solution to a network problem is constrained by the political desires of users, management, or staff. Such constraints can be the most daunting of all, as they are often illogical. However troublesome they may seem, political constraints must be considered as part of the network project. Depending on your position in the project, you may have options on how to deal with this type of constraint. As a consultant you may be able to defer to management in dealing with politics, or even refuse the project. As an employee, however, you are more likely to be an integral part of the organization, not easily separated from political issues.

Existing components in the system will often act as constraints. Users suffer from inertia, not wanting to accept changes in the ways they do their work. Applications written to be used locally on a device or for a particular network technology or protocol may have to be modified to function on the new network. Device interfaces and drivers may have to be changed or upgraded. Existing networks bring their performance and functional limitations to the project. By knowing early in the process what parts of the existing system you have to incorporate or support in the new network, you can determine which architectural/design choices will work and, just as important, which will not work.

Part of the initial conditions for your network project may be determining its performance target: multi-tier performance or single-tier performance (Figure 3.2). *Multi-tier performance networks* typically have one or a few applications, users/groups, and/or devices whose performance requirements are significantly greater than other performance requirements for that network. As a result there is a threshold between low- and high-performance requirements for this type of network. Typically, this set of high-performance requirements drives how and where performance is architected into the network.

On the other hand, *single-tier performance networks* do not have a distinctive set of applications, users, or hosts that have significantly greater performance requirements for that network; therefore, there is no threshold between low- and high-performance for this type of network. This is significant in that, without a set of high-performance requirements to drive how and where performance is architected into the network, performance is architected to support everyone equally.

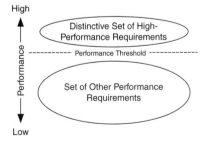

Multi-Tier Performance Network: Where one or a few applications, users/groups, and/or devices whose performance requirements are significantly greater than other performance requirements for that network

Single-Tier Performance Network: No distinctive set of applications, users, or hosts that have significantly greater performance requirements for that network.

FIGURE 3.2   Determining Performance Targets: Single or Multi-Tier Performance

This is one of the fundamental concepts in this book, which we discuss in greater detail in the architecture and design processes. For many networks you may need to consider both types in your architecture and design.

Determining the initial conditions for the network leads you into the requirements analysis process. You should know some of the initial conditions and will have to learn others. As you start digging for answers, you are gathering information for the analysis process.

3.2.2 Setting Customer Expectations

At this point in the analysis process it is important to begin to set customer expectations. This consists of:

- a rapid, initial evaluation of the problem, and
- estimating resources and schedule

This is not intended to be an in-depth estimate, but rather a quick evaluation to catch obvious problems. How quick the evaluation is depends, in part, on your role in the project. If you are a consultant or advisor, you may have to be very quick, on the order of hours or days. If you are the network architect/designer for the organization's network, you may have weeks to do the evaluation. In general, this evaluation can be done on the order of a few days. The intent is to inform customers, early in the process, when their expectations are unrealistic. This helps to realign the customer, if necessary, and avoids backloading of the project.

There will be times when you find that the customers' definition of the problem, and their expectations, is quite correct. Usually, however, their expectations need to be adjusted somewhat. And there may be times when you find that their expectations and your expectations are so far apart that it is better not to continue on that project. It is better to discover this early in the project.

When they are possible, problem statements can be quite useful for your project. *Problem statements* are descriptions of each of the problems being addressed by your network project. Problem statements form the basis of the network project. Requirements should be coupled to problem statements during the requirements process. In doing so, we ensure that each requirement is associated to one or more problems, and that each problem has some requirements applied to it.

3.2.3   **Working with Users**

In working with users, your first inclination may be to think "this takes too much time," "they are not cooperative," "they don't know what they want," and so on, but this is a vital, if sometimes painful, part of the process. By initially spending time with users, you gain a better understanding of their behavior patterns and environment. For the end users, discussing your network plans with them helps them to understand what you are trying to accomplish and builds lines of personal communication that will be useful when you are installing, debugging, and operating the network later on.

While it can be challenging to communicate with users (including administration and management), there are some successful techniques that you can use:

- developing a survey to email, FAX, or mail to users
- following up on the survey with one-on-one telephone calls or conference calls
- Following up calls with face-to-face meetings with selected individuals or groups
- Whiteboard sessions to elicit ideas from users
- Spending time with users while they work to better understand what they do and how they do it

A key trade-off is the amount of time spent versus the quality of information gathered. Working with your users, administration, and management pays off in another way, in getting them to see that you are taking an active, systems approach in the network project, not just developing a network "in the dark." In order for the system to meet users' needs, users must be able to communicate these needs to you; the applications have to be designed to work across the network; and devices must be chosen with the system in mind. Since the network is central to the system, your role in bringing the systems approach to the users is important. In a sense, you are fostering support for the network, its architecture and design, and its role in the system.

Therefore, it is important not to take a hit-and-run approach, talking to the users only to get their requirements and not following up with them. By building relationships with the users, administration, and management, through discussing their requirements, advising them of results and anticipated actions, and informing them of progress with the network project, you are developing advocates for your network. This may be vital when you need to upgrade the network in the future, or if you have to defend your architectural and design decisions.

While gathering requirements, look for warning signals, also known as "red flags." For example, warning signals occur when there is a lack of precision or clarity in requirements, such as the following:

- Misuse of "real time"
- Availability as solely a percentage (99.99%)
- "High performance" without verification
- Highly variable, inconsistent requirements
- Unrealistic expectations from the customer

When you encounter such warning signals, you should attempt, whenever possible, to clarify the meaning of the statement. Later in this chapter we discuss ways to clarify several red flags.

When you are gathering requirements and interacting with users, it is a good time to assess the opinion that users have of the current network, as well as the networking and operations staff.

3.2.4 Taking Performance Measurements

Whenever possible, it is helpful to measure performance levels of applications and devices that will be used in the planned network. This is often done either by testing applications and devices on a separate, controlled network (e.g., testbed network) or by measuring their performance levels on the existing network.

Building a small testbed network to measure application and device performance can serve multiple purposes. Since a testbed network is controlled, you can ensure that there is sufficient capacity available for your applications and devices. Thus, the network does not limit the performance of the applications and devices under test. You will be able to measure peak performance, from which you can derive performance requirements for those applications and devices.

Measurements of peak application and device performance can be used to determine how much degradation in performance is experienced on the existing network. Such measurements become a validation of performance problems on the existing network.

Along with performance measurements, you can often capture all of the traffic from an application session, by promiscuous monitoring of the network. This information is useful in characterizing and modeling application and user behaviors, discussed in Section 3.4. Tools that can help capture traffic include Sniffer, Ethereal, and Etherpeak.

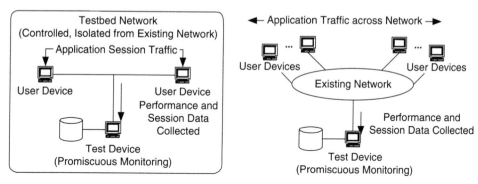

FIGURE 3.3   Measuring Performance Using a Testbed and on the Existing Network

If a testbed network cannot be built to measure performance, measurements can be made on the existing network (if permitted by management). While you will be able to get performance data using this technique, the existing network will limit application and device performance. This technique is still quite useful to capture traffic to characterize and model application and user behaviors. These two techniques are shown in Figure 3.3.

3.2.5   Tracking and Managing Requirements

Requirements also need to be tracked and managed. A listing of requirements should be kept up to date, in a location where everyone involved in the process has access to them. The Web is a great tool for posting, tracking, and managing requirements. There are a number of methods used to track and manage requirements; two of these are shown below. First is paragraph form, where a requirement is changed within its original paragraph. Example 3.1 shows a requirement managed in this form.

Example 3.1. A Requirement for Upgrades to Network Equipment Is Shown Below.

NR - 1.0-102. ~~All~~ (technology A 3/7/2007) network equipment shall be capable of software (~~or firmware 4/1/2000~~) (deleted 4/17/2007) based upgrades to allow it to support changes to ~~high-speed~~ (any 5/20/2007) data service features and functions.

This requirement has been changed as part of the analysis process. As you can see, changes were made at various times, reflecting the evolution of requirements as you talk to users, management, and staff. In this example one requirement (for software-based upgrades) was changed on 4/1/2007 to include firmware-based upgrades, which was then deleted on 4/17/2007, restoring it to its original form. It is important to note that, while a requirement evolves, the description of that requirement keeps all changes visible. In this example you can tell what the original requirement was and how it has changed. Thus, if someone wants to make a change that was attempted before, he or she will know that beforehand.

Another method to track and manage requirements is to use a tabular form. In this method the requirement is kept in its original form, and any changes to it are added to a table. Figure 3.4 shows how this is done, using the requirement from Example 3.1.

Other software tools can be used for this process, such as databases and spreadsheets. The key point here is that requirements documents should be living documents, updated on a regular basis to reflect the changing nature of the network and system.

As a list of what the system needs from the network architecture and design, these requirements will be used as the foundation for the rest of this book. Initial conditions, constraints, and any assumptions about the environment of the network project should be included with the list of requirements. This helps to determine the system components for which we need to get more information.

ID/Name	Date	Type	Description
NR - 1.0-102	01Jan2007	Original	All network equipment shall be capable of software-based upgrades to allow it to support changes to high-speed data service features and functions.
	07Mar2007	Change	"All network equipment" changed to "Technology A"
	01Apr2007	Change	"software-based upgrades" changed to "software or firmware-based upgrades"
	17Apr2007	Deletion	Change of 01Apr2000 deleted
	20May2007	Change	"high-speed" changed to "any"

FIGURE 3.4   Requirements Tracking and Management in Tabular Form

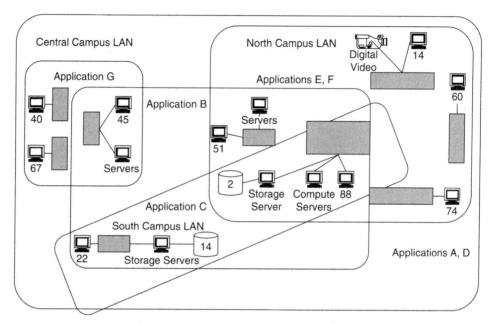

FIGURE 3.5   An Example Metropolitan-Area Map

3.2.6 **Mapping Location Information**

As part of the analysis process, the locations of applications and devices will be mapped to show their relative physical locations. In Chapter 2 we introduced the concept of mapping applications and devices. While gathering requirements, you should note (when possible) the locations of servers and specialized devices, and where specific applications are being used. Figure 3.5 shows an example of how this is done with a metropolitan-area environment with devices and applications.

3.3 **Developing Service Metrics**

After gathering requirements for our network, the next step is to analyze these requirements in order to distinguish between various performance levels in the network. We will develop and use performance thresholds and limits to distinguish between low and high performance, and also use performance characteristics to identify predictable and guaranteed performance levels. Performance thresholds and limits and performance characteristics are measured in the system with service metrics.

Service metrics are either actual measurable quantities in the network or are derived from measured quantities. These service metrics are important, as they are where "the rubber meets the road"—where requirements from all layers in the system are distilled into configurable and measurable quantities.

Recall from Chapter 2 that in order for a performance characteristic to be useful, it must be configurable, measurable, and verifiable within the network. This is particularly true when parts of the network are outside the control of the network administrator—for example, when a service provider is used to supply a service such as Frame Relay in the network, or when parts of the network (or the entire network) are outsourced. In cases such as these, service metrics can be used to ensure that you are getting the service you are requesting (and paying for) from the service provider or outsourcing agent.

The types of service metrics you use will depend on your design and the types of equipment (network devices) you implement in your network, but at this point in the analysis process, you can influence or require what will be measured in the network and (to some extent) how it will be measured.

Service metrics for RMA include:

- Reliability, in terms of mean time between failures (MTBF) and mean time between mission-critical failures (MTBCF)
- Maintainability, in terms of mean time to repair (MTTR)
- Availability, in terms of MTBF, MTBCF, MTTR
- Optionally, uptime and downtime (as a percent of total time), error and loss rates at various levels, such as packet error rate, bit error rate (BER), cell loss ratio (CLR), cell misinsertion ratio (CMR), frame and packet loss rates

Service metrics for capacity include:

- Data rates, in terms of peak data rate (PDR), sustained data rate (SDR), and minimum data rate (MDR)
- Data sizes, including burst sizes and durations

Service metrics for delay include:

- End-to-end or round-trip delay
- Latency
- Delay variation

As configurable and measurable quantities in the network, service metrics can be described in terms of variables in network devices. There are also mechanisms to configure and measure these variables. As we see in Chapter 7 on network management, current mechanisms to configure and measure service metrics are found within network management platforms that use the simple network management protocol (SNMP) and the common management information protocol (CMIP), both of which access variables described in management information bases, or MIBs. MIBs describe generic and enterprise-specific management variables.

Examples of variables used as service metrics include:

- Bytes in/out (per interface)
- IP packets in/out (per interface)
- Dropped Internet control message protocol (ICMP) messages/unit time (per interface)
- Service-level agreement (SLA) metrics (per user)

  - Capacity limit
  - Burst tolerance
  - Delay
  - Downtime

3.3.1 Measurement Tools

In addition to the management protocols and MIBs, we can use commonly available tools to help measure service metrics. One such tool is the utility *ping* (available in TCP/IP releases), which roughly measures round-trip delays between selected sources and destinations in the network. Another tool is *pathchar* (available from ee.lbl.gov), which combines round-trip delay and per-link capacity measurements with path traces, as does another popular utility *traceroute*. Another popular tool to analyze TCP traffic is *TCPdump*. There are also proprietary, enterprise, and technology-specific tools that may be used in addition to those described here.

For example, one method to monitor availability in the network is to use ping to estimate delay and packet loss (see Figure 3.6). Ping tells us the approximate round-trip delay, as well as when ICMP echo packets (ping packets) are lost in the network or at the destination. While not an exact method, it is fairly simple to set up and use and provides an early warning mechanism for RMA problems.

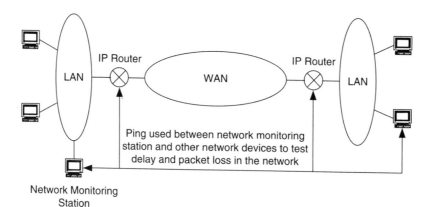

Network Monitoring
Station

FIGURE 3.6   Using Ping and IP Packet Loss as Service Metrics for RMA

	Service Metric	Where Metric Will be Measured in System	Measurement Method
1	LAN Delay	Between NM Device and Each Router in LAN	Ping
2	Wan Delay 1	Between NM Device and Local Router Interface to WAN	Ping
3	WAN Delay 2	Between NM Device and Remote Router Interface to WAN	Ping
4	LAN Packet Loss	At Each Local Router	SNMP

FIGURE 3.7   Example Service Metrics

When developing service metrics, we also want to try to determine where in the system we want to measure each metric, as well as potential mechanisms for measurement, as in Figure 3.7.

3.3.2   Where to Apply Service Metrics

Where service metrics are applied is determined in part by what you plan to achieve from them (e.g., separating responsibilities). They are useful when trying to isolate and track problems in the network, especially when there are multiple groups responsible for the network. For example, in Figure 3.6, the service metrics that are applied can also be used to separate responsibilities between an end-to-end provider, a WAN service provider, and other intermediate providers.

3.4   Characterizing Behavior

Characterizing behavior means representing how users and applications use the network, in order to develop and understand their requirements. These representations may be very simple, comprising estimates of user session duration, the number of active sessions, and data sizes; or they may be complex and detailed models of user and application behavior. The goal of characterizing behavior for our network is to determine if we can estimate network performance requirements through understanding how users and applications behave across the network.

In this section we examine some of the characteristics of users and applications that can be used to modify and better estimate network performance requirements. We then apply these user and applications characteristics during the flow analysis process.

The types of behavior that we examine include:

- User behavior
- Application behavior
- Network behavior

3.4.1   Modeling and Simulation

Developing models or simulations of user, application, and network behavior is often useful in predicting, determining, or estimating requirements and data flows. Models can range from easy, simplistic, first-order approximations to highly complex and time consuming. What you get out of a model or simulation depends on the amount of time and effort you put into it.

Modeling and simulation are useful throughout the analysis process for characterizing user, application, and existing network behaviors. They are also useful during the architecture and design processes for understanding the temporal and spatial behaviors of traffic flows, as well as understanding equipment type, placement, configuration, and behavior under stress or failure. Figure 3.8 shows an example simulation of a simple network. This example shows several devices connected to a shared media network and is based on a model developed to show performance characteristics of this network under stress.

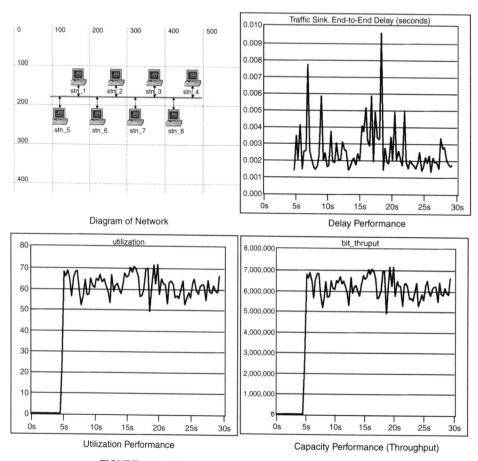

FIGURE 3.8 Simulation of Network Performance Behavior

The displays in this figure show the results of performance tests run on this simulation. Throughput, utilization, and delay are displayed graphically over time to represent the temporal behavior of the network.

Models and simulations can be developed using proprietary or publicly available tools. One clear benefit from having such models is that, once developed, they can be used again and again to help tune the system for optimal performance. Thus, although such models and simulations may take time and effort to develop, their payback over time can be substantial.

3.4.2 User Behavior

In conjunction with identifying service metrics for our network, it is useful to understand how users of the system will apply applications. Simple usage patterns can include user work times and durations; and for each application the total number of users, the frequency that a user is expected to have an application session running (usually as number of sessions per user, per day), how long an average application session will last (usually on the order of minutes), and an estimate of the expected number of simultaneous user sessions for that application.

The logic here is that we can develop a rule of thumb for scaling the expected performance of the network by examining user and application behavior. Figure 3.9 shows the characteristics of how a user uses an application. This is an example of a simple, first-order approximation of user and application behavior. In this figure an application session is described by some common characteristics. First, the sessions are shown with the times that the session is active (as boxes). The size of each box indicates the duration of activity, and the number of boxes per unit time indicates

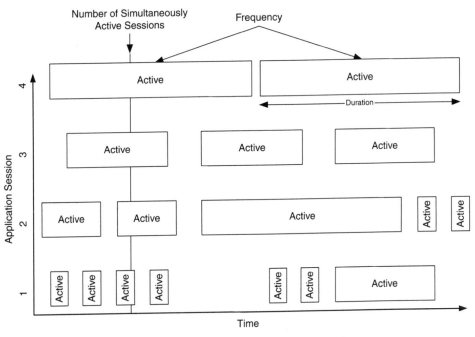

FIGURE 3.9 Characterization of User Behavior

the frequency of activity. Also shown in this figure is the number of simultaneous sessions that are active at any given point in time.

Estimating the frequency and duration of application sessions and the number of simultaneous sessions allows you to apply a modifier to the performance requirement for each application (or at least those applications you consider important enough to characterize). For example, if you can estimate the number of simultaneous sessions for an application, that estimate can be used as a multiplier for that application's capacity requirement. Similarly, if you know the duration of an application session, you can use that to help estimate the amount of time that service for that application will need to be configured within the network.

3.4.3 Application Behavior

It is also useful to determine the behavior of application sessions. Along with user behavior, application behavior can help you to modify performance requirements to achieve a better estimate of what services and performance levels you will need for your network.

In characterizing application behavior you want to consider the data sizes that the application will be processing and passing across the network; the frequency and time duration for data to be passed across the network; any traffic flow characteristics you can get for the application, such as flow directions (e.g., from client to server); and any requirements for multicasting (including broadcasts).

In applying user and application behavior you can go from a fairly simple approximation to a very complex model. For example, you can make some simplifying assumptions as to usage patterns and application behavior. One simple model is to assume that there will be only one session of an application active at any time. Another model is to apply statistical formulas to the usage pattern and application behavior. This can be quite successful when the application is well understood, such as in telephony applications.

While you can attempt to characterize behavior for all users and applications for your network, you usually get the greatest benefit by applying this analysis to the most important (mission-critical, rate-critical, real-time, interactive, high-performance) applications and their users, as their requirements typically drive the network architecture and design. While characterizing usage patterns and application behavior can be both difficult and time consuming, you will find that doing so greatly helps your understanding of the system's requirements and how to apply them. However, you should be sure that you can afford the time and effort it will take. From personal experience, I have seen quick first-order approximations developed in days, and complex, detailed models and simulations that have taken months to refine. However, many good approximations can be done on the order of a few weeks.

3.5 Developing RMA Requirements

Now we will expand on the performance requirements previously discussed, developing and quantifying requirements whenever possible. In this section we discuss two types of thresholds: general and environment specific. *General thresholds* are those that apply to most or all networks. They are rules of thumb that have been determined via experience to work in most environments. They are applied when there are no environment-specific thresholds to use. *Environment-specific* thresholds are determined for the environment of the current network project you are working on. They are specific to that environment and typically are not applicable to other networks. These thresholds are useful in distinguishing between low and high performance for the network.

3.5.1 Reliability

Reliability is a statistical indicator of the frequency of failure of the network and its components and represents the unscheduled outages of service.

One measure of reliability is mean time between mission-critical failure (MTBCF), usually expressed in hours. A related measure is the mean time between failure (MTBF), which considers all failures, regardless of their significance at the time of failure, and is a conservative approximation, useful in simple systems. MTBF can confuse the designer of a complex system. As systems become more complex and resources limitations restrict the degree of diversity or the purchase of higher-reliability components, the use of the MTBCF becomes more illuminating, although it does take more careful analysis, focusing on the system performance during specific mission scenarios. MTBF is computed as the inverse of the failure rate, which is estimated through testing or analysis in terms of failures per hours of operation. Criticality is factored in by considering the failure rates of only the components that are critical to the mission. On the surface, reliability arithmetic is a little confusing; remember that calculations for reliability of systems are really performed by adding failure rates (failures per hour) of the components and then inverting them.

3.5.2 Maintainability

Maintainability is a statistical measure of the time to restore the system to fully operational status, once it has experienced a fault. This is generally expressed as mean time to repair (MTTR). Repairing a system failure consists of several stages: detection, isolation of the failure to a component that can be replaced, the time required to deliver the necessary parts to the location of the failed component (logistics time), and the time to actually replace the component, test it, and restore full service. MTTR usually assumes the logistics time is zero; this is an assumption, which is invalid if a component must be replaced to restore service but takes days to obtain.

3.5.3 Availability

Availability (also known as operational availability) is the relationship between the frequency of mission-critical failure and the time to restore service. This is defined as the mean time between mission-critical failures (or mean time between failures) divided by the sum of mean time to repair and mean time between mission-critical failures or mean time between failures. These relationships are shown below, where A is availability.

$$A = (MTBCF)/(MTBCF + MTTR) \text{ or } A = (MTBF)/(MTBF + MTTR)$$

Some important considerations in evaluating availability are often overlooked. First of all, availability does not necessarily reflect the percentage of time that the system is operational; scheduled maintenance is not taken into account in this calculation, only unscheduled maintenance. This is significant because scheduled maintenance does not penalize the system since it can be performed when the components are not needed to perform the mission. Our real concern is the surprise nature of system failures, which is reflected in availability.

Analyzing a network's availability gives us the ability to schedule preventive maintenance and replace frequently failing components at a higher interval than the failure rate, thereby increasing the reliability of the overall system. Another way to improve availability is to reduce the MTTR, either through diversity or accelerated replacement capabilities. Several ways to achieve diversity include installing automated switchover capabilities for critical components so that they automatically switch over to a redundant unit in milliseconds once a fault is detected; however, automatic switching is an expensive feature to add to these systems. If the pressure to restore service does not warrant this level of expense, rapid replacement solutions can improve MTTR substantially over traditional troubleshooting and repair procedures: hot spares that can be manually switched vastly accelerate the restoration of service, as does prepositioning spare components in proximity to the critical component's location.

Other measures of availability include uptime, downtime, and error and loss rates.

Uptime and Downtime

A common measure of availability is expressed in terms of percent of uptime or downtime. For example, a request for proposal (RFP) from a potential customer may state a required uptime of 99.999% (commonly known as "five nines"), but what does that really mean? What do the terms *uptime* and *downtime* really mean?

When availability is represented as a percent of uptime or downtime, it is measured per week, month, or year, based on the total amount of time for that period. *Uptime* is when the system (applications, devices, networks) is available to the user (in this case, the user may also be an application or device). By available, we mean the range from having basic connectivity to actually being able to run applications across the network. How this is described in the requirements analysis is important to how it will be measured and verified. Likewise, *downtime* can range from being unable to connect across the network, to having connectivity but with loss rates high enough (or capacity low enough) that applications do not function properly. Figure 3.10 shows some commonly used availability percentages (as percent of uptime), ranging from 99% to 99.999%.

% Uptime	Amount of Allowed Downtime in Hours (h), Minutes (m), or Seconds (s) per Time Period			
	Yearly	Monthly	Weekly	Daily
99%	87.6 h	7.3 h	1.68 h	14.4 m
99.9%	8.76 h	44 m	10 m	1.4 m
99.99%	53 m	4.4 m	1 m	8.6 s
99.999%	5.3 m	26.3 s	6 s	0.86 s

FIGURE 3.10   Uptime Measured over Different Time Periods

Another way to view availability is by how much downtime can be tolerated per time period. The range shown in Figure 3.10—99% to 99.999%—covers the majority of requested uptime requirements. At the low end of this range, 99% allows the system to be down quite a bit of time (over 87 hours/year). This may be acceptable for testbeds or system prototypes but is unacceptable for most operational systems. When commercial service providers offer uptime at the low end of this range, this must be factored into the overall availability for the network.

An uptime level of 99.99% is closer to where most systems actually operate. At this level 1 minute of downtime is allowed per week, which equates to a few transients per week, or one minor interruption per month (where a transient is a short-lived network event [on the order of seconds], such as traffic being rerouted, or a period of congestion). Many networks that once had uptime requirements below 99.99% are now relying on the network much more and are revising uptime requirements to 99.99% or greater.

At 99.999%, most systems begin to push their operational limits. This level of performance, which indicates that the network is highly relied upon (e.g., for mission-critical applications), will impact the network architecture and design in several areas, as discussed in later chapters.

Finally, an uptime beyond 99.999% approaches the current fringe of performance, where the effort and costs to support such a high degree of uptime can skyrocket. There are even some applications that cannot tolerate any downtime at all while in session. For these types of applications, uptime is 100% while in session. An example of such an application is the remote control of an event (e.g., piloting a vehicle, performing an operation), where downtime may result in a loss of the vehicle or possible loss of life (one of the criteria for a mission-critical application). In cases like this, however, the times of high availability are often known well in advance (scheduled) and can be planned for.

We should note at this point that many system outages are very brief in time (transients) and may not impact users or their applications. In some cases the users may not even know that a problem existed, as the outage may manifest itself merely as a pause in an application. Yet such events are part of the reliability estimate, especially in networks where there are strict limits on reliability. Therefore, while a 10-minute weekly downtime (or 99.9% uptime) would be noticeable (e.g., application sessions dropping) if it occurred all at once, it could actually be a distribution of several 15-second transients, each of which results in applications stalling for several seconds.

With this information and the previous table of uptime estimates we can present a general threshold for uptime. The general threshold for uptime, based on practical experience, is 99.99%. When applying this general threshold, uptime requirements less than 99.99% are considered low performance, and uptime requirements greater than or equal to 99.99% are considered high performance. Remember that this general threshold is used in the absence of any environment-specific thresholds that may be developed for your network as part of the requirements analysis process.

Measuring Uptime

At the beginning of this section we asked, "What does that (99.999% uptime) really mean?" In Chapter 1, requirements for services include that they be configurable, measurable, and verifiable within the system. This is one of the biggest problems with a requirement for percent of uptime or downtime: how can it be configured, measured, or verified?

In terms of measuring uptime this question may be asked in three parts: when should it be measured (frequency), where should it be measured, and how should it be measured (service metrics)? First let's consider the frequency of measurement. A problem with expressing uptime solely as a percentage is that it does not include a time factor. Consider, for example, a requirement for 99.99% uptime. Without a time factor, that can mean a downtime of 53 minutes per year, 4.4 minutes per month, or 1 minute per week. Without stating a time factor, there can be a single outage of up to 53 minutes. As long as that is the only outage during the year, this availability requirement may be met. Some networks can tolerate a cumulative downtime of 53 minutes per year but could not handle a single downtime of that magnitude. There is a big difference between one large outage and several smaller outages.

Stating a time factor (frequency) along with uptime makes that requirement more valid. For networks that cannot tolerate large outages but can tolerate several small outages, 99.99% uptime measured weekly may make more sense than simply 99.99% uptime. By stating "measured weekly," you are forcing the requirement that outages can be no larger than 1 minute total per week.

Next let's consider where uptime should be measured. Stating where uptime is measured is as important as stating its frequency. If nothing is said about where it is measured, the assumption is that a downtime anywhere in the network counts against overall uptime. For some networks this may be the case and as such should be explicitly stated as a requirement. For many networks, however, uptime is more effective when it is selectively applied to parts of the network. For example, uptime to servers or specialized devices may be more important than general uptime across

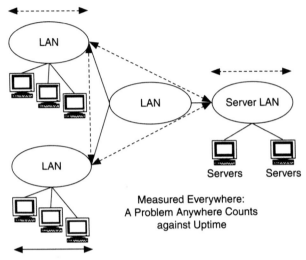

FIGURE 3.11   Uptime Measured Everywhere

the network. If this is the case, it should be included as part of the performance requirement.

Figure 3.11 shows an example where uptime would apply everywhere in the network.

The loss of service to any device in this situation would count against overall uptime. In Figure 3.12, uptime has been refined to apply only between each user

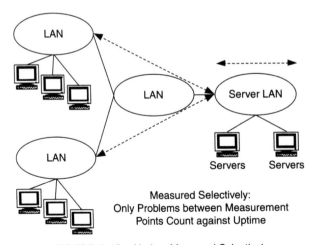

FIGURE 3.12   Uptime Measured Selectively

LAN and the server LAN. In this example, if service is lost between the user LANs, it would not count against an overall uptime requirement.

In our two examples we show a trade-off between being able to apply uptime everywhere and having a precise and more achievable application of uptime. It is possible, however, to have both apply to the same network. We could apply one standard everywhere in the network and have another standard that is applied selectively.

Often, uptime is measured end-to-end, either between user devices (generic computing devices) or between network devices (routers, switches, or network security/monitoring stations). For example, it may be measured end-to-end, at router interfaces, where the routers are separated by multiple networks. Measurement points include the LAN/WAN interface, router entry/exit points, and at monitoring stations distributed throughout the network. Determining where to measure uptime is particularly important when service providers are embedded in the system or when services are demarcated between well-defined areas of the network.

Finally, how you measure uptime is also important. As we show later in this section, it may be measured in terms of lack of connectivity or as a loss rate (bit error rate, cell, frame, or packet loss rates). The method you use to measure uptime impacts how it can be configured within the network devices, as well as how it can be verified.

When developing your requirements for uptime, keep in mind that some downtime on the network needs to be scheduled, in order to make changes to the network, upgrade hardware and software, or to run tests. Scheduled downtime for maintenance should not count against the overall uptime of the network, and the amount of planned downtime (frequency and duration) should be included in your performance requirement.

Indeed, given the ways that we specify where, when, and how uptime is measured, we can actually have multiple uptime requirements in the network. For example, there may be a general requirement across the entire network, measured everywhere, and another, higher-performance requirement, measured only between vital devices in the network.

Thus, a requirement for uptime might look something like this:
Network Uptime (see Figures 3.11 and 3.12):

1. 99.99% uptime, measured weekly, measured at every router interface and user device in the network.

2. 99.999% uptime, measured weekly, for access to the server farm network, measured at the router interface at the server farm, at server NICs. The application

ping will also be used to test connectivity between each user LAN and the server LAN.

3.   Note that these requirements do not apply to scheduled downtime periods for maintenance.

3.5.4   Thresholds and Limits

RMA requirements may include descriptions of thresholds and/or limits. RMA requirements are gathered and/or derived for each of the applications in your network from discussions with users of each application, as well as from documentation on the applications and testing of the applications on the existing network or on a testbed network. From the requirements you can often determine environment-specific thresholds (or limits) on each application by plotting application performance levels. From this you may determine what constitutes low- and high-performance RMA for your network. In the absence of environment-specific thresholds you can use the general thresholds presented in this chapter.

In addition, check RMA guarantees (if any) for services and/or technologies that exist in the current network or that are likely to be in the planned network. For example, Pacific Bell's switched multimegabit data service (SMDS) has a stated availability, in terms of mean time between service outages or greater than or equal to 3500 hours, with a mean time to restore of less than or equal to 3.5 hours. On the other hand, the Bellcore specification for SMDS calls for an availability of 99.9%. From our earlier discussion we can see that both of these specifications describe similar availability characteristics, with the MTBCF/MTTR specification being more specific.

Some of the estimation techniques we used require knowledge of which technologies and/or services exist or are planned for the system. Since at this point in the process we really do not know which technologies and/or services we will be using for our network (as those are determined in the architecture and design processes), these techniques may be used on the technologies and/or services that are in the current network, or on a set of candidate technologies and/or services for our planned network. Later in the architecture and design processes, when we have chosen technologies and/or services for our network, we can apply the information gathered here for each of those technologies/services.

An example of a general threshold for RMA is for uptime. Users normally expect the system to be operational as close to 100% of the time as possible. Uptime can get close to 100%, within a tenth, hundredth, or sometimes a thousandth of a percent, but with trade-offs of system complexity and cost. Earlier in this chapter

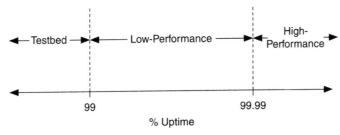

FIGURE 3.13   Thresholds between Testbed, Low-, and High-Performance Uptime

we described a general threshold for uptime, based on experience and observation, of 99.99%. In general, requirements for uptime that are greater than or equal to 99.99% are considered to be high performance, those that are less than 99.99% are low performance. In addition, a general threshold of approximately 99.5% can be used to distinguish a low-performance requirement from that of prototypes and testbeds. These thresholds are shown in Figure 3.13.

Note that any environment-specific thresholds that are developed for your network would supersede these general thresholds.

Error or loss rate is used as a measurement of uptime. For example, for an uptime requirement of 99.99%, packet or cell loss can be used to measure this performance. For many applications, experience has shown that a 2% packet loss is sufficient to lose application sessions. This can be considered downtime and in fact is a more practical measurement and verification of uptime than attempts at mathematical representations.

If you are using a 2% loss threshold and measuring packet loss in the network, it is counted as downtime when the packet loss is greater than 2%. For 99.99% measured weekly, the network can have 2% or greater packet loss for 1 minute per week (see Section 3.5.3).

In addition to the above thresholds, performance and service guarantees should also be listed as application requirements. Determining uptime requirements is an iterative process. As users, devices, applications, and networks evolve, their requirements will need to be adjusted.

3.6 Developing Delay Requirements

For applications that have delay requirements, we use the terms *end-to-end delay*, *round-trip delay*, and *delay variation* as measures of delay in the network.

We begin by introducing some useful general thresholds and limits for delay: interaction delay, human response time, and network propagation delay. These thresholds and limits are helpful in distinguishing low- and high-performance delay requirements for your network.

Interaction delay (INTD) is an estimate of how long a user is willing to wait for a response from the system during an interactive session. Here a session is defined as the time period during which an application is active. The interaction delay depends on user behavior, the user's environment, and the types of applications being used. Interaction delays may range from 100s of milliseconds to a minute or more. In general, a useful range is 10 to 30 seconds.

INTD is important when building a network targeted toward interactive applications. An INTD estimate is useful in characterizing applications that are loosely interactive, those where waiting to receive information is expected. This applies to transaction-processing applications, as well as Web, file transfer, and some database processing. For applications such as these, the user will notice some degree of delay, and INTD is an estimate of how long users are willing to wait. An upper limit to INTD is a measure of the tolerance level of users.

Human response time (HRT) is an estimate of the time threshold at which users begin to perceive delay in the system. Thus, when the system response time is less than HRT, users generally do not perceive any delay in the system. For delays greater than HRT, users generally do notice the system delay. A good estimate of HRT, based on experience and observation, is approximately 100 ms. This is an important delay threshold, as it distinguishes between when users will or will not notice delay in the system. Note that when users notice system delay, they become aware of the system. When architecting and designing a network where one of the goals is to hide the system from the user, then HRT becomes a vital requirement for the system. An example of this is in grid computing, where the system is abstracted from the users.

HRT is particularly important for highly interactive applications, where wait times may not or should not be perceived by users. This is usually the case when the application supports an interactive environment for users, such as in visualization, virtual reality, and collaborative applications, but may also apply to applications where system delays greater than HRT result in loss of productivity.

Network propagation delay is an estimate of how long it takes for a signal to cross a physical medium or link—for example, the propagation delay across a DS3 link. This provides a lower limit to the end-to-end and round-trip network and system delays. Propagation delay is dependent on distance and technology. It is useful as a lower delay limit, for it tells us when an application may not work well across the

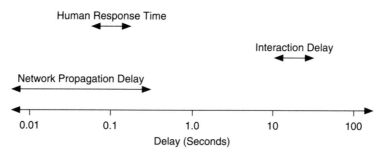

FIGURE 3.14 Delay Estimates for User Requirements

network, as its network propagation delay requirement is more stringent than the actual or planned propagation delay of the network.

These delay thresholds and limits are shown in Figure 3.14. Any or all of these delay estimates may be applied to a network. For example, we can use HRT as a limit for all services, constraining the architecture and design to provide delay characteristics less than HRT for that network. Or we can choose a value for INTD that defines and limits interactive service. In all cases, network propagation delay provides a lower limit for delay. Any of these delay estimates may also be used as guarantees on service.

These delay estimates come from experience and are presented here for you to consider. You may disagree with their values or find other useful estimates for delay. You are encouraged to develop your own estimates or improve upon those presented here. Since you know the network, system, and environment for your network project, you are in the best position to apply these estimates to your network. We can use the estimates for HRT and INTD to help us distinguish between *interactive burst* and *interactive bulk* applications. When both the responsiveness of the application (how frequently and quickly the application interacts with the user) and the end-to-end or round-trip delay (whichever is available to measure the system) are limited by one of these delay characteristics, we estimate that the application is interactive burst or interactive bulk.

In Figure 3.15 HRT and INTD are used as thresholds to separate interactive burst and interactive bulk applications. Between these two delay estimates, ranging from 100 ms to 10–30 seconds, is a gray area where the application could be considered either interactive burst or interactive bulk.

The use of INTD and HRT is probably the most straightforward way to distinguish between interactive burst and interactive bulk applications.

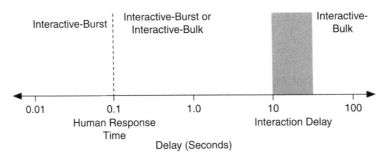

FIGURE 3.15   Performance Regions for Interactive Burst and Interactive Bulk Applications

3.6.1   End-to-End and Round-Trip Delays

End-to-end and round-trip delays are composed of many sources of delay, including propagation, queuing, transmission, I/O, switching, and processing. While it would be useful to be able to monitor and measure each source of delay, it is not practical for most networks. Therefore, totals such as end-to-end and round-trip delay are used. For many networks, especially IP networks, the round-trip delay is measured using various versions of the utility *ping*. *Ping* provides a useful, easily measured, and readily available form of round-trip delay.

Recall that we used HRT, INTD, and network propagation delay as thresholds and limits to distinguish between performance levels for delay requirements. They are based on combinations of:

- Physical limits of the network—for example, the size of the network and the distances between applications, users, and/or devices
- Device hardware and software performance
- Network protocol performance
- Application behavior at particular delay thresholds
- User interaction with the system at particular delay thresholds

A guideline for developing delay requirements is to determine the limiting factor from the delay thresholds and limits. The limiting factor will be the ultimate delay bottleneck within the system. As limiting factors are found, they can often be reduced or eliminated, revealing the next limiting factor. This process is repeated until a limiting factor is found that cannot be reduced or eliminated, or until system delay is at an acceptable level.

Given that physical limits on delay are absolute limits (the speeds of electromagnetic radiation through various media are well known), they may impact or negate other delay thresholds. For example, if an application requires a round-trip delay of 80 ms in order to support an interactive virtual reality (VR) environment, and the application session is being distributed between Los Angeles and Tokyo, the round-trip delay of the network (approximately 120 ms) will exceed the application delay requirement, regardless of the network architecture and design. Thus, either the application has to take into account the round-trip delay between Los Angeles and Tokyo, possibly by modifying the code, algorithms, or usage model, or the application sessions cannot be distributed between these sites. Knowing this early in the architecture process allows the application developers or network engineers to adapt to the physical limits of the network.

Now let's say that the distance of the network above is reduced, and the physical limitation on the delay is now 10 ms (e.g., the network is now between Los Angeles and San Francisco). However, through testing the application on the current network, a round-trip delay of 100 ms is expected within the system (primarily due to the devices used). What can be done? Device hardware and software performance can be quite difficult to identify, understand, and improve upon. In architecting and designing a network we need to try to consider each piece in the end-to-end path of communications (traffic flows), which may consist of a variety of devices. What can we look for that will reduce the likely sources of delay in the system, without an unreasonable amount of time, effort, and cost? Areas to check for sources of delay that can be modified or tuned include computer OSs, network protocols, and device peripherals.

What we can look for in these areas are OSs that are notoriously slow and poorly written, protocols that are poorly implemented, and devices and/or peripherals that are mismatched or misconfigured. This type of information obviously will not come from the manufacturer but can often be found in mailing lists, newsgroups, independent testing, and academic research, all of which are increasingly available via the Web. By doing some research, you can rapidly learn a lot about performance problems with devices. Make your own observations and analyses, and draw your own conclusions. As we will see later in this book, support services such as network management, routing, and security will also play a role in network delay.

Delay thresholds based on application behavior and user interaction are generally more flexible than physical or device delays. Recall that values for INTD and HRT are estimates (estimated range for INTD), so there is some flexibility to tailor them to your environment. While in the previous example the round-trip physical delay was the ultimate limit, when the distance of the network was reduced so that the round-trip delay was on the order of 10 ms, the application behavior (interactive VR environment), with its 40 ms delay requirement, may become the limiting factor. If this is acceptable to the users, then the delay estimates are (from our high-level view) optimized for that environment.

3.6.2 Delay Variation

Delay variation is often coupled with end-to-end or round-trip delay to give an overall delay performance requirement for applications that are sensitive to the interarrival time of information. Some examples of such applications are those that produce or use video, audio, and telemetry information. For delay variation coupled with end-to-end or round-trip delay, when no information is available about the delay variation requirement, a good rule of thumb is to use 1% to 2% of the end-to-end delay as the delay variation.

For example, an estimate for delay variation (in the absence of any known requirements), when the end-to-end delay is 40 ms, is approximately 400 to 800 microseconds. This would be a rough approximation, however, and should be verified if possible.

3.7 Developing Capacity Requirements

In evaluating application capacity requirements we want to consider applications that require large amounts of capacity as well as those that require a specific value (peak, minimum, sustained) or range of capacities. When an application requires a large amount of capacity, it is important to know when the application has a real (measurable, verifiable) requirement for high capacity and when it (or the transport protocol it is using) will simply attempt to utilize whatever capacity is available.

Applications that use TCP as their transport mechanism, without any additional conditions or modifications from the higher-layer protocols (or from the application itself), receive their performance levels based on the current state of the network (i.e., best effort). This is done by communicating and adjusting TCP transmission parameters (across the TCP control channel between the two devices in the TCP session) throughout the TCP session in reaction to conditions of apparent congestion in the network.

3.7.1 Estimating Data Rates

Estimating a data (or maybe more accurately, information) rate is based on how much information you know about the transmission characteristics (e.g., traffic flow) of the application and how accurate the estimation needs to be. Commonly used data rates include peak data rate (PDR), sustained data rate (SDR), minimum data rate (MDR), or combinations of these. These data rates may be measured at one or more layers in the network (e.g., physical, data-link, network, transport, or session).

The data rates of all applications are bounded by some limiting factor. This may be the application itself, or it may be the line rate of the network interface on the device the application is running. Or, it might be the performance level of a server that the application uses. So the real question is where the limits are in the system for that application. If the application itself supports a very fast data rate (which can be determined by running the application on a test network), then you can go through a process of elimination to determine which component, on the device or somewhere else, is acting as the performance bottleneck. In a sense, this is a local optimization of the network. In this case you are doing it for a single application in a closed network environment.

Many applications rely on the transport protocol, such as TCP, to provide an "as fast as possible" data rate. We have an intuitive feel for some of these applications (e.g., FTP, telnet) —for example, we can be fairly certain that a telnet session will not have a data rate of 100 Mb/s; likewise, an FTP session should not run at 10 Kb/s if there is greater capacity available.

What we can do to estimate data rates for applications is consider their data sizes and estimated completion times. Data sizes and completion times are based on what users may want or expect, or may be measured on the existing network.

Taking an application that has nebulous capacity and delay characteristics, such as Web access, we can estimate a data rate from user- and application-provided data sizes and completion times (e.g., INTD). We may ask a number of users for examples of pages that they expect to access, or information that they would download, and how long they are willing to wait for each event. From this information we could create entries in a table like the one below (Figure 3.16). From estimates such as those in Figure 3.17, we can estimate upper and lower limits for an application's data rates, or for an average rate.

For other applications the characteristics of the data transfers may be better known, such as the sizes of the data sets being transferred as well as the frequency and duration of such transfers. This may apply to transaction-based applications, such as credit card processing, banking applications, and distributed computing.

Consider a remote interactive data-processing application that connects to retail stores and processes customer information, such as credit card entries. We can consider an event (task) as the processing of a single customer's credit card information. Then, the completion time of the task is on the order of INTD

Application	Average Completion Time (Seconds)	Average Data Size (Bytes)
Distributed Computing (Batch Mode)	10^3	10^7
Web Transactions	10	10^4
Database Entries/Queries	2–5	10^3
Payroll Entries	10	10^2
Teleconference	10^3	10^5

FIGURE 3.16   Completion Times and Data Sizes for Selected Applications

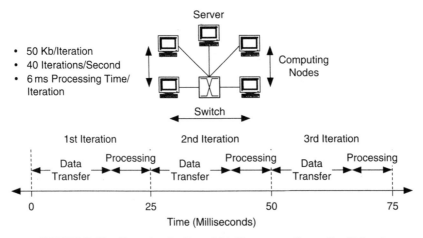

FIGURE 3.17   Example of a Shared, Multiprocessor Computing Network

discussed earlier—approximately 10 to 30 seconds, although it may be expected by the users (store personnel) to be much smaller, say on the order of 5 to 10 seconds, and the data size for each task is fairly small, on the order of 100 to 1000 bytes.

Another example is a computing environment in which multiple devices share the processing for a task. At each iteration of the task, data are transferred between devices. Here we may know the frequency of data transfer, the size of each transfer (which may also be constant), and how much time is required to process the data (which may indicate how much time a transfer may take). A shared, multiprocessor computing network is shown in Figure 3.17.

For some applications the capacity characteristics are well known, and estimating a data rate can be relatively easy to do. Applications that involve voice and/or

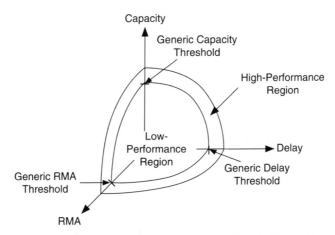

FIGURE 3.18   Performance Envelope with Generic Thresholds

video usually have known capacity requirements. The rates of such applications are likely to be constant, so that their peak and minimum data rates are the same, or there will be a known range of values. For example, an MPEG-2 low-level constrained-parameter bitstream (CPB) will have a rate of 4 Mb/s, or a main-level CPB will have a rate between 15 and 20 Mb/s.

There are currently no general thresholds or limits on capacity, to determine low and high performance capacity. It is not obvious why this should be so, except that RMA and delay have a direct impact on the user's perception of system performance, while capacity has a secondary impact through affecting RMA and delay. There will often be, however, environment-specific thresholds on capacity, determining low and high performance for that network.

Generic performance thresholds can be added to the performance envelope we developed in Chapter 1. These thresholds, as shown in Figure 3.18, are used to separate the envelope into low- and high-performance regions. This gives us a visual interpretation of the relative performance requirements for our network and can be used to relate performance requirements to management.

3.8   Developing Supplemental Performance Requirements

Three supplemental performance requirements were introduced in Chapter 2: operational suitability, supportability, and confidence. These performance requirements

Operations and Support	
Operations	**Support**
Management	Management
Personnel	Maintenance Support
Tools	Technical Documentation
Consumables	Storage
Transportation	Supply Support
Leasing	Modifications
Facilities	

FIGURE 3.19   Elements of Operations and Support

are part of the overall set of operations and support elements shown in Figure 3.19. *Operational suitability* is a measure of how well our network design can be configured, monitored, and adjusted by the customer's operators. *Supportability* is a measure of how well the customer can keep the system performing, as designed, over the entire life of the system. *Confidence* is a measure of the ability of the network to deliver data without error or loss at the required throughput.

3.8.1 Operational Suitability

Ensuring that your customer can operate the planned network is seldom an easy task and is one that the customer never thinks about until asked. Two major factors influence the operational suitability: network architecture/design and the quality of the human operators.

It is possible to develop a network that cannot be operated consistently and effectively. Complex minute-to-minute adjustments can swamp even the most competent staff. The lack of any effective monitoring tools or control systems to integrate actions across geographically dispersed sites can transform the most advanced design into a dysfunctional mass of cables and computers and recriminations and lawsuits. Development of the network must consider network management that permits the operators to adjust the network and to reconfigure it when they need to. If they need to do it every few minutes, network management must be easy to operate and must present the controls in an easily understood way.

An undersized operations staff can be quickly worn out and frustrated by a network that requires constant and precise tending. Components that never need adjustment except when they are installed do not need to clutter the integrated control console. System monitoring is essential to adjusting system performance by its operators; displays must be accessible, and the data displayed must use well-understood representations. Should there be a single (or redundant) operations console or should the system be operated from any Web browser within the network? To what degree is automation incorporated to reduce the operators' workload or to improve the response to changing conditions over what a human can provide? Is system adjustment so infrequent that no integrated control system is required? These issues are discussed in detail in Chapter 7.

A Marine colonel who managed a major system development program kept a picture on his wall of the most pathetic, bedraggled Marine recruit he had ever seen. This "sad sack" was standing on an empty parade ground holding a bag of trash in one hand and a stick with a nail in the other to use to pick paper off the ground. The caption read, "Remember. No matter what you dream, what you plan, this man must execute." Operators are more essential than any technology to successful communications over a network.

In most cases a new network design is the result of obsolescence or an order of magnitude increase in performance requirements. These new components and tools are likely to be radically different from those currently in use by the customer, and so the current staff is also likely to be obsolete or inadequately sized. It is almost always necessary to retrain or replace the operations staff during the transition period; it may also be necessary to radically expand that staff if a much larger-scale network is required to meet the customer's growing needs for communications. Keep in mind that replacement of humans in the system is much more difficult than replacing routers with switches, or multimode fiber with Category 6 copper cable.

These are activities that must be planned before the transition and implementation period and usually have a significant lead time, but they must be accomplished before the network achieves its initial operational capability (IOC). It is essential that the network engineer systematically uncover the customer's needs and constraints in these areas, document them, and then factor them into the design. These factors have a significant influence on the degree of automation that is incorporated into the design and the assumed skill level needed to operate the network.

Presenting this information during the design review helps to ensure that the customer understands what it takes to operate the network. It also ensures that any changes to the design (i.e., increased automation to compensate for a small staff) are made early in the process rather than cobbled onto the final product or into an endless cycle of change orders during delivery.

One of the key benefits to a skilled and motivated operations staff is their ability to apply the basic network architecture/design to meet new situations unforeseen during the development phase. Absent this set of skills, the network engineer's design must be even more robust and have a high degree of automation to ensure that the system is protected from the operators. A set of operators who respect the documented procedures and understand the system architecture and how the components work together can be trusted to improvise when new situations occur, as they always do. A set of unskilled operators requires a system design that is constraining to ensure ongoing performance.

A common customer edict is that the new network be operated with the same personnel as the old network or that, at a minimum, the operations staff be no more expensive than the current staff. It is essential that the design engineer meet the operations staff to develop an opinion about their skill level and ability to understand new technologies and to adopt new procedures and tools. There is a trade-off between system automation and workforce, the trade-off being that lesser qualified operators can be used. Some operations personnel are unwilling or incapable of learning to operate the new systems; new personnel must be brought in to perform these functions. Requirements for operator selection, qualification, and training (both initial and refresher) may seem burdensome but are absolutely necessary. If the requirement to retain the same staff is hard and fast, then a system design using advanced components and architectures must take this into account.

Operational suitability requirements must be collected from interviews with the operators and owners. If new staff are going to be used, then interviews with people of approximately the same skill level should be substituted in the interviews. These must be operators, not the design engineering team, who may lack the experience necessary to see how the system looks from the operator's point of view.

Articulating a concept of operations is very useful in defining the customer's needs, conveying the overall approach to the design team, and ensuring that the customer has fully conveyed his or her strategy to the designers. Such a document should be no more than 10 pages long and should address the operator skill level, the shift work organization, the tempo of operations, the degree to which the operator is expected to reconfigure the system, and how it is done. Some additional questions to be considered during the requirements analysis process include the following:

- How are operators going to monitor performance to ensure that they detect failures, faults, or outages before the customer does, or do the operators rely on the users to detect faults and report them?

- How does the end user interact with the system and the operators, including reporting problems, and how are these reports tracked and responses provided? If multiple levels of quality of service are available, how does the end user request an increase or authorize a reduction in quality of service?

- At what point does an operations problem transition into a maintenance action, and how does this occur so it is not neglected?

- How does the operations staff monitor system capacity and alert management to the need to expand capacity beyond the resources available to them? What types of time-averaged trend analysis will be performed to anticipate growth of demand?

3.8.2 Supportability

A key component of the customer's satisfaction with the network, as delivered, is its ability to maintain the high level of performance achieved on the day of delivery throughout the design life of the network. A relatively unsophisticated customer will recognize the poor quality of a design and implementation only when it is frequently out of service; an experienced and knowledgeable customer will examine the design carefully before authorizing implementation and will want to know if it will persistently provide quality performance for its entire life cycle. That customer will also want to know what it takes to operate the design and what it takes to support continued operations. A sophisticated customer will understand the implications of an operations concept and a support concept and will respect the designer's commitment to ongoing performance after the implementation is complete and the engineers are paid.

Supportability is driven by five major factors: (1) the reliability, maintainability, and operational availability (RMA) characteristics of the architecture/design; (2) workforce, including training and staffing levels; (3) system procedures and technical documentation; (4) tools, both standard and special; and (5) spare and repair parts.

Two classes of maintenance need to be performed on the network, once it is deployed: preventive and corrective. Eventually, the maintenance requirements are defined as the design is solidified. Requirements for maintenance, during this stage of the system definition, are generally qualitative in nature, such as:

- All components will be located where they can be maintained in place with a minimum of disruption to the system as a whole.

- Spare parts will be supplied to ensure the replacement of any component whose failure would jeopardize mission performance.

RMA

The first step in defining RMA requirements is to articulate a representative sample of mission scenarios in which the network is going to be used. These are documented in an anecdotal narrative which describes how the usage will occur, when it will occur, what is necessary for the mission to succeed, and how important it is to the network users. This last item includes how often the network will be used and the level of priority assigned to this mission.

For example, the network described in Section 2.5.3 may have users in one building who require access to data in another building which are necessary to pay employees; this data flow path is necessary only from 4 to 5 p.m. on Friday afternoon so that payroll can be accomplished locally over the weekend and employees paid on Monday morning. So this becomes mission-critical during that period and, as a fall-back position, may continue as such until the local processing must start or else the payroll will not be accomplished on Monday morning, resulting in disgruntled employees and all the unpleasantness which that can bring on. This path is no longer mission-critical on Monday afternoon and so could fail or be shut down for maintenance at that point, providing it does not interfere with other functions.

One possible design consideration would be to include an automated end-to-end system test prior to the start of this critical period which would advise the operators when a system failure has occurred that, if not corrected, could delay their paycheck for the next week. Many architectural and design features can be incorporated, but only if the architect/designer knows how the system is going to be used.

Based on the mission scenarios, reliability block diagrams (RBD) can be constructed for each mission, showing serial and parallel relationships between components and the performance of the mission. During the requirements analysis phase these are at a very high level and reflect functions to accomplish the mission, rather than components to accomplish the mission. A sample RBD is presented in Figure 3.20.

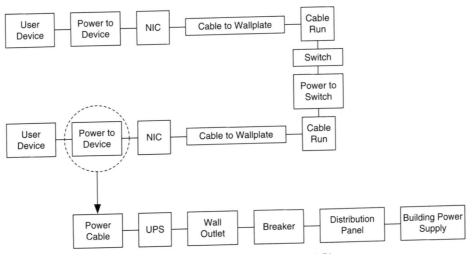

FIGURE 3.20   A Sample Reliability Block Diagram

Once a design is developed and the architectural details laid out, failure modes and their effects should be estimated and a criticality analysis (FMECA) conducted to identify the primary ways in which the system can fail to perform its mission. These can then lead the designer to establish detection modes that would reduce the occurrence of failures or accelerate the restoration of service. A template for FMECA data is shown in Figure 3.21.

Component Name	
Indenture Level	
Reference Drawing	
Mission	

Date	
Sheet Number	
Compiled By	
Approved By	

ID	Item/ Functional ID/ Nomenclature	Function	Failure Modes and Causes	Mission Phase or Op Mode	Local Effect	End Effects	Failure Detection Mode	Compensating Provisions	Severity Class	Remarks

FIGURE 3.21   A Template for FMECA Data

In performing the RMA analysis of the design it is essential to remember that RMA is a tool to help the designer understand system performance so he or she can make informed decisions.

Workforce

As with operational suitability, discussions of supportability often focus on retaining the existing workforce and/or keeping the budget the same. With the introduction of sophisticated and new technologies, this may present problems. Workforce retraining or replacement may be required in the implementation. Another approach is to rebalance maintenance activities by using contracted expert services in those areas where the existing workforce lacks the skills. In some cases it may make sense to outsource the maintenance totally, particularly in situations where the network is a supporting function of the owner's primary line of business and there is no interest in developing a highly skilled, expensive, internal workforce. During the requirements analysis phase the principal objective is to get a clear picture of the customer's constraints on changing the workforce.

The personnel who will operate and maintain the network need to be properly trained and to possess the appropriate qualifications. One approach to defining requirements in this area is to survey the existing workforce skills, depth, and formal training, document these features, and use them as the baseline for the new network maintenance workforce. Any changes needed then can be handled as engineering changes to the baseline requirements and the existing workforce.

Procedures and Documentation

In general, three classes of documentation are required to support the network. System and component technical documentation describes the characteristics, parts, and the like of the complete set of equipment that makes up the design. Maintenance procedures describe both the periodic preventive maintenance actions needed to keep the system running properly and their scheduled performance. Casualty procedures describe the abnormal (hopefully) procedures to follow when system faults occur. These are designed to minimize damage to the system and to restore service as quickly as possible; prior planning for expected failure modes will do more to restore service quickly than any other investment during implementation.

Technical documentation is usually provided by the vendor of the components and is usually adequate. During implementation the documentation should be inspected to ensure that spare and repair parts are identified so that if they need to be ordered quickly in response to a fault or failure, the parts list is available.

Technical documentation to describe the integration of network components is generally new material that the engineering team must generate as part of the testing, deployment, and integration of the new network.

Maintenance procedures must support both component- and system-level maintenance. The documentation must identify the frequency and procedures for performing preventive maintenance as well the procedures for reconfiguring the network to temporarily operate at a reduced capability while replacement components are swapped out for overhaul and maintenance. Such procedures identify the tools and initial conditions required to start the procedure, the testing to be performed prior to returning the system to a normal state, and the indicators that the maintenance has been performed properly or improperly.

Casualty procedures describe the planned actions for the operators to perform when a system fault occurs. These are broken down into immediate actions and supplemental actions. They are designed to place the system in a safe state and to operate it at reduced capability until the fault can be isolated and repaired with full service restored.

During the requirements analysis phase the scope of each of these classes of documentation should be documented as a basic set of requirements.

Tools

The provisioning of common and special test equipment and tools is a consequence of the network architecture and design. At this stage the requirements in this area represent possible constraints on the architecture and design. They should be stated in terms of the growth over the set of tools currently possessed by the existing maintenance staff. New tools should be acquired together with the components they are required to service, instead of separately, to ensure that they work properly with the planned network configuration.

Special test equipment, monitoring, and diagnostic software requirements should be defined during this phase in terms of their ability to improve response time to system performance issues, including failures and faults. This may represent a development effort or, at a minimum, an integration effort as the network is deployed. It would be reasonable at this point to specify a capability to detect system faults and performance degradation and to display status and key metrics at the operator's console, or via a Web browser from a central server. Another requirement for consideration is the ability to monitor, reconfigure, or to reset routing components using out-of-bandwidth connections, such as an analog line and a modem tied into a maintenance port on the network routing devices. This has an impact on which devices meet these requirements, and for a network with components at a long distance from the operators, it may permit maintenance without physical visits.

Repair and Spare Parts

Requirements to be imposed on the spare and repair parts inventory at this stage are qualitative constraints, not a list of parts to be delivered. Some sample requirements that customers might define at this point include the following:

- Spare and repair parts shall be stored in the network operations facility and cannot exceed, in volume, the space allocated, which is n cubic feet.

- Initial spare and repair parts shall not exceed 15% of system acquisition costs.

- Contract vehicles for replacement spare and repair parts shall be in place prior to the initial operational capability.

Specific requirements for maintenance are generally driven by the network architecture and design and are documented in a maintenance plan, based on the design. Eventually, the spare and repair parts provisioning is derived from the actual design and a maintenance analysis of the design.

Support Concept

The support concept describes the way in which the network is supported. Defining the concept clearly may help articulate the customer constraints and helps identify alternative approaches to support that can be accommodated in the design.

A commonly accepted maintenance support concept is the three-tier model. At the local level the operators can perform a set of minimal maintenance actions. They can monitor for component failure and isolate the problem. Since they are often on-site, or at least in proximity to the components, they can handle immediate actions for system faults or casualties and some supplemental actions, such as rerouting circuits or replacing certain line replaceable units.

The second tier is intermediate-level maintenance, which includes the ability to repair some components or provide a place for on-site repair by factory service representatives, if they are working locally. This tier involves staffing with specialized skills and a limited set of equipment. This is frequently handled via service contracts with the vendor or a third party who is sufficiently local as to be able to arrive on-site within a short period of time. The third tier is the factory service which generally involves a contract for service and shipping the equipment back to a maintenance location for refurbishment or repair.

Level	Location	Who	Tools and Test Equipment	Corrective Maintenance	Preventive Maintenance
Organizational	Operations Sites	Operators	• Common tools • Operator consoles and controls • Inexpensive special tools	• Day-to-day monitoring • Troubleshooting • Fault isolation • Replacing LRUs • Reconfiguring system	• Monitoring performance • Minor on-site cleaning and adjustments • Scheduled replacement of LRUs
Intermediate	On call to work onsite	Trained personnel whose primary role is maintenance	Special or expensive portable tools with limited use	On-site repair of offline equipment	• Major on-site upgrades where shipment to factory is impractical • Supplement operators
Depot	Vendor or factory	Vendor or factory personnel	Equipment to refurbish components	Overhaul and refurbishment	Scheduled overhaul or disassembly of LRUs

FIGURE 3.22   The Three-Tier Maintenance Structure

In the three-tier approach (Figure 3.22) the local operators simply identify the failed component, pull the line replaceable unit containing it, and replace it to restore service. The failed local repair unit (LRU) is then shipped to the second tier or even to the factory for repair or refurbishment. Documentation must be provided to the Tier 1 workforce describing how to pull and replace components, and they must have a limited set of tools and special equipment to accomplish these functions.

The degree to which contracted services are used should also be addressed by the support concept. Usually, at this stage of the requirements analysis, it is sufficient to document the current model for support and identify any changes that are likely to be required to support the new network.

3.8.3 Confidence

Confidence is a measure of the network's ability to deliver data without error or loss at the required throughput. This can be estimated in terms of error and/or loss rates. While error/loss rates are more commonly used at the network device level, we can also derive some general performance estimates from them. As with other performance estimates, the ability to estimate uptime is strongly based on our ability to measure it within the system. For these rates, this is done

- Per link or circuit, such as for bit error rates (BERs)
- Packet loss rates between network-layer routers
- End-to-end, between computing devices or applications

Determining what is an acceptable error or loss rate depends on the application's ability to tolerate errors or information loss. This, in turn, implies reliability and dependencies between the various layers in the network. For example, an application that transfers data in the network may rely on the transport layer to provide guaranteed transmission. If the transport layer used is the transmission control protocol (TCP), then reliability of transmission is based on TCP's ability to recover from errors in the network or on notification of transmission failures. If the transport protocol is the user datagram protocol (UDP), however, there is no reliability guarantee from the transport layer, and reliability is passed down to the data-link and physical layers or must be provided by the application itself.

Loss is often measured at the physical, link, and network layers and reported as a percentage of available traffic in the network. Thus, we could establish cell, frame, or packet loss thresholds and time periods, as shown in Figure 3.23.

Interestingly, we could use the well-known *ping* utility as a possible measurement tool. A *ping* loss rate can be used as an indicator that the network is approaching a loss threshold and that a more accurate measurement (e.g., SNMP polling of router statistics or remote monitoring [RMON] variables) is needed.

While *ping* can be useful in this mode, the loss of ICMP packets (ping is composed of two parts, ICMPEcho Request and Response) can be affected by how network devices (such as routers) handle them. For example, *ping* packets may be among the first packets to be selectively dropped by a router when it gets congested. The important point here is to use utilities such as *ping* with an awareness that it (like all applications) is imperfect and may not always accurately represent the state of the system. That is why it may be better used as a threshold indicator, triggering another method of measurement when the threshold is crossed, as it would have less of a direct impact on the accuracy and loss measurements, while still being quite useful.

There are some applications that will tolerate some loss of information. Applications that transfer video and/or voice, such as teleconferencing or telelearning,

Packet Loss Rate (% of Total Network Traffic)	Maximum Total Time (Per Week)
2% or Greater	Up to 1 Minute
Less than 2%	Remainder of Week

FIGURE 3.23 An Example Loss Threshold

will allow some loss in order to preserve the time continuity of the session. Some non-mission-critical telemetry applications also allow for data loss.

3.9 Environment-Specific Thresholds and Limits

General thresholds and limits give us some common estimates for low- and high-performance requirements for our network. They are useful when there is a lack of information about users, applications, and devices for the network, but often there is information about what the performance thresholds should be. With this information we can develop thresholds and limits specific to that network.

Environment-specific thresholds and limits are an acknowledgment that each network is unique, and that the requirements of users, applications, and devices are specific to the environment that they are in. The environment takes into account concepts such as the kind of work that users do, or what their objectives are (e.g., what motivates them). Thus, an academic research environment is quite different from a retail (sales) environment, which is different from a manufacturing environment, and so on. The thresholds that distinguish between low and high performance are unique to each environment.

Because each environment is unique, what may be considered high performance for one environment may be low performance for another. Recognizing the uniqueness of each environment (and thus, network) you work in is a good habit to develop, especially if you are involved with many different networks.

As with general thresholds, the reason for developing environment-specific thresholds is to determine which applications have high-performance requirements. We have spent a lot of time on this; why is it so important? For each network project that we work on, we need to:

1. Determine if there are any high-performance applications and devices, and if so, how important are they to the success of that environment? How important is it that they be supported? If there are not any high (multi-tier) performance applications, then the network will be supporting a set of single-tier performance applications and devices.

2. If there are high (multi-tier)-performance applications and devices, and they are crucial to the success of that environment, then it is likely that our network architecture and design will focus on supporting those applications and devices, as well as their users.

Thus, our ability to determine which users, applications, and devices are important to the success of the organization that the network will be supporting, and determining if those applications and devices are relatively high performance for that environment, or roughly the same as all other applications and devices there, will impact the success of the resulting network architecture and design.

3.9.1 Comparing Application Requirements

Developing environment-specific thresholds and limits is based on comparing the various performance requirements of applications. Typically, one, two, or all of the performance characteristics (capacity, delay, and RMA) for the applications are plotted, and the plot is used to compare relative performance requirements and develop a threshold or limits for that characteristic.

For example, consider a plot of capacity requirements for applications in a network. These may be a subset of all the applications for that environment, such as the top five or six in order of performance or importance. Figure 3.24 shows the resulting plot. There is a cluster of applications in the capacity range 50 Kb/s— around 1 Mb/s, and then isolated applications at around 4 Mb/s and 6.5 Mb/s. We could choose to pick the top one or two applications and place a threshold between them and the rest of the applications. Most likely, the top two would be grouped together and a threshold placed around 2 to 3 Mb/s.

As you can see from Figure 3.24, the capacity requirements of the applications are spread across a range of values. We could choose to develop a (environment-specific) performance limit for this group of applications, or a threshold between low and high performance, or both. Note that, for delay, an upper limit for high performance is actually the lowest delay value, not the highest value.

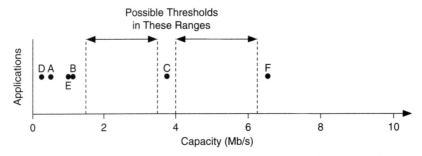

FIGURE 3.24 A Plot of Capacity Requirements with Possible Thresholds

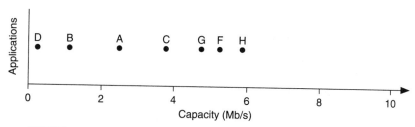

FIGURE 3.25   A Plot of Capacity Requirements with No Distinct Groupings

In this figure, we could estimate a couple of possible capacity thresholds. The most likely would be grouping Applications C and F, and placing a threshold around 2 to 3 Mb/s. This value is subjective and may need to be approved by the users or management. Sometimes the threshold or limit is obvious; at other times it may be difficult to determine. Consider, for example, the following plot of application capacities (Figure 3.25).

In this figure, the capacity requirements are also spread out over a range of values, but in this case there is no clear separation between low and high performance. When performance requirements are not clearly separated, you may not be able to develop a threshold.

3.10   Requirements for Predictable and Guaranteed Performance

Along with determining performance requirements, thresholds, and limits, we must also consider if there are any requirements for predictable or guaranteed performance. You may recall from Chapter 1 that predictable service (of which performance is a part) requires some predictability and reliability—more than best effort—while guaranteed service has accountability as part of its specification. The performance requirements for both of these service types are much more strict than the standard best-effort service. Thus, when specifying predictable and/or guaranteed performance for a network, you want to be certain that the customer really needs or wants it and is aware of the costs (financial, manpower, intellectual, and possibly schedule) to implement and maintain it.

3.10.1   Requirements for Predictable Performance

Several of the examples discussed in this chapter may be considered predictable. Depending on how important the users and applications are to the success of an organization, their requirements may need to be predictable, requiring more support for their traffic flows. This would mean that, in the network architecture and design, their flows are handled differently from best effort. How that will be done is covered later, but for now it is sufficient to be able to identify and specify such predictable performance requirements.

There have been several indicators of predictable performance so far in this book. We have talked about mission-critical, rate-critical, real-time, and interactive applications. These terms indicate predictable or guaranteed capacity, delay, and RMA, respectively. We have also talked about developing general and environment-specific thresholds and limits to separate low and high performance for multi-tier performance networks. Those applications that are characterized as high performance are also candidates for predictable service. In fact, the threshold between low and high performance can often be the threshold between best-effort and predictable service.

Therefore, whether or not you specify performance requirements as predictable is based on

- Determining if the application is mission-critical, rate-critical, real-time, or interactive
- Determining if there are any environment-specific performance thresholds or limits
- Applying general thresholds and limits, if necessary
- Discussing the results with your customer(s) (users, management, etc.) to agree on which requirements should be considered predictable

3.10.2 Requirements for Guaranteed Performance

Guaranteed performance requirements are the most strict requirements for the network, not necessarily in terms of the level of performance but rather in terms of what is needed to support (or guarantee) that performance to the device, application, or user. As with predictable requirements, guaranteed requirements are indicated when mission-critical, rate-critical, real-time, and/or interactive applications are identified, as well as when high (multi-tier) performance requirements are identified.

What makes a performance requirement guaranteed is the degree to which that requirement needs to be supported in the network. Support for guaranteed requirements has to have accountability built into it. This means the following:

- There needs to be some agreement, usually between users of the application and providers of the network service that supports the application, about

  1. What the performance requirements are

  2. When and where they apply

  3. How they will be measured and verified

  4. What happens when a requirement is not met

  This agreement may be in the form of a service-level agreement (SLA), commonly used by service providers.

- The requirements must be considered end-to-end, between source and destination. More on this can be found in the chapter on flow analysis (Chapter 4).

The factors used to determine guaranteed performance requirements are the same as for predictable performance requirements, with particular emphasis on the last factor (discussing the results with your customer(s)). Getting agreement from your customer(s) on which performance requirements need to be guaranteed is especially important, as the impact on resources can be substantial.

As we will see, how you specify requirements here can have a serious impact on the network architecture and design to follow. Therefore, the more effort you put into this, the better your resulting architecture and design will be.

3.11   Requirements Mapping

Another part of the requirements analysis process is mapping requirements. In Chapter 2 we discussed the importance of determining the locations of important devices and applications. As part of the analysis process we will bring that location information together into a map of where devices are (or are likely to be) and where applications apply (or are likely to apply).

Requirements are mapped to a geographical description of the environment. This may be a building or campus but can also be abstracted to metropolitan or wide-area views. In fact, there can be multiple views of the environment, each focusing on a particular geographic area. For example, one map may be a wide-area view, showing the cities where the devices and applications apply. Each city may then have its own map, showing the campuses and/or buildings (Figure 3.26).

Figure 3.27 shows an example of a requirements map. On this map of a campus the locations of devices (servers and specialized devices) and applications are placed. From this map we can begin to correlate which parts of the campus will be using which applications and devices, and we can estimate where traffic flows might occur, within an application, between applications, and between devices.

Note that on this map, groups of generic computing devices are also shown. Showing individual desktop or laptop devices is not practical and is not likely to provide important information. Showing groups, however, gives an indication of how many devices (and users) are in a particular location. This is useful in the flow analysis process.

The degenerate case of a requirements map is one where all applications apply everywhere, and there are no servers or specialized devices to show. There is little, if any, information that can be determined by such a map.

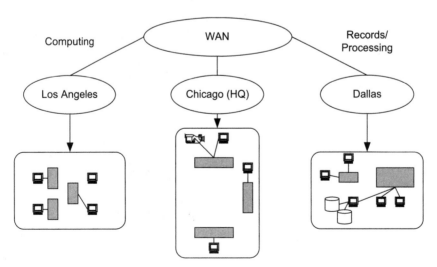

FIGURE 3.26   Multiple Requirements Maps

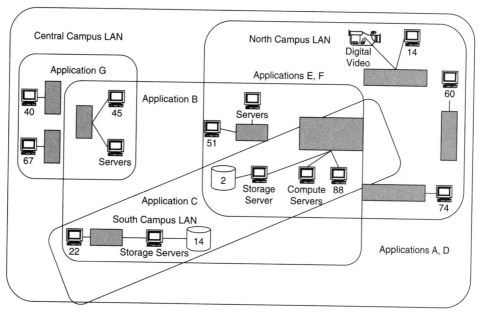

FIGURE 3.27   A Campus Requirements Map

3.12   Developing the Requirements Specification

The requirements specification and requirements map are the results of the analysis process. The first part of the process is determining any initial conditions for the project. This includes the type of network project, scope of the project, project goals, and political, administrative, and financial forces acting on the project. Part of the initial conditions of the project may be determining whether the network needs single-tier or multi-tier performance. We would also make a rapid, initial evaluation of the problem(s) in the network, if any, and estimate resources and schedule.

Thus, before we have gathered any requirements for the network, we should have some or all of this information documented. Consider the example of a building network from Chapter 2. The first part of the requirements specification may look like Figure 3.28.

The second part of the requirements specification comprises the gathered and derived requirements for the network. In this example some requirements were

Requirements Specification	
Section 1: Initial Conditions	
Project Type	Upgrade of building network
Project Scope	Single building, two floors, approximately 150 users
Project Goals	Improve performance to all users, particularly some mission-critical applications, and increase security to Internet
Other Conditions	Financial TBD
Problem Evaluation and Definition	Application performance has been a recurring problem, so management wants to upgrade network and has suggested upgrading interfaces to Fast Ethernet. Some users have GigE interfaces on their workstations.

FIGURE 3.28 A Template for Initial Conditions

learned in our initial discussion with the customer (management and staff). These requirements are shown in Figure 3.29, using the template from Chapter 2.

It is not always the case that requirements can be gathered from early meetings. To get requirements from users, we usually ask them questions about their

Requirements Specification							
Section 2: Listing of Requirements							
ID/ Name	Date	Type	Description	Gathered/ Derived	Locations	Status	Priority
1	14Jan01	User	User distribution is: 60 engineers, 15 HR and Finance, 30 Manufacturing, 10 Management, 30 Sales/Marketing, 5 Other	Gathered from Management	TBD	Info	TBD
2	14Jan01	Network	Each area of the building must support Fast Ethernet connections to the backbone	Gathered from Management	TBD	TBD	TBD
3	14Jan01	Application	Database, Visualization, Manufacturing, and Payroll applications are considered mission-critical for this company. More information needed.	Gathered from Management	TBD	TBD	TBD
4	14Jan01	Application	Payroll application (PAY1) requires 100% uptime (while in operation) between Finance and outside payroll company	Gathered from Management	TBD	TBD	TBD
5	14Jan01	Network	Company must be kept secure from Internet attacks	Gathered from Management	TBD	TBD	TBD

FIGURE 3.29 Requirements Gathered from the Initial Meeting with the Customer

1. List applications that you use	How often? (times per day)	How long each time?
Application 1 -		
Application 2 -		
Application 3 -		
Application 4 -		
Application 5 -		
2. List computers or other devices that you use that are connected to network	Network interface	Operating system
Device 1 (Desktop/Laptop) -		
Device 2 -		
3. Have you experienced any problems with the network? If so, please give a brief description of each problem		
Problems -		
4. What capabilities would you like to see in the network (performance, features)		
Performance - Features - Other -		
5. Do you have any issues or problems with security? If so, please give a brief description of each problem.		
Security Problems -		
6. Any other suggestions, issues, or comments?		
Suggestions/ Issues/ Comments		

FIGURE 3.30   A Template for the Questionnaire

environment. For this example, a questionnaire was developed and sent to all employees of the company. Figure 3.30 shows such a questionnaire.

Of course, not everyone will respond to the questionnaire. Experience has shown that anywhere from 10% to 40% will respond. This depends on how long the questionnaire is, how difficult it is to fill out, and how large the organization is. Also, you tend to get most of the responses within a few days, but some trickle in

			Requirements Specification				
			Part 2: Listing of Requirements				
ID/ Name	**Date**	**Type**	**Description**	**Gathered/ Derived**	**Locations**	**Status**	**Priority**
6	20Jan01	Application	Inventory application (INV1) for manufacturing requirements not determined at this time	Gathered from Users (MAN)	TBD	TBD	TBD
7	25Jan01	Device	Engineering users have workstations with GigE NICs	Gathered from Users (ENG)	TBD	TBD	TBD
8	02Feb01	Application	Other general applications: mail, word processing, internal and external Web access. More information needed	Gathered from Network Staff	TBD	TBD	TBD

FIGURE 3.31   Additional Requirements Gathered from the Questionnaire

over a longer period of time (e.g., a few weeks). You can update the requirements a few times based on the results of new responses.

The results of the example questionnaire are shown in Figures 3.31 and 3.32. These requirements were refined and added to by meeting with each of the groups (including meetings with management and network staff) in the company.

			Requirements Specification				
			Part 2: Listing of Requirements				
ID/ Name	**Date**	**Type**	**Description**	**Gathered/ Derived**	**Locations**	**Status**	**Priority**
9	01Feb01	Application	Database application (DB1) requires a minimum of 150 Kb/s per session	Gathered from Various Users	TBD	TBD	TBD
10	02Feb01	Network	Company requires a minimum of T1 access to Internet	Gathered from Network Staff	TBD	TBD	TBD
11	02Feb01	Network	Current network will be completely replaced, so there are no requirements from existing network	Gathered from Network Staff	N/A	Info	TBD
12	05Feb01	Application	Visualization application (VIS1) for Finance requires up to 40 Mb/s capacity and 100 ms round-trip delay	Derived from Application	TBD	TBD	TBD

FIGURE 3.32   Additional Requirements Gathered from Meetings with Users and Staff

3.13   Conclusions

The process of requirements analysis provides you with the means for analyzing your network and the environment in which it is contained. You learned about gathering and managing user, application, device, and network requirements. This includes determining the initial conditions for the project and setting and managing your customer(s) expectations about the network. Initial conditions vary, depending on the network, system, and environment, as well as whether the network is new or an upgrade of an existing network. Armed with the initial conditions, you can gather requirements from the users, administration, and management, and map application requirements to determine their dependencies.

You learned about determining the variables to measure (service metrics) and how to make measurements. Your choices of service metrics will lead to defining variables for network monitoring and management. We discussed modeling and simulation, and how they and other approximation techniques can be used to describe user and application behavior.

Building on the service metrics, we learned about developing performance requirements for capacity, delay, and RMA, including developing performance thresholds and limits. These are useful in distinguishing between low- and high-performance requirements for your network. We also learned about general and environment-specific thresholds and limits and how to determine them. Some general thresholds are presented for your use. We also discussed predictable and guaranteed performance requirements and their importance. Finally, we discussed mapping requirements to geographic locations, in preparation for traffic flow analysis.

In the next chapter, we bring all of these concepts together to develop a requirements specification for the network.

3.14   Exercises

1. Initial conditions for your network project consist of the following categories: type of network project, scope of network project, and architecture/design goals. Develop three sets of initial conditions (each containing one element from each category) and give an example network project for each set.

2. For each set of application performance requirements shown in Figure 3.33, classify the network as single-tier or multi-tier performance.

Application Set	Performance Requirements		
	Capacity	Reliability	Delay
Application Set 1:			
Application 1	150 Kb/s	N/A	N/A
Application 2	200 Kb/s	N/A	N/A
Application 3	90 Kb/s	N/A	N/A
Application 4	120 Kb/s	N/A	N/A
Application Set 2:			
Application 1	75 Kb/s	99.999%	N/A
Application 2	150 Kb/s	N/A	N/A
Application 3	250 Kb/s	99.999%	N/A
Application 4	200 Kb/s	N/A	N/A
Application Set 3:			
Application 1	1.1 Mb/s	99.95%	40 ms
Application 2	800 Kb/s	N/A	N/A
Application 3	950 Kb/s	N/A	100 ms
Application 4	120 Kb/s	N/A	N/A

FIGURE 3.33   Application Performance Requirements for Exercise 2

3. Your customer is a hospital that wants to upgrade its LAN. Develop a questionnaire to gather requirements from users, hospital management, and staff. What kinds of questions would you ask to better understand their environment?

4. Consider a network project where you cannot talk to users or staff. What resources can you use to gather user, application, device, and network requirements? Briefly outline a method for gathering and deriving requirements in the absence of user/staff involvement.

5. You want to test the performance of Web sessions across a wireless access network, between PCs and an IP router that terminates point-to-point protocol (PPP) and PPP over Ethernet (PPPoE) sessions, as shown in Figure 3.34. Describe how you would test performance, both on a testbed and on the existing network. List any equipment, software, and networking devices you would use.

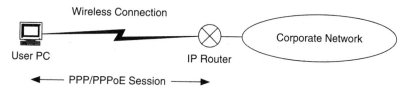

FIGURE 3.34   Wireless Connections to Corporate Network Using PPP and PPPoE

6. Show how the following changes to the requirement below would be tracked/managed. Use either the paragraph or tabular form to record changes.

   Requirement: 12Oct2002. Network must be capable of supporting up to 2000 Fast Ethernet interfaces, aggregated to a 1 Gb/s or greater capacity backbone spanning all 12 buildings across the campus.
   a. Change "Fast Ethernet" to "Fast Ethernet or Gigabit Ethernet," dated 5Jan2003.
   b. Delete "12 buildings across the campus," dated 7Jan2003.
   c. Change "2000" to "3500," dated 10Feb2003.
   d. Add "10 buildings listed in Appendix A," dated 20Jan2003.
   e. Change "Fast Ethernet" to "Fast Ethernet or Gigabit Ethernet" to "10, 100, or 1000 Mb/s," dated 5Mar2003.
   f. Change "aggregated" to "aggregated within each building," dated 21Apr2003.

7. Service metrics are used to monitor, measure, and verify services in the network and determine if performance requirements are being met. Therefore, service metrics must be meaningful to the network operators, managers, users, and staff. For each performance requirement below, describe a service metric that could be used to measure and verify the requirement.
   a. Reliability of a T1 link between an enterprise network and its ISP, with IP routers on each end of the T1.
   b. Round-trip delay between devices on network A and servers on server LAN B.
   c. Average traffic rate in and out of a compute server, measured across all four of its LAN interfaces over 15-minute intervals.

8. Given an MTBCF requirement of 8000 hours and an MTTR requirement of 4 hours, calculate an availability requirement.

9. Describe two ways to make an uptime requirement of 99.999% more precise.

10. You are developing a network for the FAA for a telemetry processing application that consists of two components: an automated guidance-control system that will analyze telemetry data from airplanes, and a motion visualization system used by controllers at their workstations (Figure 3.35). In your analysis of this application you have determined that the application requires a maximum one-way delay of

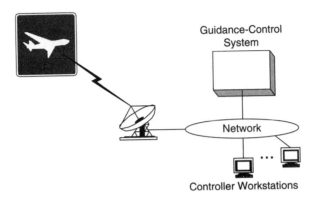

FIGURE 3.35   A Diagram of the System for Exercise 10

20 ms between an airplane and the guidance-control system. In addition, controllers interact with airplanes via the motion visualization system with delays on the order of HRT. Develop upper and lower delay bounds for this application, and show them on a graph.

CHAPTER CONTENTS

4

Flow Analysis

The results of requirements analysis—the requirements specification and requirements map—list and describe requirements that have been gathered and derived for a network. Many of these are performance requirements (capacity, delay, and RMA) for users, their applications, and devices. Such performance requirements, along with the locations of users, applications, and devices from the requirements map, form the basis for estimating where traffic will flow through the network. *Flow analysis* is the process of characterizing traffic flows for a network: where they are likely to occur and what levels of performance they will require.

The intent of flow analysis is not to show every possible flow in a network, but rather to show those flows that will have the greatest impact on the network architecture and design. This is often a small fraction of the total set of flows for a network.

4.1 Objectives

In this chapter you will learn how to identify and characterize traffic flows. We discuss individual, composite, and critical flows and how to determine when each applies. You will learn mechanisms to help identify and characterize flows, including data sources and sinks and flow models. Finally, you will learn about flow specifications, where performance requirements are combined for a flow or group of flows. Flow specifications are used as input to the network architecture and design processes, covered later in this book.

4.1.1 Preparation

To be able to understand and apply the concepts in this chapter, you should be familiar with client–server, peer-to-peer, distributed computing, and other models for how applications and devices interact with one another.

4.2   Background

Now that we have the user, application, device, and network requirements developed, listed, and mapped in the requirements specification, we further analyze these requirements based on their end-to-end characteristics. We use the concept of a *flow*, which, for an end-to-end connection, has constant addressing and service requirements, to combine performance requirements in a useful way. These characteristics are analyzed and combined, per flow, into a flow specification or flowspec. This is used for capacity and service planning.

This chapter introduces flows and flow concepts, data sources and sinks, and flow models which will help us to identify, size, and describe flows. We also develop cumulative performance requirements for each flow.

4.3   Flows

Flows (also known as *traffic flows* or *data flows*) are sets of network traffic (application, protocol, and control information) that have common attributes, such as source/destination address, type of information, directionality, or other end-to-end information.

Figure 4.1 illustrates this concept.

Information within a flow is transmitted during a single session of an application. Flows are end-to-end, between source and destination applications/devices/users. Since they can be identified by their end-to-end information, they can be directly linked to an application, device, or network, or associated with an end user. We can also examine flows on a link-by-link or network-by-network basis. This is useful when we want to combine flow requirements at the network or network-element levels.

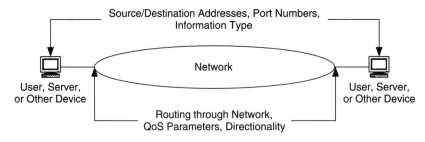

FIGURE 4.1   Flow Attributes Apply End-to-End and Throughout Network

Flow Characteristics		
Performance Requirements	Capacity (e.g., Bandwidth)	
	Delay (e.g., Latency)	
	Reliability (e.g., Availability)	
	Quality of Service Levels	
Importance/ Priority Levels	Business/Enterprise/Provider	
	Political	
Other	Directionality	
	Common Sets of Users, Applications, Devices	
	Scheduling (e.g., Time-of-Day)	
	Protocols Used	
	Addresses/Ports	
	Security/Privacy Requirements	

FIGURE 4.2   Common Flow Characteristics

Common flow characteristics are shown in Figure 4.2.

Flow analysis is an integral part of the overall analysis process. Flows are where performance requirements, services, and service metrics are combined with location information to show where performance and service are needed in the network. Flow analysis provides an end-to-end perspective on requirements and shows where requirements combine and interact. It also provides some insight into the degrees of hierarchy and diversity needed in the architecture and design. In addition, as we will see in the design process, this analysis also provides information that can be useful in choosing interconnection strategies, such as switching, routing, or hybrid mechanisms.

Most flows are bidirectional and can be represented as either a single, double-sided arrow with one or two sets of performance requirements, or as two separate flows, each with its own set of requirements. A single-sided arrow with one set of performance requirements represents a unidirectional flow. Figure 4.3 shows these cases.

Flows provide a different perspective on traffic movement in networks: they have logical as well as physical components; and they allow traffic to be coupled with users, applications, or devices. Flows are becoming increasingly important in the analysis, architecture, and design processes.

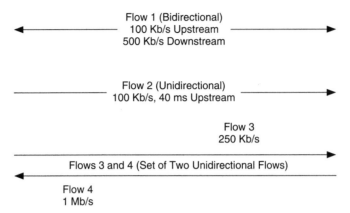

FIGURE 4.3 Flows Are Represented as Unidirectional or Bidirectional Arrows with Performance Requirements

We examine two types of flows: individual and composite. We will see that the aggregation of requirements and flows in the network due to hierarchy leads to composite flows, and that this can happen in the access network as well as in the backbone.

4.3.1 Individual and Composite Flows

An *individual flow* is the flow for a single session of an application. An individual flow is the basic unit of traffic flows in this book; they are either considered individually or combined into a composite flow. When an individual flow has guaranteed requirements, those requirements are usually left with the individual flow and are not consolidated with other requirements or flows into a composite flow (Figure 4.4).

This is done so that the flow's guaranteed requirements can be treated separately from the rest of the flows. Individual flows are derived directly from the requirements specification, or are estimated from our best knowledge about the application, users, devices, and their locations.

FIGURE 4.4 Individual Flow for a Single Application with Guaranteed Requirements

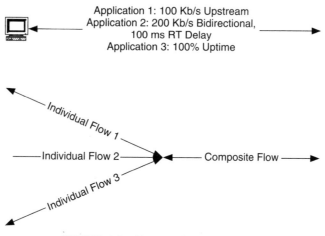

FIGURE 4.5 Example Composite Flows

A *composite flow* is a combination of requirements from multiple applications, or of individual flows, that share a common link, path, or network. Most flows in a network are composites (Figure 4.5).

More examples of flows are presented in Figure 4.6. The first example is an individual flow, consisting of a one-way delay requirement for a single session

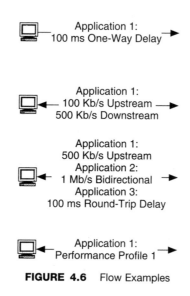

FIGURE 4.6 Flow Examples

of an application. Note that this flow is unidirectional. The second example is also of an individual flow, but in this case the capacity requirements are given in each direction. Since they are different, they are listed independently. The definitions of upstream and downstream as used here denote directionality based on the source and destination of the flow, where *upstream* indicates the direction toward the source and *downstream* is the direction toward the destination. Upstream is often toward the core of the network, while downstream is often toward the edge of the network, particularly in service provider networks. Another way to show a bidirectional flow is with two separate arrows, one upstream and the other downstream, each with its own performance requirement.

The third example is a composite flow, listing requirements from three separate applications at the same source. The last example uses a performance profile to describe the flow's performance requirements. A profile is often used when many flows have the same requirement, as this makes it easier to apply the same requirements to multiple flows: A pointer to the profile is sufficient to describe the requirements, instead of having them written out each time. This is especially useful when the requirements are long or when they are consistent across many flows. The flow in this example could be either an individual or a composite flow, depending on the contents of the profile.

Performance requirements for individual flows and composite flows are determined through development of a flow specification for the network, which is discussed at the end of this chapter.

4.3.2 Critical Flows

Some flows can be considered more important than others, in that they are higher in performance or have strict requirements (e.g., mission-critical, rate-critical, real-time, interactive, high-performance), while some flows may serve more important users, their applications, and devices. Such flows are called *critical flows*. In this chapter we examine how to determine when flows are critical. When prioritizing which flows get attention in the network architecture and design, critical flows usually come first. This is usually the case; however, individual flows with guaranteed requirements might also be considered first in the architecture and design. Prioritizing flows is discussed at the end of this chapter.

Flows are described in this fashion in order to make it easier to understand and combine requirements. Composite flows combine the requirements of individual flows, while individual flows can show guaranteed requirements that need to be considered throughout the end-to-end path of the flow. All of these flows are important in the architecture and design of the network. The descriptions of the types of flows that we develop in the flow specification help us to define the architecture and choose the technologies and services that best fit the customer's needs.

Throughout this chapter we analyze flow requirements to determine where they apply and when they contribute to composite flows, and, if they do, how to combine their performance requirements accordingly. Some networks have flows that indicate single-tier performance, others have flows that indicate multi-tier performance, and still others have predictable (stochastic) and/or guaranteed performance. Often the few flows that require high, predictable, and/or guaranteed performance are the ones that drive the architecture and design from a service (capacity, delay, and RMA) perspective, while all flows drive the architecture and design from a capacity perspective. The architecture and design processes accommodate both of these perspectives.

4.4   Identifying and Developing Flows

Flows can usually be identified and developed from information in the requirements specification: user, application, device, and network requirements; user and application behavior (usage patterns, models); user, application, and device location information; and performance requirements. The more thorough this information is, the better the resulting flows will be.

At this point in the analysis process we have sets of requirements and mappings of application and/or device locations. We have not made any choices of networking technologies, network devices, or vendors. It is important that during the flow analysis process we do not constrain flows to existing networks, topologies, or technologies. We want to be free in determining the compositions and locations of flows for our network, so that the flows drive our architectural and design choices. Thus, flows are determined based on the requirements and locations of the applications and devices that generate (source) or terminate (sink) each traffic flow.

The process for identifying and developing flows consists of identifying one or more applications and/or devices that you believe will generate and/or terminate traffic flows. Once you have chosen which applications and devices to focus on, you use their requirements from the requirements specification and their locations from the requirements map. Based on how and where each application and device is used, you may be able to determine which devices generate flows and which devices terminate flows (flow sources and sinks). Some common flow models are provided in Section 4.6 to help you with this process. Once you have identified each flow and determined its composition and location, you combine the performance requirements of flows into a flow specification. This process is shown in Figure 4.7.

From an application perspective, some common approaches to identifying flows include:

- Focusing on a particular application, application group, device, or function (e.g., videoconferencing or storage)
- Developing a "profile" of common or selected applications that can be applied across a user population
- Choosing the top N (e.g., 3, 5, 10, etc.) applications to be applied across the entire network

You may choose to consider some or all approaches for your network. Each approach is outlined in the following sections.

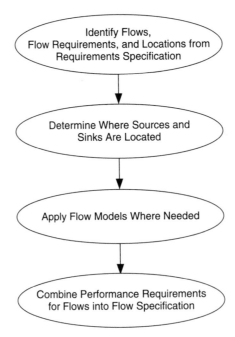

FIGURE 4.7   The Process for Identifying and Developing Flows

4.4.1 Focusing on a Particular Application

When focusing on an application, application group, device, or function, the idea here is to consider one or more applications that will likely drive the architecture and design—namely, those that are high performance, mission-critical, rate-critical, real-time, interactive, predictable, and/or guaranteed. By focusing on one or a few applications, you can spend more time determining their flows, as opposed to spreading your time out across many applications. Choose what to focus on and select the relevant information from the requirements specification.

Example: Data Migration

From requirements specification, for a single session of each application:

Application 1: Staging data from user devices

Capacity 100 Kb/s; Delay Unknown; Reliability 100%

Application 1: Migrating data between servers

Capacity 500 Kb/s; Delay Unknown; Reliability 100%

Application 2: Migration to remote (tertiary) storage

Capacity 10Mb/s; Delay N/A; Reliability 100%

You can use the location information to map out where the users, applications, and devices are, and develop a map if you don't already have one. Figure 4.8 is an example of such a map.

Using the information on user and application behavior, you determine or estimate where flows will occur. This can be between networks, device groups (better), or individual devices (best). Figure 4.9 shows where flows will occur between devices for Application 1.

Once flows are mapped, you apply performance information to each flow. Figure 4.10 shows this for the Central Campus portion of the storage application environment. Whereas Figure 4.9 shows flows between devices, Figure 4.10 simplifies this view by showing flows between buildings. Either method can be used, depending on the size of the environment and the number of flows you need to show. Usually the between-device method (Figure 4.9) is used first to estimate where flows will be, and then the second method (Figure 4.10) is used to simplify the flow diagram.

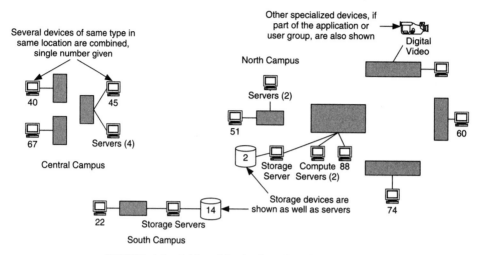

FIGURE 4.8 A Map of Device Locations for a Network

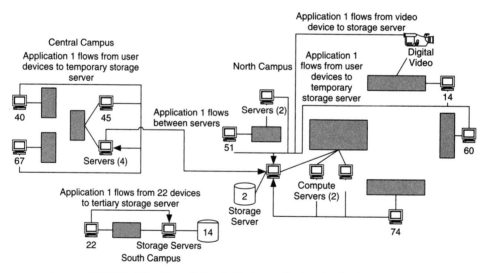

FIGURE 4.9 Flows Estimated between Devices for Application 1

In Figure 4.10 flows F1, F2, and F3 represent the single-session performance requirement for each building for Application 1. At some point in this process the performance requirement will need to be modified to represent the estimated performance required by all users in each building (40, 67, and 45 users in the

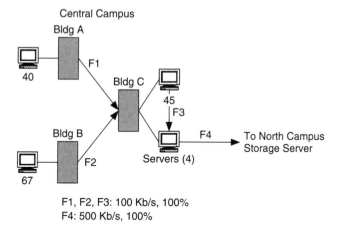

F1, F2, F3: 100 Kb/s, 100%
F4: 500 Kb/s, 100%

FIGURE 4.10   Performance Information Added to Central Campus Flows for Application 1

buildings at Central Campus). F4 represents the performance requirement for the server–server flow between Central and North Campuses.

Note that in this figure flows F1 and F2 are between Buildings A/B and C, while flow F3 is between devices. Since the 45 user devices and four servers are in the same building, we have to show the flows between devices. If we were showing flows within Building C, it would look like Figure 4.11.

This diagram also introduces a *flow aggregation point*, which allows us to show multiple flows being consolidated at a location. This is useful in the design process,

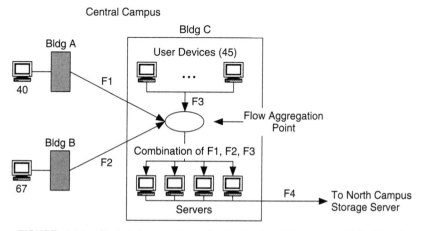

FIGURE 4.11   Central Campus Flows for Application 1 Expanded with Building C

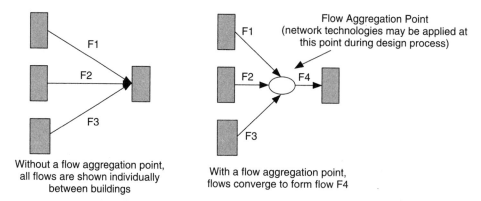

FIGURE 4.12   Consolidating Flows Using a Flow Aggregation Point

when we are looking at technologies and interconnection strategies for such locations in the network. For example, Figure 4.12 shows what flows will look like between buildings with and without a flow aggregation point.

4.4.2 Developing a Profile

Sometimes a set of common applications apply to a group of users or to the entire set of users. When this is the case a profile or template can be developed for those applications, and each flow that fits the profile is identified with that profile's tag. Thus, instead of trying to replicate flow information for similar flows, you can use the profile, saving time and effort.

There are also times when flows have the same performance requirements, regardless of whether or not they share the same set of applications. When flows have the same performance requirements, a profile can be used to simplify their information as well.

Figure 4.13 shows a profile applied across the user population for Application 1. Instead of showing identical performance requirements at each flow, a common profile is shown for flows with the same performance requirements. This helps to reduce duplication of information on the map, also reducing clutter.

In this figure, P1 is the tag associated with flows having the following performance requirements: capacity $= 100\,\text{Kb/s}$, reliability $= 100\%$. There are six flows in this diagram with those performance requirements, all of which are tagged as P1. Other flows in this figure have different performance requirements. Flow F4 (also shown in Figures 4.10 and 4.11) has different performance requirements: capacity $= 500\,\text{kb/s}$, reliability $= 100\%$. Flow 5 combines the performance

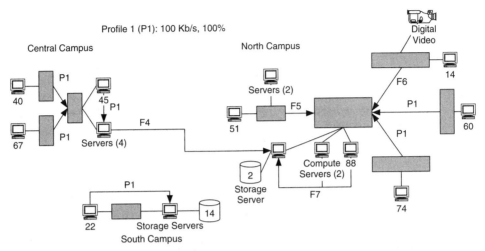

FIGURE 4.13 A Performance Profile (P1) Applied to Multiple Flows with the Same Performance Characteristics

requirements of 51 users (which, for Application 1, would be P1) with those of the two servers in that building. Flow F6 combines the performance requirements of 14 users (again, this would be P1) with that of the digital video device. F7, like F5, combines the performance requirements of users (88 in this building) with those of the two compute servers.

Note that Figure 4.13 shows flows as arrows between buildings and between devices within a building (except for flow F4, which in this example is easier to show as a flow between devices than as a flow between buildings). We could also choose to show the flows only between devices, as in Figure 4.9. If you compare these two figures, you will see that showing arrows between buildings simplifies the diagram. However, you may need to complement such a diagram with diagrams of flows within buildings, such as that shown in Figure 4.11.

4.4.3 Choosing the Top *N* Applications

Finally, choosing the top *N* applications for your network is a combination of the first two approaches. It is similar to the first approach, however; instead of one particular application (or maybe two applications), you use three, five, or perhaps ten. It is also similar to the second approach, in that the result can also be an application profile. These applications are the "top *N*" in terms of helping with the success of that organization, which may be inferred by their degrees of usage, number of users, number of devices/servers, or performance requirements.

Example: Top 5 Applications

1. Web Browsing

2. Email

3. File Transfer

4. Word Processing

5. Database Transactions

This approach reduces the set of possible applications to a number that can be analyzed. However, whenever you eliminate applications from this set, you need to ask the question, "If I meet the requirements of these top N applications, will the requirements for those applications I eliminated be met?" The intent of this approach is to determine which applications represent the most important requirements for that network. These "top N" applications are likely to be the performance drivers for the network. As such, if you meet the needs of these applications, you are likely to meet the needs of all applications for that network. This is described in more detail during the development of the flow specification.

The list of "top N" applications should be as precise as you can make it. For example, Application 5 above (Database Transactions) may actually be time-card data entry into an ERP database. This would be a more precise description, resulting in more precise flow composition and location information. Whenever possible, include usage scenarios for each application.

You may also use different approaches for different parts of the network. For example, it is common to include the top N applications that apply everywhere as well as profiles for selected locations and to focus on an application, device, or group in other locations, as in Figure 4.14.

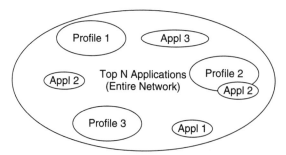

FIGURE 4.14   A Project May Incorporate Multiple Approaches in Choosing Applications

4.5   Data Sources and Sinks

Data sources and sinks can help provide directionality to flows. A *data source* generates a traffic flow, and a *data sink* terminates a traffic flow. To help show data sources and sinks in a diagram, the convention shown in Figure 4.15 is used. Data sources are represented as a circle with a dot in the center, and a data sink is represented as a circle with a cross (i.e., star or asterisk) in the center. These are two-dimensional representations of a plane with an arrow coming out of it, as in traffic flowing out of a source, or a plane with an arrow going into it, as in traffic flowing into a sink. By using these symbols we can show data sources and sinks on a two-dimensional map, without the need for arrows.

Almost all devices on a network produce and accept data, acting as both data sources and sinks, and there are some devices that typically act as either a source or sink. In addition, a device may be primarily a data source or sink for a particular application.

Some examples of data sources are devices that do a lot of computing or processing and generate large amounts of information, such as computing servers, mainframes, parallel systems, or computing clusters. Other (specialized) devices, like cameras, video production equipment, application servers, and medical instruments, do not necessarily do a lot of computing (in the traditional sense) but can still generate a lot of data, video, and audio that will be transmitted on the network (Figure 4.16).

A good example of a data sink is a data storage or archival device. This may be a single device, acting as a front end for groups of disks or tape devices. Devices that manipulate or display large quantities of information, such as video editing or display devices, also act as data sinks (Figure 4.17).

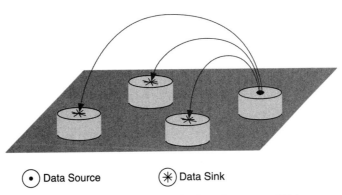

⊙ Data Source   ✳ Data Sink

FIGURE 4.15   Conventions for Data Sources and Sinks

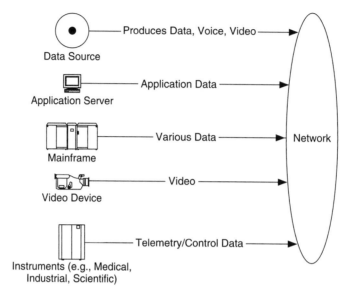

FIGURE 4.16   Example Data Sources

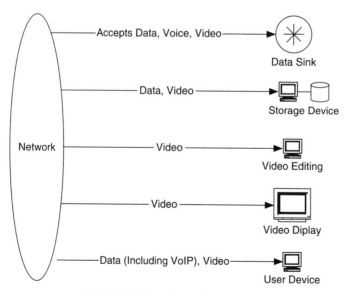

FIGURE 4.17   Example Data Sinks

Example 4.1. Data Sources and Sinks for Data Migration Applications.

As an example, let's consider the data migration applications. Recall that Figure 4.8 shows device location information for these applications. Shown on this map are storage and compute servers, a video source, and groups of desktop devices for each building. Note that a total number of desktop devices are given; this is done to simplify the map and flows. If more detail is needed, this group could be separated into multiple groups, based on their requirements, or single devices can be separated out. If necessary, a new map could be generated for just that building, with substantially more detail.

This service has two applications. Application 1 is the frequent migration of data on users' desktops, servers, and other devices, to storage servers at each campus. As part of this application, data are migrated from the server at Central Campus to the server at North Campus.

The server at South Campus is also the archival (or long-term) server for these campuses. Application 2 is the migration of data that have been collected over a period of time (e.g., 1 day) from the server at Central Campus to the archival server at South Campus.

When, for Application 1, we add the data sources and sinks to Figure 4.13, we get the diagram in Figure 4.18. In this figure all devices are labeled as a data source, sink, or both. All of the user devices at each campus are data sources. The servers at Central Campus act as a data sink for flows from user devices at that campus, and as a data source when data migrates to the server at North Campus (flow F4). The server at South Campus is a

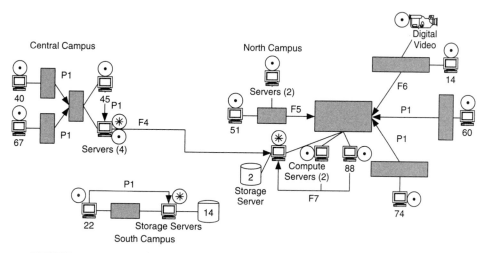

FIGURE 4.18   Data Sources, Sinks, and Flows Added to the First Part of the Application

data sink for user flows at that campus, and the servers at North Campus are data sinks for all devices at that campus, including servers and digital video, as well as for flow F4 from Central Campus.

With the sources and sinks on the map, along with arrows between them to indicate potential traffic flows, we are beginning to have an idea of where flows occur in this network for this application.

We do the same thing for Application 2, with the result shown in Figure 4.19. For this part of the application the desktop devices and video source are not involved, so they are not shown as either sources or sinks of data. The server at Central Campus that was a data sink for Application 1 now becomes a data source for Application 2, sending data to the archival server (shown as a data sink). The flows for this part of the application are much simpler, merely a single flow between the storage server and archival device. This is shown in two ways: as a flow between buildings (Option 1, the standard convention used so far in this example), and as a flow between devices at separate buildings (Option 2). While Option 2 is not common practice, it is used here since there are only two devices (and one flow) for this application.

These applications are shown as separate events in order to clarify the flows and the roles of the storage servers. We could, however, put both parts of the application together on the same map. We would want to make sure that the resultant map is still clear about when devices are data sources and sinks.

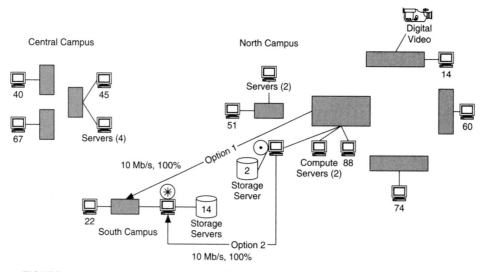

FIGURE 4.19 Data Sources, Sinks, and Flows Added to Application 2 (Two Options Shown)

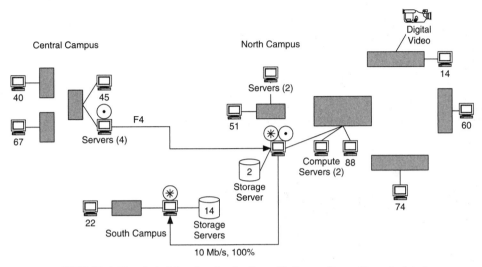

FIGURE 4.20   Data Migration Application with Server–Server Flows Isolated

One way to simplify this map is to focus only on flows between storage servers, data sources, and sinks. Figure 4.20 shows this case, with both applications on the same map.

You may have noticed in our example that flows occur at different times of the day, and can vary in schedule (when they occur), frequency (how often they occur), and duration (how long they last). The occurrence of traffic flows can be cyclic (e.g., every Monday morning before 10 a.m., at the end of each month, or during the end-of-the-year closeout). Understanding when flows occur and how they impact your customer's business or operation is critical. For example, if 90% of the revenue for a business is generated during the last four weeks before Christmas, you may need to focus flow development on what is happening to applications during that time.

This leads to the concept of developing worst-case and typical-usage scenarios. This is similar to developing for single-tier or multi-tier performance, as discussed in Chapter 3. Worst-case scenarios are like the aforementioned one—for a business whose revenue is highly seasonal. This is similar to developing for the highest-performance applications and devices, in that you focus on times when the network requires its greatest performance to support the work being done. Architecting/designing a network for the worst-case scenario can be expensive and will result in over-engineering the network for most of its life cycle. Therefore, the customer must be fully aware of the reasons for, and supportive of, building toward a worst-case scenario.

Typical-usage scenarios describe an average (typical) workload for the network. This is similar to developing for single-tier performance, in that you focus on times when average, everyday work is being done. Recall from Chapter 3 that single-tier performance focuses on those applications and devices that are in general use and that make up a background level of traffic on the network. Often both worst-case and typical-usage scenarios are developed for a network.

Using data sources and sinks to help map flows for an application provides a great start to generating the flows for your network. Flow models, described next, are another great tool that you can use to help describe flows.

4.6   Flow Models

Another method to help describe flows in the network is to compare them to general, well-known flow models. *Flow models* are groups of flows that exhibit specific, consistent behavior characteristics. The flows within a flow model apply to a single application. Directionality, hierarchy, and diversity are the primary characteristics of flow models. *Directionality* describes the preference (of lack thereof) of a flow to have more requirements in one direction than another. Hierarchy and diversity are based on the definitions from Chapter 1.

While network architectures and designs typically treat traffic flows as having equal requirements in each direction, we find that many flows (especially from newer applications) have substantially different requirements in each direction. Most flows are asymmetric, and some access and transmission technologies (such as digital subscriber loop [xDSL] or WDM) can be optimized for such flows.

Flow models help describe the degrees of hierarchy and diversity of flows for applications. They show where flows combine, where they can be grouped together, and where flows occur between *peers*, which are devices at the same level in the hierarchy. They also can help us to identify which flows are critical flows; these, as you may recall, are considered more important than others, in that they are higher in performance, have strict requirements, or serve more important users, applications, and devices.

Flow models can also be useful to help quickly identify and categorize flows in an environment, so that we may easily recognize its flow characteristics. In this way they are like application groups, discussed in Chapter 2.

Flow models that we examine are:

- Peer-to-peer
- Client–server
- Hierarchical client–server
- Distributed computing

For each model we consider the directionality and hierarchy of its flows. We also, when possible, identify which flows in each model are critical, or important, flows.

These flow models are a subset of many possible models that you could use to characterize the flows for your network. We could include, for example, real-time (or near real-time or interactive) flows as a model, as well as streaming media. You are encouraged to develop an exhaustive list of flow models for your network projects.

4.6.1 Peer-to-Peer

Our first flow model, *peer-to-peer*, is one where the users and applications are fairly consistent in their flow behaviors throughout the network. They are, in effect, peers, in that they act at the same level in the hierarchy. Since they (users and/or applications) are fairly consistent, their flows are also fairly consistent. Thus, we can consider the flows in a peer-to-peer flow model to be equivalent (Figure 4.21). This has two important implications:

- We cannot distinguish between flows in this model. Therefore, either all of the flows or none of the flows is critical
- Since the flows are equivalent, they can be described by a single specification (e.g., profile)

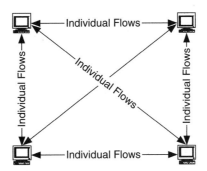

FIGURE 4.21   Peer-to-Peer Flow Model

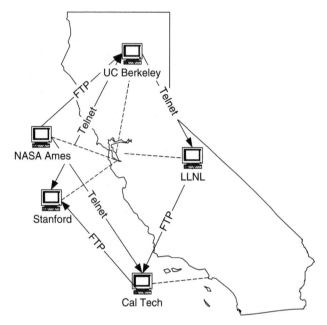

FIGURE 4.22   An Example of Peer-to-Peer Flows in the Early Internet

There are several examples of peer-to-peer flow behavior. The first is the early Internet, a portion of which is shown in Figure 4.22. In the early Internet, applications like FTP and telnet were predominant, and each device on the network was a potential source and destination of the flows for these applications. Another example is of file-sharing applications on the Internet. Basically, anywhere devices communicate directly with each other is considered peer-to-peer.

The peer-to-peer flow model is our default when we do not have any other information about the flows in our network. In a sense, it is part of the degenerate case for our requirements map (since there are no flow-specific requirements that can be determined). This flow model can also be used to describe flows when all users in a group need equal access to one another for an application. In addition to the file-sharing and remote access applications already described, this could also be a multimedia, tele*services application (e.g., teleseminars, telelearning, teleconferencing), where any of the participants may source or sink data to or from any other participant. Although each of the tele*services just noted can be considered a one-to-many application, there are components of each that can be applied as a set of one-to-one conversations. For example, while telelearning consists of a number of users (students) receiving and transmitting from and to a teacher, another

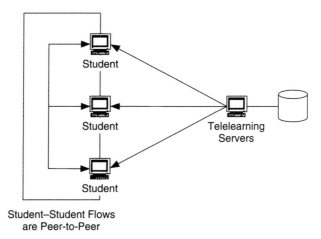

Student–Student Flows
are Peer-to-Peer

FIGURE 4.23 Peer-to-Peer Flows in a Telelearning Environment

component to this application is the ability to have side conversations among students. This part of the application is peer-to-peer (Figure 4.23). This flow model is useful, in that it indicates that a performance profile may be used for those flows, and that there are no (or several) critical flows for that application.

4.6.2 Client–Server

The client–server flow model is currently the most generally applicable model. This model has both directionality and hierarchy. Flows in this model are bidirectional, between clients and the server, in the form of requests and responses. This flow model is *client–server* in that the flows are asymmetric and hierarchically focused toward the client. Thus, requests tend to be small relative to responses. Depending on the type of application, the flows may be considered almost unidirectional, from the server to the clients. Figure 4.24 illustrates the client–server flow model.

Since the flows in the client–server model are asymmetric, with the predominant or important flows in the direction from the server to the clients, the server can be considered a data source, and the clients are data sinks. The server would be shown as a data source on the requirements map, with flows generating from it to its clients on other areas of the map. Since the predominant or important flows are from the server to the clients, these are the critical flows for this model. When there is a requirement to transmit information to multiple clients concurrently, multicasting at some layer in the network must be considered to optimize flows for this model.

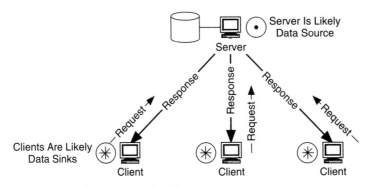

FIGURE 4.24   Client–Server Flow Model

This model is the traditional view of client–server operations, exemplified by ERP applications such as SAP, and e-commerce applications. Applications such as these are highly dependent on network performance when they are configured to work across significant distances, as when a company is dispersed across multiple locations, spanning cities, states, or countries. If the network does not properly support client–server applications, the customer must resort to distributing the client–server architecture (e.g., distributed ERP), which can be expensive.

Video editing exemplifies a client–server flow model. A video server can store video to be edited, and clients make requests to that server for video to edit. The server passes video to the clients, which may be sent back up to the server upon completion, or may be sent elsewhere for more processing (Figure 4.25).

Another view of client–server flows is with Web applications. While the early Internet started with peer-to-peer flows from applications such as FTP and telnet, this usage evolved to become more client–server-like with the use of FTP servers, followed by applications such as gopher and Archie. Now, with the widespread use of Web applications, many flows in the Internet are between Web servers and their clients. As TCP/IP assumes more network operating system (NOS) roles, print and file services across enterprise networks and the Internet will become more client–server oriented. For example, in the early days, a person who wanted to access information from an organization would have used the application FTP to a known site to download information. Then this changed into accessing an FTP or gopher server, and then to accessing a Web server. Today a person may access large quantities of information from an organization without ever entering that organization's network, through accessing external Web servers.

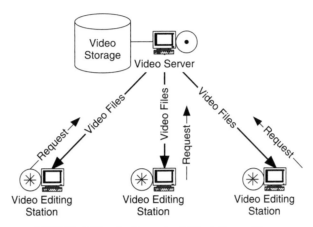

FIGURE 4.25   An Example of Client–Server Flows

However, a better flow model for Web traffic has multiple levels of tiers, with traffic flows within some of the tiers. This is the hierarchical client–server model, described in the following section.

4.6.3   Hierarchical Client–Server

As the flows within a client–server flow model become more hierarchical, in terms of adding layers, or tiers, to the flows, then their behavior can be represented as a hierarchical client–server flow model. A *hierarchical client–server flow model* has the characteristics of a client–server flow model but also has multiple layers, or tiers, between servers. In this model there may also be flows from a server to a support server or management device, as shown in Figure 4.26. These flows (server-to-server and server-to-manager) may be considered critical, in addition to the server-to-client flows. With the additional layer(s) of hierarchy in this model the servers can now be either data sources or sinks (or both). More information may be needed about the application(s) in order to determine the status of these servers. This model is important in that it recognizes server-to-server and server-to-manager flows.

A hierarchical client–server flow model is indicated when multiple applications work together and share information to accomplish a task, or when multiple client–server applications (or multiple sessions of the same client–server application) are managed by a higher-level application. An operations support system (OSS) managing several back-office applications may often be modeled in this fashion.

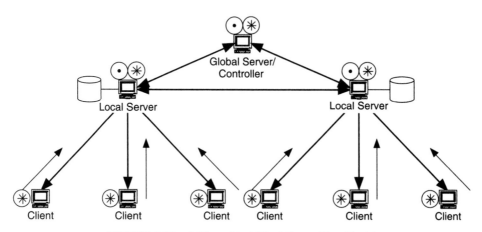

FIGURE 4.26   A Hierarchical Client–Server Flow Model

Critical flows for this model are dependent on application behavior. If the applications are inherently client–server, and the servers are there merely to support multiple sessions, then the client–server flows may be the only critical flows. However, when the servers communicate with each other (e.g., to update a common database or share data between applications), then the server-to-server flows may be critical, possibly in addition to the client–server flows. And when there is communication to a manager (e.g., to synchronize processing or information), then the server-to-manager flows may also be critical.

We have shown that the Internet has evolved from an early peer-to-peer flow model to a client–server flow model with the acceptance of Web applications. As client–server traffic has grown, however, Web servers have been replicated and distributed across the Internet, resulting in an increase in server-to-server flows. This is being done to increase the effectiveness of Web access, in part by spreading access across multiple devices and in part by locating devices closer to the access portion of the Internet, thus bypassing part or all of the core. As a result, the Internet is evolving to more of a hierarchical client–server flow model.

Such hierarchical Web services are shown in Figure 4.27. In this figure, content delivery networks (CDN) and mirrors (introduced in Chapter 1) are used to migrate Web content between servers and provide local access to content for users.

In this figure, the servers can provide the same function or different functions. For example, Web-based three-tier application servers can run application and Web services on the same device, while running database services on another device. In this case the flows between servers (application/Web and database) are critical for operation.

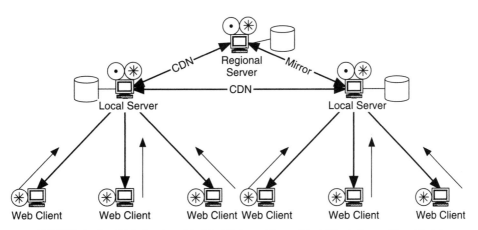

FIGURE 4.27   Web Services Modeled Using a Hierarchical Client–Server Flow Model

This type of flow model can also be seen with the visualization application group described in Chapter 2. An example of this is in the visualization of scientific simulations. Consider the simulations of a multi-part problem. These can be found in climate modeling, fluid flow analysis, structural analysis, and others.

In climate modeling there may be a simulation consisting of multiple parts—atmosphere, earth, and ocean—as shown in Figure 4.28. Each part of the simulation in this figure may be developed on a separate computing device, probably at different locations (based on where the various scientists are located). Since each component affects the others, at the boundaries between atmosphere, earth, and ocean, data must be passed between the computing/visualization servers for each part. The flows would look like those in Figure 4.29. In this figure, if the parts of

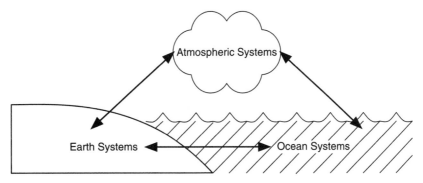

FIGURE 4.28   Components of a Climate Modeling Problem

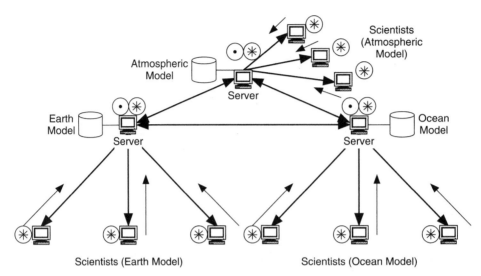

FIGURE 4.29   A Hierarchical Client–Server Model for Scientific Visualization

the simulation are being solved at different locations, then the server-to-server flows may cross long (WAN) distances, impacting both local- and wide-area networks.

4.6.4   Distributed-Computing

The distributed-computing flow model, shown in Figure 4.30, is the most specialized of the flow models. A distributed-computing flow model can have the inverse of the characteristics of the client–server flow model, or a hybrid of peer-to-peer and client–server flow models. In this model, flows may be primarily between a task manager and its computing devices (like a client–server model) or between the computing devices (like a peer-to-peer model). The type of model depends on how the distributed computing is done. The important characteristics of this model are that the flows can be client–server but are reversed in direction, and that the computing devices may have strict performance requirements.

We can make distinctions in the distributed-computing flow model based on the relationship between the task manager and the computing devices and what the task is. This relationship can result in the computing devices being closely coupled, where there are frequent transfers of information between devices, or loosely coupled, where there may be little to no transfer of information between computing devices. Tasks may range from having a coarse granularity, where each task is dedicated to a single computing device, to having a fine granularity, where a task is subdivided among several devices and the computing is done concurrently.

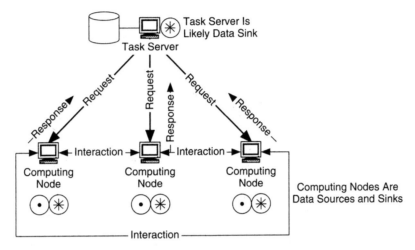

FIGURE 4.30   A Distributed-Computing Flow Model

When the task has a coarse granularity and the computing device relationship is loosely coupled, then the distributed–computing flow model takes the form of a computing cluster or computing resource management system, where tasks are allocated to each computing device based on resource availability. Thus, each computing device communicates with the cluster server or resource manager. Figure 4.31 shows the flows for an example of a computing cluster.

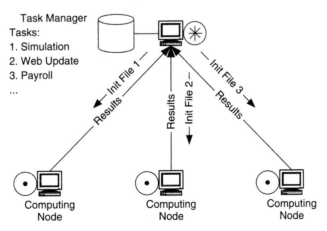

FIGURE 4.31   Flows for a Computing Cluster

The flows in this type of distributed-computing flow model are similar to those in the client–server flow model, where communications are primarily between each client and the server. A difference here is that the direction of the flows is not necessarily from the computing server to its clients. In fact, the size of the task initialization file (which is, in a sense, a request) sent from the server to each computing device may be much smaller than the size of the results of the computation, which is sent from the computing device to the server. In this model the flow directionality is asymmetric, but in the opposite direction from the client–server flow model. Also, each of the flows between the computing devices and their server is independent of the other flows. There is no synchronization among individual flows. The critical flows for this model are from the computing devices to their server. Since the flows for this model are asymmetric, in the direction toward the server, the server acts as a data sink, while the computing devices act as data sources.

When the task has a fine granularity and the computing node relationship is closely coupled, then the distributed-computing flow model behaves like a simplified parallel processing system, where each task is subdivided, based on the degree of parallelism in the application and the topology of the problem, among several computing devices. These devices work concurrently on the problem, exchanging information with neighbor devices and expecting (and waiting for) updated information. The task manager sets up the computing devices and starts the task with an initialization file, as in Figure 4.32.

Flows in this type of distributed-computing flow model can have the most stringent performance requirements of any of the models. Since computing devices may block (halt their computations) while waiting for information from neighbor devices, the timing of information transfer between computing devices becomes critical. This has a direct impact on the delay and delay variation requirements for the network connecting the devices. Although each individual flow has direction-ality, collectively there is little or no overall directionality. Individual flows in this model can be grouped to indicate which neighbor devices a computing device will communicate with for a given problem or topology. For example, a problem may be configured such that a computing device will communicate with one, two, four, or six of its closest neighbors.

For this model, critical flows are between computing devices. When a device will transfer the same information to several neighbors simultaneously, multicasting should be considered to optimize flow performance. There are no clear data sources or sinks for this model. The climate-modeling problem shown in Figure 4.28 could

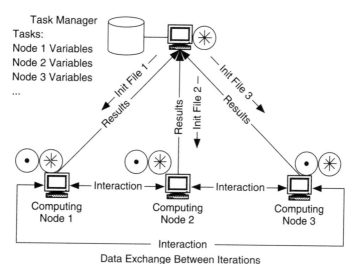

FIGURE 4.32 Flows for Parallel Computing

also be considered with a distributed-computing flow model, depending on the task granularity and degree of coupling within the system.

Flow requirements will vary between the computing cluster and parallel system models, depending on the degrees of coupling and the granularity in the task. Depending on the application and amount of analysis you want to put into this model, you can use the computing cluster and parallel system models as they are, or modify the task granularity and degree of coupling to suit your needs.

4.7 Flow Prioritization

In developing and describing flows for your network, you may find it useful to prioritize flows. Flow prioritization means ranking flows based on their importance, which can be described in various ways, depending on your environment. Flows can be prioritized according to importance, based on the characteristics shown in Figure 4.2. Some common prioritizations include:

- Business objectives and the impact of a flow on the customer's business
- Political objectives
- One or more of the performance requirements of the flow (a subset of capacity, delay, RMA, and quality of service).

- Security requirements for each flow
- The numbers of users, applications, and/or devices that a flow serves

The purpose for prioritizing flows is to determine which flows get the most resources or which flows get resources first. Typically, the primary resource is funding. This is an entirely new way of looking at how to allocate funding for parts of the network. By basing resource allocations on flows, which are directly representative of the users, their applications, and their devices, the resulting network architecture and design more accurately represent user, application, and device requirements.

You may use more than one parameter for prioritization, creating multiple levels of priority. It is common to start by prioritizing based on the number of users that a flow supports, and then adding another parameter, such as a performance requirement (e.g., capacity). Some example prioritizations are presented in Figures 4.33 and 4.34.

In Figure 4.34 the flows are prioritized by the number of users the flow supports. This information would have been determined from the requirements specification and requirements map, by comparing user, application, and device requirements, and mapping them to common flows. For this network there is a funding level ($750 K), which is distributed to each flow based on the number of users supported.

Another example prioritizes flows based on performance requirements, in this case reliability. Figure 4.35 shows a set of flows that have been prioritized this way. In this example there are three levels of reliability: 99.95%, 99.5%, and N/A

Flow ID	Performance Requirements			Number of Users
	Reliability	Capacity	Delay	
F1	N/A	1.2 Mb/s	10 ms	1200
F2	99.5%	100 Kb/s	N/A	550
F3	99.5%	15 Kb/s	100 ms	100
CF1	99.95%	500 Kb/s	100 ms	1750
CF2	N/A	100 Kb/s	100 ms	2100
CF3	N/A	3 Mb/s	100 ms	50

Total Budget for Network Project: $750 K

FIGURE 4.33   An Example of Flow Information for Prioritization

Flow ID	Performance Requirements			Number of Users	Budget	Priority
	Reliability	Capacity	Delay			
CF2	N/A	100 Kb/s	100 ms	2100	$274 K	1
CF1	99.95%	500 Kb/s	100 ms	1750	$228 K	2
F1	N/A	1.2 Mb/s	10 ms	1200	$157 K	3
F2	99.5%	100 Kb/s	N/A	550	$72 K	4
F3	99.5%	15 Kb/s	100 ms	100	$13 K	5
CF3	N/A	3 Mb/s	100 ms	50	$6 K	6

Total Budget for Network Project: $750 K

FIGURE 4.34   Flows Prioritized by the Number of Users Served

Flow ID	Performance Requirements			Number of Users	Budget	Priority
	Reliability	Capacity	Delay			
CF1	99.95%	500 Kb/s	100 ms	1750	$375 K	1
F2	99.5%	100 Kb/s	N/A	550	$141 K	2
F3	99.5%	15 Kb/s	100 ms	100	$141 K	2
F1	N/A	1.2 Mb/s	10 ms	1200	$31 K	3
CF2	N/A	100 Kb/s	100 ms	2100	$31 K	3
CF3	N/A	3 Mb/s	100 ms	50	$31 K	3

Total Budget for Network Project: $750 K

FIGURE 4.35   Flows Prioritized by Reliability

(not applicable). Budget allocations for each level are: highest level, 1/2 of budget; middle level, 3/8 of budget; and lowest level, 1/8 of budget.

Funding can be applied to this list of flows in a variety of ways. It can be applied based on the level of reliability, in which case all flows with equal levels of reliability get equal amounts of funding. This allocation can then be refined by including another parameter, such as the users or applications supported.

How per-flow funding relates to purchasing equipment is discussed in the network design chapter of this book (Chapter 10).

4.8   The Flow Specification

The results of identifying, defining, and describing flows are combined into a flow specification, or flowspec. A flow specification lists the flows for a network, along with their performance requirements and priority levels (if any). Flow specifications describe flows with best-effort, predictable, and guaranteed requirements, including mission-critical, rate-critical, real-time, interactive, and low and high performance. The flow specification combines performance requirements for composite flows, when there are multiple applications requirements within the flow. It can also be used to combine requirements for all flows in a section of a path. There is much information embedded within a flow specification.

Flow specifications can take one of three types: one-part, or unitary; two-part; or multi-part. Each type of flowspec has a different level of detail, based on whether the flows have best-effort, predictable, and/or guaranteed requirements.

A *one-part flowspec* describes flows that have only best-effort requirements. A *two-part flowspec* describes flows that have predictable requirements and may include flows that have best-effort requirements. A *multi-part flowspec* describes flows that have guaranteed requirements and may include flows that have predictable and/or best-effort requirements (Figure 4.36).

These flow specifications range in complexity. One-part and two-part flowspecs can be relatively straightforward, whereas multi-part flowspecs can be quite complex. Two-part flowspecs are usually a good balance between ease of development and amount of detail. Many networks can be adequately represented with a one-part flowspec, when performance requirements and flows are not well understood.

As networks become integrated into the rest of the system, however, flows will incorporate more reliability and delay requirements, and the two-part and multi-part flowspecs can better represent the network. This is the case today for many networks. In developing the flowspec we use the information in the requirements specification and requirements map as the basis for flows, and apply the methods described in this chapter to identify and describe flows.

Flow Specification Type	Types of Flows	Performance Description
One-Part	Best-Effort Individual and Composite	Capacity Only
Two-Part	Best-Effort and Stochastic, Individual and Composite	Reliability, Capacity, and Delay
Multi-part	Best-Effort, Stochastic, and Guaranteed, Individual and Composite	Reliability, Capacity, and Delay

FIGURE 4.36   Descriptions of Flow Specifications

4.8.1 Flowspec Algorithm

Flowspecs are used to combine performance requirements of multiple applications for a composite flow or multiple flows in a section of a path. The *flowspec algorithm* is a mechanism to combine these performance requirements (capacity, delay, and RMA) for flows in such a way as to describe the optimal composite performance for that flow or group of flows.

The flowspec algorithm applies the following rules:

1. Best-effort flows consist only of capacity requirements; therefore, only capacities are used in best-effort calculations.

2. For flows with predictable requirements we use all available performance requirements (capacity, delay, and RMA) in the calculations. Performance requirements are combined for each characteristic so as to maximize the overall performance of each flow.

3. For flows with guaranteed requirements we list each individual requirement (as an individual flow), not combining them with other requirements.

The first condition is based on the nature of best-effort traffic—that it is unpredictable and unreliable. RMA and delay requirements cannot be supported in a best-effort environment. The best that can be expected is that capacity requirements may be supported through capacity planning (also known as traffic engineering) or by over-engineering the capacity of the network to support these requirements.

The second condition is at the heart of the flowspec—that for each performance characteristic, capacity, delay, and RMA, the requirements are combined to maximize the performance of the flow or group of flows. How the requirements are combined to maximize performance is discussed later in this chapter.

The third condition is based on the nature of guaranteed requirements. Since flows with such requirements must be supported end-to-end, their requirements are kept separate so that we can identify them in the network architecture and design.

When a one-part flowspec is developed (for flows with best-effort requirements), then capacities of the flows are combined. There should be no RMA or delay requirements for these flows. Capacities are added together, forming a total best-effort capacity (C_{BE}), as shown in Figure 4.37.

A two-part flowspec builds on a one-part flowspec, adding predictable capacities, delay, and RMA. When a two-part flowspec is developed (for flows with best-effort and predictable requirements), the best-effort flows are combined in

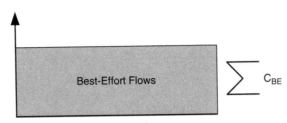

FIGURE 4.37   A One-Part Flow Specification

the same way as for the one-part flowspec. For the predictable requirements, the capacities are added together as with the best-effort flows, so that the flowspec has a total capacity for best-effort flows (C_{BE}) and another capacity for predictable flows (C_p). For the delay and RMA requirements for predictable flows, the goal is to maximize each requirement. For delay, the minimum delay (i.e., the highest-performance delay) of all of the delay requirements is taken as the predictable delay (D_p) for the flowspec, and the maximum RMA (i.e., the highest-performance RMA) of all of the RMA requirements is taken as the predictable RMA (R_p) for the flowspec. Figure 4.38 illustrates this for a two-part flowspec.

A multi-part flowspec is the most complex of the flowspecs, building on a two-part flowspec to add guaranteed requirements. Best-effort capacity, along with predictable capacity, delay, and RMA, is generated in the same fashion as for a two-part flowspec, and each set (i) of guaranteed performance requirements is added individually (shown as C_i, R_i, D_i) to the flowspec, as shown in Figure 4.39.

Sets of guaranteed performance requirements (C_i, R_i, D_i) are listed individually in the flowspec to show that they will be supported as individual requirements and not grouped with other requirements. This is necessary for us to be able to fully support each guaranteed requirement throughout the network.

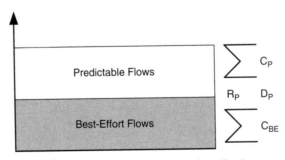

FIGURE 4.38   A Two-Part Flow Specification

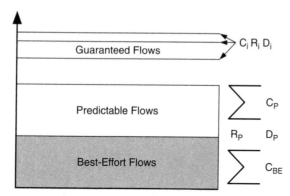

FIGURE 4.39   A Multi-Part Flow Specification

4.8.2   Capacity and Service Planning

Capacity and service plans are written descriptions of the network performance required for the flows described in the flowspec. A *capacity plan* describes network performance in terms of capacity only. It is used in conjunction with a one-part flowspec. A *service plan* describes network performance in terms of sets of capacity, delay, and RMA. It is used in conjunction with two–part and multi-part flowspecs.

While a flowspec lists flows and combines their performance requirements, capacity and service plans describe what may be needed in order to support such requirements. As we see in the chapter on performance (Chapter 8), there are many mechanisms we may choose to support performance requirements in the network.

4.9   Example Application of Flow Analysis

We now bring the concepts of flow analysis together for an example network, in this case a network to support computing and storage management. For this network project the computing and storage devices already exist in multiple buildings on a campus. The buildings and devices that will be using this network for computing and storage management are shown in Figure 4.40.

From the requirements analysis process, we have been able to determine that there are four types of flows for this network:

Type 1: Flows between high-performance computing devices. There are compute servers that are the high-performance devices for this network. The first type of flow consists of traffic flows between these devices. Flows are sometimes (approximately

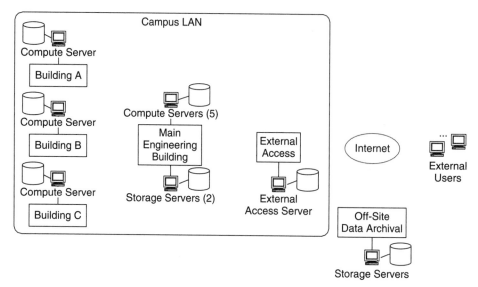

FIGURE 4.40   Building and Device Locations for the Example

10% of the time) synchronized between pairs of devices. At other times these devices may draw data from the local data store of another computing device, from the storage server at the Main Engineering building, or request a computing or data management task from a device. Most computing tasks are controlled from Main Engineering.

Type 2: Data migration from computing to storage at Main Engineering. These flows may be from each compute server as its task is completed; from the local data store at each compute server at a specific time; or from the compute server at Main Engineering at the completion of a combined (multi-server) task.

Type 3: Data migration to external server. Final data sets, or extracts of final data sets, are pushed from the Main Engineering storage server to a storage server at a building where external (Internet) access is managed. Data at this external access server are used to feed other campuses and for remote (off-site) data archival.

Type 4: Data archival and Internet access. These are flows from the external access server to users on the Internet, as well as flows to off-site archival servers.

These flow types are added to our map, as shown in Figure 4.41.

From discussions with various users of these applications, we learned that flow usually runs in this order: type 1–type 2–type 3–type 4. For flow type 1, a Main Engineering compute server may act as a server for the compute servers in Buildings A–C and for getting data from the storage servers in Main Engineering. This follows a hierarchical client–server flow model. Compute servers from Buildings

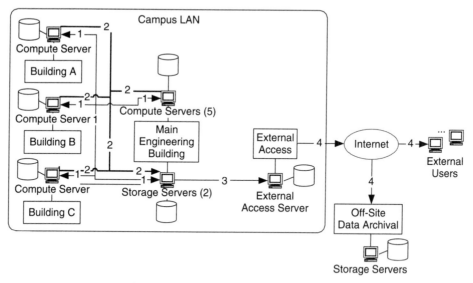

FIGURE 4.41   The Map with Flow Types Added

A–C and Main Engineering may also act as synchronized peers, using a distributed-computing flow model.

From discussions with engineering users we found that the computing application runs in either batch or interactive mode, from about 10 minutes to several hours, generating files of sizes ranging from 1 to 2 MB (synchronization or sync files), 10 to 100 MB (interactive updates), and 100 MB to over 1 GB for final data sets.

Interactivity for the computing application is needed to steer or direct the computation. This requires synchronization on the order of HRT (100 ms), and updates on the order of 1 second. Users expect to have up to two tasks running concurrently.

For flow type 2, data are stored at the storage servers in Main Engineering. Data can be from interactive updates, final data sets, and extracts (selected subsets of the final data set). Data also migrate from local stores at each computer server, usually every few hours.

For flow type 3, full data sets as well as extracts of the data sets are migrated to the external access server. Extracts are approximately 80% of the size of a full data set. Data sets are migrated hourly.

For flow type 4, users from other campuses, via the Internet, access data. Data sets are archived at an off-site facility. The system is expected to support the download of a full final data set within a few minutes.

Performance Envelope from Requirements Analysis

Characteristics of flow type 1. Flows of type 1 involve the frequent passing of 1–2 MB sync files with delays on the order of HRT, 10–100 MB update files on the order of 1 second, and final data sets of 500 MB–1 GB on the order of minutes to hours, with up to two tasks running concurrently. From this information we can estimate a range for capacity performance for these flows. Each of these flows is multiplied by 2 for concurrency.

Sync files: $(1 \text{ to } 2 \text{ MB})(8 \text{ b/B})(2 \text{ concurrent tasks})/10^{-1} \text{s} = 160 \text{ to } 320 \text{ Mb/s}$

Update files: $(10 \text{ to } 100 \text{ MB})(8 \text{ b/B})(2 \text{ concurrent tasks})/1 \text{s} = 160 \text{ Mb/s to } 1.6 \text{ Gb/s}$

Final data sets: $(500 \text{ to } 1000 \text{ MB})(8 \text{ b/B})(2 \text{ concurrent tasks})/(10^2 \text{ to } 10^4 \text{ s}) = 800 \text{ Kb/s to } 160 \text{ Mb/s}$

Characteristics of flow type 2. These flows involve migrating (pushing) updates, final data sets, and extracts. The delay characteristics of these flows are much less strict than for the computing function, with delays ranging from 10 to 10^4 seconds.

Update files: $(10 \text{ to } 100 \text{ MB})(8 \text{ b/B})/(10 \text{ to } 10^4 \text{ s}) = 8 \text{ Kb/s to } 80 \text{ Mb/s}$

Final data sets: Same as for flow type 1

The performance envelope for final data sets, updates, and synchronization files is shown in Figure 4.42.

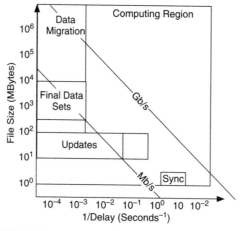

FIGURE 4.42   The Performance Envelope for the Example

Flow Models

For flow type 1 between compute servers and the Main Engineering storage servers, flows can follow distributed-computing and hierarchical client–server computing flow models, as shown in Figure 4.43.

In the distributed-computing model each device can act as a data source and sink, and data transfer is synchronized between devices at about 100 ms. In the hierarchical client–server model, data sets can flow from the storage server to the compute servers in Main Engineering, which then pass down to compute servers in Buildings A–C. There is no synchronization for this model.

Flow type 2 consists of data pushes from each compute server to the storage server in Main Engineering. Each compute server is a data source, while the Main Engineering storage server is a data sink (Figure 4.44).

For flow type 3, the storage servers in Main Engineering are data sources, and the external access server is a data sink (Figure 4.45).

For flow type 4 a client–server flow model exists between external users of the data, including off-site archival, and the external access server (Figure 4.46).

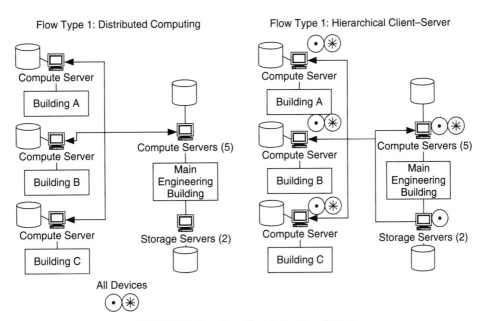

FIGURE 4.43   Flow Models for Flow Type 1

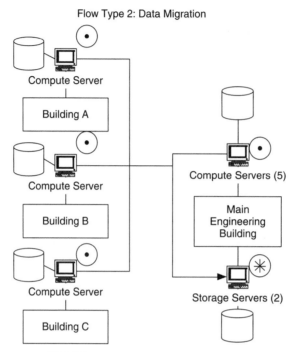

Flow Type 2: Data Migration

FIGURE 4.44   Flow Model for Flow Type 2

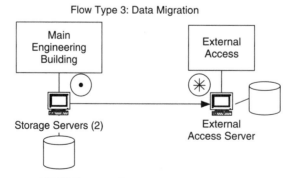

Flow Type 3: Data Migration

FIGURE 4.45   Flow Model for Flow Type 3

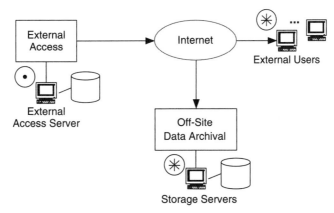

FIGURE 4.46   Flow Model for Flow Type 4

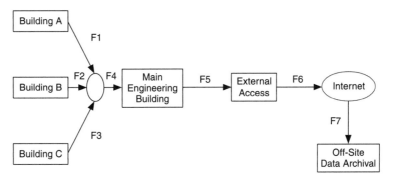

FIGURE 4.47   A Flow Map for the Example

Flow Map

Figure 4.47 is an example of a flow map that describes flows between buildings. Note that all devices have been removed from this map. This is often done for larger networks, as the number of devices on a map can become unwieldy. Also, a flow aggregation point has been added between Buildings A–C and Main Engineering. This is done to show the aggregated performance requirements at Main Engineering (flow F4).

For this flow map, flows F1, F2, and F3 have the same performance requirements, consisting of flow types 1 and 2. Flow F4 is an aggregate of flows F1, F2, and F3 (flow types 1 and 2). Flow F5 consists of flow type 3, and flows F6 and F7 are flows of flow type 4.

Next we combine the performance requirements from each of the flow types and apply them to flows F1 through F7, as shown in Figure 4.48.

Flow ID	Performance Requirements	
	Capacity (Mb/s)	Delay (ms)
F1: Flow Type 1		
Synchronization Files	320	100
Update Files	1600	1000
Final Files	160	10^5
Result for Flow Type 1	1600	100
F1: Flow Type 2		
Update Files	80	10^4
Final Files	160	10^5
Result for Flow Type 2	160	10^4
Result for F1	**1760**	**100**
Result for F2	**1760**	**100**
Result for F3	**1760**	**100**
F4: Flow Type 1	1600	100
F4: Flow Type 2		
Update Files	320	10^4
Final Files	640	10^5
Result for Flow Type 2	640	10^4
Result for F4	**2240**	**100**
Result for F5	**16**	**10^3**
Result for F6	**80**	**10^2**
Result for F7	**16**	**10^3**

FIGURE 4.48 Performance Requirements for Flows

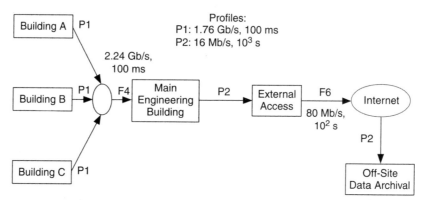

FIGURE 4.49   Performance Requirements Added to the Flow Map

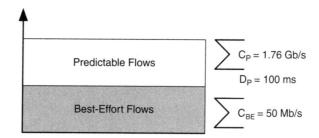

FIGURE 4.50   Two-Part Flowspec for Each Flow with Performance Profile P1

When these performance requirements are added to the flow map from Figure 4.47, we get Figure 4.49. Two performance profiles were generated for multiple flows: P1 for flows F1, F2, and F3; and P2 for flows F5 and F7.

A two-part flowspec for each flow that has a performance profile of P1 (F1, F2, and F3) would look like Figure 4.50.

4.10   Conclusions

Flow analysis takes an end-to-end perspective of network performance requirements, combining capacity, delay, and RMA requirements into a specification that is used as input to the network architecture and design, to evaluate and help select technologies and diversity strategies for the network. In building the flow specification we use various techniques, including data sources and sinks and flow models, to identify and determine individual and composite flows as well as critical flows.

Flow analysis is the final part of the analysis process. We began this process by gathering, deriving, managing, and tracking requirements for the network, from users, applications, devices, and networks that will be part of the planned network. In developing requirements for the network, we considered performance requirements (in terms of capacity, delay, and RMA) and the many ways to categorize requirements for users, applications, devices, and networks. This information, along with initial conditions, problem definitions, and goals, was collected in the requirements specification and mapped out in a requirements map.

Performance requirements, on a per-application basis or grouped by user, application, device, or network, are added to the directionality, hierarchy, and diversity of traffic flows to characterize them. Some tools, such as data sources and sinks, flow models, and flow aggregation points, can be used to help us determine which flows are important in a network and where flows are likely to occur. You are encouraged to develop other tools to aid in analyzing flows, or modify those presented in this book to fit your needs.

While flow analysis is presented here as part of the overall analysis process, in preparation to architect and design a network, it should be noted that flow analysis can be performed on any network, regardless of what state it is in. Notice that throughout the flow analysis process, no network technologies, topologies, or underlying infrastructures were shown or mentioned. Flow analysis allows us to separate traffic movement and performance requirements from an existing network, giving us the freedom to determine what flows should look like when the network does not restrict movement or performance. If you analyze flows on an existing network (regardless of whether or not you are developing a new network or upgrading the existing network), the results of this analysis will indicate if the existing network needs to be modified to fit the traffic flows.

Now that we have an idea of what to expect of the network in terms of requirements and flows, we are prepared to begin the process of network architecture.

4.11 Exercises

1. Show flows for each set of devices and applications below. Label each as either a unidirectional or bidirectional flow.
    a. Client–server application: Downstream (from server to client): 1.2 Mb/s capacity; upstream (from client to server): 15 Kb/s capacity.
    b. Streaming video (UDP) from video server to a subscriber's PC: 300 Kb/s capacity, 40 ms delay (one-way).

    c. Downloading pages from the Web: Downstream: 250 Kb/s capacity, 5 second delay; upstream: 100 Kb/s capacity.

    d. Transaction processing from point-of-sale machine to server: Upstream (from PoS machine to server): 30 Kb/s capacity, 100 ms round-trip delay; downstream: 50 Kb/s capacity.

2. Devices can act as both data sources and sinks, depending on the application and flow. Which of the following devices (for the applications given) are data sinks? Data sources?

    a. A storage device receiving streaming video from a camera

    b. A video editing unit, using video from the storage device in (a)

    c. A Web server and its clients

    d. A storage disk farm

3. Which flow models apply to each set of flows described below?

    a. Users on the Internet accessing the same Web server

    b. Forty workstations processing batch jobs overnight, managed by a central mainframe

    c. Email use across the Internet

    d. A transaction-processing application, authorizing credit card transactions between a company's retail stores and its headquarters

4. For each of the examples in Exercise 3, give the most likely direction(s) for the flows described by each flow model.

5. Develop a flow model for real-time/near-real-time flows. How would you characterize the flows for this model? What are likely data sources and sinks? Apply your model to a videoconferencing application.

6. You are developing a network for a company's online transaction processing (OLTP) application (e.g., a retail sales network). Its current system is a mainframe that has several terminals connected to it, either directly or through a terminal server, as in Figure 4.51. It is moving to a hierarchical client–server network, where there will be

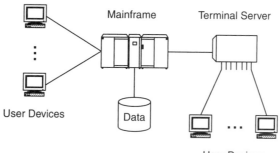

FIGURE 4.51   A Mainframe Environment for an OLTP Application

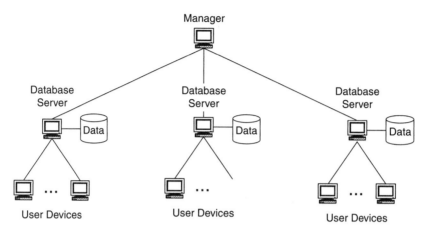

FIGURE 4.52   A Hierarchical Client–Server Environment for an OLTP Application

multiple regional database servers, each acting in a client–server fashion and updating each other's regions via a database manager, as in Figure 4.52.

a. Show the probable data sources and sinks for both environments.
b. How does migrating from the mainframe environment to the hierarchical client–server environment modify the traffic flows in the network?
c. In what ways does the network environment improve the traffic flows?
d. What are some of the potential trade-offs between the two environments—for example, in security, management, and performance?

CHAPTER CONTENTS

5

Network Architecture

Network architecture is the high-level, end-to-end structure for the network. This includes the relationships within and between major architectural components of the network, such as addressing and routing, network management, performance, and security. Determining the network architecture is the next part of the process of developing our network, and is, as we will see, key in integrating requirements and flows into the structure of a network.

5.1 Objectives

In this chapter you will learn about network architecture: what is contained within the architecture of a network and how to develop this architecture. We discuss the concept of relationships within and between components of the architecture. You will learn the factors that make up these relationships and how they apply to each architectural component. We also present several architectural models for you to use as a starting point in developing your network architecture.

This chapter introduces several concepts around network architecture, some of which may be new to you. In addition, many terms for addressing and routing, performance, network management, and security are presented in this chapter but will be detailed in Chapters 6 through 9.

5.1.1 Preparation

To be able to understand and apply the concepts in this chapter, you should be familiar with the basic concepts and mechanisms of performance (e.g., QoS), security and privacy, network management, routing, and addressing.

5.2 Background

What is network architecture? In general, architecture is the art and science of designing and constructing, or the discipline dealing with the principles of design and building. This applies to network architecture, as there is art and science in designing and constructing a network. A more specific definition for network architecture is an understanding of the relationships between (architectural) components of the network. Network architecture also guides the technical design of the network, through the application of high-level design principles. Applying these high-level design principles to the building blocks of the network helps us to develop the overall structure and function. We discuss the nature of these relationships, design principles, and building blocks in this chapter.

Defining the building blocks is essential to the success of network architecture. It is intuitive to consider these to be the physical entities (routers, switches, multiplexers, servers, etc.) in the network, especially since they are readily mapped to network technologies and purchased from vendors. However, this common view of network architecture constrains the functions of a network (addressing/routing, security, network management, performance) to operate within this physical structure. This forces functions into suboptimal configurations, as happens when one network function decreases or negates the effectiveness of another. For example, security mechanisms co-located with routers or switches, without consideration of routing or performance, can seriously impact those functions.

A different approach is to define the network building blocks as functional instead of physical entities. In doing so, the set of high-level design principles that constitute the network architecture is applied to how the network functions and operates.

This has several advantages over the physical approach. Network functions are closely coupled to users, their applications, and their devices. This allows user requirements to be directly represented in the network architecture. In fact, the success of a network can be defined by how well user, application, and device requirements are supported through these functions.

In addition, network functions, as well as user, application, and device requirements, often have a common basis in traffic flows. As part of the network architecture, the characterization of traffic flows can indicate when and where network functions will operate on common flows, and thus may impact one another and the overall effectiveness of the network. By focusing on functions in the network architecture, these interactions are better understood. Interactions, both within a function and between functions, are used to optimize the network architecture.

In this chapter we discuss how to describe, understand, and optimize the functions of a network, their interactions within the network, and how they can be meaningfully combined for that network. In this approach each network function is developed and optimized as its own *component architecture*. Component architectures are then combined into a *reference architecture*, by analyzing and optimizing interactions among components.

Since this approach focuses on network functions and their interactions, it is scalable to the largest networks. This process can be applied to the entire network, part of a network, or focused on a particular function. It provides a set of architectural guidelines that can be used to formulate the technical design of a network, consistent with Internet architecture philosophies.

5.2.1   Architecture and Design

It is easy to confuse architecture and design. They are similar in many ways, and designs are often just more detailed versions of the architecture. There are, however, ways in which they differ. Figure 5.1 compares some of the similarities and differences between architecture and design.

Some of these differences reflect the concept that the design is more detailed. For example, whereas the scope of architecture is typically broad, designs tend to be more focused. Network architecture shows a high-level view of the network, including locations of major or important components, while a network design has details about each portion of the network or focuses on a particular section of the network (e.g., storage, servers, computing). As the design focuses on selected parts of the network, the level of detail about that part increases.

Architecture and design are similar in one important way: they both attempt to solve multidimensional problems based on the results of the network analysis process. Figure 5.2 shows that a solution space can be made up of many variables (e.g., performance, security, and network management) and that network

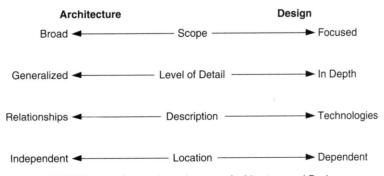

FIGURE 5.1   Comparisons between Architecture and Design

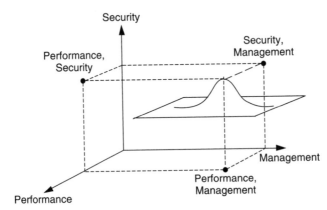

FIGURE 5.2   Architecture and Design Solutions Are Multidimensional

architecture solutions are based on relationships between these variables. We discuss these relationships throughout the architecture process.

In terms of what is described, however, the architecture can differ substantially from the design. Network architecture describes relationships, whereas a design usually specifies technologies, protocols, and network devices. So we can begin to see how the architecture and design complement each other, for it is important to understand how various components of the network will work together before actually specifying the equipment to be deployed.

Another way that architecture can differ from design is in the need for location information. While there are some parts of the architecture where location is important (e.g., external interfaces, locations of existing devices and applications), the relationships between components are generally location independent. In fact, inserting location information into the network architecture can be constraining. For a network design, however, location information is important. (In the design there is a sufficient amount of detail that locations play an important part of the decision-making process.)

Good network design is a process by which an extremely complex and non-linear system is conceptualized. Even the most experienced network designer must first conceptualize a big picture and then develop the detailed designs of the components. The network architecture represents that big picture and can only be developed by creating an environment that balances the requirements of the customers with the capabilities of network technologies and the personnel that will run and maintain the system.

The network architecture is not only necessary for a solid design; it is also essential to sustaining the required performance over time. Network personnel must grasp the big picture and understand it to be able to make the network perform as designed. To be successful, architecture development must be approached in a systematic manner.

Poor network architecture and design reflects the personality of a "wizard" who opens his bag of network tricks and pulls a couple of them out. Network architecture and design development is no longer simple enough for tricks to work; it must be done in a systematic and reproducible manner. Even if a complex network architecture/design is tricked into existence, it cannot be maintained. Smart customers have passed beyond the stage where they will hire a "wizard" to work magic. They have been burned (or heard about being burned) by the unpredictability of this behavior. Now that network services are essential to business, predictable, reliable, high-quality performance is what customers are looking for.

5.3   Component Architectures

Component architecture is a description of how and where each function of a network is applied within that network. It consists of a set of mechanisms (hardware and software) by which that function is applied to the network, where each mechanism may be applied, and a set of internal relationships between these mechanisms.

Each *function* of a network represents a major capability of that network. This book explores four functions that are major capabilities of networks: addressing/routing, network management, performance, and security. Other general functions, such as infrastructure and storage, could also be developed as component architectures. And there certainly can be functions specific to each network that you may wish to develop.

Mechanisms are hardware and software that help a network to achieve each capability. Some example mechanisms are shown in Figure 5.3 and are examined in detail in Chapters 6 through 9 on component architectures.

Internal relationships consist of interactions (trade-offs, dependencies, and constraints), protocols, and messages between mechanisms, and are used to optimize each function within the network. *Trade-offs* are decision points in the development of each component architecture. They are used to prioritize and decide which mechanisms are to be applied. *Dependencies* occur when one mechanism relies on another mechanism for its operation. *Constraints* are restrictions that one mechanism

Function	Description of Capability	Example Subset of Mechanisms Used to Achieve Capability
Addressing/Routing	Provides robust and flexible connectivity between devices	• Addressing: Ways to allocate and aggregate address space • Routing: Routers, routing protocols, ways to manipulate routing flows
Network Management	Provides monitoring, configuring, and troubleshooting for the network	• Network management protocols • Network management devices • Ways to configure network management in the network
Performance	Provides network resources to support requirements for capacity, delay, RMA	• Quality of Service • Service-Level Agreements • Policies
Security	Restricts unauthorized access, usage, and visibility within network to reduce the threat and effects of attacks	• Firewalls • Security policies and procedures • Filters and access control lists

FIGURE 5.3   Functions, Capabilities, and Mechanisms

places on another. These relationship characteristics help to describe the behaviors of the mechanisms within a component architecture, as well as the overall behavior of the function itself.

Developing a component architecture consists of determining the mechanisms that make up each component, how each mechanism works, as well as how that component works as a whole. For example, consider some of the mechanisms for performance: quality of service (QoS), service-level agreements (SLAs), and policies. In order to determine how performance will work for a network, we need to determine how each mechanism works, and how they work together to provide performance for the network and system. In Figure 5.4 QoS is applied at each network device to control its resources in support of SLAs and policies, SLAs tie subscribers to service levels, and policies (usually located at one or more databases within the network) provide a high-level framework for service levels, SLAs, and QoS.

Interactions within a component are based on what mechanisms require in order to communicate and operate with each other. Using the example for performance in Figure 5.4 we would determine if there are any information flows between QoS, SLAs, and Policies. If such flows exist (and they usually do), then we would determine where and how these flows occur. This is important to know, for when we are developing an architecture for a component, its communications

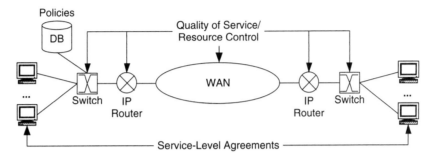

FIGURE 5.4   Examples of Performance Mechanisms in a Network

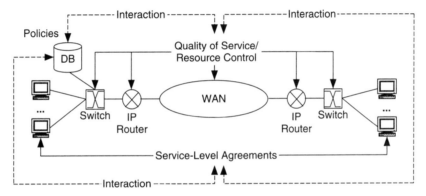

FIGURE 5.5   Interactions between Performance Mechanisms

requirements within that component will help drive that architecture. Figure 5.5 gives an example of where interactions occur between performance mechanisms.

Trade-offs are decision points in the development of each component—decisions made to prioritize and choose among features and functions of each mechanism and to optimize each component's architecture. There are often several trade-offs within a component, and much of the refining of the network architecture occurs here. For example, a common trade-off in network management entails the choice between centralizing and distributing management capabilities. As mentioned in Chapter 1, trade-offs are fundamental to network architecture as well as to network design. We therefore spend much time on trade-offs in this chapter and throughout the rest of the book.

Dependencies are requirements that describe how one mechanism depends on one or more other mechanisms in order to function. Determining such dependencies helps us to decide when trade-offs are acceptable or unacceptable. For example, there are dependencies between addressing and routing, as proper routing function depends on how internal and external addressing is done.

Constraints are a set of restrictions within each component architecture. For example, SLAs are constrained by the type and placement of QoS within the network. Such constraints are useful in determining the boundaries under which each component operates.

Although the functions described in this chapter are limited to addressing/routing, network management, performance, and security, there are often other functions—such as network storage, computing, or application services—that can also be described by this component architecture approach. Functions may be defined by you and may be specific to the network you are working on. Experience has shown that addressing/routing, network management, performance, and security are common across most networks. By developing the relationships between these functions, we begin to develop a high-level, end-to-end view of the network and system.

Developing component architectures requires input, in terms of sets of user, application, and device requirements, estimated traffic flows, and architectural goals defined for each individual network. For example, user, application, and device requirements for performance and security are used as criteria to evaluate mechanisms for the performance and security component architectures. This input forms a common foundation for all network functions, from which all component architectures are developed. Figure 5.6 illustrates that component architectures, requirements, flows, and goals are all interwoven through the reference architecture.

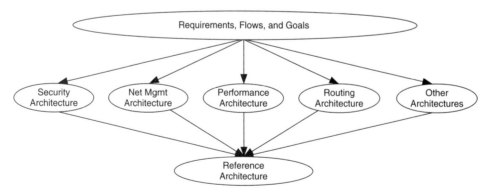

FIGURE 5.6 Component Architectures and the Reference Architecture Are Derived from Network Requirements, Flows, and Goals

Based on the requirements, flows, and goals for the network, a set of candidate mechanisms for each function is evaluated, and the desired mechanisms are chosen.

To facilitate determining where each mechanism may be applied, the network is divided into regions. Network functions have a common basis in traffic flows; thus, characterizing regions by traffic flows allows each region to be applied in a similar fashion to all functions.

Commonly used regions include access (edge), distribution, core (backbone), and external interfaces and DMZs. From a traffic flow perspective, access regions are where most traffic flows are generated and terminated. Distribution regions are where traffic flows are aggregated and terminated for common services, such as application or storage servers. Core regions provide transit for aggregates of traffic flows; individual traffic flows are rarely generated or terminated in this region. External interfaces or DMZs are aggregation points for traffic flows external to that network.

The characteristics of each region help to identify where mechanisms are applied. For example, since traffic flows are often generated and terminated at access regions, performance mechanisms that work on a per-flow basis, such as access control and traffic shaping, would apply to these regions. In the core region, where traffic flows are aggregated, performance mechanisms that work on groups or classes of flows, such as differentiated services, would apply.

When mechanisms have been chosen and applied the internal relationships between these mechanisms are determined and analyzed.

In practice, mechanisms, locations, and relationship characteristics are listed in tabular form, one set of tables for each component architecture. An example of internal relationships, in this case the set of dependencies between performance mechanisms, is presented in Figure 5.7.

There should be a chart for each characteristic, showing whether or not it would apply, and if it did apply, how it would work between each of the components. For example, let's consider a chart on dependencies. In developing this chart we would first start by looking at mechanisms for a particular component—for example, performance. We would consider any dependencies between mechanisms within each component. We would continue down the list, doing the same thing for each type of interaction. These relationships are explored in detail in the chapters on each architectural component.

As we go through the next four sections (5.3.1 through 5.3.4), you will be introduced to many terms for the mechanisms of each network function. Although each mechanism is presented briefly in this chapter, we discuss them in detail over the next four chapters.

Dependencies between Performance Mechanisms

	QoS	SLAs	Policies
QoS		QoS dependencies on SLAs—e.g., QoS at network devices may need to enforce SLA values	QoS dependencies on policies—e.g., QoS at network devices may need to enforce policies
SLAs	SLA dependencies on QoS—e.g., can an SLA be enforceable via available QoS mechanisms?		SLA dependencies on policies—e.g., SLAs may need to map to network policies
Policies	Policy dependencies on QoS—e.g., can a policy be enforceable via available QoS mechanisms?	Policy dependencies on SLAs	

FIGURE 5.7   A Sample Chart for Listing Dependencies between Performance Mechanisms

In developing each component architecture, we need to consider the dynamic nature of networks. For example, how will the network be reconfigured to handle a security attack? What happens when traffic flows change and congestion occurs? How much of each function can be automated?

Each component architecture will have policies associated with it. Security, routing, performance, and network management policies can have elements in common. Documenting policies early in the architectural process helps you to understand the relationships between component architectures.

5.3.1 Addressing/Routing Component Architecture

Addressing is applying identifiers (addresses) to devices at various protocol layers (e.g., data-link and network), while *routing* is learning about the connectivity within and between networks and applying this connectivity information to forward IP packets toward their destinations. The addressing/routing component architecture describes how user and management traffic flows are forwarded through the network, and how hierarchy, separation, and grouping of users and devices are supported.

This component architecture is important in that it determines how user and management traffic flows are propagated throughout the network. As you can imagine, this is closely tied to the network management architecture (for management flows) and performance architecture (for user flows). This architecture also helps to determine the degrees of hierarchy and diversity in the network, and how areas of the network are subdivided.

There are several addressing and routing mechanisms that could be considered for this component architecture. From an addressing perspective, mechanisms include subnetting, variable-length subnetting, supernetting, dynamic addressing, private addressing, virtual LANs (VLANs), IPv6, and network address translation (NAT). From a routing (forwarding) perspective, mechanisms include switching and routing, default route propagation, classless interdomain routing (CIDR), multicasts, mobile IP, route filtering, peering, routing policies, confederations, and IGP and EGP selection and location.

Depending on the type of network being developed, the set of candidate addressing and routing mechanisms for a component architecture can be quite different. For example, a service provider network may focus on mechanisms such as supernetting, CIDR, multicasts, peering, routing policies, and confederations, whereas a medium-sized enterprise network would more likely focus on classful or private addressing and NAT, VLANs, switching, and the selection and locations of routing protocols (particularly interior gateway protocols, or IGPs).

In terms of addressing, *classful addressing* is applying predetermined mask lengths to addresses in order to support a range of network sizes; *subnetting* is using part of the device (host) address space to create another layer of hierarchy; *variable-length subnetting* is subnetting where multiple subnet masks are used, creating subnets of different sizes; *supernetting* is aggregating network addresses, by changing the address mask, to decrease the number of bits allocated to the network; *dynamic addressing* is providing addresses on demand; *private IP addressing* is using IP addresses that cannot be advertised and forwarded by network and user devices in the public domain (i.e., the Internet); *virtual LANs* are addresses that can be dynamically changed and reconfigured to accommodate changes in the network; *IPv6* is the next generation of IP addresses; and *network address translation* is the mapping of IP addresses from one realm to another. Typically this is between public and private address space.

In terms of forwarding, *switching* and *routing* are common forwarding mechanisms; *default route propagation* is a technique used to inform the network of the default route (or route of last resort); CIDR is routing based on arbitrary address mask sizes (classless); *multicasts* are packets targeted toward multiple destinations; *mobile IP* is providing network (IP) connectivity for devices that move, roam, or are portable; *route filtering* is the technique of applying filters (statements) to hide networks from the rest of an autonomous system, or to add, delete, or modify routes in the routing table; *peering* is an arrangement between networks or autonomous systems (peers) to mutually pass traffic and adhere to *routing policies*, which are high-level statements about relationships between networks or autonomous systems; and *IGP and EGP selection and location* entail comparing and contrasting IGPs, in order to select the appropriate protocols for the network and where to apply them in the network.

Two types of interactions between mechanisms are predominant within this component architecture: trade-offs between addressing and routing mechanisms, and trade-offs within addressing or within routing. Addressing and routing mechanisms influence the selection of routing protocols and where they are applied. They also form an addressing hierarchy upon which the routing hierarchy is overlaid.

Areas of the network where dynamic addressing, private addressing, and network address translation mechanisms are applied impact how routing will (or will not) be provided to those areas.

The addressing/routing component architecture is discussed in detail in Chapter 6.

5.3.2 Network Management Component Architecture

Network management is providing functions to control, plan, allocate, deploy, coordinate, and monitor network resources. Network management is part of most or all of the network devices. As such, the network management architecture is important as it determines how and where management mechanisms are applied in the network. It is likely that the other architectural components (e.g., IT security) will require some degree of monitoring and management and will interact with network management.

The network management component architecture describes how the system, including the other network functions, is monitored and managed. This consists of an information model that describes the types of data used to monitor and manage each of the elements in the system, mechanisms to connect to devices in order to access data, and the flows of management data through the network.

Network management mechanisms include monitoring and data collection; instrumentation to access, transfer, act upon, and modify data; device and service configuration; and data processing, display, and storage. Network management mechanisms include

- Monitoring: Obtaining values for end-to-end, per-link, and per-element network management characteristics

- Instrumentation: Determining the set of tools and utilities needed to monitor and probe the network for management data

- Configuration: Setting parameters in a network device for operation and control of that element

- FCAPS components: The set of fault, configuration, accounting, performance, and security management components

- In-band and out-of-band management: Whether management data flow along the same path as user traffic or have a separate path

- Centralized and distributed management: Whether the management system is in a single hardware platform or is distributed across the network among multiple platforms

- Scaling network management traffic: Determining how much network capacity should be reserved for network management

- Checks and balances: Using multiple mechanisms to verify that variables are represented correctly

- Managing network management data: Offloading old data, keeping track of storage availability for data, updating data types.

- MIB selection: Determining which management information bases, and how much of each management information base, to use

- Integration into OSS: How the management system will communicate with higher-level operations support system

As we will see in Chapter 7, many interactions exist within the network management component. These include trade-offs of routing management traffic flows along the same paths as user traffic flows (in-band), or along separate paths (out-of-band), and centralizing all management mechanisms by placing them on a single hardware platform or distributing them throughout the network on multiple platforms.

5.3.3 Performance Component Architecture

Performance consists of the set of mechanisms used to configure, operate, manage, provision, and account for resources in the network that allocate performance to users, applications, and devices. This includes capacity planning and traffic engineering, as well as a variety of service mechanisms. Performance may be applied at any of the protocol layers, and often applies across multiple layers. Therefore, there may be mechanisms targeted toward the network layer, physical or data-link layers, as well as the transport layer and above.

The performance component architecture describes how network resources will be allocated to user and management traffic flows. This consists of prioritizing, scheduling, and conditioning traffic flows within the network, either end-to-end between source and destination for each flow, or between network devices on a per-hop basis. It also consists of mechanisms to correlate user, application, and device requirements to traffic flows, as well as traffic engineering, access control, quality of service, policies, and service-level agreements (SLAs).

Quality of service, or QoS, is determining, setting, and acting upon priority levels for traffic flows. *Resource control* refers to mechanisms that will allocate, control, and manage network resources for traffic. *Service-level agreements* (SLAs) are informal or formal contracts between a provider and user that define the terms of the provider's responsibility to the user and the type and extent of accountability if those responsibilities are not met. *Policies* are sets (again, formal or informal) of high-level statements about how network resources are to be allocated among users.

This architectural component is important in that it provides the mechanisms to control the network resources allocated to users, applications, and devices. This may be as simple as determining the amount of capacity available in various regions of the network, or as complex as determining the capacity, delay, and RMA characteristics on a per-flow basis.

As we discuss in detail in Chapter 8, interactions within this component architecture include the trade-offs between end-to-end and per-hop prioritization, scheduling, and conditioning of traffic flows, and whether flows are treated individually, aggregated into groups, or a combination of the two. As we will see, these interactions are closely coupled at the network (IP) layer to the use of differentiated services (DiffServ) and integrated services (IntServ) within the network. Differentiated and integrated services are performance mechanisms standardized through the Internet Engineering Task Force (IETF) that target individual and aggregate performance requirements.

When policies, SLAs, and differentiated services are chosen for the network, part of this component architecture describes the placement of databases for SLA and policy information, including policy decision points (PDPs), policy enforcement points (PEPs), and DiffServ edge devices.

5.3.4 Security Component Architecture

Security is a requirement to guarantee the confidentiality, integrity, and availability of user, application, device, and network information and physical resources. This is often coupled with *privacy*, which is a requirement to protect the sanctity of user, application, device, and network information.

The security component architecture describes how system resources are to be protected from theft, damage, denial of service (DOS), or unauthorized access. This consists of the mechanisms used to apply security, which may include such hardware and software capabilities as virtual private networks (VPNs), encryption, firewalls, routing filters, and network address translation (NAT).

Each of these mechanisms can be targeted toward specific areas of the network, such as at external interfaces or at aggregation points for traffic flows. In many instances security mechanisms are deployed in regions, often termed *security zones* or *cells*, where each region or security zone represents a particular level of sensitivity and access control. Security zones may be within one another, overlapping, or completely separate, depending on the security requirements and goals for that network. We cover security zones, as part of the security component architecture, in detail in Chapter 9.

The security and privacy architecture is important in that it determines to what degree security and privacy will be implemented in the network, where the critical areas that need to be secured are, and how it will impact and interact with the other architectural components.

The security mechanisms that we consider are

- Security threat analysis: The process to determine which components of the system need to be protected and the types of security risks (threats) they should be protected from

- Security policies and procedures: Formal statements on rules for system, network, and information access and use, in order to minimize exposure to security threats

- Physical security and awareness: The protection of devices from physical access, damage, and theft (including isolating all or parts of the network from outside access); and getting users educated and involved with the day-to-day aspects of security in their network and helping them to understand the potential risks of violating security policies and procedures

- Protocol and application security: Securing management and network protocols and applications from unauthorized access and misuse

- Encryption: Making data unreadable if they are intercepted, by applying cipher algorithms together with a secret key
- Network perimeter security: Protecting the external interfaces between your network and external networks
- Remote access security: Securing network access based on traditional dial-in, point-to-point sessions, and virtual private network connections

5.3.5 Optimizing Component Architectures

Determining and understanding the set of internal relationships enable each component architecture to be optimized for a particular network. This is based on input for that particular network, the requirements, estimated traffic flows, and goals for that network.

Having chosen a set of mechanisms for a component architecture and determined possible interactions between these mechanisms, the requirements, flows, and goals for the network are used to prioritize the mechanisms and interactions.

User, application, and device requirements usually incorporate some degree of performance, security, and network management requirements. Such requirements are directly related to selecting and placing mechanisms within a component architecture, and prioritizing interactions.

Estimated traffic flows for the network—determined through modeling and simulation, experience with the existing system, or via a set of heuristics—can indicate aggregation points for traffic or places where high-priority flows (e.g., mission-critical, real-time, secure, or OAM) are likely to occur. By understanding the types of flows in the network and where they are likely to occur, each component architecture can be developed to focus mechanisms that will optimally support high-priority flows.

Architectural goals for the network are derived from requirements, determined from discussions with users, management, and staff, or taken as an extension of the scope and scale of the existing network. When goals are developed from a variety of sources, they provide a broad perspective on which functions are most important in a network.

Thus, requirements, flows, and goals strongly influence which mechanisms are preferred and where they are applied for each component architecture.

5.4 Reference Architecture

A *reference architecture* is a description of the complete network architecture and contains all of the component architectures (i.e., functions) being considered for that network. It is a compilation of the internal and external relationships developed during the network architecture process (Figure 5.8).

There can be more, fewer, or different component architectures than are described in this book, depending on the focus of your network. For example, the component architecture labeled "Others" in Figure 5.8 could be an Infrastructure Architecture or Storage Architecture. This flexibility allows you to choose those component architectures that best fit the requirements of that network.

In Figure 5.8 each component architecture defines the internal relationships for a particular function, whereas the reference architecture combines these components. As we will see, component architectures can be weighted to determine their relative priority levels.

Once the component architectures are developed for a network, their relationships with one another are then determined. These external relationships are defined by the interactions between pairs of component architectures, their trade-offs,

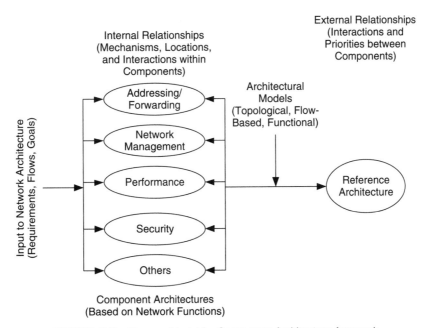

FIGURE 5.8   Process Model for Component Architecture Approach

dependencies, and constraints. Typically, all of the component architectures for a network are closely coupled to each other. This is reflected in their external relationships.

Just as internal relationships are used to optimize each component architecture for the network, external relationships are used to optimize the sum of all component architectures. Thus, the reference architecture, developed by combining component architectures, incorporates the effects that functions have on one another.

Depending on the requirements, traffic flows, and goals for a particular network, the reference architecture is either balanced across all functions or weighted to favor one or more functions. In a network architecture that is balanced across all functions, constraints and dependencies between functions are minimized, and trade-offs between functions are balanced so that no individual function is prioritized over the others.

When one or more functions are weighted in favor over others, the external relationships reflect this. For example, in a network where performance is the primary architectural goal, the external relationships between performance and the other functions would be weighted so that interactions (trade-offs in particular) favor performance.

This is a powerful capability that is missing in traditional approaches. Not only does it provide the ability to decide which functions are prioritized higher than others, but this becomes an *informed decision*, where the effects on other functions, as well as on the reference architecture, are understood and documented as part of the network architecture.

Consider a network where the set of requirements, flows, and goals indicates that low delay and jitter performance are high priorities. Yet, in this same network, routing, network management, and security can negatively impact delay and jitter performance. In traditional network architecture the interactions between performance and the other functions are often not well understood, resulting in a network where security, network management, and routing mechanisms increase delay and jitter, and so the network does not meet its requirements or goals.

However, by developing each function as its own composite architecture, delay and jitter can be optimized in the performance component architecture, and then this component architecture can be prioritized over the others, so that when interactions are identified between performance and the other functions, performance is chosen.

5.4.1 **External Relationships**

To some degree, each function depends upon and supports the other functions within a network, as well as the requirements from users, applications, and devices. This is reflected in the external relationships between their component architectures.

The addressing/routing component architecture supports traffic flows from each of the other functions. Based on the mechanisms used in the network management and security component architectures, their traffic flows may take separate paths from user traffic flows, and this capability needs to be incorporated into the addressing/routing component architecture.

In addition, routing can be configured so that traffic flows with differing performance requirements take separate paths through the network, coupling addressing/routing with performance. This is evident in routing protocols that integrate performance mechanisms, such as multi-protocol label switching (MPLS).

Each component architecture depends on network management to support the access and transport of management data for that component. In practice, the monitoring and management of addressing/routing, performance, and security are often achieved through an integrated approach within the network management component architecture. In this approach, network management supports flows of management data for each function equally. In some cases, however, multiple priority levels are assigned to the access and transport of management data for the various functions.

The performance component architecture provides network resources to support the other functions, as well as user, application, and device traffic flows. By considering performance requirements at various levels of granularity (e.g., network-wide, per-function, per-user/application/device, or per-flow), this component architecture determines how performance mechanisms are used to allocate resources at the proper level of granularity.

For example, the performance component architecture for a service provider network may focus on traffic engineering to achieve a systemwide balance for bandwidth allocation. In addition, this network may include SLAs, access control, and traffic prioritization, scheduling, and conditioning to provide bandwidth and delay performance to select groups of users or applications.

The security component architecture supports the security and privacy requirements of each of the other functions. For addressing/routing, performance, and network management, network devices are where traffic flows are aggregated and controlled, and they often require a high degree of security, in terms of additional access controls and protocol (e.g., SNMP) security.

5.4.2 Optimizing the Reference Architecture

Requirements, flows, and goals for a network are used to optimize the reference architecture, much the same way that each component architecture is optimized. However, for the reference architecture, interactions occur between pairs of component architectures. There are numerous trade-offs, dependencies, and constraints that occur between addressing/routing, network management, performance, and security. Some examples of common interactions between pairs of component architectures are presented below.

Interactions between performance and security. By their nature, security mechanisms are often intrusive, inspecting and controlling network traffic and access. Such actions require network resources and processing, increasing network delay. As security is increased, by adding more mechanisms to the network, performance is decreased. Whereas capacity can sometimes be increased to offset a decrease in performance, delay is difficult to mitigate.

When performance is a high priority, particularly when there is a need to measure end-to-end performance between select users, applications, or devices, performance mechanisms may preclude the use of security in particular areas of the network. Some security mechanisms interrupt or terminate and regenerate traffic flows, seriously impacting the ability to provide end-to-end performance across a security interface. As a result, security can constrain performance mechanisms to within a security perimeter.

Interactions between network management and security. Network management requires frequent access to network devices, and as such, is a potential security problem. Management access can be provided out-of-band via a separate management network, with its own security mechanisms. When management access is in-band, however, any additional security mechanisms for network management may impact performance for user traffic flows. When manageability is a high priority, a separate security component architecture for network management may be indicated.

Interactions between network management and performance. In-band network management directly impacts the performance of user traffic flows, as management traffic flows compete with user traffic flows for network resources. This is often a problem in centralized network management architectures, as all management traffic flows are aggregated to a common management device. As management traffic flows are aggregated, their network resource requirements can become quite large, particularly during periods of network problems. Thus, a trade-off of centralized management is between over-engineering bandwidth, providing prioritization mechanisms for performance, or reducing performance expectations.

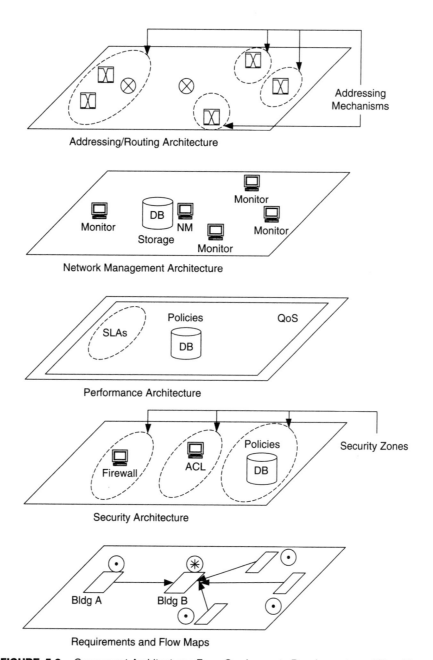

Addressing Mechanisms

Addressing/Routing Architecture

Monitor

DB Storage NM Monitor

Monitor

Monitor

Network Management Architecture

Policies QoS

SLAs

DB

Performance Architecture

Policies Security Zones

Firewall ACL DB

Security Architecture

Bldg A Bldg B

Requirements and Flow Maps

FIGURE 5.9 Component Architectures Form Overlays onto Requirements and Flow Maps

Interactions between addressing/routing and performance. Performance can be closely coupled with routing through mechanisms such as MPLS, differentiated and integrated services, and signaling via the resource reservation protocol (RSVP). However, when routing protocol simplicity is a high priority, performance may be decoupled from routing.

The result of this approach is a network architecture that shows how each function is optimally applied to the network, how the functions interact with each other, and how they can be balanced or prioritized in the reference architecture.

When the architectural process is completed, you will have a set of component architectures that lie on top of your requirements and flow maps, as shown in Figure 5.9. This set of overlays describes how each function is supported in the network, where mechanisms are to be applied, and how they interact with one another.

5.5   Architectural Models

In developing the architecture for your network there are several architectural models that you can use as a starting point, either as the foundation of your architecture or to build upon what you already have. Three types of architectural models are presented here: topological models, which are based on a geographical or topological arrangement and are often used as starting points in the development of the network architecture; flow-based models, which take particular advantage of traffic flows from the flow specification; and functional models, which focus on one or more functions or features planned for in the network. It is likely that your reference architecture will contain more than one architectural model.

5.5.1 Topological Models

There are two popular topological models: the LAN/MAN/WAN and Access/Distribution/Core models. The *LAN/MAN/WAN architectural model* is simple and intuitive and is based on the geographical and/or topological separation of networks. Figure 5.10 shows this model. Its important feature is that, by concentrating on LAN/MAN/WAN boundaries, it focuses on the features and requirements of those boundaries, and on compartmentalizing functions, service, performance, and features of the network along those boundaries.

Both the LAN/MAN/WAN model and the Access/Distribution/Core model (shown in the following figure) indicate as well the degree of hierarchy intended

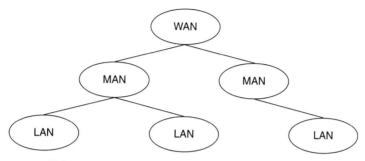

FIGURE 5.10   The LAN/MAN/WAN Architectural Model

for the network. Either model can be collapsed to show fewer than three levels or expanded to show as many levels as necessary. For example, the LAN/MAN/WAN model is often used as a LAN/WAN model, or the LAN component is separated into campus, buildings, or even floors.

Interface control descriptions, or ICDs, are useful in managing the development of this architectural model. ICDs define and describe LAN/MAN/WAN boundaries. This consists of the network devices, links, networks, and any other elements used to interconnect LANs, MANs, and WANs.

The *Access/Distribution/Core architectural model* has some similarities to and differences from the LAN/MAN/WAN model. It is similar to the LAN/MAN/WAN model in that it compartmentalizes some functions, service, performance, and features of the network, although not to the degree of the LAN/MAN/WAN model. The Access/Distribution/Core model, however, focuses on function instead of location, as Figure 5.11 shows. A characteristic of this model that is important to

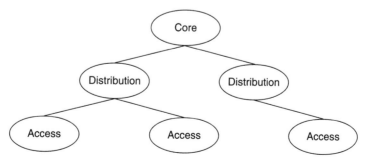

FIGURE 5.11   The Access/Distribution/Core Architectural Model

note is that it can be used to reflect the behavior of the network at its access, distribution, and core areas.

The access area is closest to the users and their applications and is where most traffic flows are sourced and sinked. Thus, flows and requirements can be treated on an individual basis more easily than in the distribution and core areas.

The distribution area can also source and sink flows, but they are more likely to be to or from multiple-user devices, such as servers or specialized devices. Few users are normally directly connected to the distribution area. As such, this area is often used to consolidate flows. As we will see, performance mechanisms that support individual and combined flows can both be used here.

The core of the network is used for bulk transport of traffic, and flows are not usually sourced or sinked at the core. Thus, any view of individual flows is lost at the core, unless specifically planned for (as with flows that have guaranteed requirements).

Both the LAN/MAN/WAN and Access/Distribution/Core models are used as starting points in the network architecture, as both are intuitive and easy to apply. They can be restrictive, however, in that they place strict boundaries between areas. When applying these models, therefore, keep in mind that you may have to be creative in how you define each area, so that it fits the requirements for that area.

5.5.2 Flow-Based Models

Flow-based architectural models are based on their counterparts, the flow models discussed in Chapter 4. If you used these models during the flow analysis, it may be easy to apply them here. While each model has the features of its flow counterpart, it also has architectural features that were not discussed in the flow models.

The flow-based models we present are peer-to-peer, client–server, hierarchical client–server, and distributed computing.

The *peer-to-peer architectural model* is based on the peer-to-peer flow model, where the users and applications are fairly consistent in their flow behaviors throughout the network. The important characteristics of this model are in the architectural features, flows, function, features, and services. Since the users and applications in this model are consistent throughout the network, there are no obvious locations for architectural features. This pushes the functions, features, and services toward the edge of the network, close to users and their devices, and also makes flows end-to-end, between users and their devices. This resembles the Core portion of the Access/Distribution/Core model. Figure 5.12 shows this

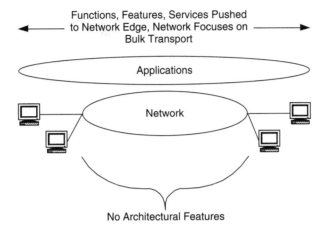

FIGURE 5.12   The Peer-to-Peer Architectural Model

architectural model. Ad hoc networks exemplify this model, as they lack a fixed infrastructure, forcing nodes to communicate in a peer-to-peer fashion.

The *client–server architectural model* also follows its flow model, but in this case there are obvious locations for architectural features—in particular, where flows combine. Therefore, functions, features, and services are focused at server locations, the interfaces to client LANs, and client–server flows, as shown in Figure 5.13.

The characteristics of the client–server model also apply to the *hierarchical client–server architectural model*. In addition to the functions, features, and services being focused at server locations and client–server flows, they are also focused at the server–server flows (see Figure 5.14).

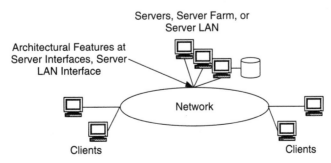

FIGURE 5.13   The Client–Server Architectural Model

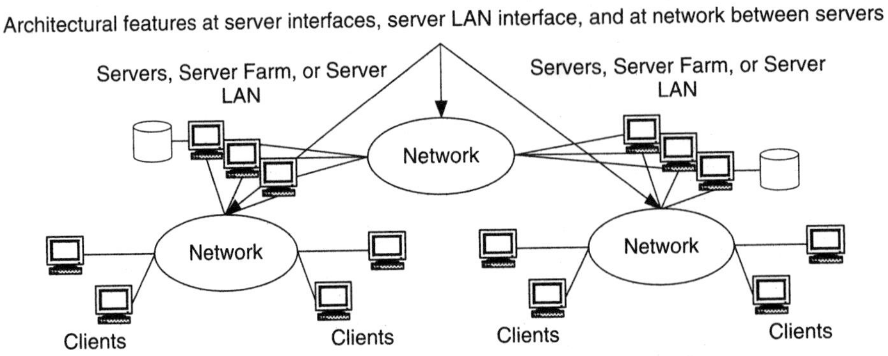

Architectural features at server interfaces, server LAN interface, and at network between servers

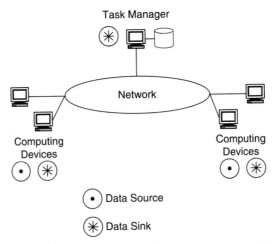

FIGURE 5.14   The Hierarchical Client–Server Architectural Model

FIGURE 5.15   The Distributed-Computing Architectural Model

In the *distributed-computing architectural model* (Figure 5.15) the data sources and sinks are obvious locations for architectural features.

Flow-based models, like the topological models, are intuitive and can be easy to apply. Since they are associated with flows, they should map well to any flow maps you created as part of the requirements analysis process. These models are fairly general, and you may have to modify them to fit the specific requirements of your network.

5.5.3 Functional Models

Functional architectural models focus on supporting particular functions in the network. In this section we present service-provider, intranet/extranet, single-/ multi-tiered performance, and end-to-end models.

The *service-provider architectural model* is based on service-provider functions, focusing on privacy and security, service delivery to customers (users), and billing. In this model, interactions between providers (the networks) and with users are compartmentalized. While this model represents a service-provider architecture, many enterprise networks are evolving to this model, applying it across organizations, departments, and buildings. Figure 5.16 illustrates this model.

The *intranet/extranet architectural model* focuses on security and privacy, including the separation of users, devices, and applications based on secure access. Note that in this model there can be several levels of hierarchy (security/privacy) (Figure 5.17).

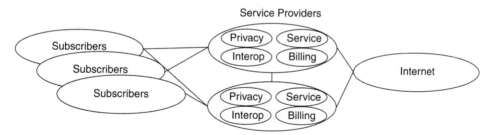

FIGURE 5.16 The Service-Provider Architectural Model

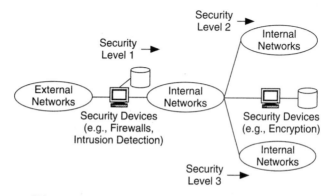

FIGURE 5.17 The Intranet/Extranet Architectural Model

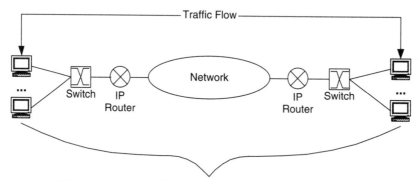

FIGURE 5.18 The End-to-End Architectural Model

The *single-/multi-tiered performance architectural model* focuses on identifying networks or parts of a network as having a single tier of performance, multiple tiers of performance, or having components of both. This model is based on results from the requirements and flow analyses, where single- and multi-tiered performance is determined. Recall that for multi-tiered performance, multiple applications, devices, and users can drive the network architecture and design, in terms of performance, while single-tier performance focuses on supporting (usually a majority of) applications, devices, and users that have a consistent set of performance requirements. These have two very different sets of architectural requirements.

Finally, the *end-to-end architectural model* focuses on all components in the end-to-end path of a traffic flow. This model is most closely aligned to the flow-based perspective of networking (Figure 5.18).

Functional models are the most difficult to apply to a network, in that you must understand where each function will be located. For example, to apply the end-to-end model you first have to define where end-to-end is for each set of users, applications, or devices that will be a part of end-to-end. An advantage of using such models is that they are likely to be the most closely related to the requirements you developed during the requirements analysis process.

5.5.4 Using the Architectural Models

Typically, a few of the models from the previous three sections are combined to provide a comprehensive architectural view of the network. This is usually achieved by starting with one of the topological models and then adding flow-based and functional models as required. This is shown in Figure 5.19.

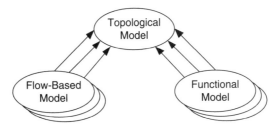

FIGURE 5.19   Functional and Flow-Based Models Complement the Topological Models

The result of combining models and developing the relationships between architectural components is the reference architecture (Figure 5.20).

In developing the reference architecture for a network, we use as input information from the requirements specification, requirements map, and flow specification, along with the architectural models and component architectures. Since at this point in the process we have not developed any of the component architectures, we will focus on the architectural models. As each component architecture is developed, it would be integrated into the reference architecture.

As mentioned in the previous section, we normally start with one of the topological models—LAN/MAN/WAN or Access/Distribution/Core—and add to that elements from one or more of the functional and/or flow-based models. The topological models are a good starting point, as they can be used to describe the

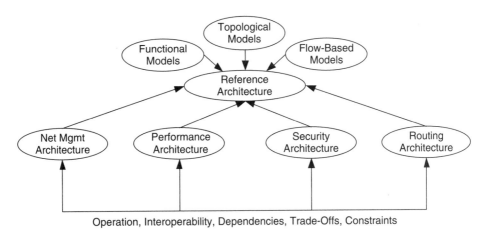

FIGURE 5.20   The Reference Architecture Combines Component Architectures and Models

entire network in a general fashion. While the functional and flow-based models can also be used to describe an entire network, they tend to be focused on a particular area of the network and are thus used to add detail to a more general description.

Nine models have been presented in this chapter (two topological, four flow-based, and three functional models) to provide you with as many options as possible to develop your reference architecture. In practice, one or two models are typically sufficient for many networks. You may choose to apply a model to describe the entire network, with additional models for specific areas (e.g., a client–server model for access to a server farm, or a distributed-computing model for computing centers).

Consider, for example, the Access/Distribution/Core model. The areas of this model focus on different functions in the network, such as traffic flow sources and sinks in the access network, server and/or specialized device flows in the distribution network, and bulk transport of traffic (no sources or sinks) in the core network. We would combine this model with the requirements specification and requirements map to determine which areas of the network are likely to be access, distribution, and core networks. Determining the core network is often relatively easy, while determining the distribution and access networks can be more of a challenge. In some cases there may not be a distribution network, but only access and core networks.

From a flow perspective, the core network will not source or sink any flows, the distribution network will source and sink server and specialized device flows, and the access network will source and sink generic computing device flows, as shown in Figure 5.21.

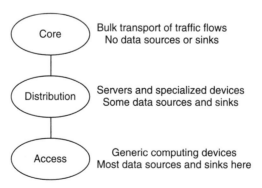

FIGURE 5.21   The Access/Distribution/Core Model from a Flow Perspective

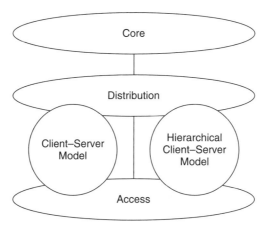

FIGURE 5.22   Where Client–Server and Hierarchical Client–Server Models May Overlap with the Access/Distribution/Core Model

Given this perspective, we can identify potential distribution networks as places where servers and specialized devices are located. We can then apply flow-based models to distribution and access networks that have client–server and hierarchical client–server flows (identified in the flow specification). As shown in Figure 5.22, these models overlap with the distribution and access networks. Usually the client–server and hierarchical client–server models apply across the distribution and access areas but may at times also apply across the core. However, even when these models apply across the core, they may not impact the architecture of the core network.

As a general rule of thumb, Figure 5.23 shows where the functional and flow-based models may overlap with the Access/Distribution/Core model. This figure does not imply the concurrent use of these models within one network architecture, but rather where each model may overlap with the Access/Distribution/ Core model.

The results of the requirements and flow analyses are used as input to the network architecture, which then lead to the development of the network design. Network architecture and design are attempts to solve nonlinear problems, and figuring out where to begin can be difficult. You cannot start at the top without some understanding of the capabilities of the individual components, and you cannot easily pick components until you understand the top-down requirements. Optimally we try to converge on an understanding of all of the pieces and then start at the top and work our way down to the individual components.

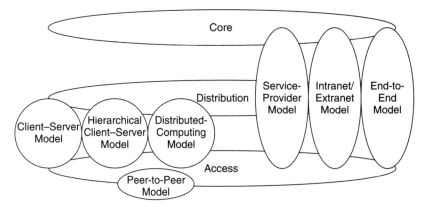

FIGURE 5.23 The Access/Distribution/Core Model with Functional and Flow-Based Models Added

---

Example 5.1. Applying Architectural Models.

Consider the flow map from the storage example in Chapter 4, shown here in Figure 5.24.

From this flow map we can determine where flows are sourced or sink and where servers are located. This information can be used with the Access/Distribution/Core architectural model, with the results shown in Figure 5.25.

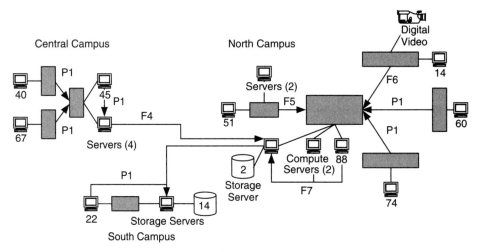

FIGURE 5.24 The Flow Map from the Storage Example in Chapter 4

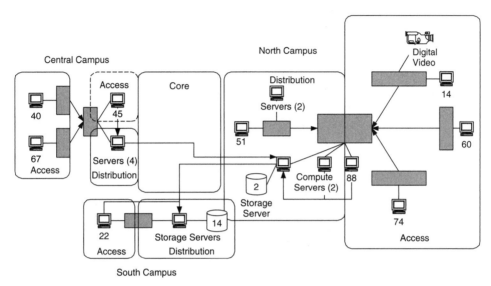

FIGURE 5.25   Access, Distribution, and Core Areas Defined for the Example

For this flow map, the access areas are where user devices (including the digital video camera) are located, as these devices are the primary sources of data for storage. Distribution areas are where servers are located in each campus, as these are sinks (as well as sources) of data from multiple devices. The core area is shown between buildings, as this is where bulk data transport is needed, and there are no obvious data sources or sinks. Although as shown the core area is not located at any building on the campuses, any network devices that would connect to the core area would be located at the junction between core and distributions areas at each campus.

In this example we could also apply a distributed-computing architectural model between servers and their clients. The distributed-computing model is chosen here over the client–server model (which seems more intuitive) as the flows are primarily in the direction from the user devices to the storage servers. When this model is applied, we get the configuration in Figure 5.26.

There are three areas where the distributed-computing model can apply in this example, one at each campus. Note that in each area the flows within it are from user devices to servers. At North Campus there are also server-to-server flows; therefore, we could have modified either the distributed-computing or hierarchical client–server models to apply there.

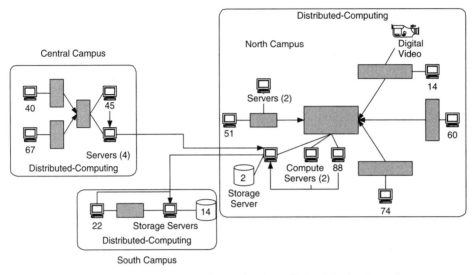

FIGURE 5.26   Distributed-Computing Areas Defined for the Example

5.6   Systems and Network Architectures

You may find that, in the process of developing a network architecture, you may also need to develop a systems architecture. A systems architecture (also known as an enterprise architecture) is a superset of a network architecture, in that it also describes relationships, but the components are major functions of the system, such as storage, clients/servers, or databases, as well as of the network. In addition, devices and applications may be expanded to include particular functions, such as storage. For example, a systems architecture may include a storage architecture, describing servers, applications, a storage-area network (SAN), and how they interact with other components of the system.

From this perspective, the systems architecture considers the total or comprehensive picture, including the network, servers/clients, storage, servers, applications, and databases (Figure 5.27). Potentially, each component in the system could have its own architecture. There are likely to be other components, depending on the environment that the network is supporting.

In contrast, the network architecture considers the relationships within and between each of the network architectural components (Figure 5.28). From this perspective, Figure 5.28 is one of the components of Figure 5.27. You may find that

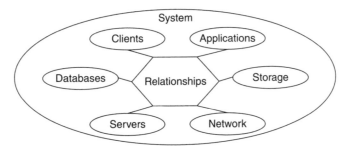

FIGURE 5.27   Systems Architecture

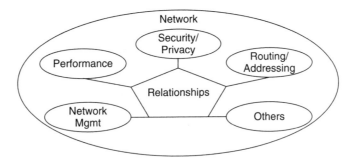

FIGURE 5.28   Network Architecture

you have the start of a systems architecture with your network architecture. You can then use the network architecture as a core from which to build the systems architecture. The goal here is for you to be aware that the network architecture process may lead to areas outside of networking. When that happens, you can choose to ignore those areas, try to incorporate them into the network architecture, or expand your architecture to include a systems architecture.

Chapters 6 through 9 discuss each of these network architectural components.

5.7 Conclusions

The component approach to network architecture defines the building blocks of architecture as network functions instead of physical entities. In this way, the underlying requirements, flows, and goals for the network, instead of technologies, drive the network architecture.

This approach focuses on relationships within each component and between components, providing an understanding of how each function not only operates within a network, but also how it *interoperates* with other functions. By weighting the interactions between components (through assigning a priority to each component), the network architecture can be tailored to meet the specific needs of a network.

Component architectures and the resulting reference architecture can be further refined and validated through network modeling and simulation. This allows internal and external relationships to be studied at length and supports a logical progression through the architectural process.

Implementation of the process reveals numerous interactions between component architectures. Interactions that are particularly subtle and complex, such as in grid networking, are an evolving area of research in component architectures. Refining these interactions is an area of ongoing work.

The next four chapters focus on component architectures. The addressing and routing architecture is covered in Chapter 6, as it helps to lay the foundation for how IP is handled in the network, upon which all other component architectures depend. In Chapter 7 we cover the network management architecture, and in Chapter 8 the performance architecture. We wrap up our development of component architectures with Chapter 9, the security architecture.

5.8   Exercises

1. Network architecture defines the building blocks of a network as physical or functional entities. Give examples of physical and functional entities that you would use as building blocks for a network. How does each approach (physical and functional) differ?

2. A network's architecture differs from its design, in terms of its scope, level of detail, description, and location information. Describe how an architecture and design differ in each characteristic.

3. A component architecture is a description of how and where each network function is applied within that network. Besides addressing/routing, network management, performance, and security, list three other possible component architectures for a network. What does each component architecture describe? Show each function and capability, and give two examples of mechanisms (as in Figure 5.3).

4. Give examples of external relationships between each of the following component architectures: addressing/routing, network management, performance, and security.

5. What are the differences between the LAN/MAN/WAN and Access/Distribution/ Core architectural models? Under what conditions might each be applied to a network?

6. Consider the development of a demilitarized zone (DMZ), also known as an isolation LAN (iLAN), between two different networks (two different autonomous systems [ASs], managed by different organizations). The purpose of a DMZ is to separate and isolate the two networks. Briefly outline what you consider to be the most important addressing/routing, network management, performance, and security requirements and issues for a DMZ.

7. For Exercise 6, what are some potential external relationships between addressing/routing, network management, performance, and security for this DMZ? How do the component architectures need to work together to achieve the goal of effectively isolating and separating the two autonomous systems?

CHAPTER CONTENTS

6

Addressing and Routing Architecture

We begin examining component architectures with the addressing and routing architecture. IP addressing and routing are the cornerstones of a network, upon which much of the performance, network management, and security component architectures are built.

6.1 Objectives

In this chapter you will learn about the architecture for addressing and routing. We discuss some fundamental concepts about addressing and routing for IP networks, and examine various mechanisms to provide flexible and comprehensive addressing within the network, as well as to manipulate routing flows through the network. As with the other component architectures, we discuss possible interactions within this architecture (internal relationships) and between this and other component architectures (external relationships).

6.1.1 Preparation

To be able to understand and apply the concepts in this chapter, you should be familiar with addressing and routing concepts for TCP/IP networks. While the addressing mechanisms discussed in this chapter are relatively straightforward, you should have some background in IP addressing, and a good addressing reference is provided below. In addition, you should have some background in routing protocols, particularly RIP/RIPv2, OSFP, and BGP4. Some recommended sources of information include:

- *Everything You Wanted to Know about IP Addressing*, by Chuck Semeria, available from 3Com at www.3com.com.
- *Interconnections*, Second Edition, by Radia Perlman, Addison-Wesley Publishing, January 2000.

- *Routing in the Internet*, by Christian Huitema, Prentice Hall, January 2000.

- *OSPF: Anatomy of an Internet Routing Protocol*, by John T. Moy, Addison-Wesley Publishing, January 1998.

- *BGP4 Inter-Domain Routing in the Internet*, by John W. Stewart, Addison-Wesley Publishing, January 1999.

- *Requirements for Internet Hosts—Communication Layers*, STD 0003, R. Braden, Ed., October 1989.

- *Requirements for IP Version 4 Routers*, RFC 1812, F. Baker, Ed., June 1995.

The host requirements and router requirements RFC and STD listed here are heavy reading but thoroughly describe the vital characteristics of hosts and routers on IP networks.

While IPv6 is on the horizon, particularly for government and service provider networks, the addressing and routing mechanisms discussed in this chapter focus on IPv4.

6.2   Background

The final architectural component that we discuss is a combination of addressing and routing. Addressing and routing can be considered separated architectures; however, they are closely coupled in the network, so they are considered here as parts of a single architecture. In this book the addressing and routing architecture is focused on the network (IP) layer. Addressing, however, does have elements at the link and physical layers (e.g., Ethernet addresses). Routing also has its counterparts—bridging and switching—that occur primarily at the physical, data-link, and network layers, but (switching) can occur at any layer in the protocol stack. Therefore, as you go through this chapter, remember that the concepts discussed can be applied at many layers in the network.

What are addressing and routing? *Addressing* is assigning local or global, private or public, temporary or persistent, identifiers to devices. *Routing* consists of learning about the reachability within and between networks and then applying this reachability information to forward IP packets toward their destinations. These two processes, in combination with the addressing element of the architecture, provide a complete picture of network connectivity.

In this section we provide some fundamental concepts behind addressing and routing for your review. These fundamental concepts are necessary to understand the rest of this chapter and are sometimes overlooked in texts on routing and routing protocols.

This chapter begins with a discussion of requirements for addressing and routing in the network architecture, and then explains mechanisms (functional areas and boundaries) to establish routing flows for the network. A relationship between boundaries and routing flows is then developed, which leads to discussions on the characteristics of routing flows and how such characteristics may be manipulated. We then examine various addressing and routing mechanisms, including a comparison of popular routing protocols. This chapter then ends with development of the addressing and routing architecture.

6.2.1 Addressing Fundamentals

A network address is an identifier used to temporarily or persistently locate a device on a network, in order to communicate with that device. For IP, addresses consist of an address identifier and an associated mask, usually presented in dotted-decimal notation (Figure 6.1). An address mask identifies which bits in the address are considered part of the network and (by default) which bits are considered part of the device.

The combination of an address and its mask allows the address to be separated into a network portion and a host portion. This is important, as it provides a way to determine when an address is on the local network, and when it is on a remote network. This local/remote decision is discussed in routing fundamentals later.

In this book addresses are sometimes shown in their binary formats, so that we can better understand how some of the addressing and routing mechanisms work. In this form, each decimal address is represented by its binary equivalent. Figure 6.2 shows the IP address from the previous figure, represented in binary as well as dotted-decimal formats.

FIGURE 6.1   IP Addresses Consist of a Unique Identifier and a Mask

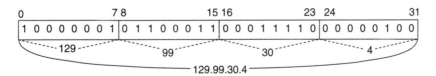

FIGURE 6.2   An IP Address in Binary and Dotted-Decimal Formats

Example 6.1. Address and Class Calculations.

For a network address of 136.178.10.1, let's represent this address in binary form. The bits in each octet (byte) represent a power of 2, from 2^0 (i.e., 1) through 2^7 (128), as shown below.

Power of 2	2^7	2^6	2^5	2^4	2^3	2^2	2^1	2^0
Decimal Value	128	64	32	16	8	4	2	1

To represent the first octet of this address, 136, in binary, we can successively subtract the largest possible power of 2, until we get to 0. In this case the largest power of 2 is 2^7, or 128. Subtracting 128 from 136 leaves us with 8, which is 2^3. Thus, 136 in binary is 10001000, as shown below:

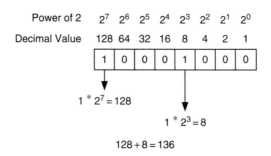

Continuing in this fashion, we get the following binary representation for 136.178.10.1:

$136 = 2^7 + 2^3$	$178 = 2^7 + 2^5 + 2^4 + 2^1$	$10 = 2^3 + 2^1$	$1 = 2^0$
1 0 0 0 1 0 0 0	1 0 1 1 0 0 1 0	0 0 0 0 1 0 1 0	0 0 0 0 0 0 0 1

The numbers can be shown together as 10001000 10110010 00001010 00000001.

Addresses can be local or global, private or public, temporary or persistent. Most networks implement both local and global addresses. Local addresses are those that are important in local communications, such as link-layer addresses like Ethernet. These addresses are not advertised outside the local network. The isolation of link-layer addresses is an example of hierarchy in networking. However, in order for devices outside that network to communicate with devices in the network, global addresses are needed that can be advertised outside the local network. IP addresses are used for this purpose.

IP addresses, which have been traditionally global in scope, can now be separated into public and private address spaces. *Public IP addresses* are those that can be advertised and forwarded by network devices in the public domain (i.e., the Internet). *Private IP addresses* are those that cannot be advertised and forwarded by network devices in the public domain. Private IP address space has been allocated out of previously public IP address space. Why and how this works is explained later in this chapter.

Addresses may also be temporary or persistent. Link-layer addresses (such as Ethernet) are intended to be persistent for the life of the device (where the device may be a network interface card [NIC]). IP addresses can be either temporary or persistent, usually depending on how they are configured within the network. Temporary addresses are usually assigned using a dynamic addressing mechanism such as the dynamic host configuration protocol (DHCP). The degree to which addresses are temporary depends on how DHCP is configured for that network. An address may be updated each time a device becomes active on the network, may be updated periodically while a device is on the network, or may be assigned once (it which case it becomes persistent). Persistent addresses are usually assigned to devices as part of their overall configuration and are not updated unless changes in the network require new addresses be assigned (usually a painful process).

Figure 6.3 lists these address terms and their meanings.

6.2.2 Routing Fundamentals

As mentioned earlier, routing entails learning about reachability within and between networks and then applying this reachability information to forward IP packets toward their destinations. In order for routers to forward IP packets to their destinations, they first need to know what they are connected to, which networks are available, and how to get to them. This is reachability. Routers learn reachability either statically or dynamically. To learn reachability statically, routers must have the information configured into them by network personnel. Static routes, discussed later, exemplify how reachability is statically configured in a router. Typically, however, reachability is learned dynamically through the use of a routing protocol. Routing protocols, such as RIP/RIPv2, OSPF, and BGP4, provide the mechanism for routers to learn reachability.

Once routers learn about reachability within and between networks, this information is used to forward packets toward their destinations. Routers store

Address Type	Meaning
Local Addresses	Addresses that are recognized locally, at the LAN or subnet. Such addresses are usually at the data-link (e.g., Ethernet) layer.
Global Addresses	Addresses that are recognized worldwide. Such addresses are usually at the network (IP) layer.
Private Addresses	Network-layer addresses that are not routed through the public Internet. Private addresses are used in Network Address Translation (NAT).
Public Addresses	Network-layer addresses that are routed through the public Internet.
Temporary Addresses	Addresses that are assigned for a short duration of time, e.g., dynamically via the Dynamic Host Configuration Protocol (DHCP)
Persistent Addresses	Addresses that are assigned for a long duration of time or permanently configured within the device.

FIGURE 6.3   Address Terms and Meanings

reachability information and update it from time to time, or upon a change in the state of routing in the network. A routing table, or list of routes, metrics, and how they can be reached, is a common mechanism routers use to keep such information.

Routers forward packets based on reachability. Traditionally, a router looks at the network portion of a packet's destination address to determine where it needs to be sent. The router compares this destination to the contents of its routing table, and chooses the best route for that destination. If there are multiple possible routes, the best route is the one with the longest (or more explicit) match. Figure 6.4 gives an example of this.

In this example Company A has the address 129.29.0.0 with a network mask of 255.255.0.0, which is 16 bits in length. Company B has the address 129.99.10.0 with a network mask of 255.255.255.0, which is 24 bits in length. IP packets arriving from the Internet will be examined at ISP Z's router, where the destination addresses of these packets are compared with entries in the routing table.

In comparing a packet's destination address with entries in a routing table, the longest match to the destination address is chosen. For example, an IP packet arriving at ISP Z with a destination address of 129.99.10.1 matches both entries in the routing table shown in Figure 6.4. When the network mask of the first entry in the routing table, 255.255.0.0, is applied to 129.99.0.0, we get 129.99 as the

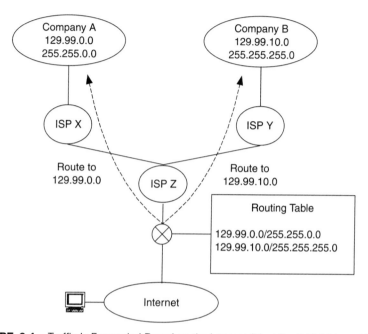

FIGURE 6.4   Traffic Is Forwarded Based on the Longest (Most Explicit) Address Match

network. This matches the first two octets of the IP packet with 129.99.10.1 as its address. Likewise, when the network mask of the second entry in the routing table, 255.255.255.0, is applied to 129.99.10.0, we get 129.99.10 as the network. This also matches our IP packet, with 129.99.10.1 as its address, but it matches the first three octets—a longer (more explicit) match. As a result, packets with a destination address of 129.99.10.1 are forwarded to ISP Y.

Usually there is also a *default route*, which is the route used when there is no other route for that destination. It is the route of last resort and is useful when a lot of traffic flows toward one upstream router or network (e.g., a home or business connection to an ISP).

Routers may also look at labels in a packet and use that information for routing. Multi-protocol label switching (MPLS), discussed later in this book, uses this mechanism.

Routing is converging with switching, and at times it is difficult to understand the differences between the two. A comparison of routing and switching is presented in Chapter 11.

Addressing and routing are used together to form an overall picture of connectivity for the network. An example of this is the local/remote decision to determine where to initially send packets. In the local/remote decision, a device (such as a user's computer) needs to decide if the destination of a packet is local (on the same network) or remote. The destination IP address and mask (discussed earlier) are used to determine the network portion of the destination address. This is compared with the network portion of the sending device's IP address. If they are the same, the destination is on the same network (i.e., is local). If the network portions of the IP addresses are different, they are on different networks (remote).

Why is this important? Part of the fundamental behavior of IP is in this local/remote decision (Figure 6.5). IP requires that, if the destination address is local, then there is a lower-layer mechanism to directly transport that packet. As part of this requirement, every device on an IP network (or subnet, as we see later) must be able to directly communicate with every other device on that network. This means that the underlying network must have a mechanism to allow every device to communicate with every other device. This has implications for how address resolution at the lower layers is done, as we see later in this book.

IP also requires that, if the destination address is remote, then there is a router that can forward that packet toward its destination. Thus, a device on the network needs to know about which router or routers it can forward packets to. This can be learned by the device, through listening to routing protocol updates, or can be configured in the device. This router is termed the *next-hop router* for that network. In Figure 6.5 devices on the same subnet, 129.99.0.0, must be directly connected at the MAC/PHY layers. Devices are on the same subnet when they have the same network address, determined by applying the network mask to their addresses. In the example in Figure 6.5 devices 129.99.0.1 and 129.99.0.2 are on the same

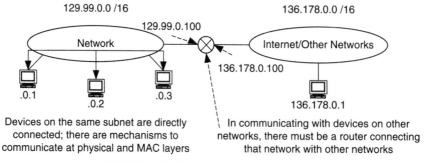

FIGURE 6.5   Basic Tenets of IP Forwarding

network, as the network mask (/16 or 255.255.0.0) applied to each address resolves a network of 129.99.0.0. IP assumes this connectivity and passes IP datagrams down to the MAC and PHY layers for transport.

When devices are on different networks, there must be a router that can forward traffic between these networks. In the example, traffic between 129.99.0.0 and 136.178.0.0 passes through the adjoining router, which has interfaces on both networks.

6.3   Addressing Mechanisms

In this section we discuss some of the popular mechanisms for addressing networks: classful addressing, subnetting, variable-length subnetting, supernetting and classless interdomain routing (CIDR), private addressing and network address translation (NAT), and dynamic addressing. Although these mechanisms all basically share the same theme (manipulating address space), we treat them as separate in order to highlight their differences.

It should be noted that the concept of classful addressing is a bit outdated. We discuss it here in order to give some background on newer mechanisms and to provide insight into the addressing process.

6.3.1   Classful Addressing

Classful addressing is applying predetermined mask lengths to addresses in order to support a range of network sizes. The result is a set of classes of addresses (A, B, C, D, and E), each of which supports a different maximum network size. A class identifier at the beginning (first octet) of the address determines its class. A Class A address is indicated when the first bit of the first octet is 0 (network addresses 1 through 127), a Class B address is when the first bit is 1 and the second bit is 0 (network addresses 128 through 191), and a Class C address is when the first bit is 1, the second bit is 1, and the third bit is 0 (network addresses 192 through 223). The structures of Classes A, B, and C are shown in Figure 6.6. Classes D and E are not shown here, as they are used for special purposes (Class D is used for multicast) or reserved.

Classful addresses default to a natural mask which coincides with the class boundary and reflects that class's network and host space allocations. The natural mask is different for each class. For Class A addresses the natural mask is 255.0.0.0, indicating that the bits in the first octet represent the network for that class. Since the first bit of the first octet is used to indicate a Class A address, and neither all 0s

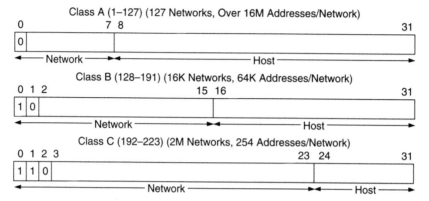

FIGURE 6.6   Classful Addressing Uses Traditional Class Boundaries to Form Class A, B, or C Addresses

nor all 1s can be used as network addresses (they represent broadcasts), there can be 2^7-2 or 126 possible networks. The device (host) portion of the mask is the remaining three octets, so there can be up to $2^{24}-2$ or over 16 million possible device addresses per network for Class A networks. So, Class A provides for a few very large networks.

The natural mask for Class B addresses is 255.255.0.0, so the first two octets represent the network for that class. Since the first two bits are used to identify the class, there can be $2^{14}-2$ or 16,382 possible networks. The device portion of the mask is the remaining two octets, so there can be up to $2^{16}-2$ or 65,534 possible device addresses per network. So, Class B provides for tens of thousands of (still quite large) networks. At one time this seemed like a lot of networks—but not anymore.

The natural mask for Class C addresses is 255.255.255.0, so the first three octets represent the network for that class. Since the first three bits are used to identify the class, there can be $2^{21}-2$ or slightly over 2 million possible networks. The device portion of the mask is the remaining octet, so there can be up to 2^8-2 or 254 possible device addresses per network. So, Class C provides for millions of small networks.

There are two additional classes of address space (Classes D and E) that are used or reserved for special purposes. Class D is used for multicast addresses, and Class E is reserved. Class D address spaces are calculated in the same way as the other classes, so Class D is indicated when the first, second, and third bits of the first octet are 1, and the fourth bit is 0 (network addresses 224 through 239).

Classful addressing was the first step to add hierarchy to addressing. Although the three classes can address from very small to very large networks, there are some fundamental problems with this scheme. First, Class A and B networks can address large numbers of devices. As it turns out, networks do not scale well to the size of a Class A or B, and further hierarchy is needed. And, as Class A and B address space ran out, the use of Class C address space impacted routing in the Internet. Clearly, something more than classful addressing was needed.

Example 6.2. Determining Class and Natural Mask.

For the network address from Example 6.1, 136.178.10.1, let's determine its class and natural mask. Recall from Example 6.1 the binary representation of 136.178.10.1:

$136 = 2^7 + 2^3$	$178 = 2^7 + 2^5 + 2^4 + 2^1$	$10 = 2^3 + 2^1$	$1 = 2^0$
1 0 0 0 1 0 0 0	1 0 1 1 0 0 1 0	0 0 0 0 1 0 1 0	0 0 0 0 0 0 0 1

Looking at the first three bits (from left to right) of the first octet, we see that they are 100. Since the first bit must be 0 for a Class A address, 136.178.10.1 is not Class A. The first two bits are 10, which are consistent with Class B; therefore 136.178.10.1 is a Class B address. The natural mask for this address is the natural mask for Class B, 255.255.0.0.

There are limitations in allocating addresses based on Class A, B, and C boundaries. First, since there are relatively few Class A and B addresses, they have already been allocated. This leaves new networks with only Class C address space. Thus, a network may require many Class C addresses. Second, these class boundaries are not an efficient use of network addresses. Many networks require more addresses than a single Class C can provide, yet are not large enough to justify a Class A or B, even if such network addresses were available. There are networks that have Class A or B addresses but can only use a small fraction of the total address space. There needed to be a more flexible method to match address space to the requirements of each network. This was accomplished by expanding the network mask to create subnets and variable-length subnets, as described next.

6.3.2 Subnetting

The next step in adding hierarchy to addressing is to allow a classful network address to be segmented into smaller sections. Subnetting (RFC 950) accomplishes this. *Subnetting* is using part of the device (host) address space to create another level of hierarchy. Changing the address mask increases the number of bits allocated to the network, creating the subnet. The resultant mask now includes a *subnet mask*, and the network segments that are created are termed *subnets*.

What is essentially happening in subnetting is that, by changing the address mask to increase the number of bits allocated to the network and thereby decreasing the number of bits allocated to devices, subnetting takes address space away from devices and gives it to the network.

Subnetting can be done on Class A, B, or C networks, although it is rare to subnet a Class C network (since there are only 254 addresses for devices anyway). The result of subnetting is a set of equal-sized subnets, where the length of the subnet mask determines the number of subnets and the size of each subnet. An example of this for Class B networks is shown in Figure 6.7.

Subnetting adds hierarchy to a network. A network in which all devices are addressed with the same network address can have problems scaling to a large number of devices. The term "large" is relative: some networks have problems

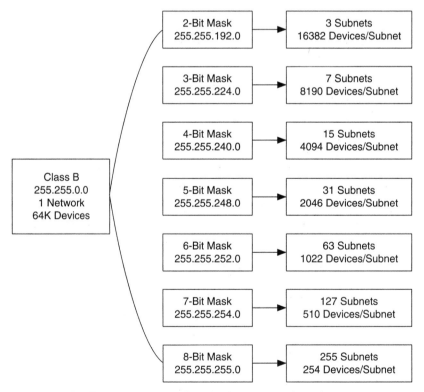

FIGURE 6.7 Masks and Sizes for Subnetting a Class B Network

with a few dozen devices, while others can scale to hundreds of devices without problems. The problems are usually related to traffic loads and behavior at the link and physical layers. The behaviors of users, applications, and devices are reflected in the traffic flows on the network, and the characteristics of these flows (including their sources and sinks) impact the scalability of the network. How network devices are configured at the link layer affects how they communicate at that layer. Problems at the link layer, such as jabbering devices or broadcast/multicast storms, impact scalability of the network. Subnetting helps to reduce the problem by segmenting the network into subnets connected by routers. Routers terminate the link and physical layers, thus stopping problems in one subnet from impacting other subnets.

Subnet masks (and therefore subnets) are recognized only within that network. When routes to that network are advertised, the natural mask is used. This is desirable; since subnetting is used to provide hierarchy within that network, there is no need to reveal that hierarchy outside of the network.

Example 6.3. Creating Subnets.

Let's subnet 129.99.0.0 into seven subnets. 129.99.0.0 is a Class B (how do we know this?) address with a natural mask of 255.255.0.0. To create subnets, we increase the mask into the third octet by enough bits to get seven subnets. From Figure 6.7, we see that three bits will give us seven subnets, using an extended mask (subnet mask) of 255.255.224.0, as shown below.

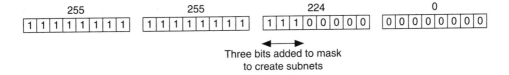

Each subnet is shown below in binary and dotted-decimal forms.

Subnet 1: 10000001 01100011 00100000 00000000 ⟶ 129.99.32.0   255.255.224.0
Subnet 2: 10000001 01100011 01000000 00000000 ⟶ 129.99.64.0   255.255.224.0
Subnet 3: 10000001 01100011 01100000 00000000 ⟶ 129.99.96.0   255.255.224.0
Subnet 4: 10000001 01100011 10000000 00000000 ⟶ 129.99.128.0 255.255.224.0
Subnet 5: 10000001 01100011 10100000 00000000 ⟶ 129.99.160.0 255.255.224.0
Subnet 6: 10000001 01100011 11000000 00000000 ⟶ 129.99.192.0 255.255.224.0
Subnet 7: 10000001 01100011 11100000 00000000 ⟶ 129.99.224.0 255.255.224.0

6.3.3 Variable-Length Subnetting

Subnetting segments of a network into a number of equal-sized subnets is often inefficient. If a goal of subnetting is to create subnets that are scaled to the sizes of groups (workgroups) in the organization, so that a subnet can be allocated to each group, then it is desirable to have subnets of different sizes. *Variable-length subnetting* is subnetting where multiple variable-length subnet masks (VLSM) are used, creating subnets of different sizes.

This practice allows for a better mapping of subnets to workgroups. For example, the following organization has a number of workgroups of varying sizes.

Workgroup	Groups	Size/Group (Devices)
Engineering	3	400 (1200 total)
Marketing	1	1950
Administration	1	200
Sales	15	35–90 (1350 total)
R&D	1	150
Support	22	10–40 (880 total)
Total:	43	Total: 5730

This organization has a Class B address (136.178.0.0, mask 255.255.0.0) and would like to give one subnet to each group. If we were to use only the natural mask, this network would support 65,534 devices, which is far more than needed. However, it is likely that the network would have problems scaling to that size. We cannot implement subnets of equal size, given the requirement of one subnet per group. In order to support the largest group (Marketing, with 1950 devices), we would need a 5-bit or smaller subnet mask. But this would give a maximum of 31 possible subnets (with a 5-bit mask). In order to have enough subnets, we would need a 6-bit or larger subnet mask, but then the size of the subnet would not be large enough for Marketing. By using variable-length subnetting, we can tailor the subnets to the sizes of the groups and the quantity of subnets we need.

For this example we choose to use a combination of 4-bit and 8-bit subnet masks. With a 4-bit mask (255.255.240.0), we would have 15 subnets, each with a maximum of 4096 devices. This would be sufficient for Engineering and Marketing. The 8-bit subnet mask (255.255.255.0) provides subnets that can have a maximum of 254 devices each, sufficient for each of the groups Sales, R&D, and Support.

The subnet allocations are as follows: The 4-bit mask (255.255.240.0) is used to allocate the following 15 subnets:

136.178.16.0	136.178.96.0	136.178.176.0
136.178.32.0	136.178.112.0	136.178.192.0
136.178.48.0	136.178.128.0	136.178.208.0
136.178.64.0	136.178.144.0	136.178.224.0
136.178.80.0	136.178.160.0	136.178.240.0

Not all of these subnets would be used at this time. We would allocate three subnets to Engineering (136.178.16.0, 136.178.32.0, and 136.178.48.0), one subnet to Marketing (136.178.64.0), and we probably should allocate one to Administration (136.178.80.0), as it would be close to the maximum number of devices for an 8-bit subnet.

For the 8-bit mask, we would take one of the 4-bit subnets and apply the 8-bit mask to it. We could take the next 4-bit subnet available (136.178.96.0) and apply an 8-bit mask (255.255.255.0), yielding the following 8-bit subnets:

136.178.97.0	136.178.102.0	136.178.107.0
136.178.98.0	136.178.103.0	136.178.108.0
136.178.99.0	136.178.104.0	136.178.109.0
136.178.100.0	136.178.105.0	136.178.110.0
136.178.101.0	136.178.106.0	136.178.111.0

These are all the 8-bit subnets between 136.178.96.0 and 136.178.112.0. Each can support up to 254 devices. We would allocate 15 of these subnets (136.178.97.0 through 136.178.110.0) to Sales, and the last one (136.178.111.0) to R&D. At this point we need to create more 8-bit subnets (22 subnets for Support), so we would repeat this procedure for the next two available 4-bit subnets (136.178.112.0 and 136.178.128.0). For 136.178.112.0:

136.178.113.0	136.178.118.0	136.178.123.0
136.178.114.0	136.178.119.0	136.178.124.0
136.178.115.0	136.178.120.0	136.178.125.0
136.178.116.0	136.178.121.0	136.178.126.0
136.178.117.0	136.178.122.0	136.178.127.0

and for 136.178.128.0:

136.178.129.0	136.178.134.0	136.178.139.0
136.178.130.0	136.178.129.0	136.178.140.0
136.178.131.0	136.178.136.0	136.178.141.0
136.178.132.0	136.178.137.0	136.178.142.0
136.178.133.0	136.178.138.0	136.178.143.0

The 22 subnets for Support would be 136.178.113.0 through 136.178.127.0, and 136.178.129.0 through 136.178.129.0. The remaining 4-bit and 8-bit subnets would be available for future growth.

6.3.4 Supernetting

As mentioned earlier, there are not many Class A and B networks (on the order of tens of thousands). As these network were allocated, it became necessary to allocate several Class C network addresses in place of a single Class A or B. Recall that there are millions of Class C networks that can be allocated.

What happens when Class C addresses are used in lieu of Class A or B addresses? Consider, for example, the addressing strategy for a company with 10,000 devices. A single Class B could support up to 65,534 devices, which would be plenty for this company, but a Class B is not available, so Class C addresses are used instead. A single Class C can support up to 254 devices, so 40 Class C networks are needed (40 networks × 254 addresses/network = 10,160 total addresses).

When 40 Class C networks are allocated to this company (e.g., 192.92.240.0 through 192.92.279.0), routes to each network have to be advertised to the Internet. Thus, instead of an advertisement for a single Class B network for this company, we now have advertisements for 40 Class C networks. Each route advertisement would be added to the routers in the Internet, using memory and processing resources. As you may imagine, the number of routes would grow exponentially, as would the memory and processing requirements in the routers. In fact, this was a problem in the Internet in the 1990s. There were predictions that the Internet would collapse in 1995, yet this did not happen. Through the ingenuity of Internet engineers at that time, a mechanism was found to alleviate this problem. The solution was supernetting.

Supernetting is aggregating network addresses, by changing the address mask to decrease the number of bits recognized as the network. By decreasing the number of bits recognized as the network, we are in effect ignoring part of the network address, which results in aggregating network addresses.

Let's see how this works. Consider a block of 16 contiguous Class C addresses (you will shortly see why 16 was chosen, and why it is contiguous), 192.92.240.0 through 192.92.255.0, with their natural mask 255.255.255.0:

192.92.240.0	192.92.248.0
192.92.241.0	192.92.249.0
192.92.242.0	192.92.250.0
192.92.243.0	192.92.251.0
192.92.244.0	192.92.252.0
192.92.245.0	192.92.253.0
192.92.246.0	192.92.254.0
192.92.247.0	192.92.255.0

Notice that the first, second, and last octets of this group of addresses do not change. They are 192, 92, and 0, respectively. The third octet does change for each address. If we look at the binary representation of this octet for these addresses, we get Figure 6.8.

Notice that the first four bits in this octet do not change, but the last four bits do. Also notice that the last four bits are represented in their full range of

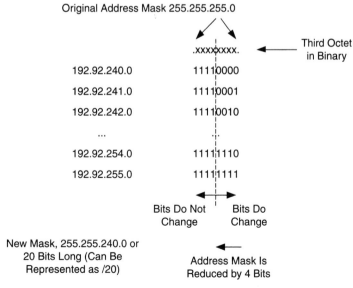

FIGURE 6.8 Modifying the Address Mask for Supernetting

values, from (binary) 0000 to 1111. Therefore, if we choose to ignore the last four bits in this octet, we get a single address that represents the full range of 16 addresses. That address is 192.92.240.0 (the first address of the group), and its mask is 255.255.240.0 (the natural mask minus the last four bits). This mask is termed the *supernet mask*.

How does that work? Let's first look at 192.92.240.0 with its natural mask, 255.255.255.0. These addresses are shown in Figure 6.9 as decimal and binary representations. When the natural mask is applied to the address, we get a single Class C network with 254 device addresses. If we look at this network with the new supernet mask, we get Figure 6.10.

The difference here is that, with the new supernet mask, the last four bits of the third octet are not recognized as part of the network; therefore they can be

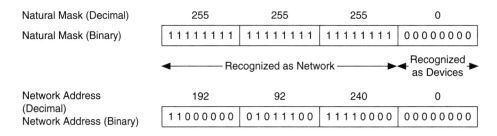

Result: A Single, "Normal" Class C Network

FIGURE 6.9   An IP Address Shown with Its Natural Mask

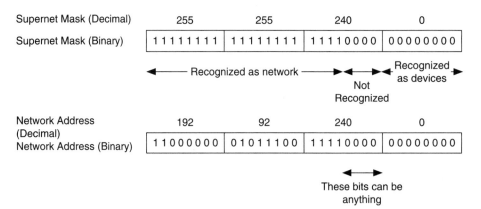

FIGURE 6.10   An IP Address Shown with a Supernet Mask

anything (0000 to 1111). As a result, we get a set of 16 addresses, ranging from 192.92.240.0 (where the last four bits of the third octet are 0000) to 192.92.255.0 (where the last four bits of the third octet are 1111). Thus, the single advertisement of 192.92.240.0 with supernet mask 255.255.240.0 is the equivalent of 16 advertisements for addresses 192.92.240.0 through 192.92.255.0.

Supernetting reduced the number of advertisements in the Internet and changed the way that most people view addressing. If we can change the mask length to aggregate networks, why do we need class boundaries at all? The answer is that we don't. The term *classless interdomain routing* (CIDR) is used to denote the absence of class boundaries in network routing. The dotted-decimal notation for masks can be replaced by noting the length of the mask in bits. For example, the supernet mask 255.255.240.0 shown previously would be described as a 20-bit mask, and the combination of address and mask would be 192.92.240.0/20. The block of networks that are addressed in this way is termed a *CIDR block*. Using this convention, a single Class C network would have a mask length of 24 bits (/24), and a single Class B network would have a mask length of 16 bits (/16). When a mask is shown as a length in bits it is called an *address prefix*.

By describing networks in this way we are really creating arbitrary hierarchies in the network. By changing the mask length we can change the degree of aggregation of networks. This is now common practice in the Internet community.

There are some conventions that are followed in supernetting: The number of addresses in a CIDR block is a power of 2, and the block of addresses is contiguous, meaning that there are no holes in this address space.

The number of addresses in a CIDR block is a power of 2, based on the number of bits that is not recognized by the mask. If we look at 192.92.240.0 with a /24 (the natural mask), we get one network: 192.92.240.0. With a /23 mask, we ignore the last bit of the third octet, and we get two networks: 192.92.240.0 and 192.92.240.1. As you can see in Figure 6.11, this can continue for /22, /21 and so on. Each time we increase the number of possible networks by a factor of 2.

When the address space is not contiguous (i.e., there are one or more network addresses missing from the CIDR block), there is the potential for problems. In our discussion on supernetting it should be clear that, in the process of changing the mask length, we ignore some of the bits in the address. The bits that are ignored can take on any value, and the result is that a range of networks are assumed. If one or more of the networks in that range are not part of the CIDR block (e.g., that network address is being used by somebody else), it is still advertised as part of the range of addresses in that block.

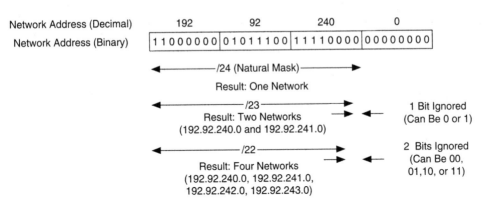

FIGURE 6.11   The Address Prefix Size Determines the CIDR Block Size

For example, the advertisement 200.1.128.0/17 is equivalent to a range of 2^7 or 128 networks, from 200.1.128.0 to 200.1.255.0. If one of these addresses, say 200.1.200.0/24, is already allocated to another customer, it is still included in the advertisement 200.1.128.0/17. Does this mean that advertisements cannot have any such "holes" in them? No. Fortunately, this method still works. As discussed at the beginning of this chapter, routers choose the best match for a destination. Given a number of routes (in the router's forwarding table) that would work, the router chooses the one that is the longest match to the destination address of the packet. If the single network 200.1.200.0/24, which is in the CIDR block advertisement 200.1.128.0/17, is owned by somebody else, packets with a destination address of 200.1.200.0/24 are forwarded to the 200.1.200.0 network, as it is a better (longer) match than 200.1.128.0/17.

6.3.5   Private Addressing and NAT

Private IP addresses are those that cannot be advertised and forwarded by network devices in the public domain. This was originally established to help with address space depletion in the Internet, for if networks that would normally be allocated public address space instead use private address space, those public addresses would remain available.

The IETF has defined (in RFC 1918) three blocks of private address space:

10.0.0.0 through 10.255.255.255 (10/8 prefix)

172.16.0.0 through 172.31.255.255 (172.16/12 prefix)

192.168.0.0 through 192.168.255.255 (192.168/16 prefix)

There is a side benefit of using private addresses. It turns out that because these addresses are not advertised and forwarded in the Internet, they have an additional degree of security. What is needed for private addressing to work, however, is a mechanism to translate addresses from the private address space to the public address space. Network address translation (NAT) is such a mechanism. NAT maps IP addresses between public and private spaces.

In translating between public and private address spaces, NAT creates bindings between addresses. These can be one-to-one address bindings (known as static NAT), one-to-many address bindings (known as dynamic NAT), and address and port bindings (known as network address port translation, or NAPT). Often combinations of static, dynamic, and NAPT bindings are used in a network. For example, dynamic NAT is often used for user devices, and static NAT for servers.

6.4   Routing Mechanisms

The routing mechanisms we consider here are establishing routing flows, identifying and classifying routing boundaries, and manipulating routing flows.

6.4.1   Establishing Routing Flows

In preparing to discuss boundaries and route manipulation, we want to understand how flows will likely be routed through the network. As we see later in this chapter, addressing and routing are both closely coupled to the flow of routing information in the network, and the addressing and routing architecture is based partially on establishing these flows.

Determining routing flows begins with the flow analysis process. When you develop flows in the flow specification and flow map, they form the foundation for routing flows (traffic flows being what is routed through the network).

The process of establishing routing flows in the network consists of segmenting the network into functional areas and workgroups, identifying boundaries between these areas, and then forming the relationships between boundaries and routing flows.

Functional areas (FA) are groups within the system that share a similar function. Groups may be of users (workgroups), applications, devices, or combinations of these, and they may share similar jobs/tasks, physical locations, or functions within the network (e.g., backbone routing). *Workgroups* (WG) are groups of users that have common locations, applications, and requirements, or that belong to the same organization.

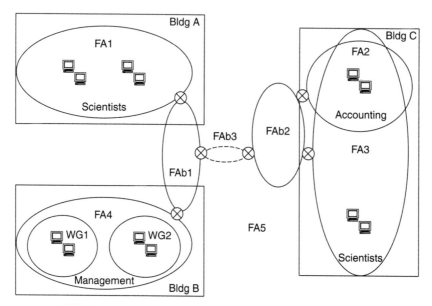

FIGURE 6.12   An Example of Workgroups and Functional Areas

The purpose of functional areas is to simplify the routing architecture. They can cross physical boundaries, such as rooms, floors, and buildings. A workgroup is similar to a functional area, but one level lower in hierarchy.

Consider Figure 6.12. In this figure there are multiple workgroups, in this case based on organizations within a company. Functional areas are created: the Scientists and Accounting groups in Building C, the two Management workgroups in Building B, the Scientists groups across Buildings A and C, and the backbone between the buildings. Notice that functional areas are connected with routers.

6.4.2 Identifying and Classifying Routing Boundaries

Routing boundaries are physical or logical separations of a network, based on requirements for or administration of that network. Physical boundaries can be identified by isolation LANs or demilitarized zones (DMZs); physical interfaces on network equipment; or physical security. Logical boundaries can be identified by functional areas, workgroups, administrative domains, such as autonomous systems (ASs), and routing management domains.

Autonomous systems have AS numbers associated with them. Routing management domains are often the same as ASs but can be either a subset or superset of one or more AS. Security domains are places where security devices are located; they may use public address space outside the security boundary and private address space inside.

The type of routing protocol used to pass routing information across the boundary may also distinguish boundaries. There are two general types of routing protocols. *Exterior gateway protocols* (EGPs) communicate routing information (reachability and metrics) primarily between ASs. *Interior gateway protocols* (IGPs) communicate routing information primarily within an AS. The word "primarily" is used here, for EGPs can be used within an AS, and IGPs can be used between ASs, although this is rarely done. Later in this chapter we look at ways to combine EGP and IGP use both within and between ASs.

Here we use the term *hard boundary* to describe a routing boundary where EGPs are predominantly used to pass routing information, while a *soft boundary* is a routing boundary where IGPs are predominantly used. Hard boundaries are found between ASs, between an AS and an external network (which may or may not have an AS associated with it), or at well-defined separations between networks within an AS (e.g., at interfaces between internal organizations within a company where there are different administrative domains). Hard boundaries are also found at interfaces to ISPs and are associated with DMZs. Figure 6.13 shows an example of a hard boundary.

In this example a network is used to separate an enterprise AS from an ISP. A network used to separate other networks (provide a buffer between them) is often termed an *isolation LAN* (iLAN). Another term for isolation LAN is *demilitarized*

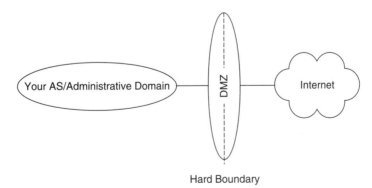

Hard Boundary

FIGURE 6.13   *An Example of a Hard Boundary*

zone, or *DMZ*. DMZ denotes a buffer area between two factions—in this case the two networks being separated. This is a common hard boundary, and one where an EGP is likely to be used. Another example is when an enterprise wants to restrict communications between certain organizations within that enterprise (e.g., to/from the accounting workgroup). While the entire organization is within an AS, the boundary between the accounting workgroup and the rest of the AS is similar to a DMZ (it could be considered an internal DMZ), so this is also a hard boundary. An EGP or IGP may be used in this case.

Soft boundaries are typically found within a single AS and are usually placed at the junction of FAs or WGs, as in Figure 6.14. In this figure all of the interfaces between functional areas are soft boundaries.

Why are we interested in determining routing boundaries for our network? Routing boundaries are important because they are the focal points for routing flows. Recall from our examples that between functional areas and between ASs, hard and soft boundaries are located at routers, which aggregate routing traffic. These are also locations where hierarchies are established in the network. Figure 6.15 shows boundaries and routing flows for a network.

Routing flows are flows of routing information, passed between functional areas as well as between ASs. This routing information includes routing initialization, updates, transients, and background traffic such as hello or keepalive messages. Routing boundaries and flows are important to the development of the architecture and design, because routing flows can be manipulated at routing boundaries.

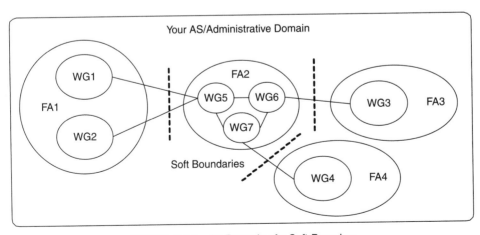

FIGURE 6.14   An Example of a Soft Boundary

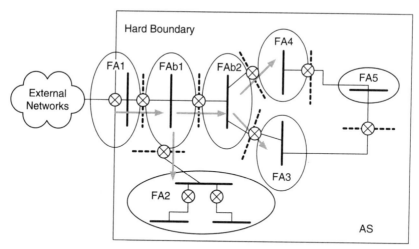

FIGURE 6.15   Boundaries and Routing Flows in a Network

6.4.3 **Manipulating Routing Flows**

Manipulating (i.e., controlling) routing flows within the network is vital to the proper operation and performance of the network. The right combination of addressing and routing is important in this process, to localize routing flows whenever possible.

There are several techniques for manipulating routing flows at hard and soft boundaries. We can supply a default route through our network via default route propagation. We can use route filtering to hide routes, and route aggregation to simplify advertisements. We can develop peering relationships between networks or ASs across boundaries. We can also develop routing policies and policy enforcement.

A *default route* is the route used when there is no other route for that destination. Usually, this is the route with the highest available capacity to external networks. *Default route propagation* is the technique used to inform the network (or subnets or FAs) of the default path; propagation begins at the exit point for the network.

Route filtering is the technique of applying route filters to hide networks from the rest of an AS, or to add, delete, or modify routes in the routing table. A *route filter* is a statement, configured in one or more routers, that identifies one or more IP parameters (e.g., an IP source or destination address) and an action (e.g., drop or forward) to be taken when traffic matches these parameters. Route filtering is commonly used at hard boundaries. When the IGP OSPF is used, route filtering should not be used to hide networks internal to the OSPF network. This is due to the nature of the route-calculation algorithm in OSPF, which is discussed later in this chapter.

Route aggregation is the technique exchanging of routing information between ASs, usually between service providers with transit networks, and between large customer networks. This technique is typically used at hard boundaries and may include policy information. Historically, on the Internet, peering was the free and open exchange of routes between large transit networks, but changes in the structure and operation of the Internet have modified peering arrangements, so that now they are somewhat competitive.

Policies are higher-level abstractions of the route filter technique described previously. Just as a route filter takes an action (e.g., drop, accept, modify) on traffic that matches one or more parameters (e.g., IP addresses), a policy takes a similar action on traffic that matches one or more AS parameters (e.g., AS number or list of AS numbers and metrics, time of day, cost).

Policies allow an AS to accept or deny traffic, or to modify routing information passed between ASs, based on high-level parameters. This allows decisions about routing traffic to be made on a basis other than route metrics. Policies are typically applied across hard boundaries and are currently used with the EGP border gateway protocol version 4 (BGPv4), discussed later in this chapter.

For example, consider a group of interconnected ASs, as in Figure 6.16. Router 1 peers with Routers 2 and 3. Routers 2 and 3 enforce a policy that traffic from AS1 must transit AS2 in order to get to AS4, and this traffic cannot transit AS3.

To illustrate these route-manipulation techniques, we discuss each as applied to the example in Figure 6.17.

The routing requirements for AS1 are as follows:

1.1.   Primary Internet access for AS1 is through ISPa.

1.2.   Redundant (secondary) Internet access for AS1 is through ISPb.

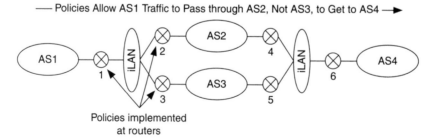

FIGURE 6.16   Policy Enforcement between Autonomous Systems

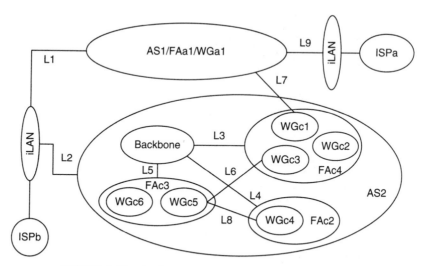

FIGURE 6.17   An Example for Route Manipulation Techniques

1.3. Allow AS2 traffic to transit (go through) AS1 to get redundant Internet access via ISPa.

1.4. Only allow communication between workgroup WGa1 in AS1 and workgroup WGc1 in AS2 via link L7.

1.1 and 1.2 are solved by establishing peering agreements with both ISPa and ISPb. This agreement specifies that ISPa should propagate a default route to AS1 with a lower routing cost than ISPb. Also, within this peering agreement, AS1 will advertise an aggregate route for its subnets to ISPa with a lower cost than to ISPb. Peering is done across a hard boundary; therefore, it is typically accomplished with an EGP (e.g., BGP4).

For 1.3, a third peering agreement is developed between AS1 and AS2 via links L1 and L2. AS1 accepts aggregate routes from AS2 and passes them through AS1 to ISPa at a higher cost than the cost AS2 uses to ISPb. The earlier peering agreement is modified to allow AS1 to send AS2's routes to it. ISPa agrees to propagate AS2's routes to the Internet at a higher cost than to ISPb.

For 1.4, a fourth peering agreement is established between AS1 and AS2 via link L7. AS1 accepts route advertisements from AS2/WGc1 for subnets within this WG via link L7. Route filtering is applied to block any other traffic.

The results of applying route manipulation techniques to the routing requirements of AS1 are shown in Figure 6.18.

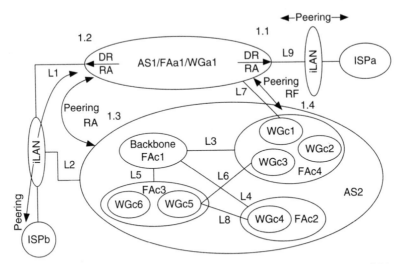

FIGURE 6.18   The Results of Route Manipulation Techniques Applied to AS1

The routing requirements for AS2 are as follows:

2.1.   Workgroup WGc5 can only communicate with workgroup WGc4 via link L8.

2.2.   Allow only traffic from AS1 that is received over link L7 and is destined for workgroup WGc1 to pass; block all other traffic.

2.3.   Allow functional area FAc3 to use functional area FAc4 as an alternate path to the Internet via link L6.

2.4.   Do not allow functional area FAc2 to use functional area FAc3 as an alternate path to the Internet via link L8.

2.5.   Do not advertise workgroup WGc2.

2.6.   Workgroup WGc1 can only communicate with AS1/WGa1 via link L7; deny all other traffic.

2.7.   All other functional areas must use functional area FAc1 as the default path.

2.8.   Use AS1 as a transient AS for redundant access to the Internet via ISPa.

2.9.   Use ISPb as a primary access to the Internet.

Requirement 2.1 is solved by applying route filtering at both workgroups WGc5 and WGc4 to force this routing to take place and to prevent other workgroups from using link L8. For 2.2, a peering agreement with AS1 is established, and route filtering is applied at link L7. 2.3 is solved by having functional area FAc4 propagate a default route via link L6 to functional area FAc3 with a higher cost than functional area FAc3 is getting from FAc1. In 2.4, route filtering is applied to functional areas FAc2 and FAc3, as was done in problem 2.1.

For 2.5, route filters are applied at routers that connect to workgroup WGc2, in order to keep that workgroup from being advertised. In 2.6, route filtering is used again, this time to force communications via link L7. Be careful to not allow workgroup WGc1 to use link L7 as access to the Internet. In 2.7, FAc1 propagates a default route to all functional areas. All functional areas will aggregate route advertisements at the soft boundaries.

For 2.8, another peering agreement (agreement number 5) is established with AS1 to allow AS2 to use AS1 as a transit AS to access ISPa in the event that ISPb fails. AS2 must advertise aggregate routes to AS1 with a higher cost than to ISPb.

In 2.9, a peering agreement is established between ISPb and AS2. AS2 will advertise aggregate routes to ISPb, ISPb will advertise a default to AS2, and ISPb will propagate AS2's routes to the Internet.

The results of applying route manipulation techniques to the routing requirements of AS2 are shown in Figure 6.19.

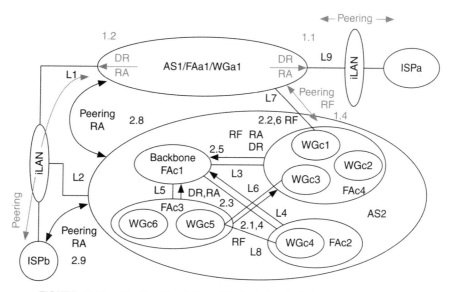

FIGURE 6.19 The Results of Route Manipulation Techniques Applied to AS2

6.5 Addressing Strategies

During the requirements analysis process, it is important to gather information about device growth expectations, so that you can avoid having to change addressing schemes and reconfigure device addresses during the life cycle of the network.

When applying subnetting, variable-length subnetting, classful addressing, supernetting, private addressing and NAT, and dynamic addressing, we want to make sure that our network addresses and masks will scale to the sizes of the areas they will be assigned to. We also want to establish the degrees of hierarchy in the network. To scale the network addressing, we will use the numbers of

- Functional areas within the network
- Workgroups within each functional area
- Subnets within each workgroup
- Total numbers of subnets (current and future) in the organization
- Total numbers of devices (current and future) within each subnet

By establishing the scaling and hierarchies for our network, we are applying addressing not only systemwide, but also across functional areas, workgroups, and subnets. The intent here is to look at addressing from many perspectives, so that we do not lose the detail of any particular area, nor fail to see the overall addressing picture. While each of the addressing strategies could be applied to any area of the network, there are areas where each strategy is more appropriate. Figure 6.20 shows where each strategy applies.

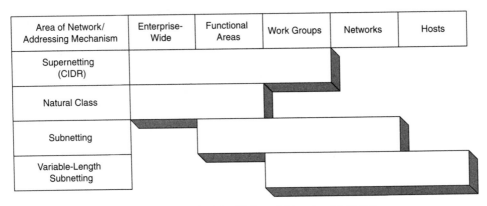

Area of Network/ Addressing Mechanism	Enterprise- Wide	Functional Areas	Work Groups	Networks	Hosts
Supernetting (CIDR)					
Natural Class					
Subnetting					
Variable-Length Subnetting					

FIGURE 6.20 Applying Various Addressing Strategies

At the bottom of the hierarchy, where devices and subnets are addressed, variable-length subnetting can provide the flexibility needed to map addresses to a variety of network/device sizes. In the middle of the hierarchy, where there are functional areas and workgroups, subnetting is often sufficient. At the top end of the hierarchy, where the entire network resides (along with most external interfaces), using the natural mask for the network address or applying subnetting is usually appropriate.

The hierarchies of variable-length subnetting, both internal and external to the network, are shown in Figure 6.21.

In this figure, a hub router connects a number of workgroup routers to an ISP. This hub router can interconnect up to ten networks but is currently connected to only five. Each workgroup router should be configured to support four networks, each network having 10 to 20 devices attached to it. We have been assigned the CIDR block 192.92.240.0/20, which we are expected to summarize to the ISP router.

We can break this network into addressing areas, based on the numbers of functional areas, workgroup, networks, and devices. This will help us to choose address mask sizes that are appropriate for the scale of our network.

In this example there are three distinct areas to address. First, the workgroups have four networks with 10 to 20 devices per network. For this area, we could assign from the CIDR block a Class C per workgroup, subnetted with a mask

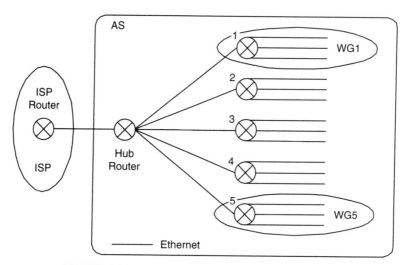

FIGURE 6.21 An Example for Variable-Length Subnetting

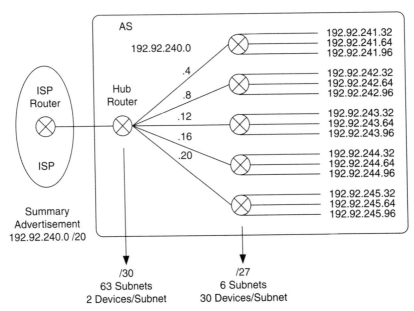

FIGURE 6.22   An Example with Variable-Length Subnetting Applied

of 255.255.255.224 (or /27), which will support up to six subnets with up to 30 devices per subnet. The next area is where the workgroup routers connect to the hub router. If addresses need to be assigned (if the routers do not support unnumbered links), we could subnet a single Class C from the CIDR block with a mask of 255.255.255.252 (or /30), supporting 63 subnets with two devices per subnet.

Since these connections are point-to-point between each workgroup router and the hub router, we only need to address two devices per connection. The third area is the connection between the hub router and the ISP router. Here we will provide the summary advertisement 192.92.240.0/20.

The result is shown in Figure 6.22.

6.6   **Routing Strategies**

This section introduces and describes popular interior and exterior routing protocols. Section 6.6.1 describes which protocols are best for which circumstances, and 6.6.2 describes how to select the appropriate ones to use within each network.

Now that we have the framework for routing developed and some addressing strategies, let's consider some strategies for applying routing protocols. This section covers the characteristics of some popular routing protocols, criteria for making selections from these protocols, and where to apply and mix these protocols.

Typically, when routing protocols are evaluated, it is on the basis of characteristics that are somewhat distant from the overall architecture, such as their convergence times; their protocol overheads, in terms of capacity (bandwidth overhead), CPU utilization, and memory utilization; and their stability. While these are important characteristics to consider, it is often difficult to relate them directly to the network architecture or design. They are, however, indirectly related to the architecture and design through two characteristics discussed several times in this book: hierarchy and diversity.

From the perspective of choosing a routing protocol, the hierarchy and diversity of the network help to determine the required complexity and features of the routing protocol. In determining the degrees of hierarchy and diversity in the network, we are indirectly applying the aforementioned characteristics to the network.

For example, convergence time for a routing protocol is directly related to the degree of diversity in the network. When used to provide redundancy, a higher degree of diversity implies a requirement for predictable or guaranteed (mission-critical) reliability. This may also be explicitly stated as a requirement from the requirements analysis. As diversity increases in importance, the routing protocol will need to converge rapidly when changes in the routing topology occur. This also indicates a need for stability in the routed network.

In distributed networks (which routed networks usually are), hierarchy tends to force decision making (e.g., routing decisions) down the tree. In the case of routing protocols, this may require an abstraction of hierarchy in the routing protocol itself, such as the area abstraction in OSPF.

We can apply degrees of hierarchy and diversity to our evaluation of routing protocols. In addition, in evaluating the routing protocols for your network, you should make sure that the network is segmented into functional areas and workgroups.

Other criteria to consider in routing protocols are the relative complexities of the protocols, or their ease of use, and the interoperability of the protocol. These criteria can be more difficult to assess subjectively, for they may be dependent on how the vendor implements the routing protocol. Some of the many trade-offs in routing protocol choices are simplicity and ease of use versus sophistication and features, and interoperability versus vendor-specific features.

Some routing protocols are relatively simple to configure and maintain. RIP, for example, is pretty much plug-and-play, as long as the network is not too large and you do not try anything complex. Easy-to-use protocols tend to have few features or options and may not scale well to high degrees of hierarchy or diversity. As routing protocols increase in features or scalability, they also become more complex, requiring greater expertise on the part of the staff who will be operating the network. The routing protocol may have some parameters that are tunable, allowing network operators to change the values of these parameters to optimize protocol performance or features. This can be a great help for networks that have extreme size, unique topology characteristics, or multi-tier performance requirements, but also requires a lot of personnel resources for monitoring and maintenance.

Interoperability is the support for OAM&P, performance, and features across multiple vendor platforms. For routing protocols, standards are the start toward interoperability. Standards are necessary, but not sufficient, for protocol interoperability. Do not assume that, when an implementation of a routing protocol supports or is based on a standard, it will interoperate with all other vendor implementations of the same protocol. To be certain of interoperability, you need to know which vendor implementations you expect to deploy in the network, and then either check to see what interoperability tests have been done (there are several test labs that perform such tests and release information to the public) or test interoperability yourself, in your own test environment.

At times it may be necessary or desirable to forsake interoperability in order to get features or performance from a particular vendor. For example, we may get a highly desirable feature with a vendor-specific routing protocol, or a degree of support from the vendor that far exceeds that with a standard protocol. However, while there are times when vendor-specific routing protocols may be considered, they should always be considered with caution. If you choose a vendor-specific (proprietary), nonstandard routing protocol, you run the risk of becoming locked into using that protocol. It may prove expensive to include or change to a standard protocol later, as the network operations staff may have to learn this new protocol, including interactions with the existing protocol. Once locked into a proprietary routing protocol, you may be forced to continue to buy and deploy that vendor's equipment, even though it may not be optimal for your network.

6.6.1 Evaluating Routing Protocols

Now we briefly examine and compare some popular IGPs and EGP: the routing information protocol (RIP and RIPv2), the open shortest-path first (OSPF) routing protocol, and the border gateway protocol version 4 (BGPv4). We also consider the limited use of static routes in the network. We do not consider any proprietary routing protocols in this book.

Static routes are routes that are configured manually, by network personnel or scripts, in network devices, and that do not change until manually deleted or modified. As such, they are not a routing protocol but are considered in this chapter because they impact the routing on a network. Many people overlook the use of static routes, yet they can be useful in some networks, primarily when a routing protocol is not needed. Some disadvantages to static routes are that they require maintenance, and they require resources on routers. This can become significant with a large number of static routes.

Routing protocols are dynamic. They learn about reachability within and between networks and update that information periodically; thus, they are needed when alternate paths exist in the network (i.e., when there is some degree of diversity). When there is only one path into or out of an area, a routing protocol cannot adapt to changes in topology. A *stub network* is a network with only one path into or out of it, as in Figure 6.23.

With stub networks, a static route can be applied between the stub network and the network it is connected to. The trade-off entailed in using static routes is not having to configure and maintain a routing protocol versus having to maintain the static routes. Since a stub network has only one path into or out of it, a default route is usually all that is needed. A static route may be used to provide this default.

Static routes can also be used to force routing along a certain path. Since a routing protocol is not used, alternate paths are not learned or used, and thus traffic is forced to use the static route. There are times when this can be useful (e.g., it

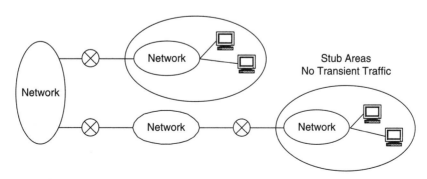

FIGURE 6.23   Stub Networks

is sometimes used to enhance security). However, it should always be used with caution.

Whenever there are multiple paths into and out of a network, then a routing protocol should be considered. Popular routing protocols, such as RIP, RIPv2, and OSPF, use either a distance-vector or link-state routing algorithm to determine reachability.

In a distance-vector routing algorithm each router maintains the "distance" (a metric to weight each hop, or connection between routers) between itself and possible destinations. A vector (or list) of these distances is computed from distance information received from other participating routers on that network. In a link-state routing algorithm each router learns about itself, its links to next-hop routers (its neighbors), and the state of each link. This information is multicasted to other participating routers, and all routers build their routing information from the sum of these multicasts. For an excellent description of routing protocol algorithms, see *Interconnections*, second edition (the full reference is listed in Section 6.1.1).

RIP and *RIPv2* are IGPs that are based on a distance-vector routing algorithm. This implies some characteristics of the dynamic behavior of RIP/RIPv2-routed networks. RIP and, to a lesser degree, RIPv2 are relatively straightforward to implement and maintain. RIP has been around for a long time (more than 30 years), having been part of the TCP/IP protocol suite shipped with most UNIX systems, and there is a lot of experience with RIP-routed networks. Given the simplicity, longevity, and experience with RIP, interoperability between various versions of RIP should not be a problem.

Due to the nature of the distance-vector routing algorithm used in RIP and RIPv2, they can be slow to converge to a new routing topology when changes occur in the network—where "slow" is on the order of minutes. They can also form routing instabilities in networks with high degrees of hierarchy or diversity, although there have been several mechanisms developed to minimize the probabilities of this happening (e.g., poison reverse, hold-down timers). For these reasons, they are not optimal for areas that have high degrees of hierarchy or diversity.

RIP/RIPv2 should be considered when there is low to medium hierarchy and diversity in the network. Degrees of hierarchy and diversity are shown in Figure 6.24.

OSPF is an IGP that is based on a link-state algorithm. Like RIP/RIPv2, the choice of routing algorithm affects the characteristics of the protocol. In the case of OSPF, the use of a link-state algorithm results in a faster convergence time when changes in the routing topology occur. Convergence times can be on the order

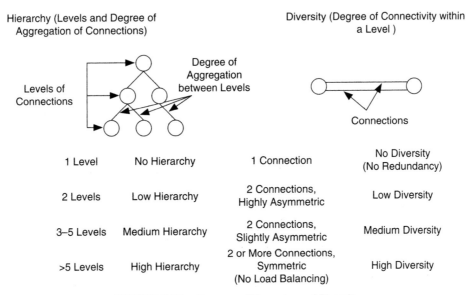

Hierarchy (Levels and Degree of
Aggregation of Connections)

Diversity (Degree of Connectivity within
a Level)

Levels of
Connections

Degree of
Aggregation
between Levels

Connections

1 Level	No Hierarchy	1 Connection	No Diversity (No Redundancy)
2 Levels	Low Hierarchy	2 Connections, Highly Asymmetric	Low Diversity
3–5 Levels	Medium Hierarchy	2 Connections, Slightly Asymmetric	Medium Diversity
>5 Levels	High Hierarchy	2 or More Connections, Symmetric (No Load Balancing)	High Diversity

FIGURE 6.24   Degrees of Hierarchy and Diversity

of seconds, one to two orders of magnitude faster than RIP/RIPv2. For an area with high hierarchy or diversity, a fast convergence time may be the single most important feature of a routing protocol and would indicate the use of OSPF.

OSPF also supports an area abstraction, which provides a hierarchy for routing information. The OSPF hierarchy connects these areas via a backbone area, and routing information is internalized within each area. This reduces the size of routing information flows across the OSPF network. In addition to the area abstraction, OSPF supports equal-cost multipath, allowing multiple paths to be used to the same destination when their OSPF costs are the same.

There are trade-offs for OSPF's rapid convergence times and area abstraction. One trade-off is in complexity. OSPF can require a substantial amount (relative to RIP) of configuration during setup, and possibly configuration tuning to reach an optimized steady-state routing topology. There is more information to understand, monitor, and use in an OSPF-routed network. This information can be helpful in isolating and troubleshooting routing problems but also requires the skills to use this information. Additionally, interoperability between various OSPF implementations is less certain than with RIP. OSPF should be considered when there is high hierarchy and diversity in the network, as shown in Figure 6.24.

BGPv4 (or *BGP*) is a path-vector-based EGP. A path-vector algorithm is similar to a distance-vector algorithm, such as that used in RIP; however, it operates on ASs or lists of ASs (paths). In addition, BGP can use policies to determine actions to be taken on paths.

BGP exchanges routing information by establishing peering connections using TCP with a user-defined list. BGP is used to enforce network transport policies for an AS, such as allowing all routes from a certain AS to use this AS as a transit route; rejecting all routes that have been learned from a certain AS; and only announcing certain routes from this AS to other peers.

The configuration of BGP depends on the complexity of your policy definitions. Once these are configured, then BGP will operate within those policies in a dynamic manner. BGP is best suited as an inter-AS (interdomain) routing protocol, although there are times when it is used within an AS.

BGP operates between ASs, yet there may be a number of routers (termed *border routers*) that connect to external networks. As such, there needs to be a mechanism for border routers from the same AS to communicate path information, so that it can be passed to multiple ASs (see Figure 6.25).

Therefore, there are two types of BGP: external BGP and internal BGP. External BGP (eBGP) is the "normal" operational mode of BGP: passing path information between ASs. Internal BGP (iBGP) is used to form tunnels between border routers within an AS, in order to pass path information across that AS. Why is this necessary? BGP communicates path information and policies, which are not (as yet) recognized by IGPs. Thus, if border routers within an AS were forced to use an IGP to communicate (e.g., OSPF), the path and policy information would be lost in translating between BGP and OSPF. Therefore, tunnels are used so that border routers do not need to translate BGP to an IGP.

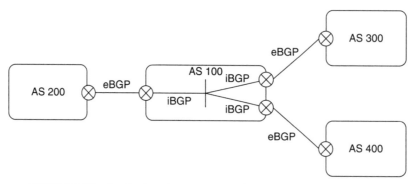

FIGURE 6.25   Application of Internal BGP (iBGP) and External BGP (eBGP)

6.6.2 Choosing and Applying Routing Protocols

This section presents some recommendations for choosing and applying routing protocols for your network. They were developed to simplify the application of routing protocols whenever possible. These recommendations are:

1. Minimize the number of routing protocols used in the network. Two should be the maximum number of protocols allowed, with only one IGP.

2. Start with the simplest routing strategy and routing mechanism/protocol.

3. As the complexity in routing and choices of routing protocols increase, reevaluate the previous decisions.

Minimizing the number of routing protocols is straightforward: don't overcomplicate the routing architecture by applying too many routing protocols. How many routing protocols are too many is based on the ability of the customers—specifically those responsible for OAM&P of the network—to support those protocols. It does not make sense to architect and design a complicated network that cannot be managed by the network staff. Many networks focus on a single IGP within their AS and an EGP for external communications. However, as we will see, there are times when multiple IGPs within an AS and even a mix of IGPs and EGP together within an AS can work, as long as the trade-offs in complexity and support are well understood.

We also want to start with the simplest routing strategy and work up to more complex strategies when necessary. The simplest strategy is to use static routes, and this would be considered first, for stub areas. If there are no stub areas in the network, or when a routing protocol is indicated, then RIP or RIPv2 should be considered. Recall that RIP or RIPv2 is recommended for low to medium hierarchy and diversity networks. When the network increases to a high degree of hierarchy and diversity, then OSPF should be considered. The approach is to apply static routes first, for stub areas, then RIP/RIPv2 when network hierarchy and diversity are low to medium, and then OSPF when network hierarchy and diversity are high. BGP is applied when an EGP is required in the network.

Since we are starting with the simplest routing mechanism (static routes) and working our way up to more complex mechanisms, we usually start with the outer edges of the network, where hierarchy and diversity are lowest, and work our way toward the center, or backbone, of the network, where hierarchy and diversity are highest (Figure 6.26).

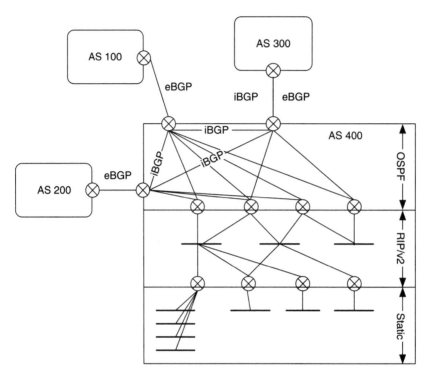

FIGURE 6.26   An Example Application of Static Routes, IGPs, and EGPs in a Network

The idea is to start simple and add a more complex routing protocol only when needed. When a more complex routing protocol is needed, however, we have to reevaluate previous choices, not just add the protocol to the network. As a result of reevaluating previous choices, we may decide to keep them and simply add the new routing protocol to the network, or we may decide to replace the previous routing protocol with the new one. The intent is to keep the number of routing protocols at a minimum, and to avoid having multiple instances of the same routing protocol in different areas of the network. With this in mind, recommendation 3 may be extended to state:

3a. When static routes have previously been chosen, and RIP/RIPv2 has been chosen as the routing protocol for another area of the network, then RIP/RIPv2 replaces static routes for those areas where static routes were chosen.

3b. When RIP/RIPv2 has previously been chosen, and OSPF has been chosen as the routing protocol for another area of the network, then OSPF replaces RIP/RIPv2 for those areas where RIP/RIPv2 was chosen.

3c. BGP, when required for a backbone network, may replace OSPF or RIP/RIPv2 if either had been previously chosen for the backbone.

While we recommend keeping the number of routing protocols in the network to a minimum, there are times when the benefits of having more than one IGP may outweigh the costs of their support and maintenance. When the network hierarchy and diversity are high enough to warrant changing the routing protocol from RIP/RIPv2 to OSPF, the areas where RIP/RIPv2 or static routes are already assigned are then reevaluated. There may be areas where OSPF is beneficial, or other areas where it does not offer any additional benefits and may increase support or maintenance costs.

There may also be times when applying BGP within the network, with either RIP/RIPv2 or OSPF, is appropriate. Applying BGP within the network may be considered when the network is so large that it should be fragmented into multiple ASs, or when the organizations within the network want administrative, management, or security autonomy. In such cases the boundary between the organizations could be treated as a hard boundary.

One thing to consider when mixing routing protocols is how information is to be translated between routing protocols. Information such as network masks, protocol metrics, policies, or AS information can easily be lost or misrepresented when translating between routing protocols. There is currently no standard metric translation between dissimilar routing protocols.

In applying routing protocols we start by evaluating the degrees of hierarchy and diversity of each functional area and considering any other factors for that functional area or features of the routing protocols that may apply. When a change is made in the choice of routing protocol, such as from static routes to RIP/RIPv2, from RIP/RIPv2 to OSPF, or from RIP/RIPv2/OSPF to BGP, we need to reevaluate functional areas where routing protocols or static routes have already been chosen. In general, RIP/RIPv2 supersedes static routes, and OSPF supersedes RIP/RIPv2. But remember that you can also consider combining the protocols within the network. Figure 6.27 illustrates the process of applying routing protocols.

Functional areas that contain only backbone networks should be considered last, as they are usually the most complex. It is therefore likely that the backbone

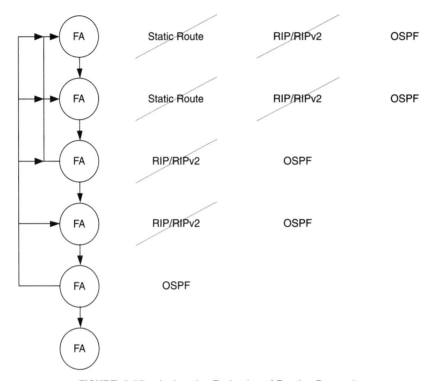

FIGURE 6.27   An Iterative Evaluation of Routing Protocols

networks will require the most complex routing protocols. This is where BGP may be considered. In general, for the backbone network:

1. If all functional areas are using the same routing protocol, that protocol should be considered first for the backbone.

2. When multiple routing protocols are chosen for the network, consider the more complex protocol for the backbone first.

3. When the backbone interconnects ASs, or when organizations require autonomy in interfacing to the backbone, consider BGP as the routing protocol for the backbone.

The decisions developed in choosing and applying routing protocols should be documented as part of the addressing and routing architecture. Showing the decisions for each area of the network, as in Figures 6.26 and 6.27, is a start toward this documentation.

6.7   Architectural Considerations

In developing our addressing and routing architecture we need to evaluate the sets of internal and external relationships for this component architecture.

6.7.1   Internal Relationships

Depending on the type of network being developed, the set of candidate addressing and forwarding mechanisms for a component architecture can be quite different. For example, a service-provider network may focus on mechanisms such as super-netting, CIDR, multicasts, peering, routing policies, and confederations, whereas the focus of a medium-sized enterprise network would more likely be on private addressing and network address translation, subnetting, VLANs, switching, and the choice and locations of routing protocols.

Two types of interactions are predominant within this component architecture: trade-offs between addressing and forwarding mechanisms, and trade-offs within addressing or within forwarding. Addressing and forwarding mechanisms influence the choice of routing protocols and where they are applied. They also form an addressing hierarchy upon which the routing hierarchy is overlaid.

An example of this is shown in Figure 6.28. This figure illustrates interactions within the addressing/forwarding architecture. Within this architecture, routing

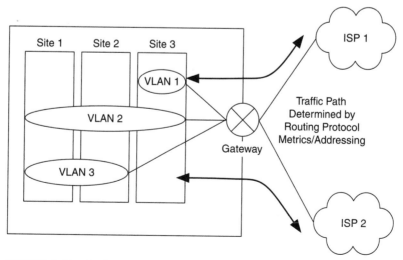

FIGURE 6.28   An Example of Interactions within Addressing/Routing Architecture

protocol selection, either by itself or in combination with VLAN addressing, determines ISP path selection.

Areas of the network where dynamic addressing, private addressing, and network address translation mechanisms are applied will impact how routing will (or will not) be provided in those areas.

6.7.2   External Relationships

External relationships are trade-offs, dependencies, and constraints between the addressing/routing architecture and each of the other component architectures (network management, performance, security, and any other component architectures you may develop). There are common external relationships between addressing/ routing and each of the other component architectures, some of which follow here.

Interactions between addressing/routing and network management. Addressing/routing can be used to configure boundaries for network management. For example, autonomous system (AS) boundaries indicate where one management domain ends and another begins.

Interactions between addressing/routing and performance. Performance can be closely coupled with addressing/routing through mechanisms such as MPLS, Differentiated and Integrated Services, and RSVP. However, when routing protocol simplicity is a high priority, performance may be decoupled from addressing/routing. Performance can also be coupled with addressing/routing through the use of IPv6, which provides information fields that can be used by performance mechanisms.

Interactions between addressing/routing and security. Security mechanisms are often intrusive as they intercept, inspect, and control network access and traffic. As such, they can impact the routing behavior of the network. Just as security perimeters or zones bound performance (from Chapter 8), they can also bound routing.

Network address translation (NAT) can be used to enhance security as well as provide private addressing space for a network. By forming a boundary between private and public address spaces, with translation of addresses between these spaces, outside access to the network can be more controlled.

Addressing and routing can impact security in three ways:

1. In terms of accessing the network from the outside (firewalls, IP hiding, and NAT)

2. In how protective measures are implemented on servers (e.g., access control lists restrict access based on IP address and subnet)

3. In their ability to trace an attack inside the perimeter

The use of dynamic addressing can create problems in tracing network events. Positioning some services (e.g., public address Web servers) outside the firewall or behind the firewall (with only http permitted through the firewall) is an important decision. Wrappers will not work if the IP address space is dynamic when you want to control access. Also, permitting only certain protocols to talk to a server from within a well-known address space is an option if the network is designed with this in mind. Lastly, properly routing hostile packets is an option with the right architecture.

6.8   Conclusions

Addressing and routing provide the basic functionality for forwarding user and network management traffic through the network. In developing the addressing/routing architecture, it is important to understand the fundamental concepts behind addressing and routing, and how they are used to provide hierarchy and diversity in the network.

This chapter provides some new ways of looking at routing, routing flows, and routing protocols. We used workgroups and functional areas to develop hard and soft boundaries for routing flows, and then applied a number of techniques to manipulate these flows. These mechanisms, combined with evaluating and choosing routing protocols for the network, as well as where to apply the various addressing strategies, provide a picture of addressing and routing for the network that will enable you to optimize the forwarding of traffic flows through your network.

6.9   Exercises

1. Represent each address below in binary format. What is the class of each address?
   a. 192.12.102.0
   b. 10.20.30.100
   c. 130.5.77.15

2. For each of the following address/prefix length pairs, give its natural mask (in dotted-decimal notation), its subnet/supernet mask (also in dotted-decimal notation), and the range of networks or subnets permitted by the mask. Also describe any problems and limitations with the address/mask pairs, if any.
   a. 129.99.0.0/16
   b. 136.178.0.0/22
   c. 198.9.9.0/28
   d. 192.92.240.0/20
   e. 192.92.243/20

3. Subnet 136.178.0.0 into 16 subnets. Show the binary and dotted-decimal forms of each subnet, as well as the subnet mask.
   Refer to Figure 6.29 for Exercises 4 through 7.

4. Where are the functional areas for this network design?

5. Where are the potential logical and physical boundaries for this network design?

6. Given the network address 129.99.0.0/16, develop a variable-length addressing scheme that best fits the design, with the following numbers of users:

AS Number	Location	Department	Users
1	Chicago Campus Building 1	Legal	120
		Accounting	370
	Chicago Campus Building 2	HQ	1580
		Engineering	200
2	Toronto	Sales	75
	Boston	Sales	110
3	Philadelphia	Operations1	2150
		Operations2	975
		Sales	575

7. You are using BGP-4 in the WAN between AS1, AS2, and AS3. Describe in plain text or as BGP-4 policy statements how you would:
   a. Permit AS3 to communicate with AS1 but not allow AS2 to communicate with AS1
   b. Allow both AS2 and AS3 Internet access through AS1 only between 6 p.m. and 6 a.m. EST each night
   Refer to RFC 1771 for specifics on the BGP-4 specification.

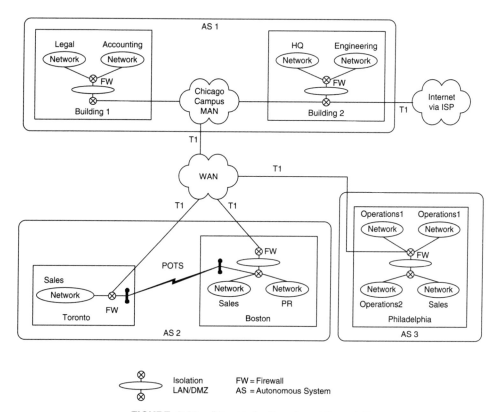

FIGURE 6.29 Diagram for Exercises 4 through 7

8. Consider the following. You are an ISP and have a group of addresses (CIDR blocks) to allocate to your customers. You have allocated addresses to a number of customers from a CIDR block of 198.9.128.0/18 (equivalent to the block of Class C addresses 198.9.128.0 through 198.9.191.0). Now one of your clients wants to stop using your ISP service and move to another ISP, while keeping the /24 that you had allocated to it (198.9.145.0/24). You are in a dilemma, as you cannot take back this address (the client's lawyers are better than yours!), yet advertising a CIDR block that contains that address seems to break the rules of CIDR routing.
   a. Show how routing based on the longest (most specific) match allows you to continue advertising this CIDR block.
   b. Show what happens to the ex-customer's traffic if there is a bug in the Internet and its route gets dropped.

9. Many network designs are requiring redundant access to the Internet, with the backup connection either in a hot-standby mode or with load balancing between

the two connections. Using BGP-4, outline a strategy for providing a backup Internet connection for the following cases:

a.   The backup Internet connection is in a hot-standby mode and can be made operational with a change in the routing configuration

b.   The backup Internet connection is fully operational, and there is load-balancing between the primary and backup connections

CHAPTER CONTENTS

Network Management Architecture

Our next component architecture is for network management. Proper network management is critical to the success of any network, and, as you will see, there are many factors to consider in providing network management.

7.1 Objectives

In this chapter you will learn about network management and the network management architecture. We discuss the various functions of network management and the mechanisms used to achieve these functions. We discuss and compare a number of variations for the network management architecture, as well as the internal and external relationships for network management.

7.1.1 Preparation

To be able to understand and apply the concepts in this chapter, you should be familiar with network management protocols (SNMP and optionally CMIP/CMOT), the utilities ping, Traceroute, and TCPdump, management information base (MIB) structures and parameters, and operations support system (OSS) functions. Some recommended sources of information include:

- *Snmp, Snmpv2, Snmpv3, and Rmon 1 and 2*, by William Stallings, Addison-Wesley, January 1999.

- *Understanding Snmp Mibs*, by David Perkins and Evan McGinnis, Prentice Hall, December 1996.

- *Simple Network Management Protocol (SNMP)*, STD 0015,[1] by J. D. Case, M. Fedor, M. L. Schoffstall, C. Davin, May 1990.

---

[1] All IETF RFCs and STDs can be found at www.ietf.org.

7.2 Background

Network management (NM) consists of the set of functions to control, plan, allocate, deploy, coordinate, and monitor network resources. Network management used to be an afterthought in many network architectures. For example, most network architectures and designs were developed without a thought about users being malicious, which was generally true up until a few years ago. Consider the changes that have recently been made in SNMP security. Today, and in the future, networks are a resource whose integrity must be measurable and verifiable.

The network management architecture, as with the other component architectures, begins with the requirements and flow analyses. Areas that should be addressed during the analysis process include:

- Which network management protocol to apply
- Implementing high-level asset management as part of the network management architecture
- Reconfiguring the network often to meet various different requirements
- The need to monitor the entire system from a single location or device
- Testing service-provider compliance with SLAs and policies
- The need for proactive monitoring (discovering performance problems before users, applications, and devices are impacted by them)
- Requirements for out-of-band access

We begin this chapter by defining and characterizing management for a network architecture, and how to plan for monitoring, configuring, and troubleshooting the planned network. We then examine network management protocols and instrumentation requirements. This will lead to considerations for developing the network management architecture.

7.3 Defining Network Management

Network management can be viewed as a structure consisting of multiple layers:

- *Business Management*: The management of the business aspects of a network—for example, the management of budgets/resources, planning, and agreements.

- *Service Management*: The management of delivery of services to users—for example, for service providers this would include the management of access bandwidth, data storage, and application delivery.
- *Network Management*: The management of all network devices across the entire network.
- *Element Management*: The management of a collection of similar network devices—for example, access routers or subscriber management systems.
- *Network-Element Management*: The management of individual network devices—for example, a single router, switch, or hub.

This structure is a top-down approach, with the most abstract component (business management) at the top of the hierarchy, and the most specified, concrete component (network-element management) at the bottom of this hierarchy. This is shown in Figure 7.1.

Correspondingly, as the components become more abstract, the ways that they are applied and measured (their information elements) change. Thus, at the bottom of this hierarchy, (network-element, element, network) management is applied with variables and parameters, while at the top of this hierarchy (service, business), management is applied in more abstract terms, using policies. This is common to all architectural components, and we will find that policies can be used for each component.

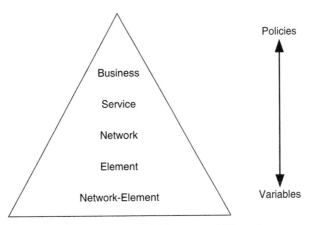

FIGURE 7.1   Network Management Hierarchy

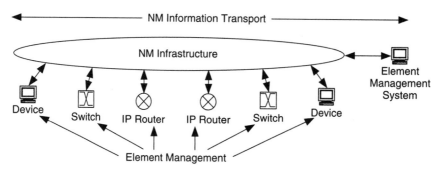

FIGURE 7.2   Network Management Is Composed of Managing Elements and Transporting Management Data

Network management can be divided into two basic functions: the transport of management information across the system, and the management of NM information elements (Figure 7.2).

These functions, as shown in Figure 7.2, consist of a variety of tasks—monitoring, configuring, troubleshooting, and planning—that are performed by users, administrators, and network personnel. One of the first challenges in developing a network management architecture is to define what network management really means to the organizations that will be performing the tasks and receiving the end services—namely, the users, or customers, of the system.

There are four categories of network management tasks that we consider here, corresponding to the four tasks mentioned above:

- Monitoring for event notification
- Monitoring for trend analysis and planning
- Configuration of network parameters
- Troubleshooting the network

7.3.1   Network Devices and Characteristics

A *network device* is an individual component of the network that participates at one or more of the protocol layers. This includes end devices, routers, switches, DSUs, hubs, and NICs. Network devices have characteristics that can be measured. They are grouped into end-to-end, per-link, per-network or per-element characteristics, as shown in Figure 7.3.

End-to-end characteristics are those that can be measured across multiple network devices in the path of one or more traffic flows, and may be extended across

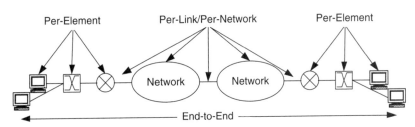

FIGURE 7.3   Network Characteristics Can Be per-Element, per-Link, per-Network, or End-to-End

the entire network or between devices. Examples of end-to-end characteristics for network devices are availability, capacity, delay, delay variation (jitter), throughput, error rates, and network utilization. These characteristics may be modified or added to, depending on the types of traffic on the network.

Per-link/per-network and per-element characteristics are those that are specific to the type of element or connection between elements being monitored. These characteristics may be used individually, or may be combined to form an end-to-end characteristic. Examples of per-link characteristics are propagation delay and link utilization, while examples of per-element characteristics include (for an IP router) IP forwarding rates (e.g., in IP packets/second), buffer utilization for the router, and any logs of authentication failures.

Management of network devices and networks includes network planning (e.g., cell site planning for wireless), initial resource allocation (e.g., frequency or bandwidth allocations), and FCAPS from the telecommunication network management model: fault, configuration, accounting, performance, and security management.

7.4 Network Management Mechanisms

We now take a look at some of the popular management mechanisms, including network management protocols. There are currently two major network management protocols: the simple network management protocol (SNMP) and the common management information protocol (CMIP). CMIP includes CMIP over TCP/IP (CMOT). These network management protocols provide the mechanism for retrieving, changing, and transport of network management data across the network.

SNMP has seen widespread use and forms the basis for many popular commercial and public network management systems. It provides facilities for collecting and configuring parameters from network devices. These are done through the SNMP commands *get* (to collect the value of a parameter), *get-next* (to collect the value of the next parameter in the list), and *set* (to change the value of a parameter). There are also provisions for the unsolicited notification of events, through the use of traps. A *trap* is a user-configurable threshold for a parameter. When this threshold is crossed, the values for one or more parameters are sent to a specified location. A benefit of trap generation is that polling for certain parameters can be stopped or the polling interval lengthened, and instead an automatic notice is sent to the management system when an event occurs.

Parameters that are accessible via SNMP are grouped into management information bases, or MIBs. Parameters can be part of *the* standard MIB (MIB-II), other standard MIBs (typically based on a type of network device, technology, or protocol), remote monitoring MIBs, or enterprise-specific MIBs, which have parameters specific to a particular vendor's product.

SNMP version 3 (SNMPv3) builds on the previous versions of SNMP, providing more secure authentication, the ability to retrieve blocks of parameters, and trap generation for most parameters. When SNMP is mentioned in this book, it refers to SNMPv3 unless otherwise noted.

CMIP/CMOT provides for parameter collection and setting, as with SNMP, but also allows for more types of operations. Many CMIP/CMOT features, such as globally unique object naming, object classification, alarm reporting, audit trails, and test management, can also be provided by SNMP by creating new MIBs and tools to support such abstractions.

In general, SNMP is simpler to configure and use than CMIP/CMOT, helping to make it widely accepted. It is usually easier to instrument network devices with SNMP. SNMP is used in monitoring, instrumentation, and configuration mechanisms, all of which are discussed below.

7.4.1 Monitoring Mechanisms

Monitoring is obtaining values for end-to-end, per-link, and per-element characteristics. The monitoring process involves collecting data about the desired characteristics, processing some or all of this data, displaying the (processed) data, and archiving a subset of this data.

Data are usually collected through a polling (actively probing network devices for management data) or monitoring process involving a network management protocol (e.g., SNMP) or proxy service. As we see later in this chapter, several techniques may be used to get this data as well as to ensure that the data are current and valid. When the data are gathered, they may or may not reflect the characteristics we wish to monitor. Values for some characteristics may have to be derived from the gathered data, while other values may be modified (e.g., added, subtracted, time-averaged). This is processing of the data.

Sets of raw (unprocessed) and processed data will need to be displayed. There are different types of displays you may use, including standard monitor displays, field-of-view or wide-screen displays, and special-purpose displays. Along with choosing displays you will also want to consider how the data will be shown to the user, administrator, or manager. There are several techniques to display data, such as logs and textual displays, graphs and charts (both static and moving), and alarms. Some data may be abstracted by symbols, such as showing parts of the network as a cloud.

At some time during this process some or all of the data are saved to a (semi-) permanent media or system. This part of the process may have multiple steps, including *primary storage*, the staging of data for short periods of time, which could be at the network management server; *secondary storage*, the aggregation of data from multiple primary storage sites, at a storage server for the network; and *tertiary storage*, which is usually the most permanent—and slowest—storage within the network. Secondary and tertiary storage are often termed *storage archives*. Figure 7.4 shows each part of this process occurring on a separate device, but they may all be combined on a single device.

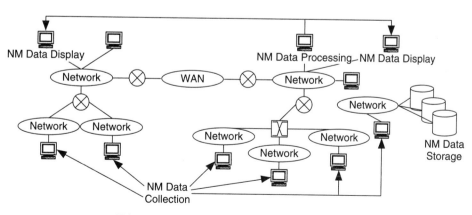

FIGURE 7.4   Elements of the Monitoring Process

Monitoring for Event Notification

An *event* is something that occurs in the network that is noteworthy. This may be a problem or failure in a network device, across the network, or when a characteristic crosses a threshold value. It may only be something that is informational to the user, administrator, or manager, such as notification of an upgrade. Events may be noted in a log file, on a display, or by issuing an alarm, depending on the priority level of the event. Events are similar to transients, which are short-lived changes in the behavior of the network. Thresholds or boundaries may be set on end-to-end, per-link, or per-element characteristics for short-term or immediate notification of events and transients. This is termed here *real-time analysis*.

Figure 7.5 shows an example of such monitoring. Ping is used to gather round-trip delay information, which is presented as a chart on the monitoring system. A threshold of 100 ms has been chosen for this display. When this threshold is crossed, it triggers an alarm to notify the network manager that a problem may exist in the network.

Real-time analysis usually requires short *polling intervals* (time periods between active probing of the network and network devices for management data), and there is a trade-off between the number of characteristics and network devices polled for real-time analysis versus the amount of resources (capacity, CPU, memory, storage) needed to support such analysis.

In some cases the amount of network data generated (and the resulting traffic) by the periodic polling of multiple characteristics on many network devices can

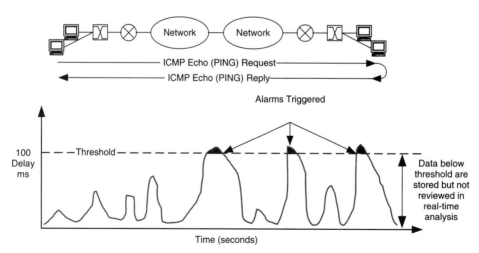

FIGURE 7.5   Monitoring for Event Notification

impact the overall performance of the network. For example, consider a network that has 100 network devices, where each element has an average of four interfaces and each interface is monitored for eight characteristics. This would add up to

(100 network devices)*(4 interfaces/network device)*(8 characteristics/interface)

= 3200 characteristics

If each of the 3200 characteristics generates an average of 8 bytes of data and an estimated 60 bytes of protocol overhead, the amount of data generated per polling session would be

(3200 characteristics)*(8 bytes + 60 bytes)

= 217.6 KB of traffic, or 1.74 Mb of traffic

If we plan to poll with a polling interval of 5 seconds, at best this 1.74 Mb of traffic would be spread out over the 5 seconds, or 384 Kb/second. It is more likely, however, that most of the data will arrive shortly after the polls are generated, so the traffic may be more like a spike of 1.74 Mb for the second after the polls occur.

For a period of one day, the total amount of traffic will be

(1.75 Mb/polling interval)*(720 polling intervals/hour)*(24 hours/day)

= 30.2 Gb of traffic

And the amount of data stored would be

(3200 characteristics/polling interval)*(8 bytes)*(720 polling intervals/day)*

(24 hours/day) = 442 MB data stored per day

Over the course of a year, this would add up to over 161 GB of data. And this is a conservative estimate for mid-range enterprise environment.

Monitoring for Trend Analysis and Planning

The same end-to-end, per-link, and per-element characteristics used for event monitoring can also be put to work in trend analysis. *Trend analysis* utilizes network management data to determine long-term network behaviors or trends. This is helpful in planning for future network growth.

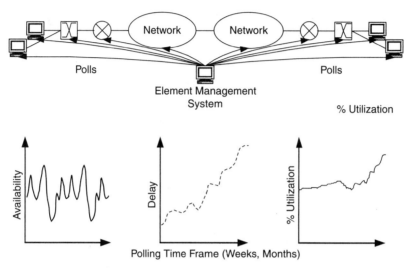

FIGURE 7.6   Monitoring for Metrics and Planning

In doing continuous, uninterrupted data collection, usually with long polling intervals (minutes or hours instead of seconds), we can begin by establishing baselines for trends, and then use these baselines to plot trend behavior. This is shown in Figure 7.6. This figure shows long-term trends for availability, delay, and percent of utilization. Polls for each characteristic are saved to network management on a regular basis, and over a long period of time (usually weeks or months, but sometimes up to years) trends in these characteristics begin to emerge. In Figure 7.6, upward trends are clearly visible for delay and percent of utilization.

7.4.2   Instrumentation Mechanisms

Instrumentation is the set of tools and utilities needed to monitor and probe the network for management data. Instrumentation mechanisms include access to network management data via SNMP, monitoring tools, and direct access. Instrumentation can be coupled with monitoring, display, processing. and storage to form a complete management system.

SNMP (currently in version 3) provides access to management information base (MIB) variables, including those in MIB-II, other standard MIBs (e.g., DS1 MIB), enterprise-specific MIBs, and other monitoring MIBs (remote monitoring (RMON), and switch monitoring (SMON). SNMP is the most common method for accessing network management data. There are several commercially available and publicly available monitoring software packages available that use SNMP for data access.

Monitoring tools include utilities such as ping, Traceroute, and TCPdump, while direct-access mechanisms include telnet, FTP, TFTP, and connections via a console port.

An example of a base set of parameters to monitor can be developed from the standard MIB-II. The following parameters can be collected on a per-interface basis:

ifInOctets	Number of bytes received
ifOutOctets	Number of bytes sent
ifInUcastPkts	Number of unicast packets received
ifOutUcastPkts	Number of unicast packets sent
ifInNUcastPkts	Number of multicast/broadcast packets received
ifOutNUcastPkts	Number of multicast/broadcast packets sent
ifInErrors	Number of errored packets received
ifOutErrors	Number of packets that could not be sent

These parameters can be used for both short-term event monitoring and long-term trend analysis of throughput and error rates. In addition, the following parameter may be collected to determine availability:

ifOperStatus   State of an interface (up, down, testing)

This parameter could be used in conjunction with monitoring tools such as ping to verify availability.

In developing the network management architecture, the instrumentation requirements for each type or class of network device, such as forwarding elements (e.g., routers, switches, hubs), pass-through elements (e.g., DSUs, simple concentrators, simple bridges), and passive devices such as those that use RMON, should be collected.

A consideration for the network management architecture is to ensure that the instrumentation is accurate, dependable, and simple. There are a couple of ways to ensure accuracy in the instrumentation: testing and taking alternate measurements. If a lab environment is available, some limited network conditions can be replicated and tested. For example, generating known quantities of traffic by devices and/or traffic generators and comparing the results in the routers with those from the devices/traffic generators can test packet-forwarding rates in routers.

Sometimes parameters can be verified from the current network. Taking alternate measurements of the same parameter at different points in the network is one way to verify parameters. We may be able to get link-layer data from DSUs, routers, and switches in the path of a flow, and, by comparing the various sources of data, determine if and where there are discrepancies in parameter measurements.

For a network management system to work properly, the instrumentation needs to be dependable. A network management system is useless if it is the first thing to crash when network problems occur. This may seem obvious, but few current management systems are truly robust and dependable. Ways that dependability can be enhanced in the architecture include physically separating and replicating the management components. By having multiple systems collecting, processing, displaying, and storing management data for different parts of the network, and by building hierarchy in the management data flows, the loss of any single component of the management system will have less impact on the network's manageability. This is covered in more detail later in this chapter.

7.4.3   Configuration Mechanisms

Configuration is setting parameters in a network device for operation and control of that element. Configuration mechanisms include direct access to devices, remote access to devices, and downloading configuration files (Figure 7.7):

- SNMP *set* commands

- Telnet and command line interface (CLI) access

- Access via HTTP

- Access via common object request broker architecture (CORBA)

- Use of FTP/TFTP to download configuration files

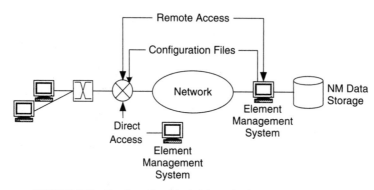

FIGURE 7.7   Configuration Mechanisms for Network Management

As part of this process, we want to generate a working set of end-to-end, per-link, and per-element characteristics, and plan for the architecture and design to have the facilities to monitor these characteristics at short- and long-term polling intervals. Later in this chapter we develop some guidelines on where monitoring facilities should be placed in the network.

Many network devices require some degree of configuration by network personnel. For each type or class of network device (e.g., Brand X router, Ethernet switch, etc.), we want to generate a table of configuration parameters, establish the methods for configuring these parameters, and understand the effects of changing each parameter (when possible). In order to properly manage a network, it is important to understand how configuration parameters affect each network device.

We also need to understand the effects of problems with network devices and how to correct such problems. Troubleshooting, which consists of problem notification, isolation, identification, and resolution, can be aided by knowing likely failure modes in the network, their effects, and any possible steps to correct them.

It should be noted that, in generating a set of working characteristics, configuration parameters, and failure modes, we are going through a detailed review of how the network will operate. The result is that you will better understand what will happen in the network.

7.5 Architectural Considerations

The network management process consists of choosing which characteristics of each type of network device to monitor/manage; instrumenting the network devices (or adding collection devices) to collect all necessary data; processing these data for viewing, storage, and/or reporting; displaying a subset of the results; and storing or archiving some subset of the data.

Network management touches all other aspects of the network. This is captured in the FCAPS model:

- Fault management
- Configuration management
- Accounting management
- Performance management
- Security management

In this model, fault management consists of processing events and alarms (where an *alarm* is an event that triggers a real-time notification to network personnel); problem identification, isolation, troubleshooting, and resolution; and returning the network to an operational state.

Configuration management consists of setting system parameters for turn-up; provisioning the network; configuration and system backups and restores; and developing and operating system databases.

Accounting management consists of monitoring and managing subscriber service usage, and service billing.

Performance management consists of implementing performance controls, based on the IP services architecture; collecting network and system performance data; analyzing this performance data; generating short- and long-term reports from this data; and controlling network and system performance parameters.

Finally, security management consists of implementing security controls, based on the security architecture; collecting and analyzing security data; and generating security reports and logs from this data.

The network management process and management model both provide input to the network management architecture. With the knowledge of what network management means for our network, we can consider the following in the architecture:

- In-band and out-of-band management
- Centralized, distributed, and hierarchical management
- Scaling network management traffic
- Checks and balances
- Managing network management data
- MIB selection
- Integration into OSS

7.5.1 In-Band and Out-of-Band Management

In-band management occurs when the traffic flows for network management follow the same network paths as the traffic flows for users and their applications. This simplifies the network management architecture, in that the same network paths can be used for both types of data, and a separate path (and possibly network) is not required (Figure 7.8).

A trade-off with in-band management is that management data flows can be impacted by the same problems that impact user traffic flows. Since part of network

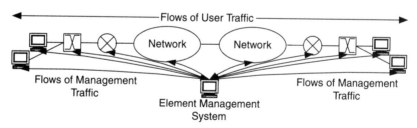

FIGURE 7.8   Traffic Flows for In-Band Management

management is troubleshooting problems in the network, this function is negatively impacted if the management data flows are delayed or blocked. So when network management is most needed, it may not be available. Also, a primary objective of the network management architecture is to be able to do event monitoring when the network is under stress—for example, when congested with traffic, suffering from network hardware/software configuration problems, or under a security attack.

Out-of-band management occurs when different paths are provided for network management data flows and user traffic flows. This type of management has the distinct advantage of allowing the management system to continue to monitor the network during most network events, even when such events disable the network. This allows you to effectively see into portions of the network that are unreachable through normal paths (i.e., user data flow paths).

Out-of-band management is usually provided via a separate network, such as frame relay or plain old telephone service (POTS) connections. Figure 7.9 illustrates

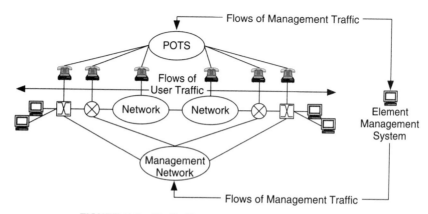

FIGURE 7.9   Traffic Flows for Out-of-Band Management

this point. An advantage of having a separate network is that additional security features can be integrated into this (network management) network. Since this network provides access to most or all network devices, having additional security here is important. Another advantage is that the out-of-band connection can be used to troubleshoot and configure network devices that are in remote locations. This saves time and resources when the user data network is down and remote network devices need to be accessed.

Whenever out-of-band management is planned, a method to check and verify its availability is needed. This can be as simple as planning to use out-of-band management on a regular basis, regardless of need. This will help to ensure that problems with out-of-band management are detected and solved while the network is still healthy.

A trade-off with out-of-band management is the added expense and complexity of a separate network for network management. One way to reduce the expense is to provide out-of-band monitoring at a low level of performance, relative to the user data network. For example, out-of-band monitoring may be achieved using phone lines. While this may be less expensive than providing dedicated network connections, it does require time to set up (e.g., call) the out-of-band connections, and the capacity of each connection may be limited.

For some networks a combination of in-band and out-of-band management is optimal (Figure 7.10). Usually this is done when the performance of the user data network is needed to support network management data flows (for monitoring the operational network), but the separate, out-of-band network is needed when the user data network is down.

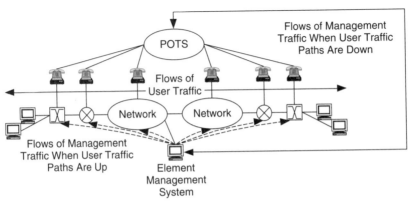

FIGURE 7.10   A Combination of In-Band and Out-of-Band Management Traffic Flows

Some trade-offs of combining in-band and out-of-band management are that the expense of a separate network is still incurred, and security issues on the user data network still need to be addressed.

7.5.2 Centralized, Distributed, and Hierarchical Management

Centralized management occurs when all management data (e.g., pings, SNMP polls/responses, Traceroute, etc.) radiate from a single (typically large) management system. The flows of management data then behave like the client–server flows discussed in Chapter 4 and shown in Figure 7.8.

The obvious advantage to centralized management is that only one management system is needed, simplifying the architecture and reducing costs (depending on the choice of management system). In centralized management the management system often has a variety of management tools associated with it.

Some trade-offs to centralized management are that the management system is a single point of failure, and that all management flows converge at the network interface of the management system, potentially causing congestion or failure.

Distributed management occurs when there are multiple separate components to the management system, and these components are strategically placed across the network, localizing network management traffic and distributing management domains. In Figure 7.11 multiple local element management systems are used to distribute management functions across several domains.

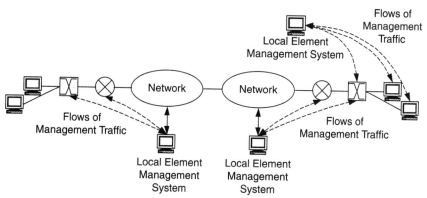

FIGURE 7.11   Distributed Management Where Each Local EMS Has Its Own Management Domain

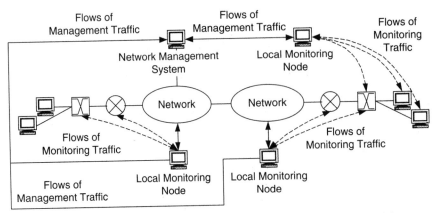

FIGURE 7.12 Distributed Management Where Monitoring Is Distributed

In distributed management the components either provide all management functions (monitoring, display, storage, and processing) or the distributed components are the monitoring devices. For example, distributed management may take the form of having multiple management systems on the network (e.g., one management system per campus or per management domain, as shown in Figure 7.11), or a single management system with several monitoring nodes, as in Figure 7.12.

Advantages to distributed management are that the monitoring devices act to localize the data collection, reducing the amounts of management data that transit the network. They may also provide redundant monitoring, so that other monitoring devices on that network can cover the loss of any single monitoring device. A trade-off with distributed management is that costs increase with the number of monitoring devices or management systems needed.

Hierarchical management occurs when the management functions (monitoring, display, storage, and processing) are separated and placed on separate devices. Management is hierarchical in that, when the functions are separated, they can be considered layers that communicate in a hierarchical client–server fashion. (See Chapter 4 for a discussion on hierarchical client–server flows.) Figure 7.13 shows the structure of a hierarchical management system.

In hierarchical management, localized monitoring devices collect management data and pass these data either directly to display and storage devices or to monitoring devices to be processed. When the management data are passed on to display and storage devices without processing, the monitoring devices act as they did in distributed management, localizing the data collection and reducing the amounts of management data that transit the network.

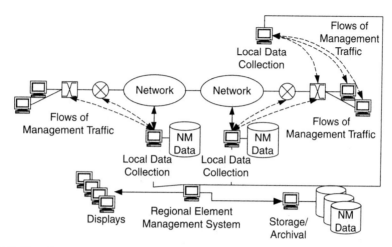

FIGURE 7.13   Hierarchical Management Separates Management into Distinct Functions That Are Distributed across Multiple Platforms

When the management data are processed before being sent to display and storage devices, then the monitoring devices act as local filters, sending only the relevant data (such as deltas on counter values or updates on events). This can substantially reduce the amount of management data in the network, which is especially important if the monitoring is in-band.

Thus, we can have monitoring devices at strategic locations throughout the network, polling local devices and network devices, collecting and processing the management data, and forwarding some or all of these data to display and storage devices. The numbers and locations of each type of device will depend on the size of the network, the amount of management data expected to be collected (discussed later in this chapter), and where the displays and storage devices are to be located in the network management architecture.

An advantage to hierarchical management is that every component can be made redundant, independent of the other components. Thus, it can be tailored to the specific needs of your network. In some networks it may be preferable to have several display devices, in other networks several processing devices or storage devices. Since these components are separate, the numbers of each can be individually determined.

A trade-off in hierarchical management is the cost, complexity, and overhead of having several management components on the network.

7.5.3 Scaling Network Management Traffic

Some recommendations are presented here to help determine and optimize the capacity requirements of network management traffic.

Recommendation 1. For a LAN environment, start with one monitoring device per IP subnet. For each subnet, estimate values for the following traffic variables:

- The number of devices and network devices to be polled
- An average number of interfaces per device
- The number of parameters to be collected
- The frequency of polling (polling interval)

Combining these variables gives you an estimate of the average data rate for management traffic per subnet. If this rate is greater than approximately 10% of the capacity (line rate) of the LAN, you may want to consider reducing the amount of management traffic generated, by reducing one or more of the above variables. When the estimated average rate is less than 1% of LAN capacity, this indicates that it may be possible to increase one or more of the above variables.

For most of the standard LAN technologies (Ethernet, Fast Ethernet, Gigabit Ethernet, Token Ring, FDDI), the management traffic rate should be targeted at 2% to 5% of the LAN capacity. As LAN capacity increases, you will have more available capacity for network management traffic and may choose to increase one or more traffic variables (Figure 7.14).

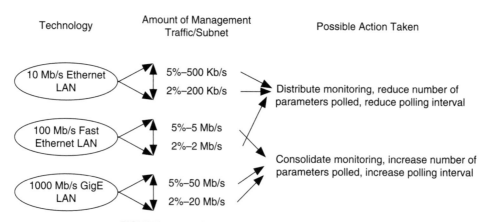

FIGURE 7.14 Scaling Network Management Traffic

Recommendation 2. For a WAN environment, start with one monitoring device per each WAN–LAN interface. This is in addition to any monitoring devices indicated in Recommendation 1. However, if a monitoring device is on a LAN subnet that is also the WAN–LAN interface, that device may be used to collect data for both the LAN and WAN. Placing a monitoring device at each WAN–LAN interface allows us to monitor the network at each location, as well as to measure, verify, and possibly guarantee services and performance requirements across the WAN.

7.5.4 Checks and Balances

Checks and balances are methods to duplicate measurements in order to verify and validate network management data. Although implementing checks and balances adds effort to the network management process, it is advisable to have more than one method for collection network management data, particularly for data considered vital to the proper operation of the network. SNMP agent and MIB implementations are vendor-implementation-specific and are not guaranteed to provide data that are consistent across all vendors.

Objectives of performing checks and balances are to locate and identify:

* Errors in recording or presenting network management data
* Rollovers of counters (e.g., returning a counter value to zero without proper notification)
* Changes in MIB variables from one software version to another

In addition, checks and balances help to normalize network management data across multiple vendors, by verifying data through measurements from multiple sources.

Collected management data should be verified for accuracy. For example, when polling for SNMP variables for an interface, consider RMON polling as well to verify this data. Consider using a traffic analyzer to verify data for various random periods of time. You may also run independent tests with traffic generators, the vendors' network devices, and data collection devices, to verify the accuracy of collected data.

7.5.5 Managing Network Management Data

Flows of network management data typically consist of SNMP parameter names and values, and the results of queries from utilities such as ping or Traceroute. These data are generated by network devices and other devices on the network, transported via SNMP to monitoring devices, and possibly forwarded to display and storage devices. It is important to the network management architecture that we understand where and how the data are generated, transported, and processed, as this will help us to determine where network management components may be placed in the network.

Management data may be generated either in a query/response (stateless) method, as with SNMP or ping queries, or in response to a prearranged set of conditions (stateful), as with SNMP traps. Large numbers of SNMP queries should be spread out over a time interval (e.g., polling interval), not only to avoid network congestion, but also to avoid over-burdening network devices and monitoring devices with the processing required to generate management data.

Management data consist of frequently generated parameters for real-time event notification and less frequently generated (or needed) parameters for trend analysis and planning. It may be that the same parameters are used for both purposes. Since frequent polling can generate large amounts of data, storage of this data can become a problem. Some recommendations for managing these data are presented below.

Recommendation 1: Local storage versus archival. Determine which management data are necessary to keep stored locally and which data may be archived. Management data are usually kept locally, cached where they can be easily and quickly retrieved, for event analysis and short-term (on the order of hours or days) trend analysis. Management data that are not being used for these purposes should be archived to secondary or tertiary storage, such as tape archives or off-site storage (Figure 7.15).

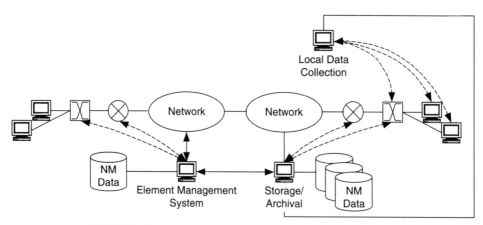

FIGURE 7.15   Local and Archival Storage for Management Data

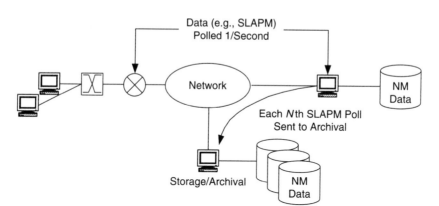

FIGURE 7.16   Selective Copying to a Separate Database

Recommendation 2: Selective copying of data. When a management parameter is being used for both event notification and trend analysis, consider copying every Nth iteration of that parameter to a separate database location, where the iteration size N is large enough to keep the size of these data relatively small, yet is small enough so that the data are useful in trend analysis. In Figure 7.16 SLA variables are polled regularly (each variable polled per second), while every Nth poll is saved in long-term storage (archival). Depending on the bandwidth and storage available for network management traffic, N can range from 10^2 to 10^5.

A trade-off in selective copying of data is that whenever data are copied, there is a risk that some data may be lost. To help protect against this you can use TCP for data transmission or send copies of data to multiple archival systems (e.g., one primary and one redundant).

If there are indications that more immediate analysis needs to be done, then either a short-term trend analysis can be performed on the locally stored data (from Recommendation 1), or the iteration size N can be temporarily shortened.

Recommendation 3: Data migration. When collecting management data for trend analysis, data can be stored local to the management device and then downloaded to storage/archival when traffic is expected to be low (e.g., at night). In Figure 7.17 polls of network management data are made in five-minute intervals and stored locally. These data are then downloaded to archival storage once or twice daily, usually when there is little user traffic on the network (e.g., at 2 a.m.).

Recommendation 4: Metadata. Metadata is additional information about the collected data, such as references to the data types, time stamps of when the data were generated, and any indications that these data references any other data.

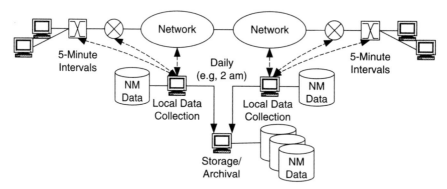

FIGURE 7.17   Data Migration

A management data-archival system should provide such additional information regarding the data that have been collected.

7.5.6   MIB Selection

MIB selection means determining which SNMP MIBs to use and apply as well as which variables in each MIB are appropriate for your network. This may, for example, be a full MIB (e.g., MIB-II is commonly used in its entirety), a subset of each MIB required for conformance to that MIB's specification (also known as *a conformance subset* of the MIB),[2] enterprise-specific MIBs (the parameters available from each vendor-element or network-element type), or possibly a subset of MIB parameters that you define to apply to your network.

For example, a subset of performance monitoring parameters can be used from the Interfaces MIB (RFC 2863): ifInOctets, ifInErrors, ifInUcastPkts, ifOutOctets, ifOutErrors, and ifOutUcastPkts. This set of six parameters is a common starting point for MIB parameters. These parameters can usually be measured on all interfaces for most network devices.

One can consider MIB variables falling into the following sets: a common set that pertains to network health, and a set that is necessary to monitor and manage those things that the network needs to support, including:

- Server, user device, and network parameters
- Network parameters that are part of SLAs, policies, and network reconfiguration

---

[2] Conformance subsets of MIBs are usually listed at the end of each MIB's specification (RFC).

7.5.7 Integration into OSS

When the network includes an interface to an operations support system (OSS), the network management architecture must consider how management is to be integrated with the OSS. The interface from network management to OSS is often termed the *northbound interface*, as it is in the direction of service and business management (see Section 7.3). This northbound interface is typically CORBA or SNMP (Figure 7.18).

7.5.8 Internal Relationships

Internal relationships for the network management architecture comprise the interactions, dependencies, trade-offs, and constraints between network management mechanisms. It is important to understand these relationships, as they are part of a complex, nonlinear system and they define and describe the behavior of this architecture.

Interactions

Interactions within network management may include interactions among components of the management system; between the network management system and network devices; and between the network management system and the OSS.

If there are multiple network management systems, or if the network management system is distributed or hierarchical, then there will be multiple components

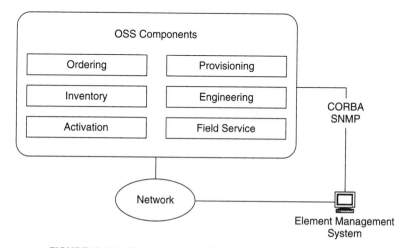

FIGURE 7.18 The Integration of Network Management with OSS

to the management system. The network architecture should include the potential locations for each component and/or management system, as well as the management data flows between components and/or management systems. The interactions here may be in the form of SNMP or CMIP/CMOT queries/responses, CORBA, HTTP, file transfers, or a proprietary protocol.

Part of network management inheres in each managed network device, in the form of management data (e.g., MIB variables) and software that allows access and transport of management data to and from the management system (e.g., SNMP agent software). Therefore, interactions between network management components (particularly monitoring devices) and managed network devices can also be considered here. We may choose to consider all of the managed network devices, depending on how many of them are expected in the network; however, we usually do not consider all managed devices in the network, as there can be quite a large number of them. As we discussed in flow analysis (Chapter 5), the devices that are most likely to be considered are those that interact with several users, such as servers and specialized equipment. Interactions here are likely to be in the form of SNMP or CMIP/CMOT queries/responses.

If your environment includes an OSS, there will likely be some interactions between network management and the OSS, for flow-through provisioning, service management, and inventory control. The network management architecture should note where the OSS would be located, which components of the network management system will interact with the OSS, and where they will be located in the network. Interactions here are likely to use CORBA, but may use SNMP or HTTP (see dependencies below).

Dependencies

Dependencies within network management may include dependencies on capacity and reliability of the network for management data flows; dependence on the amount of data storage available for management data; and dependence on the OSS for the northbound interface requirement.

Network management may be dependent on the performance of the underlying network for support of management data flows. In its most basic sense, the network must provide sufficient capacity for the estimated amount of management data. This estimate can be derived using the information we discuss in Section 10.5 (on network layout). This is particularly important when network management is centralized and all management data will be aggregated at the network management system interface. This may also be a dependency on IP services, discussed later in this section.

The amount of management data that can be stored is partly a function of how much storage will be available; thus, network management can be dependent on data storage availability.

While network management may interface with an OSS, it may also be dependent on that OSS to determine the northbound interface. For example, some OSSs require CORBA for their interface, which will have to be supported by network management. This may also be considered a constraint on network management.

Trade-Offs

Trade-offs within network management may include trade-offs between in-band and out-of-band management; and trade-offs among centralized, distributed, and hierarchical management. Trade-offs between in-band and out-of-band management include the following:

- In-band management is cheaper and simpler to implement than out-of-band management; however, when management data flows are in-band, they can be impacted by the same problems that impact user traffic flows.

- Out-of-band management is more expensive and complex to implement than in-band management (since it requires separate network connections); however, it can allow the management system to continue to monitor the network during most network events, even when such events disable the network. In addition, out-of-band management allows access to remote network devices for troubleshooting and configuration, saving the time and effort of having to be physically present at the remote location.

- Out-of-band management, by definition, requires separate network connections. This may be a benefit, in that security for the separate network can be focused on the requirements of management data flows, or it may be a liability, in that additional security (with its associated expense and overhead) is required for this network.

- When in-band and out-of-band management are combined, there is still the expense and complexity of out-of-band management, as well as the additional security requirements. However, the combination allows (typically) higher-performance in-band management to be used for monitoring (which is the high-capacity portion of network management), yet still allows out-of-band management to be used at critical times (e.g., when the user data network [including in-band paths] is down).

Trade-offs among centralized, distributed, and hierarchical management include the following:

• In centralized management only one management system is needed (all management components, as well as other tools, are on one hardware platform), simplifying the architecture and reducing costs (depending on the choice of management system) over distributed or hierarchical management systems, which may have several separate components. However, centralized management can act as a single point of failure; all management data flows are aggregated at the management system's network interface, potentially causing congestion or failure. Distributed or hierarchical management can avoid central points of failure and reduce congestion points.

• The degrees of distribution or hierarchy in management are a function of how complex and costly you are willing to allow the management system to become, and how important it is to isolate management domains and provide redundant monitoring. Costs for distributed or hierarchical management increase with the number of monitoring devices or management systems needed. However, if you are willing to accept high management costs, you can provide a fully redundant, highly flexible hierarchical management system for your network.

Constraints

Constraints include the northbound interface from network management to the OSS. This interface may be constrained by the interface requirement of the OSS. Since the OSS potentially ties together several service and business components, its interface requirements may be forced onto network management. CORBA is often required for this northbound interface.

7.5.9 External Relationships

External relationships comprise trade-offs, dependencies, and constraints between the network management architecture and each of the other component architectures (addressing/routing, performance, security, and any other component architectures you may develop). Network management should be a part of all the other architectural components as they will need some or all of the monitoring, control, and configuration capabilities that network management provides. As such, each of the other components will interact at some level with network management.

There are common external relationships between network management and each of the other component architectures, some of which are presented below.

Interactions between network management and addressing/routing. Network management depends on the addressing/routing architecture for the proper routing of management data flows through the network. If the management is in-band, then the routing of management data flows should be handled in the same fashion as the user traffic flows and does not require any special treatment in the architecture. However, if the management is out-of-band, then the routing of management data flows may need to be considered in the architecture.

Network management is often bounded by the network or networks that are under common management. A *management domain* is used to describe a set of networks under common management; *autonomous system* is another term often used. Thus, the routing and addressing architecture may define the management domain for the network, setting the boundaries for network management.

If the management is out-of-band, the separate management network may require routing and addressing as part of the architecture.

Interactions between network management and performance. Network management interacts with the performance architecture through the collection of network performance data as it seeks to verify the proper operation of performance mechanisms. This may occur through a northbound interface (described earlier) to OSS or to a policy database for performance. Performance also depends on network management to provide data on the performance and function of the network.

A trade-off between network management and performance comes in how much network resources (e.g., capacity) network management requires, as this may impact the network's ability to support various performance levels. This is particularly true when management is centralized, as management data flows in centralized management are aggregated at the management system's network interface.

Network management can depend on performance in two ways: first, when performance mechanisms support best-effort traffic (as determined in the flow specification), part of this best-effort traffic can be allocated to network management data flows; second, if a higher-priority service is desired for network management data flows, then network management will be dependent on performance mechanisms to provide the necessary support for such services. When network management data flows require high-priority service, network management may be dependent on performance mechanisms to function properly.

Interactions between network management and security. Network management is dependent on some level of security in order to be used in most operational environments. This may be security at the protocol level (e.g., SNMP security) and/or for securing access to network devices. If the management is out-of-band, the separate network that supports this management must be secured.

Network management may be constrained by security, if the security mechanisms used do not permit network management data or access across the security perimeter. This may also be considered a trade-off, when it is possible to reduce the level of security in order to support access or management data transport across the security perimeter. For example, consider the use of POTS for out-of-band access. Such dial-in access is unacceptable to many organizations, unless extra security measures are taken on each access line (e.g., dial-back, security keys, etc.).

7.6   Conclusions

While network management can appear to be a simple function, it is actually a complex set of functions with interesting architectural features. In this chapter we decomposed network management into monitoring, instrumentation, and management, and explored how each of these can be achieved within the network management architecture.

The essence of the network management architecture is in understanding what you want to monitor and manage, determining where you want to locate each network management function, and managing the flows of network management traffic. Depending on the characteristics of the network you are developing, you have a wide range of architectural solutions, from a simple, single-platform system with preconfigured monitoring and management capabilities, to a distributed, hierarchical system where you determine and configure its monitoring and management capabilities.

Based on the information in this chapter, you have the flexibility to create a network management architecture tailored to the requirements of your customer.

7.7   Exercises

1. What are the layers of network management? Give an example of management at each layer (what is managed, how it is managed).

2. What are the differences between monitoring for events and monitoring for trend analysis and planning? Give an example of each type for:
   a. Monitoring the capacity of an OC-3c WAN link
   b. Monitoring the utilization of an IP router

3. Which of the following are end-to-end characteristics? Per-link/per-network/per-element characteristics?
   a. Round-trip delay between a network management device and a computing server
   b. Percent utilization of the buffers in an IP router
   c. Maximum throughput between two devices (client and server) using a client-server application
   d. Bit error rate (BER) of a DS3 link

4. For each of the SNMP commands get, get-next, and set, and using Figure 7.19, describe what each command does, and give an example of how it is used.

5. How much storage capacity is required for the following network management configuration (Figure 7.19)?

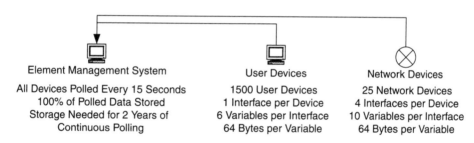

Element Management System

All Devices Polled Every 15 Seconds
100% of Polled Data Stored
Storage Needed for 2 Years of
Continuous Polling

User Devices

1500 User Devices
1 Interface per Device
6 Variables per Interface
64 Bytes per Variable

Network Devices

25 Network Devices
4 Interfaces per Device
10 Variables per Interface
64 Bytes per Variable

FIGURE 7.19   Devices for Storage Capacity Problem

6. This enterprise network currently has a network management system at the corporate network operations center (NOC), located in Minneapolis, which monitors only the 13 corporate routers. Develop a network management architecture that will allow monitoring of the routers as well as of all 190 user devices and dial-up routers, keeping the management traffic local to each area (Los Angeles, Minneapolis, and Washington, DC).

7. How much management data would be generated in a centralized management approach, assuming data collection of nine SNMP counters on all routers and ICMP ping polling of all devices (network and user), with a polling interval of 5 minutes? Each SNMP counter and ping generates 64 bytes of data.

8. Add devices for managing each of the remote sites (outside of the Minneapolis area) out-of-band from the corporate NOC.

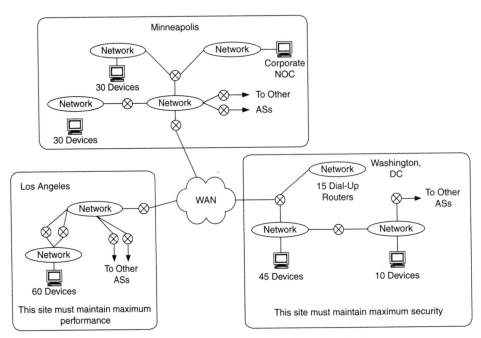

FIGURE 7.20 Diagram for Exercises 6 through 10

9. How does the addition of out-of-band management between the corporate NOC and remote sites potentially impact the security of the network?

10. Recommend two ways that the management data collected via SNMP counters from each of the routers could be verified.

CHAPTER CONTENTS

8

Performance Architecture

The performance architecture describes how user, application, device, and (existing) network requirements for performance (capacity, delay, and RMA [reliability, maintainability, and availability]) will be met within the planned network. Developing requirements for performance is a key part of the analysis process, and this component architecture is where they are supported.

The performance architecture is the newest of the component architectures, and it is rapidly evolving to include many new mechanisms to achieve network performance. And, as you will see in this chapter, this architecture is highly dependent on the other component architectures for success.

8.1 Objectives

In this chapter you will learn about what performance means in a network, including descriptions of mechanisms to achieve performance, how to determine the relationships both among these mechanisms and between performance and the other architectural components, and how to develop the performance architecture. We also develop goals for performance that will guide the development of this architecture.

8.1.1 Preparation

To be able to understand and apply the concepts in this chapter, you should be familiar with the basic concepts and mechanisms of performance. The basic concepts of performance were discussed in Chapters 1, 2, and 3, and the coupling of performance to traffic flows in Chapter 4 of this book. In addition, concepts of network architecture were presented in Chapter 5.

If you need additional information on network performance and performance mechanisms, some recommended sources include:

- *Internet QoS: Architectures and Mechanisms for Quality of Service*, by Zheng Wang, Morgan Kaufmann Publishers, March 2001.

- *Designing Quality of Service Solutions for the Enterprise*, by Eric D. Siegel, John Wiley & Sons, October 1999.

- *High-Speed Networking: A Systematic Approach to High-Bandwidth Low-Latency Communication*, by James Sterbenz and Joseph Touch, John Wiley & Sons, April 2001.

- *Queuing Systems Theory*, Volume 1, by Leonard Kleinrock, John Wiley & Sons, January 1975.

- Requests for Comments from the Differentiated Services (DiffServ) Working Group of the IETF, RFC 2474 and 2475 in particular. See www.ietf.org for these RFCs.

8.2   Background

Performance is the set of levels for capacity, delay, and RMA in a network. It is usually desirable to optimize these levels, either for all (user, application, and device) traffic flows in the network, or for one or more sets of traffic flows, based on groups of users, applications, and/or devices.

In support of performance in the network, a performance architecture is the set of performance mechanisms to configure, operate, manage, provision, and account for resources in the network that support traffic flows. The performance architecture shows where these mechanisms are applied within the network, and the sets of internal and external relationships between this and other component architectures. In this chapter we learn about network resources and about mechanisms to control and manage them.

An important part of developing this architecture is determining the performance goals for your network. For example, performance may be applied to:

- Improve the overall performance of the network (e.g., to improve response times and throughput to all users, regardless of where they are and what they are doing)

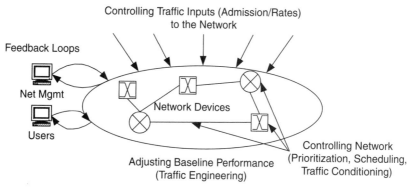

FIGURE 8.1   General Mechanisms for Performance

- Support a particular group or groups of users or applications, maybe new or planned applications
- Control resource allocation for accounting, billing, and/or management purposes

We discuss developing goals for performance later in the next section. In general, performance consists of one or more of the following: controlling traffic inputs to the network (admission and rate controls); adjusting the baseline performance of the network (traffic or capacity engineering); controlling all or part of the network for delivery of specific services (prioritizing, scheduling, and conditioning traffic flows); and implementing a feedback loop to users, applications, devices, and management to modify controls as necessary. Figure 8.1 shows these general mechanisms.

8.3 Developing Goals for Performance

For each component architecture it is important to understand why that function is needed for that particular network. This is especially important for the performance architecture. The process of developing goals for this (or any other) component architecture begins during requirements analysis and is further refined during the architecture process. Therefore, the requirements and flow specifications and maps provide important input to this process.

While performance is always desirable, we need to ensure that the performance mechanisms we incorporate into the architecture are necessary and sufficient to achieve the performance goals for that network. Therefore, toward developing this architecture, we should answer the following questions:

1. Are performance mechanisms necessary for this network?

2. What are we trying to solve, add, or differentiate by adding performance mechanisms to this network?

3. Are performance mechanisms sufficient for this network?

In determining whether or not performance mechanisms are necessary for a network, we should already have the information needed to make a decision from the requirements and flow analyses. Part of the purpose of determining whether performance mechanisms are necessary is to avoid implementing such mechanisms just because they are interesting or new. For example, it may be tempting to implement QoS mechanisms in a network, even when there are no clear goals or problems to solve.

When performance mechanisms are indicated, you should start simple and work toward a more complex architecture when warranted. Simplicity may be achieved in this architecture by implementing performance mechanisms only in selected areas of the network (e.g. at the access or distribution [server] networks), or by using only one or a few mechanisms, or by selecting only those mechanisms that are easy to implement, operate, and maintain.

There should be information in the requirements and flow analyses that can help in determining the need for performance mechanisms in a network. Some requirements include:

*   Clearly different sets of network performance requirements, per user, group, application, device, and/or flow

*   Requirements to bill and account for network service

When you plan to implement performance mechanisms in a network, you should also determine whether or not your customer is willing to pay the costs for such mechanisms. For example, does your customer have a network staff capable of configuring, operating, and maintaining QoS, SLAs, and policies? If not, are they willing to pay the cost to acquire such staff, or outsource performance (and some portion of network management)? Performance is not a capability that is implemented once and then forgotten; it requires continual support. If your customer is not willing to provide that support, it is better not to implement such mechanisms.

Experience has shown that when performance mechanisms are implemented and not supported, maintained, or kept current, performance in the network can actually degrade to a point where it would be better not to have any performance mechanisms at all. Therefore, determining the requirements for performance, and the willingness of your customer to support performance, is critical to developing this architecture.

Having established a need for performance in the network, you should also determine what problems your customer is trying to solve. This may be clearly stated in the problem definition, developed as part of the requirements analysis, or you may need to probe further to answer this question. Some common problems that are addressed by the performance architecture include:

- Improving the overall performance of a network
- Improving the performance to select users, applications, and/or devices
- Changing the network from a cost center to profitability
- Merging multiple traffic types over a common network infrastructure
- Differentiating (and possibly charging) customers for multiple levels of service

Improving the overall performance of a network is consistent with the network having single-tier performance (determined during the requirements analysis). When all users, applications, and/or devices in a network require a similar level of performance, your goal may be to improve performance to everyone.

When there are sets of users, applications, and/or devices that require greater performance than others on the same network, performance mechanisms are required to deliver multiple performance levels. Such networks have multi-tier performance.

When attempting to charge customers for service, and possibly to generate revenue for network service, performance mechanisms are needed to provide the contractual framework between subscribers and provider, and to deliver multiple performance (and charging) levels.

Performance mechanisms are also needed when a customer wants to merge multiple traffic flow types. This is common when multiple networks are being consolidated. For example, when building a new data network, your customer may want to (eventually) migrate voice and video services onto that network, eliminating the existing separate voice and video networks. Performance mechanisms are needed to be able to identify these multiple traffic flow types and provision the required network resources to support each flow.

Finally, having established the need for performance in the network, and determining what problems will be solved by implementing performance mechanisms, you should then determine if these performance mechanisms are sufficient for that network. Will they completely solve the customer's problems, or are they only a partial solution? If they are a partial solution, are there other mechanisms that are available, or will be available, within your project time frame? You may plan to implement basic performance mechanisms early in the project, and upgrade or add to those mechanisms at various stages in the project.

8.4   Performance Mechanisms

As presented in the last chapter, performance mechanisms discussed here are quality of service, resource control (prioritization, traffic management, scheduling, and queuing), service-level agreements, and policies. These mechanisms incorporate the general mechanisms shown in the previous section (Figure 8.1).

Subsets of these mechanisms are usually used together to form a comprehensive approach to providing single-tier and multi-tier performance in a network. These mechanisms provide the means to identify traffic flow types, measure their temporal characteristics, and take various actions to improve performance for individual flows, groups of flows, or for all flows in the network.

8.4.1   Quality of Service

Quality of Service, or QoS, is determining, setting, and acting upon priority levels for traffic flows. QoS is usually associated with IP but is used here to define a class of mechanisms that provision and apply priority levels in multiple layers in the network. This class includes IP QoS (including MPLS), type of service (ToS), and Frame Relay committed information rate (CIR). In this section we focus on IP QoS.

For IP-based traffic, there are two standard types of QoS: differentiated services (DiffServ, or DS) and integrated services (IntServ, or IS), intended to support two views of network service. *DiffServ* approaches QoS from the perspective of aggregating traffic flows on a per-hop basis based on traffic behavior, while *IntServ* approaches QoS from the perspective of supporting traffic flows on an individual, end-to-end basis.

In DiffServ, IP packets are marked in the type of service (ToS) byte for IPv4 or in the traffic class byte in IPv6 so that they will receive the corresponding performance at each network device (or hop). DiffServ defines a set of values (termed *differentiated services code points*, or DSCPs) for classes of traffic flows, to be used by resource control mechanisms. An important concept of DiffServ is that it applies to *aggregates* of traffic flows (e.g., composite flows), not individual traffic flows.

The main reason for this is for scalability (particularly across the Internet, but it could also be applied in a large enterprise environment). If, in a network architecture and design, all flows requiring priority service were treated individually, one trade-off in the network would be the amount of resources (e.g., memory in network devices) required to store and maintain state information for each individual flow across the network. This resource requirement grows geometrically with the network and therefore does not scale well. By aggregating flows into traffic classes, storing and maintaining state information become more tenable. State information, or state, is information about the configuration and status of flows or connections. Examples include addresses (IP or MAC-layer), time (duration of flow/connection, idle time), and temporal characteristics (data rates, packet losses).

There are three traffic classes for DiffServ: best-effort, assured forwarding (AF), and expedited forwarding (EF). Assured and expedited forwarding are the preferred traffic classes and are based on the types of performance they require. Expedited forwarding is usually targeted toward traffic that has delay requirements (e.g., real-time or interactive), while assured forwarding can be used for traffic with both delay and capacity requirements (e.g., multimedia or tele*services).

There are times, however, when a traffic flow needs to be treated individually. *Integrated services* defines values and mechanisms for allocating resources to flows across the end-to-end path of the flow. IntServ is closely tied to the flow nature of a network, by placing importance on supporting a flow at every network device in the end-to-end path of that flow. Recall from our discussion of flow analysis that end-to-end paths are defined by you, and will vary depending on what you are trying to accomplish. In defining where end-to-end applies for particular flows (e.g., flows with guaranteed requirements), you are determining where mechanisms such as IntServ could be applied.

As mentioned with DiffServ, however, the advantages of IntServ come at a price. IntServ requires support on the network devices across which the flow travels, and it requires resources (e.g., memory, processing, bandwidth) for each flow. Support across multiple networks implies coordination of service between those networks. And requiring resources for each flow means that it will not scale well in areas where flows converge (e.g., the core area of a network).

IntServ also requires a mechanism to communicate flow requirements, as well as the setup and teardown of resource allocations, across network devices in the end-to-end path of a flow. Such signaling is usually provided by the resource reservation protocol (RSVP). Other signaling mechanisms, such as that with MPLS, are also being developed for this purpose.

RSVP is used by network devices (including user devices) to request specific quality of service levels from network devices in the end-to-end path of a traffic flow. Successful RSVP requests usually result in resources being reserved at each network device along this end-to-end path, along with state information about the requested service.

Thus, a mechanism such as this is best applied in an environment where the network administrator has control of the end-to-end path of the flow, such as within an enterprise environment. Although IntServ is often dismissed because of its complexity and scalability issues, it can be used, but only when there is a strong case for it (from the requirements and flow specifications), and then with an understanding of what is required, in terms of network and personnel resources, to implement and maintain it.

A comparison of some of the functions and features of DiffServ and IntServ are presented in Figure 8.2.

DiffServ and IntServ can be applied individually or together within a network, and it is possible to combine these mechanisms in a variety of ways. For example, DiffServ may be applied across the entire network by itself, or both may be applied in different areas of the network. Additionally, both mechanisms may be applied to the same areas of the network, targeted at different types of flows. In this case DiffServ is first applied to the network, and IntServ is then overlaid onto it.

Function/Feature	Differentiated Services (DiffServ)	Integrated Services (IntServ)
Scalability	Scalable to Large Enterprise of Service-Provider Networks	Limited to Small or Medium-Size Enterprise Networks
Granularity of Control	Traffic Aggregated into Classes	Per-Flow or Groups of Flows
Scope of Control	Per Network Device (Per-Hop)	All Network Devices in End-to-End Path of Flow

FIGURE 8.2 A Comparison of DiffServ and IntServ

If we consider the Access/Core/Distribution architectural model (presented in Chapter 5) in the context of IP QoS, we can begin to see where these mechanisms might apply. The access portion of the network is where most flows are sourced and sinked—therefore, where they can be (most easily) supported individually. The core of the network is where bulk transport of flows occurs, where it would make the most sense to aggregate them. Thus, one way to look at prioritizing flows is presented in Figure 8.3, where flow aggregation via DiffServ is applied at the core, per-flow service via IntServ is applied at the access, and some translation occurs between the two at the boundary between access and core, possibly at the distribution network.

In this figure IntServ is applied as an end-to-end mechanism, where the end points are defined between devices within each access (and possibly its serving distribution) area. Therefore, it is targeted toward those flows that remain within an access network or are sourced/sinked at the distribution network. For example, this would apply for client–server flows where the servers are located at the distribution network.

For flows that cross the core network, their performance would change from IntServ at the access and distribution networks to DiffServ at the core network, and individual state would be lost as a trade-off for scalability. However, flows that remain in the access or distribution networks would still get the full benefits of

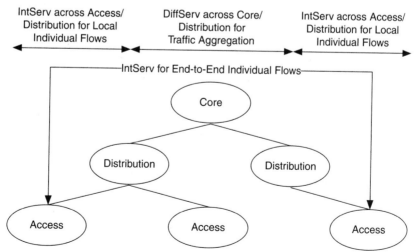

FIGURE 8.3   Where DiffServ and IntServ Apply in the Access/Distribution/Core Model

IntServ. And, importantly, IntServ could be used to signal the core network for resources for a traffic class.

It is also possible to apply both IntServ and DiffServ so that they work concurrently across the entire network. In a case like this (shown as the end-to-end flows in Figure 8.3), IntServ would only be used for a relatively small percentage of flows and would be used end-to-end. DiffServ would be used for other prioritized flows and could be aggregated at either the access or distribution network.

DiffServ and IntServ are used to apply prioritization, scheduling, and resource control to traffic flows. How these mechanisms work is described next.

8.4.2   Prioritization, Traffic Management, Scheduling, and Queuing

Prioritization, traffic management, scheduling, and queuing are at the heart of providing performance in a network. A performance architecture may include one or more of these mechanisms, in conjunction with QoS, SLAs, and policies, to provide performance to its users, applications, devices, and traffic flows. These mechanisms are usually implemented in network devices such as routers and switches but can also be applied to the network as stand-alone hardware, such as in vendor-specific admission control and traffic management devices.

Prioritization

Prioritization is the process of determining which user, application, device, flow, or connection gets service ahead of others, or gets a higher level of service. Prioritization is necessary as there will be competition between traffic flows for network resources. With a limited amount of resources available in any network, prioritization determines who gets resources first, and how much they get.

Prioritization begins during the requirements and flow analysis processes. Priority levels for users, applications, and devices should be determined as part of the requirements analysis, and priority levels for traffic flows determined during the flow analysis process. For example, you may recall (from Chapter 4) how to prioritize flows based on the various parameters, such as the numbers of users supported and performance requirements.

For a performance architecture there are two high-level views of performance: single-tier performance, where capacity, delay, and/or RMA are optimized for all traffic flows, and multi-tier performance, where capacity, delay, and/or RMA are optimized for one or more groups of traffic flows, based on groups of users, applications, and/or devices. Either or both of these views can be taken for a network architecture. As with our approach to DiffServ and IntServ, single-tier performance may apply across the entire network, with multi-tier performance in select areas, or as an addition to single-tier performance.

These two views of performance imply that there may be multiple levels (tiers) of performance required by different groups of traffic flows. Whenever there are multiple levels of performance requirements in a network (and thus multiple groups of traffic flows), there will be a need to prioritize these traffic flows. Prioritization is ranking (determining a priority level) based on importance and urgency. Ranking may be applied to users, applications, devices, or their traffic flows. A rank or priority level indicates the importance and/or urgency of that user, application, device, or flow, relative to other users, applications, devices, or flows in that network. Such priority levels are often determined during the requirements and flow analyses.

The most basic or degenerate case of prioritization is when every user, application, device, or flow has the same priority level. Such is the case in best-effort networks. When a user, application, device, or flow, or groups of these, require performance greater than the general case, then they will have higher priority levels. In addition, an individual or group at the same priority level as other individuals or groups may change its priority level due to the urgency of its work.

For example, most users on a network have a common set of applications and devices. They will often use a similar type of desktop or laptop computer, with a standard type of network interface. They will likely use email, Web, word processing, and other common applications. Such users may constitute a group of single-tier performance users, all with a single priority level. For some networks, this is as far as prioritization gets, and the performance architecture focuses on optimizing performance for everyone in this group. In some cases, however, even a single, single-tier performance group may have multiple priority levels. In such a case, priority levels can be used to grant preference to individuals who have not used the network for a period of time, or who are willing to pay a premium for preferred access.

Priority levels may be based on the type of protocol (e.g., TCP versus UDP), service, or port number, by IP or MAC-layer address, or by other information embedded within the traffic. This information can be maintained in databases and coupled with policies and SLAs (discussed later in this chapter) as part of the performance architecture.

Priority levels are used by network devices to help determine if traffic flows will be allowed on the network (admission control), scheduling of traffic flows onto the network, and conditioning of flows throughout the network.

Traffic Management

Priority levels determine the relative importance and urgency of traffic flows and how each traffic flow will be handled within the network. Traffic management consists of admission control and traffic conditioning. *Admission control* is the ability to refuse access to network resources. *Traffic conditioning* is a set of mechanisms that modify (increase or decrease) performance to traffic flows, as a precursor to scheduling.

Admission control uses priority levels to change the behavior of network access. In a best-effort network without admission control, access to the network is democratic in that all traffic flows have a (more or less) equal chance to get network resources. With admission control, however, access is permitted, denied, or sometimes delayed, based on the relative priority of that traffic.

An example of this is assigning a higher priority to real-time traffic flows, such as voice and video. In this case voice and video traffic flows are given access before other traffic flows. When network resources dedicated to these flows are fully utilized, further flows are refused (blocked). Admission control is most often applied at access areas.

In order to understand traffic conditioning functions, let's follow traffic flows across a network device that implements traffic conditioning. As traffic flows enter a network device, there must be a mechanism to identify flows and distinguish among flows. *Classification* is the ability to identify traffic flows. The classifier looks at various parts of the IP packet, such as source and destination addresses, port numbers, or protocol types. Additionally, the classifier may look deeper into a packet for the necessary information. For example, voice over IP (VoIP) signaling flows may be determined by looking for session initiation protocol (SIP) identifiers (RFC 3261) within the packets. Upon identifying traffic flows that are important for that network, packets within these flows may be *marked*, or tagged with a priority level. Examples of marking included tagging packets with DiffServ Code Points (DSCPs) for best-effort (BE), assured forwarding (AF), and expedited forwarding (EF) priority levels.

Once traffic flows have been classified, they may be metered to determine their performance levels. *Metering* is measuring the temporal performance characteristics of a traffic flow, including traffic rates and burst sizes. Performance characteristics are measured periodically and compared with expected performance boundaries, which can be from SLAs and/or policies. Metering is most often a capability provided in network devices (e.g., routers and switches) as part of their performance implementation, but can also be applied as a separate network device (some network management devices can provide metering support, for example).

For example, a traffic flow may be metered over a period of 1 second. Each second, the peak data rate for that flow is compared with a capacity boundary of 1.5 Mb/s, which was input into the network device from an SLA developed for that traffic flow.

Metering a traffic flow can determine whether or not a flow is within performance boundaries (Figure 8.4). *Conforming traffic* is within performance boundaries; *non-conforming traffic* is outside of performance boundaries. Typically, no action is taken on conforming traffic. Conforming traffic is forwarded to the appropriate output queue (as determined by its priority level) and scheduled for transmission onto the network.

When traffic is non-conforming, however (indicating that it is exceeding the specifications of an SLA), it is subject to shaping or dropping. *Shaping* is delaying traffic to change a performance characteristic, while *dropping* is discarding traffic. Non-conforming traffic may also be marked, with no other action taken. This is done so that network devices upstream (those receiving this traffic flow) can choose to shape or drop this traffic if necessary.

In order to shape non-conforming traffic, it may be sent to a shaper queue where delay is added before it is transmitted onto the network. By delaying traffic, a shaper queue changes the performance of that traffic flow. Consider an SLA for a traffic flow that specifies a peak rate of 1.5 Mb/s. (Mb/s is shown as MBits/second in the following discussion for consistency in units; in practice, the rate is usually shown as Kb/s, Mb/s, or Gb/s.) A meter is measuring that traffic flow, and calculates a rate of:

$$(200 \text{ packets/second})^*(1500 \text{ byte packets})^*(8 \text{ bits/byte}) = 2.4 \text{ MBits/second}$$

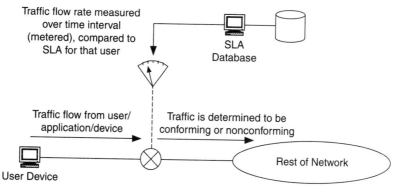

FIGURE 8.4   Traffic Metering at a Network Device

This is compared with the SLA specification (1.5 MBits/second) and found to be non-conforming. Subsequent packets are then forwarded to a shaper queue, where they are delayed by an average of 10 ms. As a result, only 100 packets can be transmitted per second, and the rate of that traffic flow becomes:

$$(100 \text{ packets/second})^*(1500 \text{ byte packets})^*(8 \text{ bits/byte}) = 1.2 \text{ MBits/second}$$

Shaping continues either for a specified period of time or until the traffic flow is again conforming.

The most serious action that can be taken on traffic is dropping, or discarding, packets. This is done when a traffic flow is seriously exceeding its performance boundary, or when the network device is congested to the point where dropping packets is necessary. Traffic conditioning functions are shown in Figure 8.5.

Scheduling

Once traffic has been prioritized and conditioned, it is forwarded to one or more output queues for transmission onto the network. *Scheduling* is the mechanism that determines the order in which traffic is processed for transmission. Scheduling uses priority levels to determine which traffic flows get processed first and most often.

Scheduling is applied at network devices throughout a network. In most network devices, such as switches and routers, scheduling is provided through network management, or as part of the QoS implementation in that device.

Scheduling may be proprietary (enterprise-specific) or standards-based. Some commonly used standard scheduling algorithms include weighted fair queuing (WFQ) and class-based queuing (CBQ). These algorithms provide some degree of fairness in queuing while allowing relative priority levels (weights).

The combination of QoS, prioritization, traffic management, and scheduling provides a comprehensive set of mechanisms that can be applied across a network

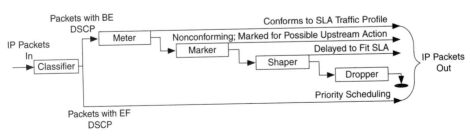

FIGURE 8.5   Traffic Conditioning Functions

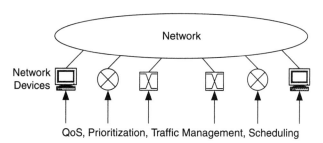

FIGURE 8.6   Performance Mechanisms Act on Network Devices

to achieve various performance levels for traffic flows (Figure 8.6). As we will see, these mechanisms are closely tied to SLAs and policies, which are discussed next.

Queuing

We complete this section with a discussion of queuing. Queuing is storing IP packets (this can also be applied to frames or cells, but for the purposes of this discussion we limit it to IP packets) within a network device while they wait for processing. There may be several locations where packets are stored (queues) within a network device, for each type of processing that the device is performing on each packet (e.g., holding packets received from the network, processing for QoS, holding packets for transmission onto the network).

There are a number of queuing mechanisms available in network devices. Each mechanism is developed to achieve a particular objective in processing packets. For example, queue mechanisms may treat all packets in the same way, may randomly select packets for processing, or may favor particular packets. In this chapter we briefly consider the following queuing mechanisms:

- First in first out (FIFO)
- Class-based queuing (CBQ)
- Weighted fair queuing (WFQ)
- Random early detect (RED)
- Weighted RED (WRED)

First in first out (FIFO) queuing is arguably the simplest queuing mechanism available. In FIFO queuing packets are stored in a single queue. For an output FIFO queue, packets are transmitted onto the network in the order that they were received (at the input queue).

In class-based queuing (CBQ), multiple queues with differing priorities are maintained. Priority levels are configurable in the network device and indicate the performance levels required for each traffic type. Packets of each priority level are placed in their respective queues. Higher-priority queues are processed before lower-priority queues, with the result that higher-priority traffic receives more network resources and thus greater performance.

Like CBQ, weighted fair queuing (WFQ) assigns priorities (weights) to queues. Typically with this mechanism, high-priority traffic flows are processed first, and lower-priority traffic flows share the remaining resources.

Generally, when a queue becomes full (e.g., during periods of congestion), packets are dropped either from the beginning of the queue (head) or end of the queue (tail). In either case, the dropping of these packets is likely to be unfair to one or a few traffic flows. As a result, random early detect (RED) was developed to randomize the packet dropping process across a queue. In addition, RED will drop packets early (before the queue is actually full) to force traffic flows (i.e., TCP flows) to adjust by reducing their transmission rate.

Weighted RED (WRED) operates in the same fashion as RED but supports multiple priority levels (one for each queue) for dropping packets.

8.4.3 Service-Level Agreements

Service-level agreements, or SLAs, are (typically) formal contracts between a provider and user that define the terms of the provider's responsibility to the user and the type and extent of accountability if those responsibilities are not met. While SLAs have traditionally been contracts between various service providers (e.g., ISPs) and their customers, this concept can also be applied to the enterprise environment. In fact, the notion of customer and provider is becoming more common in enterprise networks, as they evolve from treating networks as mere infrastructure (cost-center approach) to treating them as centers for providing services to their customers (users).

There are two common ways to apply SLAs within a network. First, an SLA can be an agreement between network management/administration and its customers (the network users). Second, an SLA can be used to define the levels of services required from third-party service providers (e.g., cable plant providers, xSPs) for the network.

SLA performance elements may be as simple as a data rate (minimum, peak) and burst tolerance (size, duration), and can be separated into upstream (in the

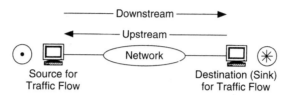

FIGURE 8.7   Upstream and Downstream Directions

direction from the destination to the source) and downstream (in the direction from the source to the destination). Figure 8.7 shows upstream and downstream for a traffic flow, along with the data sources and sinks.

While these terms can apply for any flow, they are most commonly used in service-provider networks. In such networks, the sources of most traffic flows are servers on the Internet, and most destinations are subscriber PCs at the service provider's access networks. For this case, downstream is from these servers (i.e., from the Internet) to the subscriber's PC, and upstream is from the PC to the Internet. For example, Web pages downloaded from the Internet to a subscriber's PC generate TCP traffic downstream from a Web server to the subscriber PC, and TCP acknowledgements (TCP acks) upstream from the subscriber PC to the Web server (Figure 8.8).

SLAs can include delay and RMA metrics for more complete provisioning of service. An example of an enterprise SLA is shown in Figure 8.9.

The SLA in Figure 8.9 specifies capacity, delay, and RMA levels for various types of users, their applications, and devices. A basic, or best-effort, service level is shown, where all performance characteristics are best effort. This service level is the default and would normally be provided to any user free of charge.

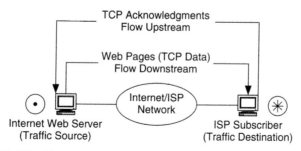

FIGURE 8.8   Upstream and Downstream Directions for Internet Web Traffic

Network Service Description for My Enterprise

Service Levels:	Capacity Performance	Delay Performance	Reliability Performance
Basic Service	As Available (Best Effort)	As Available (Best Effort)	As Available (Best Effort)
Silver Service	1.5 Mb/s (Bidirectional)	As Available (Best Effort)	As Available (Best Effort)
Gold Service	10 Mb/s (Bidirectional) (Burst to 100 Mb/s)	Max 100 ms Round-Trip (between Specified Points)	As Available (Best Effort)
Platinum Service	100/10 Mb/s Up/Down (Burst to 1 Gb/s)	Max 40 ms Round-Trip (between Specified Points)	99.999% Uptime (User–Server)

FIGURE 8.9   An Example of an Enterprise SLA

The other service levels (silver, gold, and platinum) specify increasing levels of capacity, delay, and RMA performance. Users that subscribe to these performance levels would likely be charged for usage. This may take the form of an internal charge within each organization, an allocation of resources, or both. For example, each valid subscriber to the platinum service (only a certain type of user may be allowed to use this service, based on work and needs) may be allocated N hours per month. Usage greater than N hours per month would result in a charge to that user's organization.

Figure 8.9 depicts an example of a fairly complex SLA and is used to illustrate how an SLA may be structured. In practice, SLAs are usually simpler, with two to three service levels. Depending on the requirements of an organization, however, an SLA can be more complex than our example.

An SLA is typically a contract between users and service provider about the types of services being provided. In this sense an SLA forms a feedback loop between users and provider. The service provider has the responsibility of monitoring and managing services, to ensure that users are getting what they expect (and possibly are paying for), and users are made aware of what is available to them.

Figure 8.10 shows that, when SLAs are added to the performance architecture, they provide a means for communicating among users, staff, and management about performance needs and services.

In order for SLAs to be effective as feedback loops, they need to operate in conjunction with performance monitoring and trouble reporting/ticketing, as part of the performance or network management architectures.

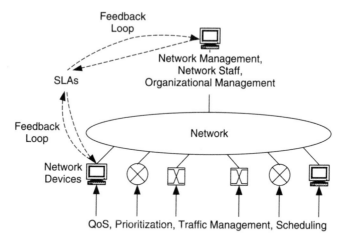

FIGURE 8.10   Performance Mechanisms with SLAs Added

8.4.4 Policies

Policies are formal or informal sets of high-level statements and rules about how network resources (and, therefore, performance) are to be allocated among users. They are used to create and manage one or more performance objectives. Policies complete the framework of performance for a network by coupling the high-level (e.g., management) view of how the network should perform, with mechanisms to implement performance at the network devices (QoS) and feedback loops with users (SLAs) (Figure 8.11).

Policies may describe what network, computing, storage, or other resources are available to users, when resources are available, or which users are permitted to access certain resources. In this sense these policies are similar to policies for security or routing.

Policy information is often implemented, stored, and managed in policy databases kept on the network. Policy information is passed between databases and network devices using Common Open Policy Service (COPS) and Lightweight Directory Access Protocol (LDAP).

8.5 Architectural Considerations

In developing our performance architecture we need to evaluate potential performance mechanisms, determine where they may apply within the network,

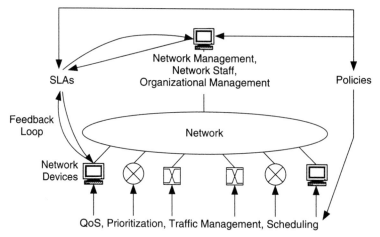

FIGURE 8.11   Performance Mechanisms with Policies Added

and examine the sets of internal and external relationships for this component architecture.

8.5.1   Evaluation of Performance Mechanisms

At this point we should have requirements, goals, type of environment, and architectural model(s), and are ready to evaluate potential performance mechanisms. When evaluating performance mechanisms, it is best to start simple (e.g., DiffServ QoS), and work toward more complex solutions only when necessary.

Where a performance mechanism will apply in a given network depends primarily on where performance requirements are located throughout the network, based on the results of the requirements and flow analyses. In addition to the requirements and flow analyses, we can also use any architectural goals that have been developed, as well as the architectural models presented in Chapter 5.

Recall that the Access/Distribution/Core architectural model separates a network based on function, where the core network supports the bulk transport of traffic flows, distribution networks support flows to and from servers, and aggregates traffic flows from the access network, and access networks are where most traffic flows are sourced and sinked. This functional separation of a network can be applied when evaluating performance mechanisms.

For example, performance mechanisms that operate on individual traffic flows (such as admission control and signaling for resources, IntServ, and Layer 2 QoS) should be considered where traffic flows are more likely to be individual (e.g., before they are aggregated), such as at access networks. Performance mechanisms that operate on aggregates of traffic flows, such as DiffServ, CBQ, WFQ RED/WRED, and MPLS, should be considered where traffic flows are more likely to be aggregated, such as at distribution and/or core networks, or at interfaces to external networks.

An example of where performance mechanisms may generally be applied is presented in Figure 8.12. Note that these applications should be considered only as general guidelines. Depending on the network, any performance mechanism may be applied at any area of a network.

Along with determining the regions of the network where each performance mechanism will apply, we also need to consider which devices will implement each mechanism. Examples include DiffServ edge devices, where traffic flows are classified and marked with DSCPs, and policy decision points (PDPs), servers where policies are configured and maintained. Policies are implemented at policy

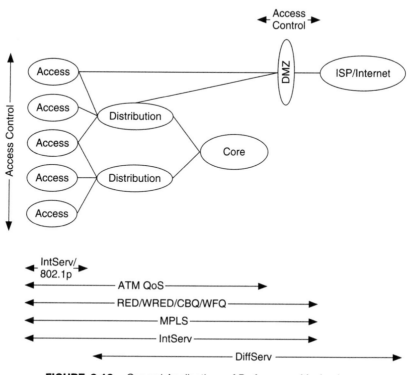

FIGURE 8.12   General Applications of Performance Mechanisms

enforcement points (PEPs), network devices that are configured for performance (e.g., through QoS).

8.5.2   Internal Relationships

Interactions within the performance architecture include trade-offs between end-to-end and per-hop prioritization, scheduling, and conditioning of traffic flows, admission control, and whether flows are treated individually or aggregated into groups. Interactions within the performance architecture include trade-offs across the following set of traffic flow functions: prioritization, scheduling, conditioning, admission control, and aggregation.

When policies, SLAs, and differentiated services are chosen, part of this component architecture describes the placement of databases for SLA and policy information, including policy decision points (PDPs), policy enforcement points (PEPs) and DiffServ edge devices.

8.5.3   External Relationships

External relationships are trade-offs, dependencies, and constraints between the performance architecture and each of the other component architectures (addressing/routing, network management, security, and any other component architectures you may develop). There are common external relationships between performance and each of the other component architectures, some of which are presented in the following paragraphs.

Interactions between performance and addressing/routing. Performance can be closely coupled with routing through mechanisms such as MPLS, differentiated and integrated services, and RSVP. However, when routing protocol simplicity is a high priority, performance may be decoupled from forwarding.

Interactions between performance and network management. Performance depends on network management to configure, monitor, manage, verify, and bill for performance levels throughout the network. Network management helps to couple QoS, SLAs, and policies by providing common communications paths and protocols for performance information. In addition, network management can tie performance management to the customer's operations support system (OSS).

SLAs need to be coupled with network management, for performance monitoring and trouble reporting/ticketing. This provides the feedback loop necessary between performance and network management, users, and management/staff.

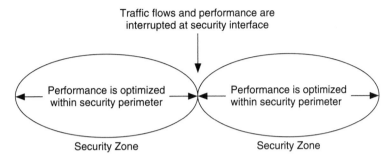

FIGURE 8.13   Performance Is Constrained by Security

Interactions between performance and security. As we will see in the security component architecture, security mechanisms are often intrusive, intercepting, inspecting, and controlling network access and traffic. Such actions require network resources and processing, increasing network delay. As security is increased, by adding more mechanisms (and mechanisms that are more intrusive) to the network, performance is decreased. Whereas capacity can sometimes be increased to offset a decrease in performance due to security, increased delay is difficult to mitigate.

When performance is high priority, particularly when there is a need to provision end-to-end performance among select users, applications, or devices, performance mechanisms may preclude the use of intrusive security mechanisms in those areas of the network.

When security mechanisms interrupt or terminate and regenerate traffic flows, they seriously impact the ability to provide end-to-end performance across the security interface. As a result, security constrains performance to operate within a security perimeter (Figure 8.13). These security perimeters, or *security zones* or *cells*, can be configured in different ways. This is discussed further in the chapter on security architecture (Chapter 9).

8.6   Conclusions

In this chapter we learned about developing the performance architecture for a network. The performance architecture consists of determining which performance mechanisms (quality of service, prioritization, scheduling, traffic conditioning, service-level agreements, and policies) apply to a particular network, where each mechanism may apply, and the relationships within the performance architecture and between performance and other component architectures.

The performance architecture is the first of the component architectures that we will be examining. As we go through each component architecture, the reference architecture (consisting of all the external relationships) for the network will emerge.

8.7 Exercises

For Exercises 1 through 6, refer to the performance requirements listed below.

Requirement 1. Two clearly different sets of network performance requirements: one high RMA, the other low RMA (for that network)

Requirement 2. A requirement to bill subscribers for network service, and to provide accounting of subscriber billing information

Requirement 3. Combining a customer's voice and data traffic over a common network

1. For each performance requirement listed, explain why performance mechanisms are needed to support the requirement.

2. DiffServ and IntServ are two approaches to providing QoS in IP networks, designed to support performance from different perspectives. For the requirements listed, which would you recommend: DiffServ? IntServ? Both or neither? Give reasons for your choices.

3. Which of the requirements indicate single-tier performance? Multi-tier performance?

4. Figure 8.5 shows the traffic conditioning functions: *classification, marking, metering, shaping*, and *dropping*. For Requirement 3 (combining voice and data traffic), outline how the process of traffic conditioning, using these five functions with DiffServ, would be applied to this requirement. Assign a DiffServ code point (DSCP) to each traffic type.

5. Combining Requirements 2 and 3, write an SLA for this network. Use the following performance requirements:
    a. Voice traffic must have an availability (RMA) of 99.999% (excluding scheduled maintenance times), measured everywhere in the network.
    b. Data traffic must have an availability (RMA) of 99.99% (excluding scheduled maintenance times), measured between user devices and servers. Include sample pricing for Requirement 2.

6. A performance architecture consists of QoS, SLA, and policy mechanisms, applied at network devices and servers, to support performance within the network (Figure 8.14). Given that there will be a policy and SLA database server, and IP

routers and Fast Ethernet switches with DiffServ QoS, outline how QoS, SLAs, and policies could be implemented to support the two sets of performance in Requirement 1.

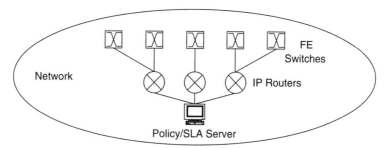

FIGURE 8.14   The Network for Exercise 6

7. List four types of problems that the performance architecture addresses. Give examples of each type of problem.

8. For the queuing mechanisms shown below, give an example of how each would be used within a network. What problem(s) is each mechanism solving?
   a. First in first out (FIFO)
   b. Class-based queuing (CBQ)
   c. Weighted fair queuing (WFQ)
   d. Random early detect (RED)
   e. Weighted RED (WRED)

CHAPTER CONTENTS

9

Security and Privacy Architecture

Security and privacy of user, application, device, and network resources and data are increasingly important areas of network architecture and design. Security is integrated within all areas of the network and impacts all other functions on the network. For the proper functioning of security within a network, it is crucial that the relationships among security mechanisms, as well as between the security architecture and other component architectures, be well understood.

Overlaying security onto a developed network was an acceptable approach in the past. Today, however, security must be integrated into the network from the beginning in order for the network to meet the needs of the users and for security to provide adequate protection.

9.1 Objectives

In this chapter you will learn about various security mechanisms (such as physical security, protocol and application security, encryption/decryption, and perimeter and remote access security), how to determine the relationships both among these mechanisms and between security and the other architectural components, and how to develop the security architecture.

9.1.1 Preparation

To be able to understand and apply the concepts in this chapter, you should be familiar with the basic concepts and mechanisms of security. Some recommended sources of information include:

- *Hacking Exposed: Network Security Secrets & Solutions*, Third Edition, by Stuart McClure, Joel Scambray, and George Kurtz, McGraw-Hill Osborne Media, September 2001.

- *Information Security Architecture: An Integrated Approach to Security in the Organization*, by Jan Killmeyer Tudor, Auerbach, September 2000.

- *Firewalls and Internet Security: Repelling the Wily Hacker*, Second Edition, by William R. Cheswick, Steven M. Bellovin, and Aviel D. Rubin, Addison-Wesley Professional, February 2003.

- *Inside Network Perimeter Security: The Definitive Guide to Firewalls, Virtual Private Networks (VPNs), Routers, and Intrusion Detection Systems*, Second Edition, by Stephen Northcutt, Karen Fredrick, Scott Winters, Lenny Zeltser, and Ronald W. Ritchey, New Riders Publishing, June 2005.

- *Computer Security Handbook*, by Seymour Bosworth and Michel Kabay, John Wiley & Sons, April 2002.

9.2   Background

Network security is defined here as the protection of networks and their services from unauthorized access, modification, destruction, or disclosure. It provides assurance that the network performs its critical functions correctly and that there are no harmful side effects. *Network privacy* is a subset of network security, focusing on protection of networks and their services from unauthorized access or disclosure. This includes all user, application, device, and network data. Whenever the term *network security* is used in this book, it includes all aspects of network privacy as well.

There are three classic security considerations: protecting the integrity, the confidentiality, and the availability of network and system resources and data. These considerations are discussed throughout this chapter and are integral to the security architecture. Effective security and privacy combine an understanding of what security means to each of the components of the system—users, applications, devices, and networks—together with the planning and implementation of security policies and mechanisms. Security in the network needs to protect network resources from being disabled, stolen, modified, or damaged. This includes protecting devices, servers, users, and system data, as well as the users' and organization's privacy and image.

Attacks against the system range from seemingly innocuous unauthorized probing and use of resources to keeping authorized users from accessing resources (denial of service), to modifying, stealing, or destroying resources.

This chapter covers how security and privacy may be determined and brought into the network architecture and design. This is an area of great interest and rapid expansion and change in the networking community, so we present concepts and mechanisms that should be valid across a wide range of security requirements. We discuss elements of security administration and various security and privacy mechanisms, consider how to develop a security plan, and examine requirements for security. We also define security policies, perform risk analysis for the architecture and design, and develop a security and privacy plan. We then discuss the security and privacy architecture.

9.3   Developing a Security and Privacy Plan

As discussed in the previous chapter, the development of each component architecture is based on our understanding of why that function is needed for that particular network. While one may argue that security is always necessary, we still need to ensure that the security mechanisms we incorporate into the architecture are optimal for achieving the security goals for that network. Therefore, toward developing a security architecture, we should answer the following questions:

1. What are we trying to solve, add, or differentiate by adding security mechanisms to this network?

2. Are security mechanisms sufficient for this network?

While it is likely that some degree of security is necessary for any network, we should have information from the threat analysis to help us decide how much security is needed. As with the performance architecture, we want to avoid implementing (security) mechanisms just because they are interesting or new.

When security mechanisms are indicated, it is best to start simple and work toward a more complex security architecture when warranted. Simplicity may be achieved in the security architecture by implementing security mechanisms only in selected areas of the network (e.g., at the access or distribution [server] networks), or by using only one or a few mechanisms, or by selecting only those mechanisms that are easy to implement, operate, and maintain.

In developing the security architecture, you should determine what problems your customer is trying to solve. This may be clearly stated in the problem definition, developed as part of the threat analysis, or you may need to probe further to answer this question. Some common areas that are addressed by the security architecture include:

- Which resources need to be protected
- What problems (threats) are we protecting against
- The likelihood of each problem (threat)

This information becomes part of your security and privacy plan for the network. This plan should be reviewed and updated periodically to reflect the current state of security threats to the network. Some organizations review their security plans yearly, others more frequently, depending on their requirements for security.

Note that there may be groups within a network that have different security needs. As a result, the security architecture may have different levels of security. This equates to the security perimeters or zones introduced in the previous chapter. How security zones are established is discussed later in this chapter.

Once you have determined which problems will be solved by each security mechanism, you should then determine if these security mechanisms are sufficient for that network. Will they completely solve the customer's problems, or are they only a partial solution? If they are a partial solution, are there other mechanisms that are available, or will be available within your project time frame? You may plan to implement basic security mechanisms early in the project, and upgrade or add to those mechanisms at various stages in the project.

9.4   Security and Privacy Administration

The preparation and ongoing administration of security and privacy in the network are quite important to the overall success of the security architecture. Like the requirements and flows analyses, understanding what your threats are and how you are going to protect against them is an important first step in developing security for your network. In this section we discuss two important components in preparing for security: threat analysis and policies and procedures.

9.4.1   Threat Analysis

A *threat analysis* is a process used to determine which components of the system need to be protected and the types of security risks (threats) they should be protected from (Figure 9.1). This information can be used to determine strategic locations in

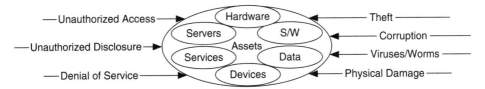

FIGURE 9.1 Potential Assets and Threats to Be Analyzed

the network architecture and design where security can reasonably and effectively be implemented.

A threat analysis typically consists of identifying the assets to be protected, as well as identifying and evaluating possible threats. Assets may include, but are not restricted to:

- User hardware (workstations/PCs)
- Servers
- Specialized devices
- Network devices (hubs, switches, routers, OAM&P)
- Software (OS, utilities, client programs)
- Services (applications, IP services)
- Data (local/remote, stored, archived, databases, data in–transit)

And threats may include, but are not restricted to:

- Unauthorized access to data/services/software/hardware
- Unauthorized disclosure of information
- Denial of service
- Theft of data/services/software/hardware
- Corruption of data/services/software/hardware
- Viruses, worms, Trojan horses
- Physical damage

One method to gather data about security and privacy for your environment is to list the threats and assets on a worksheet. This threat analysis worksheet can then be distributed to users, administration, and management, even as part of the requirements analysis process, to gather information about potential security problems.

Effect/ Likelihood	User Hardware	Servers	Network Devices	Software	Services	Data
Unauthorized Access	B/A	B/B	C/B	A/B	B/C	A/B
Unauthorized Disclosure	B/C	B/B	C/C	A/B	B/C	A/B
Denial of Service	B/B	B/B	B/B	B/B	B/B	D/D
Theft	A/D	B/D	B/D	A/B	C/C	A/B
Corruption	A/C	B/C	C/C	A/B	D/D	A/B
Viruses	B/B	B/B	B/B	B/B	B/C	D/D
Physical Damage	A/D	B/C	C/C	D/D	D/D	D/D

Effect: Likelihood:
A: Destructive B: Disabling   A: Certain   B: Likely
C: Disruptive   D: No Impact   C: Unlikely D: Impossible

FIGURE 9.2 An Example of a Threat Analysis Worksheet for a Specific Organization

An example of such a worksheet is presented in Figure 9.2. The results shown in this worksheet were determined during the requirements analysis process and are specific to a particular organization. Depending on the organization, the results of a threat analysis can be quite different from those shown in Figure 9.2. For example, a threat analysis can consist of the information and assets that need to be protected, in terms of confidentiality, integrity, and availability. This analysis can be combined with lists of threats that are currently out there, as well as potential vulnerabilities.

Threat analyses are by their nature subjective. One of the ways to minimize the degree of subjectivity is to involve representatives from various groups of the organization to participate in the analysis process. This helps to get many different perspectives into the analysis. It is also recommended that you review your threat analysis periodically, such as annually, to identify changes in your environment. As an organization grows and changes, and as the outside world changes, the degrees and types of threats to that organization will also change. A periodic threat analysis ensures that new threats are included and shows where new security mechanisms may be applied to the network. Along with this, a periodic review of security policies and procedures is also recommended. Subsequent reviews may highlight previously overlooked areas in the network, system, and environment.

9.4.2   Policies and Procedures

There are many trade-offs in security and privacy (as with all other architectural components), and it can be a two-edged sword. Sometimes security is confused with control over users and their actions. This confusion occurs when rules, regulations, and security guardians are placed above the goals and work that the organization is trying to accomplish. The road toward implementing security starts with an awareness and understanding of the possible security weaknesses in the network and then leads to the removal of these weaknesses. Weaknesses can generally be found in the areas of system and application software, the ways that security mechanisms are implemented, and in how users do their work. This last area is where educating users can be most beneficial.

Security policies and procedures are formal statements on rules for system, network, and information access and use, in order to minimize exposure to security threats. They define and document how the system can be used with minimal security risk. Importantly, they can also clarify *to users* what the security threats are, what can be done to reduce such risks, and the consequences of not helping to reduce them.

At a high level, security policies and procedures can present an organization's overall security philosophy. Examples of common high-level security philosophies are to deny specifics and accept everything else, or to accept specifics and deny everything else, as in Figure 9.3. The term *specific* refers to well-defined rules about who, what, and where security is applied. For example, it may be a list of specific routes that can be accepted into this network, or users that are permitted access to certain resources.

Security that denies specifics and accepts all else reflects an open network philosophy, requiring a thorough understanding of potential security threats, as these should be the specifics to be denied. It can be difficult to verify the security implementation for this philosophy, as it is hard to define "all else."

On the other hand, security that accepts specifics and denies all else reflects a closed network philosophy, requiring a thorough understanding of user, application, device, and network requirements, as these will become the specifics to be accepted. It is easier to validate this security implementation, as there is a finite (relatively small) set of "accepted" uses. Of the two philosophies, accept specifics/deny all else is the more common philosophy.

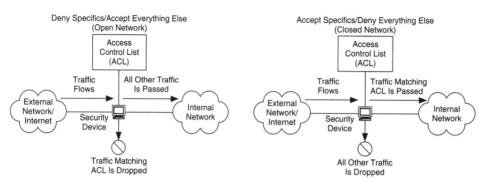

FIGURE 9.3   Example Security Philosophies

When you develop security policies and procedures, remember that, in order for them to be useful, they should be straightforward to implement for your environment (keeping in mind who will be supporting them), enforceable, and have clearly defined areas of responsibility.

Policies and procedures should include:

- Privacy statements (monitoring, logging, and access)
- Accountability statements (responsibilities, auditing)
- Authentication statements (password policies, remote access)
- Reporting violations (contact information, procedures)

Examples of security policies and procedures are acceptable use statements, security incident-handling procedures, configuration-modification policies, and network access control lists (ACLs). Each of these has a place in the security and privacy plan. These policies and procedures should describe not only how network resources can be accessed, used, and modified, but also why, to help users understand the policies they are being asked to accept and work with. Incident-handling procedures can be particularly helpful in making users aware of what to do when a security problem arises, bringing them into the security process rather than just subjecting them to it.

The list of areas for policies and procedures shown below can be used as a starting point to apply to the security architecture:

User Access to the System

- Authorization of use
- Authentication of identity and use of passwords

- Training and acceptance of responsibility for compliance
- Notices that corporate equipment is not private property
- Expectations of the right to privacy

Administrator Skills and Requirements for Certification

- Superusers as well as administrators

System Configuration and Management

- Maintenance
- Virus/Trojan protection
- Patching operating systems and applications
- Monitoring CERT advisories for notices of hacks
- Overseeing who can and cannot connect devices to the network
- Managing notice screens during login or startup
- Establishing what data get backed up
- Establishing what data get saved off-site
- Developing contingency computing plans
- Determining what to do when the system is attacked

9.5   Security and Privacy Mechanisms

There are several security mechanisms available today and many more on the horizon. However, not all mechanisms are appropriate for every environment. Each security mechanism should be evaluated for the network it is being applied to, based on the degree of protection it provides, its impact on users' ability to do work, the amount of expertise required for installation and configuration, the cost of purchasing, implementing, and operating it, and the amounts of administration and maintenance required.

In this section we cover physical security and awareness, protocol and application security, encryption/decryption, network perimeter security, and remote access security.

9.5.1 Physical Security and Awareness

Physical security is the protection of devices from physical access, damage, and theft. Devices are usually network and system hardware, such as network devices (routers, switches, hubs, etc.), servers, and specialized devices, but can also be software CDs, tapes, or peripheral devices. Physical security is the most basic form of security, and the one that is most intuitive to users. Nevertheless, it is often overlooked when developing a security plan. Physical security should be addressed as part of the network architecture even when the campus or building has access restrictions or security guards.

Ways to implement physical security include the following (see Figure 9.4):

- Access-controlled rooms (e.g., via card keys) for shared devices (servers) and specialized devices.
- Backup power sources and power conditioning
- Off-site storage and archival
- Alarm systems (e.g., fire and illegal entry alarms)

Physical security also applies to other types of physical threats, such as natural disasters (e.g., fires, earthquakes, and storms). Security from natural disasters includes protection from fire (using alarm systems and fire-abatement equipment), water (with pumping and other water-removal/protection mechanisms), and structural degradation (through having devices in racks attached to floors, walls, etc.). Addressing physical security lays the foundation for your entire network security and privacy plan.

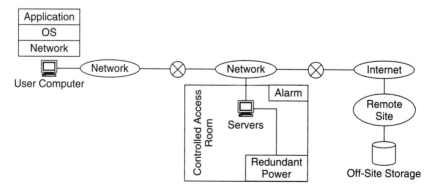

FIGURE 9.4 Areas of Physical Security

Security awareness entails getting users educated and involved with the day-to-day aspects of security in their network, and helping them to understand the potential risks of violating security policies and procedures. Security awareness can be promoted through providing sessions on security, where users have a chance to discuss the issues and voice their opinions and problems with security mechanisms, policies, and procedures, and potentially offer options for security and privacy; by providing users with bulletins or newsletters (or adding information to the organization's newsletter) on network security and what users can do to help; and by providing users with information on the latest security attacks.

9.5.2 Protocol and Application Security

In this section we consider some common protocol and application security mechanisms: IPSec, SNMP, and packet filtering.

IPSec is a protocol for providing authentication and encryption/decryption between devices at the network layer. IPSec mechanisms consist of authentication header (AH) and encapsulating security payload (ESP). There are two modes that IPSec operates in: transport and tunneling. In transport mode the IP payload is encrypted using ESP, while the IP header is left in the clear, as shown in Figure 9.5.

In tunnel mode (Figure 9.6) IPSec can be used to encapsulate packets between two virtual private network (VPN) gateways (IP_b and IP_c in the figure).

The tunneling process consists of the following:

- IPSec tunnels are created between VPN gateways IP_b and IP_c in Figure 9.6
- IP packets are encrypted using ESP

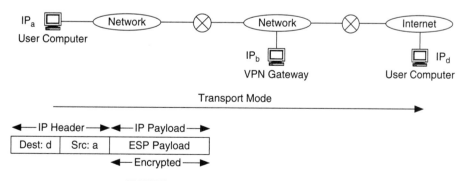

FIGURE 9.5 The Transport Mode of IPSec

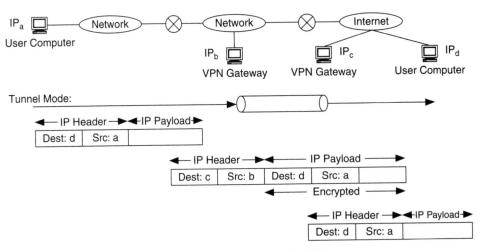

FIGURE 9.6   The Tunnel Mode of IPSec

- These packets are then encapsulated within another IP packet, and addressed with the ends of the IPSec tunnel (IP_b and IP_c)
- At the end of the tunnel (the VPN gateway serving IP_d), the original packet is unencapsulated and decrypted and sent to its destination (IP_d).

This is an example of *tunneling*, or encapsulating information within protocol headers for the purpose of isolating and protecting that information. Note that this is different from traditional protocol encapsulation, which is used to support varying functions at each protocol layer. Virtual private networks apply this tunneling concept to create multiple isolated networks across a common infrastructure.

Tunneling and VPNs are common methods for building an isolated network across a common infrastructure such as the Internet.

Security for the Simple Network Management Protocol version 3 (SNMPv3) is described in the user-based security model (USM), protecting against modification of information, masquerades, disclosure (eavesdropping), and message stream modification. SNMP Security provides the following security capabilities:

- SNMP message verification (data integrity), user identity verification (data origin authentication), and data confidentiality (via *authProtocol, authKey, privProtocol,* and *privKey*)
- Detects SNMP messages that have exceeded time thresholds (message timeliness/limited replay) (via *snmpEngineID, snmpEngineBoots,* and *snmpEngineTime*)

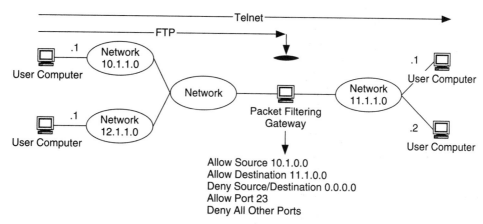

FIGURE 9.7 An Example of Packet Filtering

SNMP security also includes authentication mechanisms (*authProtocol*) and encryption/decryption mechanisms (*privProtocol*):

- HMAC-MD5-96 (128-bit message digest algorithm (MD5) cryptographic hash–function, message authentication codes (HMAC) mode, truncated to 96 bits)
- HMAC-SHA-96 (Secure Hash Algorithm)
- CBC-DES (Cipher Block Chaining Mode Symmetric Encryption/Decryption protocol

SNMP security also provides for modifying MIB views and access modes. For example, it is possible to have different MIB views definable for different groups, and access modes (RO, RW) are also definable for different groups, and are tied to MIB views.

Packet filtering is a mechanism in network devices to explicitly deny or pass packets at strategic points within the network. It is often used to deny packets to or from particular IP addresses or ports (services), as in Figure 9.7.

9.5.3 Encryption/Decryption

While other security mechanisms provide protection against unauthorized access and destruction of resources and information, encryption/decryption protects information from being usable by the attacker. *Encryption/decryption* is a security

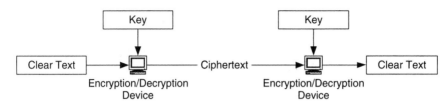

FIGURE 9.8   Encryption/Decryption of Network Traffic

mechanism where cipher algorithms are applied together with a secret key to encrypt data so that they are unreadable if they are intercepted. Data are then decrypted at or near their destination. This is shown in Figure 9.8.

As such, encryption/decryption enhances other forms of security by protecting information in case other mechanisms fail to keep unauthorized users from that information. There are two common types of encryption/decryption: public key and private key. Software implementations of public key encryption/decryption are commonly available. Examples include data encryption standard (DES) private key encryption, triple DES private key encryption, and Rivest, Shamir, and Adleman (RSA) public key encryption.

Public key infrastructure (PKI) is an example of a security infrastructure that uses both public and private keys. *Public key infrastructure* is a security infrastructure that combines security mechanisms, policies, and directives into a system that is targeted for use across unsecured public networks (e.g., the Internet), where information is encrypted through the use of a public and a private cryptographic key pair that is obtained and shared through a trusted authority. PKI is targeted toward legal, commercial, official, and confidential transactions, and includes cryptographic keys and a certificate management system. Components of this system are:

- Managing the generation and distribution of public/private keys
- Publishing public keys with UIDs as certificates in open directories
- Ensuring that specific public keys are truly linked to specific private keys
- Authenticating the holder of a public/private key pair

PKI uses one or more trusted systems known as Certification Authorities (CA), which serve as trusted third parties for PKI. The PKI infrastructure is hierarchical, with issuing authorities, registration authorities, authentication authorities, and local registration authorities.

Another example is the secure sockets library (SSL). *Secure sockets library* is a security mechanism that uses RSA-based authentication to recognize a party's digital identity and uses RC4 to encrypt and decrypt the accompanying transaction or communication. SSL has grown to become one of the leading security protocols on the Internet.

One trade-off with encryption/decryption is a reduction in network performance. Depending on the type of encryption/decryption and where it is implemented in the network, network performance (in terms of capacity and delay) can be degraded from 15% to 85% or more. Encryption/decryption usually also requires administration and maintenance, and some encryption/decryption equipment can be expensive. While this mechanism is compatible with other security mechanisms, trade-offs such as these should be considered when evaluating encryption/decryption.

9.5.4 Network Perimeter Security

For network perimeter security, or protecting the *external interfaces* between your network and external networks, we consider the use of address translation mechanisms and firewalls.

Network address translation, or NAT, is the mapping of IP addresses from one realm to another. Typically this is between public and private IP address space. Private IP address space is the set of IETF-defined private address spaces (RFC 1918):

- Class A   10.x.x.x   10/8 prefix
- Class B   172.16.x.x   172.16/12 prefix
- Class C   192.168.x.x   192.168/16 prefix

NAT is used to create bindings between addresses, such as one-to-one address binding (static NAT); one-to-many address binding (dynamic NAT); and address and port bindings (network address port translation, or NAPT).

While NAT was developed to address the issues of address space exhaustion, it was quickly adopted as a mechanism to enhance security at external interfaces. Routes to private IP address spaces are not propagated within the Internet; therefore, the use of private IP addresses hides the internal addressing structure of a network from the outside.

The security architecture should consider a combination of static and dynamic NAT and NAPT, based on the devices that are being protected. For example, static NAT is often used for bindings to multiple-user devices such as servers or high-end computing devices, while dynamic NAT is used with generic computing devices.

Firewalls are combinations of one or more security mechanisms, implemented in network devices (routers) placed at strategic locations within a network. Firewalls can be filtering gateways, application proxies with filtering gateways, or devices running specialized "firewall" software.

9.5.5   Remote Access Security

Remote access consists of traditional dial-in, point-to-point sessions, and virtual private network connections, as shown in Figure 9.9. Security for remote access includes what is commonly known as AAAA: authentication of users; authorization of resources to authenticated users; accounting of resources and service delivery; and allocation of configuration information (e.g., addresses or default route). AAAA is usually supported by a network device such as a network access server (NAS) or subscriber management system (SMS).

Remote access security is common in service-provider networks (see also the service-provider architectural model), but it is evolving into enterprise networks as enterprises recognize the need to support a remote access model for their networks.

Considerations when providing remote access are as follows (see Figure 9.10):

- Method(s) of AAAA
- Server types and placement (e.g., DMZ)
- Interactions with DNS, address pools, and other services

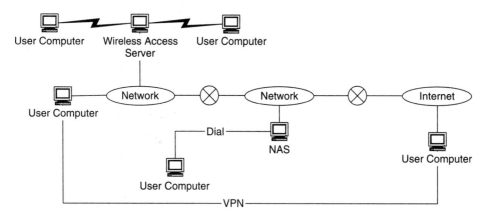

FIGURE 9.9   Remote Access Mechanisms

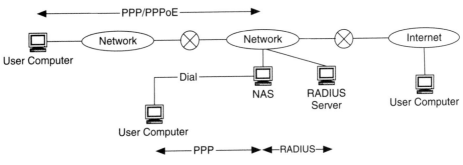

FIGURE 9.10   Remote Access Considerations

Figure 9.11 shows the protocol interaction of the point-to-point protocol (PPP), PPP over Ethernet (PPPoE), and remote access dial-in user service (RADIUS) in a remote access network.

This figure shows the process of establishing a PPPoE session, upon which a PPP session is started. PPPoE provides a shim between Ethernet and PPP, supporting the point-to-point nature of PPP sessions over a broadcast Ethernet network. Thus, a PPPoE session starts with a broadcast packet, the PPPoE active discovery initiation (PADI). This packet begins a handshake between the user's computer and NAS, consisting of PADI, PPPoE active discovery offer (PADO), PPPoE active discovery request (PADR), and PPPoE active discovery session (PADS) packets. The PPP session can begin at the completion of this part of the process.

A PPP session has three stages: link establishment, authentication, and network layer. Each stage builds on the previous one to establish the PPP session. Once PPPoE and PPP sessions have been established, the user can begin using the network.

Authentication in a remote access network is typically accomplished via a combination of PPP, PPPoE, PAP, CHAP, and RADIUS protocols. Other authentication mechanisms at the remote access network include tokens, smart cards, digital certificates, and callback. VPNs and tunnels can also be considered as part of the remote access network.

VPNs are an example of what can be considered a subarchitecture. VPNs, by themselves, can require their own set of architectural considerations. This is particularly true when they make an extranet, which is an intranet extended to include access to or from selected external organizations (e.g., customers, suppliers) but not to the general public. Such considerations include equipment types, tunneling

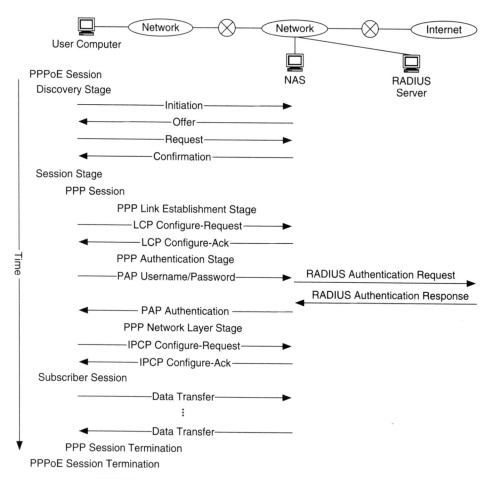

FIGURE 9.11   Process for PPP/PPPoE Session Establishment

protocols and security, VPN locations, policies on VPN provisioning and support, and the use of routing protocols such as the border gateway protocol (BGP) or multi-protocol label switching (MPLS).

Finally, remote access security should also consider wireless communications and portable computing devices using standards such as 802.11 and Homephoneline Networking Alliance (homePNA). Wireless can target a number of environments, such as mobility, portability, and nomadic computing.

9.6 Architectural Considerations

In developing our security architecture we need to evaluate potential security mechanisms, where they may apply within the network, as well as the sets of internal and external relationships for this component architecture.

9.6.1 Evaluation of Security Mechanisms

At this point we have requirements, goals, type of environment, and architectural model(s) and are ready to evaluate potential security mechanisms. As with each component architecture, when evaluating mechanisms for an architecture, it is best to start simple and work toward more complex solutions only when necessary.

Where a security mechanism will apply in a given network depends primarily on where security requirements are located throughout the network, and what the security requirements are, based on the results of the requirements analysis and the security and privacy plan.

The architectural models presented in Chapter 5 can help in determining where security mechanisms can be applied in the network. For example, the Access/Distribution/Core architectural model, which separates a network based on function, can be used as a starting point for applying security mechanisms. Using this model, security can be increased at each level, from access network to distribution networks to core networks, by either adding security mechanisms or by enhancing the amount of security provided by each mechanism. This is shown in Figure 9.12.

In this figure, security is increased from access to distribution to core areas, either by adding security mechanisms at each area or by increasing the level of security (i.e., enhancing security) at each level. For this architectural model, most

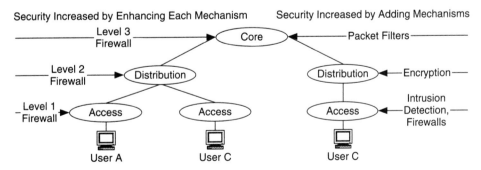

FIGURE 9.12 The Access/Distribution/Core Architectural Model as a Starting Point for Security

traffic flows are sourced/sinked at access networks, and travel across distribution and core networks. By adding mechanisms or enhancing mechanisms at each level, a traffic flow will encounter higher levels of security as it moves from access to distribution to core networks.

In Figure 9.12 traffic flows from User A to User C travel across both access and distribution networks and would encounter two levels of security: Level 1 and Level 2 firewalls, where Level 2 is greater security than Level 1. A Level 2 firewall may have a more complete access control list (ACL), stricter rules for filtering traffic, or greater logging and detection capability.

Traffic flows from User C to User A travel across access, distribution, and core networks. As traffic moves from User C to the core network, it would encounter multiple security mechanisms (intrusion detection, firewalls, encryption/decryption, and packet filters), with security increasing from access to distribution to core. In addition, as traffic moves from the core network to User A, it encounters three levels of firewalls.

In a similar fashion, the service provider and intranet/extranet architectural models can also be used to develop a framework for security in a network.

As mentioned in the last chapter, security perimeters (i.e., security zones or cells) can be developed within a network, to accommodate multiple levels of security requirements. Two common methods of developing security zones are to increase security as you move deeper into the network (an example of this is shown in Figure 9.12), or to develop zones wherever they are needed in the network, regardless of topology.

When security zones are developed to increase security as you move deeper into a network, they become embedded within each other, as shown in Figure 9.13. In a sense the security levels look like the layers of an onion, with the innermost layers having the highest level of security.

Security zones are based on the various security requirements determined during the requirements analysis process and should be described in the security and privacy plan. There may be requirements for different levels of security, coupled to groups of users, their applications, their devices, or devices that are shared among users. Security zones developed to meet such requirements may be scattered throughout the network and may even overlap one another. An example of this is presented in Figure 9.14.

In this figure five security zones are shown, based on different security requirements. The first zone (Security Level 1) covers the entire network and is intended to provide a general level of security for all users, applications, and devices. This may include intrusion detection and logging. The second zone (Security Level 2)

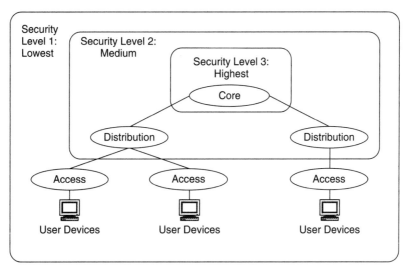

FIGURE 9.13   Security Zones Embedded within Each Other

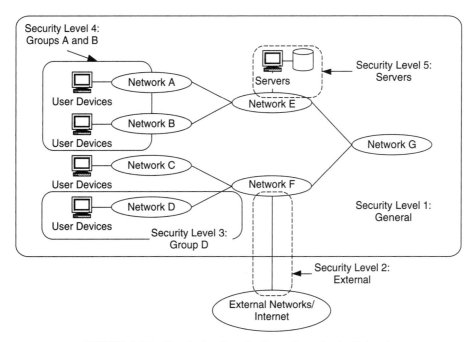

FIGURE 9.14   Developing Security Zones throughout a Network

provides a higher level of security between this network and all external networks. This may include NAT and firewalls.

The third zone (Security Level 3) provides another level of security for an entire group of users, applications, and/or devices (Group D), whose security requirements are different from the rest of the network. For example, this group may handle financial and/or proprietary information for the company. The fourth zone (Security Level 4) provides security for a subset of users, applications, and/or devices from multiple groups (Groups A and B). These are select users, applications, and/or devices whose security needs are different from others in their groups. For example, they may be working on company-classified projects, producing data that need to be protected from the rest of the groups. The third and fourth zones may apply mechanisms to protect their data, such as encryption/decryption, and may have access protection via firewalls and/or packet filtering. The fifth zone (Security Level 5) is security for devices used by multiple users, such as servers. This zone may employ monitoring, logging, and authentication to verify user access.

Figures 9.12, 9.13, and 9.14 show how security mechanisms may be applied in a network to achieve multiple security levels or zones.

9.6.2 Internal Relationships

Interactions within the security architecture include trade-offs, dependencies, and constraints among each of the security mechanisms for your network. For example, some security mechanisms require the ability to look at, add to, or modify various information fields within the packet. NAT changes IP address information between public and private address domains. Encryption/decryption mechanisms may encrypt information fields, making them unreadable to other mechanisms.

9.6.3 External Relationships

External relationships are trade-offs, dependencies, and constraints between the security architecture and each of the other component architectures (addressing/routing, network management, performance, and any other component architectures you may develop). There are some common ones, some of which are presented below.

Interactions between security and addressing/routing. NAT is an addressing mechanism that is often used to enhance security. Therefore, when it is applied for security, it also impacts addressing for the network. In addition, dynamic addressing can interfere with address-specific protective measures and with logging.

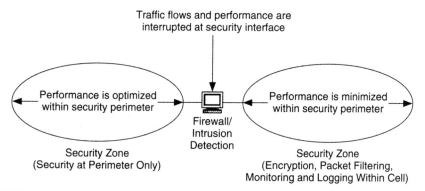

FIGURE 9.15   Security Mechanisms May Restrict or Preclude Performance within Each Zone

It is more difficult to determine what is going on when IP addresses are changed frequently.

Interactions between security and network management. Security depends on network management to configure, monitor, manage, and verify security levels throughout the network. In addition, there is a need for maintenance access even during attacks where in-band access to network devices is not available. For example, when devices are not at the same location, using dial-up for out-of-band access is a potential fall-back position to take.

Interactions between security and performance. Security and performance are often at odds, as security mechanisms can impact network performance. The security zones described earlier in this chapter can constrain performance within the areas described by the zones. When security is a high priority, security mechanisms that impact traffic flows may restrict performance mechanisms to operate within security zones, or result in performance being minimized for that zone (Figure 9.15).

When performance is high priority, particularly when there is a need to provision end-to-end performance among select users, applications, or devices, performance mechanisms may preclude the use of intrusive security mechanisms in those areas of the network.

9.7   Conclusions

In this chapter we discussed various potential security mechanisms for your security architecture, including physical security, protocol and application security, encryption/decryption, and perimeter and remote access security. Based on information from the requirements analysis, we developed input for a security and privacy plan. We also discussed elements of both internal and external relationships for the security architecture.

9.8   Exercises

For Exercises 1 through 3, refer to Figure 9.16.

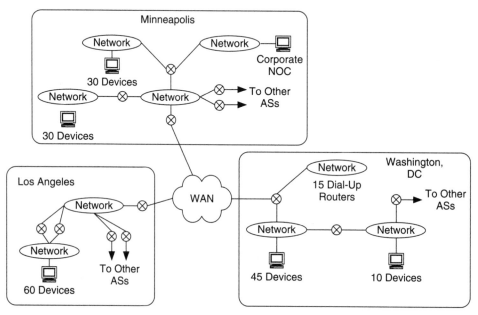

FIGURE 9.16   Network for Exercises 1 through 3

1.   Develop a sample threat analysis for the network in Figure 9.16, or for a network that you are familiar with. Show assets and potential threats as in Figure 9.2.

2.   Apply the security mechanisms from this chapter to support the following require-ments. Show where each mechanism might be applied.
   a.   An intranet between each of the routers connected to the WAN.
   b.   Remote access security for each of the 15 dial-up routers connected to the LAN in Washington, DC.
   c.   All traffic flows between Los Angeles and Minneapolis must be encrypted.

3. Outline the development of DMZs that would be applied at each site where connections are made to other autonomous systems (AS). What types of devices would be used at these sites?

4. Figure 9.17 shows five security zones required by the customer. These zones are prioritized, such that Security Zone 5 provides basic security for the entire network, and Zones 2, 3, 4, and 1 have increasing degrees of security, with Zone 1 having the highest level of security. For this network:

   a. What security mechanisms can be applied within each security zone, and at the interfaces between security zones, to achieve increasing degrees of security?

   b. Which architectural models are most applicable to this network? Show how each model can be applied.

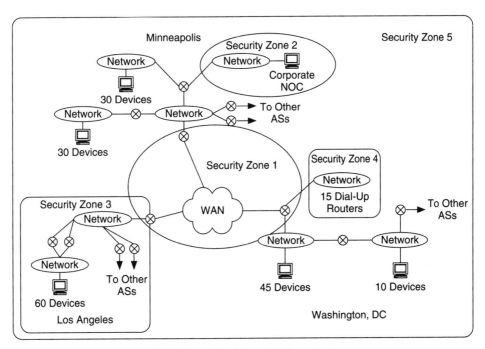

FIGURE 9.17 Network for Exercise 4

CHAPTER CONTENTS

10

Network Design

Network design adds product, vendor, location, and configuration detail to the architecture. Our analysis and architecture work done to date helps make the design process straightforward, reproducible, and well documented. In fact, when the analysis and architecture processes are done well, the design process becomes relatively easy.

Some readers may feel that the reason the design process is straightforward is that we have already done most of what is traditionally termed "design" during the analysis and architecture. This is somewhat true; however, *design decisions* made without benefit of the analysis and architecture processes are ad hoc decisions, made without a sufficient understanding of what we are trying to achieve (problem statements and objectives), what we need (requirements), and how network components will work together (architecture). Ad hoc decision making results in a lot of work at the back end of the project, in terms of resolving conflicts and trying to understand, justify, and explain the design.

By moving much of the work forward in the project life cycle to the analysis and architecture, we are better prepared to make design decisions, procure equipment and services, and provide the background material to support our decisions, and we can couple design decisions to the architecture, requirements, and problem statements. My experience is that this is always a much better position to be in, and well worth the investment in time and resources.

Unfortunately, there is a tendency for engineers to jump to a technical solution without the discipline of analysis and architecture. I have seen this happen many times, always with less than positive results. For example, I was asked to participate in a network project that entailed the development of a national WAN to replace one that is out of date. It turned out that a replacement WAN had already been developed—done quickly with lots of money spent—but its design was ad hoc, without any requirements or architectural forethought. Although it had been implemented and in place for over a year, it had never been used and would never be used. Using the processes in this book we were able to develop a replacement WAN that was highly successful, exceeding the performance and scalability expectations of the customer.

10.1   Objectives

In this chapter you will learn the network design process. This process focuses on two major areas of work for your design: evaluating vendors and service providers, along with their products and services; and diagramming the design—that is, developing detailed blueprints that provide the physical layout for all of your information developed so far. You will learn that a critical result of this work is a set of design decisions that are traceable back to your architecture decisions, requirements, and problem statements. You will also learn how to trace design decisions back to architectural decisions and how to apply metrics to design decisions.

10.1.1   Preparation

To be able to understand and apply the concepts in this chapter to your projects, you should be familiar with the analysis and architecture processes discussed throughout this book; current and emerging network and systems technologies; network topologies and their associated hierarchy and diversity characteristics; and equipment-vendor and service-provider characteristics (although we will go through much of this in this chapter).

10.2   Design Concepts

Network design is the ultimate target of our work, the culmination of network analysis and architecture processes. Whereas network analysis provides understanding, and network architecture provides conceptual (technology and topology) descriptions of the network, network design builds upon these to add physical detail and vendor, product, and service selections to the network.

The upper part of Figure 10.1 shows an example WAN architecture describing the general topology (a multiple-ring topology); strategic locations in the network (Carrier-Independent Exchange Facilities (CIEFs) and demarcation points for each Center and Center LAN); and locations of major types of equipment (switches [S], routers [R], and monitoring devices [M]. Along with such a diagram you would have descriptions of CIEFs and equipment types when needed. In addition, technology choices could be shown on this diagram and included in the corresponding description. This architecture conveys the general concepts of this WAN, including the general structure of the network (a set of carrier facilities interconnected with carrier services in multiple rings, with each CIEF acting as a hub for point-to-point

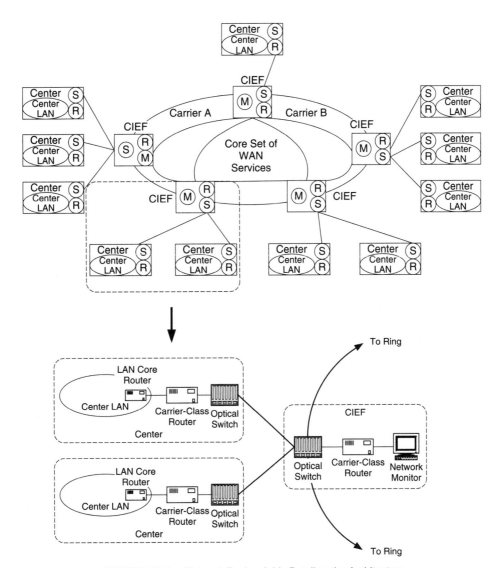

FIGURE 10.1   Network Design Adds Detail to the Architecture

connections to a number of Centers), and general locations for switches, routers, and monitors.

The lower part of Figure 10.1 is an example of how design begins to add detail to the architecture. This figure shows how Centers and CIEFs interconnect. Using generic terms like *carrier-class switches* and *routers*, the diagram indicates what these devices could actually be, based on vendor and product selections made during the design process. Some details can also be shown in terms of the configuration of the devices and how they are connected to each other. However, this diagram does not show all of the possible detail in the products, or the physical locations of equipment. It is useful to note that there can be different products of the design, providing different levels of detail depending on who is the recipient of the product.

What is shown in Figure 10.1 can be considered a *first-order product* of the design. It is not intended to be used to install or configure devices, but rather as a product for management, providing greater detail than the architecture but not so much as to be confusing. What is shown in Figure 10.1 helps describe what is being evaluated and how many devices will be needed for a particular location, and is useful for procurement and general connectivity planning.

Figure 10.2 shows a *second-order product* for one center from the same design. Note the greater amount of detail, including product types, hardware and software revision levels, device configurations, and a more explicit layout of the connectivity between devices, as well as with service providers. Second-order design products provide enough detail to fully understand the network, where devices are in relation to one another, their general locations, and where services such as QoS and VoIP should be enabled.

What is missing from a second-order product such as in Figure 10.2 is the actual location of each piece of hardware in the network design. While a second-order product may provide general locations (buildings, floors, rooms), a *third-order product* adds location detail. For example, the design could show rack layouts and where each device is located in a rack (or equivalent piece of hardware). An important part of a third-order product is showing the explicit connectivity between devices,

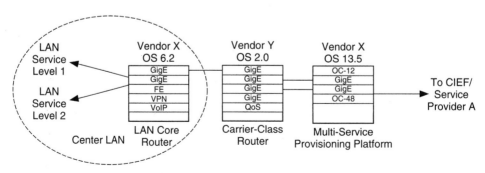

FIGURE 10.2 A Second-Order Design Product

including descriptions and diagrams of cable runs. With a third-order product you should have all of the information you need from the design to install, configure, and operate the network.

It is important to note that third-order products are the ultimate targets for the design. You may end up developing first- and second-order products as by-products while working on third-order products. Thus, it may not be more work developing first-, second-, and third-order design products, and by organizing your design products into these three categories you can support multiple recipients of the design. For example, in the process of developing highly detailed third-order design products for network implementation, you can have first-order design products for management and second-order design products for review.

10.2.1 Analogy to a Building Design

A comparison can be made between the architecture/design of a network and that of a building. For example, in designing a building, the designer/architect needs to know the general purpose for that building (e.g., residential, commercial, industrial), what type(s) of occupants the building is likely to have, approximately how many there will be, and what they will be doing (their requirements). The building design would include the building's physical layout, how space will be used, how occupants will move around within the building, and their needs for building resources (HVAC, lighting, power, water, restrooms, exits, etc.). The product of the building design is a set of blueprints that provide a physical layout for all of this information and show the relationships among components of the building (e.g., where trade-offs were made among space, power, and other resources).

A network design has these same characteristics. Instead of building occupants we have network users; what they will be doing are their requirements (their applications and devices, their work and traffic flows). The building's architecture becomes the network architecture: its topology and technologies. While a building architecture describes relationships among building functions (space, HVAC, power, plumbing, water, lighting, elevators, stairs, etc.), the network architecture describes relationships among network functions (security, network management, routing/addressing, performance, etc.). And as the product of a building's design is a set of blueprints providing the physical layout for all of its information, the network design is also a set of blueprints and diagrams, along with supporting textual descriptions for the network.

One big difference between a building design and a network design is that there is often an artistic component to a building design, while there is rarely one for a network design. There can be an artistic component to a network, such as when it is a part of an exhibit, show, or conference; however, the vast majority of networks is not seen by its users.

10.2.2   Design Products

The key products of a network design are:

- Network blueprints
- A component plan
- Vendor, vendor equipment, and service-provider selections
- Traceability
- Metrics for measuring design success

Network blueprints describe the physical aspects of your network design: locations of network devices, servers, the cable plant, physical security and secure locations; how devices are interconnected, their interface types and speeds; as well as device-specific and service-specific information. Blueprints usually also show the support infrastructure for the cable plant: building entrances, conduit, cable runs, and the like.

Network blueprints may consist of a single diagram or several diagrams of the network, depending on your needs and the size of your project. If the network design is large, you may need to have one or more high-level diagrams that show the entire network in some detail, along with more detailed diagrams that focus on specific areas of the network, such as the WAN, campus LANs, individual buildings, even floors or rooms of a building (Figure 10.3). As part of your detailed diagrams you may want to focus on strategic locations of your network, developed during the architecture process. This is the traditional and most common form of network blueprint.

For other cases you may want to have several detailed diagrams that focus not on specific areas of your network, but instead on specific functions of your network (as we discussed during the architecture process). When this is the case, it is useful to have the diagrams as overlays (diagrams on clear sheets of plastic), where you can place one diagram on top of another, in order to see how and where the functions are applied within the network, and how and where they overlap (Figure 10.4). You can use the results of the architecture process as the starting point to develop such overlays.

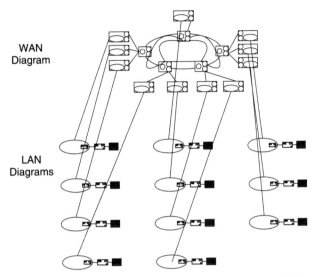

WAN
Diagram

LAN
Diagrams

FIGURE 10.3 Diagrams Focus on Geographical Areas of a Network

If you decide to describe the network design as overlays of multiple functions, then each function can have a *component plan* which describes the mechanisms associated with that function, internal interactions among those mechanisms, and external interactions among functions. Component plans can be complementary to the network blueprints, often providing function-specific information that normally would not be on blueprints. For example, a component plan that describes security for the network might include configuration information for security devices, such as sets of ACLs or VPNs, and where in the network each set would be applied.

Each way of describing the network has its advantages. Describing geographical areas of a network (e.g., WANs, LANs) is intuitive and useful for installation, operation, troubleshooting, and modification of that network. Since such diagrams have all relevant devices depicted, it is easy to see connectivity between devices, and to trace a path across the network.

Describing functions of a network has the advantage of showing all devices and services of a particular function (e.g., security) together on the same diagram. This allows network personnel to more easily see where those devices are, how that function will be provided in the network, and how those devices are interconnected. For example, in a layered, defense-in-depth, security strategy you may have different security techniques and/or degrees of security at each layer. Functional diagrams can show these security layers, which devices/services are at each layer, and how the devices (and layers) interconnect and interact.

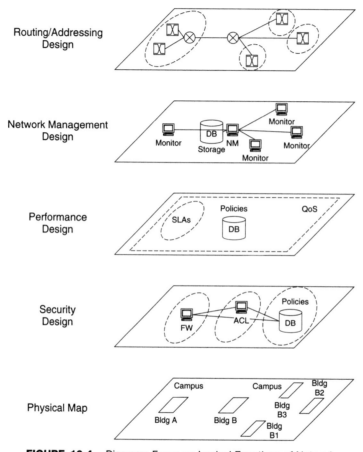

FIGURE 10.4 Diagrams Focus on Logical Functions of Network

Along with blueprints and component plans, the analysis and architecture processes provide information for you to make *vendor, vendor equipment, and service-provider selections*. In making these selections, we apply a process similar to that used to make architecture decisions. Using products from network analysis and architecture we develop an initial set of options and then develop complete sets of candidate options and evaluation criteria; gather data to apply to the evaluations; refine our evaluation criteria and develop ratings; and then apply criteria and ratings to prioritize the candidate options, reducing the number of options to one or a few optimal choices.

Once you know the equipment, vendors, and service providers for your design, you will apply configuration details to your design, which will be used during network implementation and testing. These data consist of general and vendor-specific configuration information and protocol selections (if necessary). For example, sets of ACLs mentioned earlier as part of the security component plan would be considered configuration details. Routing protocols, AS numbers, and specific routing and peering information would also be considered configuration details.

Along with these products you will also be able to show *traceability* between design decisions, architecture decisions, requirements, and problem statements. This is a powerful capability that will help you to address any questions and challenges that may arise regarding your design.

As part of the decisions regarding your design you will have associated *metrics* that are used to describe how you measure success of the design, in the same way that metrics were coupled to requirements. As part of your traceability you may also show how design metrics trace back to requirements metrics. Design metrics can also be used to validate your design.

All of the analysis and architecture work done up to this point provide you with an excellent foundation for making design decisions. This input to the design is discussed next.

Experience has shown that many network projects start at this point, without the underlying analysis and architecture work. The resulting ad hoc design decisions can be disastrous. In addition, I have found that, by applying the analysis and architecture processes, making design decisions becomes the easiest part of the project. Knowing the problems that need to be solved, the requirements for the project, and the network architecture, the design decisions can actually *flow* from this information. Of course, this should be expected: throughout the analysis and architecture processes we are preparing to make design decisions, so that when we get to the design process, we will have already put a fair bit of thought into it.

10.2.3   Input to the Design

At this point in the process we have lots of information to use for our design. These analysis and architecture processes provide products that serve as input to our design. The better these products are, the better our input is, and the better our design will be. The term "garbage in, garbage out" is quite applicable here. In Figure 10.5 architecture products feed into the two parts of the design process—evaluations and layout—producing a number of design products.

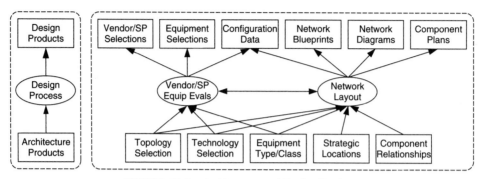

FIGURE 10.5 Architecture and Design Products

Throughout this chapter we discuss how these products are used in the design process.

10.3 Design Process

The design process consists of vendor, equipment, and service-provider evaluations and network layout. These processes build upon and add detail to architectural decisions.

Architecture products include:

- Selected topology
- Selected technologies
- Equipment types/classes
- Supporting material (e.g., traceability diagrams)
- Architectural relationships
  - Routing and addressing
  - Security
  - Network management
  - Performance
  - Others (as needed)

All of these architecture products can be combined into the reference architecture for the project.

Analysis products include:

- Requirements
- Flow information
- Problem statements
- Service information

Vendor, equipment, and service-provider evaluations build on technology and equipment type/class selections made during the architecture process, working toward vendor, service provider, and equipment selections for the design. Such information is often formalized in documents such as requests for proposal (RFPs), which are useful during equipment and service procurement. Recall that during the architecture process we developed a similar document, a request for information (RFI), which is useful in gathering the detailed product and service information needed to prepare for evaluations.

Network layout combines topology, technology, equipment types, relationships, and strategic locations to develop blueprints and component plans for your network design. To some degree, both parts of the design process can be done at the same time and using each other's products (thus the arrow shown between the evaluation and layout processes in Figure 10.5). You may want to incorporate equipment and service-provider information from your evaluations into the blueprints and component plans. Thus, the network layout is usually the last part of the design process.

We now examine each part of the design process in detail.

10.4   Vendor, Equipment, and Service-Provider Evaluations

The evaluation process presented here can be applied to vendors and service providers, their equipment and services. In general, this process consists of using products from network analysis and architecture to develop an initial set of options (termed *seeding the evaluation process*); conducting discussions to develop a complete set of candidate options, along with criteria to evaluate those options; gathering and developing data to apply to the evaluations; refining evaluation criteria and developing ratings; applying criteria and ratings to prioritize the candidate options; and modifying the set of candidate options, with the goal of selecting the optimal candidate. This process is shown in Figure 10.6.

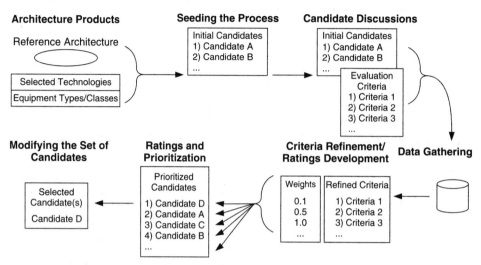

FIGURE 10.6   Vendor, Equipment, and Service-Provider Evaluation Process

This is an iterative process. There are times when an optimal candidate can be found with a single iteration of the process; at other times it may take two or three iterations to produce an optimal result. The number of iterations depends in part on the complexity of the evaluations, how well prepared you are, and how well you and your evaluation team perform the evaluation. As you get used to the process, you will be able to get results with fewer iterations.

Ideally, a template can be developed that can then be applied to each and every evaluation, making the process straightforward, predictable, and reproducible. That is what this section strives to provide. However, we also recognize that, depending on the project, some evaluations may have their own unique characteristics. In all cases I have found that this process can still provide excellent results.

Although this process can be applied to evaluate vendors, vendor equipment, and service providers, it is important to note that we do not want to combine these evaluations into one. Keep each evaluation separate—do not mix vendors, vendor equipment, and service providers—as this will confuse the evaluators and overly complicate the process. For example, some of the evaluation criteria for vendors will be different from those for service providers, and trying to apply criteria to both concurrently would be problematic.

An important part of this process is that you will develop a detailed set of information regarding how your evaluation decisions were made. This information can be used to help reduce or eliminate disagreements that may arise regarding your vendor, service provider, or equipment selections. Such disagreements tend to be more likely as the design budget increases.

Example 10.1.

It has been my experience that a large part of the design process is often spent resolving protests brought by vendors, service providers, and even a subset of the evaluators, disagreeing with a selection (often a vendor selection). The evaluation process presented here will provide you with plenty of documentation with which you can resolve or even avoid such protests.

For example, I have participated in vendor evaluations where Vendor A is the popular choice, while Vendor B has the best technical solution. Without a process for evaluating and selecting vendors, Vendor A would have been chosen as the *de facto* choice, without regard to its inferior technical solution. I have used this process to help make it obvious that the technically superior vendor should be chosen.

10.4.1 Seeding the Evaluation Process

The purpose of seeding an evaluation is to get the process started quickly. Seeding consists of generating an initial list of candidates for discussion. One person, such as the project manager, or a few select people can seed the evaluation process. Since the goal is to rapidly kick-start the evaluation process, we do not want to spend much time on this, but rather quickly put together a short list of candidates (vendors, service providers, or equipment, depending on the evaluation) for discussion. This list often consists of the most obvious candidates.

Why is this needed? I have found that it is much easier to generate discussion and develop options when some options are already on the table. This tends to focus the group and gives them something to work toward (or against).

Some or all of the analysis and architecture products shown in Section 10.3 should be directly applicable to start the evaluation process. We can use these products to determine an initial set of candidates. For example, the architecture process provides us with network technologies and network topology that were selected for the project. The selected network technologies may be available only from a subset of vendors (and their equipment) and may be supported by a subset of service providers. Similarly, the selected network topology may be supported only by a subset of service providers. In addition, only some service providers may be able to reach the strategic locations selected for the network architecture. For example, a strategic location may lie in a city that is not readily available to some providers, or it may be prohibitively expensive for them to provide service to those locations.

Architectural relationships, along with strategic locations, may have resulted in specific equipment types or classes being chosen. For example, strategic locations that require high-performance routing, security, and management indicate the need for larger-scale equipment (e.g., carrier-class equipment) where we can combine these functions, or the need for multiple instances and types of equipment to distribute these functions. The class or type of equipment chosen may indicate a particular set of vendors, maybe also particular pieces of equipment.

We also have the products of the network analysis—the requirements and flow specifications—which can be used to help determine initial candidates for evaluation.

The seeding of the evaluation process results in having some candidate vendors, vendor equipment options, or service providers to take into the next step in this process—discussions with project participants.

10.4.2 Candidate Discussions

Having developed a short list (seed) of candidates, we want to use that list to generate a more complete list of candidates, as well as begin to develop a set of criteria that we can use for evaluation.

Whereas one or a few persons can develop the seed list, the complete list should involve a much larger group of participants, including the project team, select potential users of the network, technical staff, management, and/or stakeholders. Your evaluation team should represent the scale and scope of your project.

Using the seed as a starting point, discussions are held, often involving a whiteboard or Web equivalent, to expand this list. At this point in the process it is better to include all candidates, including obviously inferior ones, and reject them during the prioritization and selection, rather than rejecting them outright. Even if the list becomes unwieldy, it can be quickly pared down once your criteria and ratings have been developed. In this way you will be able to show that you considered a sizable number of options, along with reasons for rejecting them. This can be useful later if someone contests your selection with one that happens to be on your list of rejections. Additionally, you may find that one of your not-so-obvious choices turns out to be one of the better ones.

Along with the complete set of candidates you will need to develop your set of evaluation criteria. Common examples of evaluation criteria are shown in Figure 10.7. Your set will also likely contain evaluation criteria specific to your project, your network, and your organization.

At this point in the process you should not use these criteria to evaluate your candidates. We still need to refine the criteria, as well as develop weights for the

	Evaluation Criteria
1	Costs
2	Technologies
3	Performance
4	Risks

FIGURE 10.7   An Example Set of Initial Evaluation Criteria

criteria, before applying them. But even before that we need to perform some research and data gathering to support the evaluation.

10.4.3 Data Gathering

Now that you have developed a complete (or nearly complete) set of (vendor, vendor equipment, service provider) candidates, you need to gather and develop data that will be helpful to your evaluations. Common sources and types of information are:

- Discussions with internal and external groups
- Discussions with vendors and/or service providers
- Independent (third-party) assessments of vendors, equipment, and/or service providers
- Modeling and simulation
- Information from risk assessments

Discussions with internal and external groups can provide information in addition to the candidate discussions. The intent of these discussions is to expand the amount of information by talking with more users and staff, and in greater detail. External groups may be able to relate their experiences with candidate vendors, vendor equipment, and service providers. This is especially useful when your design includes technologies or equipment that are new to you, but that others have experience with (e.g., implementation and operational experience with IPv6). External groups may be other organizations like yours, or groups with a common interest, such as user groups or technical forums.

Since we now have a list of candidates, discussions with vendors and/or service providers on that list are often useful to learn specific information about each vendor, service provider, or piece of equipment. Such discussions can also be helpful in learning what each is capable of doing for your project: providing value-added services, access to labs, testing and validation, and competitive pricing are some examples. However, vendors and service providers should not be allowed to get too close to the evaluation. They are motivated to represent their products and services in the best light and may try to steer the evaluation in their direction. Therefore, it is best to keep such discussions isolated from the evaluations (i.e., don't invite them to any meetings where the evaluations are being discussed).

Along with the above discussions, at times it is useful to get independent (third-party) assessments of vendors, equipment, and/or service providers. Independent assessments provide a prospective that is often different from what internal groups, vendors, and service providers will give. Like external groups, independent assessors may be able to provide you with implementation and operational experience with technologies and equipment that are new to you. For independent assessments I tend to choose small companies or individuals (consultants) instead of large consulting firms.

Modeling and simulation of all or part of the network architecture can provide valuable information for your evaluations. For example, you can use computer models to make comparisons of how your network will perform using different service providers, based on their services offered and on their infrastructures. You may already have some of this information if you have done modeling and simulation to refine your network analysis and/or architecture.

In addition to the above, any information from risk assessments that is applicable to vendors and/or service providers can be useful in evaluations. Your risk assessment, performed early in the analysis process, may reveal certain risks for your project. One or more of these risk factors may be applicable to your evaluation. For example, your project may be adverse to the risk of applying a new protocol, technology, or service. If vendors or service providers apply one of these, it can be used as a part of your evaluation.

All of this information is usually compiled as a document in support of the evaluations and is carried forward into criteria refinement and ratings development. In addition, this information can be very helpful in developing formal documents needed in the procurement and implementation of your design. One example of this is development of a request for purchase (RFP) for products and services.

For example, using the set of initial evaluation criteria from Figure 10.7, data gathering would probably allow us to expand that set based on input from various organizations. Vendors would probably be able to add technology and standards-specific information, while we may be able to learn about risks from other organizations that have already completed similar projects. We may be able to learn specifics regarding performance, from these same organizations or from groups that do equipment and system testing.

10.4.4 Criteria Refinement and Ratings Development

Now that you have additional information regarding your criteria (from the data gathering exercise), you can use this information to refine the criteria. Often, in gathering and developing data, we learn that there are some new criteria that should be added; that some existing criteria are not as appropriate as first thought and perhaps should be removed; or that some criteria should be modified according to the new information. The result is a refined and better set of evaluation criteria.

In order to apply these evaluation criteria to your list of candidates, you should have some way to compare and contrast the candidates. This is commonly done with a system of ratings. Ratings show how the candidates compare to one another. Ratings are applied with criteria (which you already have) and weights that show the relative importance of each criterion. In this section we are concerned with developing weights for our criteria. Although this is one of the more subjective parts of the process, it is necessary in order to make selections from your list.

In our example we had the following initial criteria: costs, technology, performance, and risks. From our data gathering we learned that costs should be separated into initial costs and recurring costs, and that other criteria should be added: standards compliance, available services, operations, and scalability. If our seed set of two candidates expanded into five design candidates, our evaluation chart would look something like Figure 10.8. Note that we have a column for relative weights, and a row to total the ratings for each candidate, both of which we have yet to complete.

In this figure we have nine criteria. Each criterion will be given a weight based on the importance of that criterion to the evaluation. This is determined through group discussion, which may include voting on suggested weights. The range of weights that you apply is not as important as maintaining consistency throughout your evaluation. One common range for weights across the set of criteria is 0–1, where 0 means that that criterion has no importance to your evaluation, 1 means that it has the highest importance to your evaluation, and any value in between indicates that criterion's degree of importance. (Note that you could decide that all criteria are equal, in which case you need not assign weights, or you could give each criterion a weight of 1.)

For our example we would take the data gathered so far, along with our refined sets of criteria and candidates, and conduct a discussion regarding how to weight each criterion. Using a range of 0–1, Figure 10.9 shows how the weights might be applied.

Evaluation Criteria		Relative Weight	Candidates				
			Candidate 1	Candidate 2	Candidate 3	Candidate 4	Candidate 5
1	Initial Costs						
2	Recurring Costs						
3	Technologies						
4	Standards Compliance						
5	Risks						
6	Performance						
7	Available Services						
8	Operations						
9	Scalability						
	Candidate Totals						

FIGURE 10.8   A Refined Set of Evaluation Criteria

Evaluation Criteria		Relative Weight (0–1)	Candidates				
			Candidate 1	Candidate 2	Candidate 3	Candidate 4	Candidate 5
1	Initial Costs	0.8					
2	Recurring Costs	1.0					
3	Technologies	0.5					
4	Standards Compliance	0.2					
5	Risks	0.9					
6	Performance	0.8					
7	Available Services	0.2					
8	Operations	0.5					
9	Scalability	0.1					
	Candidate Totals						

FIGURE 10.9   A Set of Evaluation Criteria with Relative Weights Added

In this figure recurring costs are weighted highest, followed by risks, initial costs, and performance. Operations and technology are weighted in the middle of the scale, while standards compliance, available services, and scalability are weighted the least. By looking at this comparison chart, you can see the importance the evaluation team places on each criterion.

It is useful to write down how you arrived at each weight and keep this as part of your documentation. If you are ever asked why certain criteria were weighted higher than others, you will be happy to have it documented. I have found that memory does not serve well here: There have been times when I was certain I would remember the reasons for a particular weight (it seemed obvious at the time), only to forget when asked later.

There are additional ways to develop weights for criteria. As discussed during the analysis process, some characteristics that we can apply to criteria are urgency, importance, and relevance. *Urgency* is a measure of how time-critical the criterion is; *importance* is a measure of how significant the criterion is to this project; and *relevance* is a measure of the appropriateness of this problem to the project. The default characteristic is importance.

Each criterion can be evaluated in terms of urgency, importance, and relevance, and a weight assigned to the criterion that is based on all three characteristics. Then the candidates can be evaluated as in the previous example.

In the next section our weights are used with ratings based on how each candidate fares relative to one another for a given criterion.

10.4.5 Ratings and Prioritization

Armed with our criteria and the results of our data gathering exercise we now develop ratings for each candidate. As in developing the first set of weights, this should be a group effort that includes your best technical and executive decision makers. The size of such an evaluation group is important—you don't want such a large group that nothing gets accomplished, nor one so small that decisions made by the group will be protested by others in your organization.

Example 10.2.

My experience is that a group size somewhere between six and twelve is optimal for making these types of decisions. Oddly enough, this works from small to very large designs.

One important requirement of the evaluation group is that there be no vendors or service providers present. This may seem obvious, but it is surprising how often they are able to get involved. Clearly, in order to develop fair and balanced decisions it is best to leave them out. You should have already gotten all relevant information from vendors and service providers during the data gathering process, *before* you develop and apply ratings.

To continue our exercise, we have our evaluation group together along with our evaluation chart. We then need to agree on a scale for our ratings. One common range is the same range previously used, 0–1, where 0 means that the candidate is least relevant for that criterion and 1 means that it is most relevant. Other common ranges are 1–5 or 1–10, where a weight of 1 means that that candidate is the worst or least relevant for that criterion, and 5 (or 10) means that that candidate is the best or most relevant for that criterion. You could use these ranges to rank the candidates, giving the best candidate (according to that criterion) a 1, the next best a 2, and so on.

Expanding the scale, or reversing the numbers (so that 10 is the worst or least relevant) is entirely subjective. However, it is important that your evaluation group agrees on the scale. If you have problems with this, it indicates that you will have trouble during the evaluations.

Let's say that for this example we choose a scale of 1–5, 5 being the best and 1 the worst. We then take one of the evaluation criteria (e.g., costs) and discuss each design option based on this. This should be a democratic process, where each person gets a chance to express his or her opinion and vote on each candidate. The group leader or project manager would break ties if necessary.

For a discussion on costs we may have cost information (for each candidate design) that was provided to us by an independent assessment, from other organizations that are deploying a similar design, from our own past experience, or from the vendors and service providers themselves. You should be able to compile such cost information and use it to determine a relative rating for each design candidate. You would populate the evaluation chart with ratings for all of the candidates for the cost criterion and then do the same thing for the other criteria. Once you have given ratings to each of your candidates across all of the criteria, you can multiply the weight of each criterion with the rating given to each candidate. The result would look something like Figure 10.10.

In this example each candidate is rated from 1 (worst) to 5 (best) for each criterion. Those ratings are shown as the first number in each evaluation box. Then each rating is multiplied by that candidate's relative weight, resulting in a weighted rating. These weighted ratings are shown as the second number in each evaluation box. The ratings and weighted ratings for each candidate are added together, as reflected in the candidate totals at the bottom of the figure. Although totals for both weighted and unweighted ratings are shown (for illustration), only the weighted ratings would be totaled and applied to the evaluation. Having both weighted and unweighted ratings in an actual evaluation would be confusing.

Evaluation Criteria		Relative Weight (0–1)	Candidates				
			Candidate 1	Candidate 2	Candidate 3	Candidate 4	Candidate 5
1	Initial Costs	0.8	3/2.4	5/4	4/3.2	2/1.6	1/0.8
2	Recurring Costs	1.0	4/4	5/5	3/3	1/1	2/2
3	Technologies	0.5	3/1.5	4/2.0	1/0.5	2/1.0	5/2.5
4	Standards Compliance	0.2	4/0.8	1/0.2	3/0.6	2/0.4	5/1.0
5	Risks	0.9	3/2.7	4/3.6	1/0.9	5/4.5	2/1.8
6	Performance	0.8	4/3.2	5/4.0	2/1.6	1/0.8	3/2.4
7	Available Services	0.2	5/1.0	1/0.2	3/0.6	2/0.4	4/0.8
8	Operations	0.5	3/1.5	5/2.5	4/2.0	2/1.0	1/0.5
9	Scalability	0.1	5/0.5	1/0.1	3/0.3	2/0.2	4/0.4
	Candidate Totals		34/17.6	31/21.6	24/12.7	19/10.9	27/12.2

FIGURE 10.10   A Set of Ratings for Candidates

Notice from this figure that, if we follow the unweighted ratings (the first numbers), Candidate 1 has the highest score. However, using the weighted ratings, Candidate 2 receives the highest score. This is because Candidate 2 has the highest ratings for those criteria that have the highest weights. Thus, applying weights allows you to focus the evaluation on those areas of importance to your project.

Finally, it is helpful to have a way to determine when the overall (summary) ratings are so close that you should declare a tie, and what to do when that occurs. Best practice is to declare a tie when candidates are within a few percentage points of each other.

When ratings development and application to the candidates are done well, it helps to take the politics out of the evaluation process.

Having rated our candidates, it is now time to refine the set of candidates, with the objective of selecting the optimal vendor, equipment, or service provider for our project.

10.4.6 Modifying the Set of Candidates

You now have an evaluation chart that shows how each network design candidate performed against various criteria. Weights were developed for the set of criteria. Each candidate received a rating for each criterion, which were then multiplied by that criterion's weight to form weighted ratings. The weighted ratings were combined to form a total for each candidate. The result of the evaluation is a set of overall or summary ratings that combines the individual ratings for each candidate.

Rank	Candidate	Deltas	
		Relative	Total
1	Candidate 2	0	0
2	Candidate 1	−4	−4
3	Candidate 3	−4.9	−8.9
4	Candidate 5	−0.5	−9.4
5	Candidate 4	−1.3	−10.7

FIGURE 10.11   Rankings of the Candidates after Evaluation

Summary ratings are used to prioritize the set of candidates. For example, from our previous evaluation chart we would get the prioritization shown in Figure 10.11. This figure shows the ranking of each candidate, along with the relative difference in ratings between that candidate and the one next higher in rank (relative delta), and the difference in ratings between that candidate and the top candidate (total delta). Either delta can be used to determine whether a candidate should be dropped from the set, or whether a tie should be declared. If, for this example, we had decided that a candidate had to be within one point of the next higher-ranking candidate (about 5% of the summary rating for Candidate 2) in order to declare a tie, we could see from the relative deltas that no candidates are close enough to be tied, and that Candidate 2 is the clear winner.

With a prioritized set you can eliminate candidates with bad ratings, with the goal of achieving a single optimal candidate. Usually a single candidate is chosen when it is clearly superior, that is, when its ratings are significantly better than all other candidates. Typically, on a first run of the evaluation there will not be one clearly superior candidate; instead, there may be few or several, depending in part on how many candidates you start with.

When the evaluation process yields more than one superior candidate, another iteration of the evaluation process should be performed on this reduced set. Successive iterations of the evaluation process begin with candidate discussions and continue through data gathering, criteria refinement and ratings development, ratings and prioritization, and another modification of the candidate set.

An advantage of doing another iteration of the evaluation process is that you already have most of the work done: the data sets and evaluation criteria. The work done in each successive iteration improves upon that information and should result in clearer and better ratings and prioritizations. Eventually, the evaluations should result in a single superior candidate.

Example 10.3.

Experience shows that often one or two iterations of the evaluation process will result in a single winner. If you do two evaluations and still have more than one candidate left (or worse, several candidates left), then you should reevaluate your evaluation data and how you are performing the evaluations.

10.4.7 Determining the Order of Evaluations

Remember that this process can be used to select vendors, their equipment, and service providers for your design, and that you will apply this process to only one type of evaluation at a time. However, there may be information that you gathered for one evaluation that can also be used for the other evaluations. For example, vendor information, gathered for vendor evaluations, may also be useful to evaluate specific items of equipment from that vendor. Likewise, service providers may be using network equipment similar to those you are evaluating. This may be particularly important from compatibility and end-to-end service perspectives.

This implies that there may be an optimal order for evaluations. In fact, it can be to your advantage to sequence your evaluations so that you can reuse and build upon information. A common order to evaluations (as indicated by the title to this section) is vendor, vendor equipment, and service provider. The logic for doing this is as follows:

1. You may want to choose which vendors you want for your design before making specific selections for network equipment. Vendor choices can strongly influence equipment selection.

   Of course, there is a counter argument to this: that you should not let vendor selections influence your choice of equipment. However, typically your selections for vendors and for equipment are at the very least loosely coupled.

2. Understanding which network equipment you plan to acquire will help you to make better decisions regarding service providers.

An alternative to this is to evaluate vendors and service providers concurrently. This does not mean you would combine your evaluations, but rather perform them separately during the same time frame.

10.5   Network Layout

Network layout takes topology and technology choices; architecture and design decisions; vendor, equipment, and service-provider choices; and strategic locations; and from these develops various views of your planned network design, including detailed logical diagrams, physical blueprints, and function-specific component plans. All products of this process should also show the parts of your existing network that will be incorporated into the new design.

10.5.1   Logical Diagrams

Logical diagrams show the connectivity and relationships among network devices. Relationships show how devices may interact with one another, how they may work together to provide service and support in the network, and what you might expect from them. For example, you could have a logical diagram showing the routers in your network, or showing just the border routers, or just the interfaces to all external networks. Such diagrams may also include security devices and how they will be connected to the routers, providing insight regarding how the routers and security devices would work together at an external interface.

Diagrams that focus on logical relationships do so at the expense of accuracy in physical descriptions (i.e., location accuracy). Such diagrams can provide approximate correlations between devices and their physical locations; however, they do not provide an accurate representation of physical space. I refer to such descriptions as logical diagrams and not blueprints, as they do not provide the traditional spatial accuracy and level of detail expected in blueprints. Diagrams showing logical relationships among devices are quite useful as companions to network blueprints, or as early drafts of blueprints. Figure 10.12 is an example of a network diagram.

This figure is an example of a communications closet. It shows the types of network devices planned for that closet, and how they are logically connected. For example, from the diagram you can tell that there are multiple firewalls and switches in the communications closet. You can also see the connectivity between devices, to the local networks, and to the Internet. At this stage, however, it does not describe the actual equipment or vendor selections, cable paths or types, or the physical arrangement of the devices in racks or shelves. Diagrams such as these are useful for planning purposes; however, they are not detailed enough to be considered blueprints.

Another example of a logical diagram is shown in Figure 10.13. Instead of describing a particular location, this diagram shows the logical interconnection of devices from across a network. This diagram is useful in that it describes the

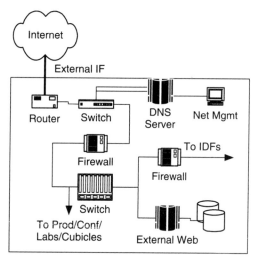

FIGURE 10.12   A Logical Diagram of a Communications Closet

hierarchy of connections, which can be easily mapped to traffic flows in the network.

10.5.2 Network Blueprints

As mentioned at the beginning of this chapter, network blueprints describe detailed physical aspects of your network design: locations of network devices, servers, cable plant, physical security, and secure locations; how devices are to be interconnected, their interface types and speeds; as well as device-specific and service-specific configuration information. There is significantly more detail in a blueprint than there is in a logical diagram.

Network blueprints can consist of a single diagram or sets of network diagrams, depending on network size. If your network design is large you may prefer to have high-level diagrams that show the entire network in some detail, along with more detailed diagrams that focus on specific network areas, such as geographical areas: a WAN, campus LANs, network backbones, individual buildings, even floors or rooms of a building. One focus of blueprints can be on strategic locations in your network.

Developing network blueprints consists of mapping strategic locations of your network onto network templates; applying topology and technology information; and adding your selections of network equipment and services.

Although these steps are described sequentially in this section, it is possible (and often desirable) to apply two or more of them concurrently. Depending on your

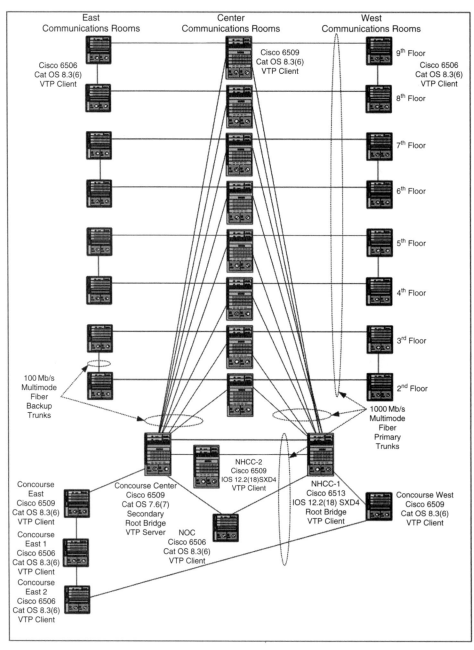

FIGURE 10.13   A Logical Diagram Showing the Interconnection of Devices across a Network

design and how far along you are with your selection process, your technology choices may be strongly coupled to one or more topologies. Also, if equipment choices have been made by this point, they are almost always strongly coupled to technology choices. Thus, you may find that you can map both equipment and technology at each strategic location as you step through the topology.

Mapping Strategic Locations

Developing network blueprints starts with collecting physical information regarding your network (diagrams of rooms, floors, buildings, and campuses; locations of physical plant, communication rooms/closets, and computing and server rooms). This information provides the templates upon which network specifics are described. Figure 10.14 shows an example of a diagram that has been used as the basis for a network blueprint. If such diagrams are not available, you will need to develop your own templates for the network blueprint. If available, you can use building or campus blueprints as the basis for your templates.

Using such templates we map the strategic locations for the network. We want to identify strategic locations as they are of particular importance to network design. From a financial perspective, these locations are likely to be where a number of network functions apply and thus where we may want multiple, high–performance (and more expensive) devices. As such, we will likely spend a higher proportion of our device budget on these locations. From a timing perspective, we typically plan to develop these locations first, as they are key to the development of the entire network. From a topological perspective, strategic locations are usually places where hierarchy is applied. Hierarchy occurs in the network through layering of the

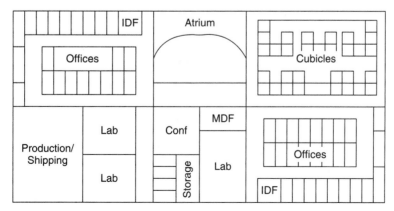

FIGURE 10.14   An Example of a Physical Diagram for a Small Enterprise

network in order to segment and isolate portions of the network, and aggregation of traffic flows as they move through the network. Since we usually impact more traffic flows (and thus more users of those flows) at strategic locations, we have the potential to impact more users at these sites.

You should already have identified likely strategic locations for your network during the architecture process and should be prepared to apply them to your physical diagrams. If not, at this point in the process you will need to determine whether or not you have strategic locations in your network and, if so, where they are.

Some examples of possible strategic locations based on network function are places where:

- Boundary points occur between security cells/zones.
- Major components of monitoring and management are located, particularly when this is for other than OAM functions.
- Multiple performance mechanisms, such as QoS and policies, are needed.
- Different classes or routers or switches interface. This indicates an aggregation of routes, networks, and/or traffic flows. This is also a strategic location based on hierarchy.
- Multiple routing protocols (EGPs and IGPs) coexist.
- Multiple network functions (e.g., security, network management, performance, routing) coexist.

The more that such examples are co-located, the more likely it is that that location is of strategic importance. Some examples of possible strategic locations based on hierarchy are at:

- LAN–MAN and LAN–WAN interfaces
- External interfaces of buildings.
- External interfaces of a campus (this may also be a LAN–MAN or LAN–WAN interface)
- Interfaces between access networks and a LAN backbone
- AS boundaries

Common strategic locations are found at external interfaces of the network, where your network connects to other networks, such as to other autonomous systems or to the Internet. In many small to medium-sized enterprise networks, this collapses to a single external interface (although multiple external interfaces may be necessary when external route diversity is required).

Such locations are strategic for several reasons: First, they are often the most significant boundary in the network (and may require different protocols for each interface, internal and external); second, they often require the presence of every major network function; third, hierarchy is often present, in that traffic flows are aggregated at these locations. This can result in co-locating relatively high-performance routers, security devices, network monitoring/management, and performance devices at this site.

Another set of common strategic locations is at the interfaces to the network backbone. Although such interfaces lie within your network, they can be places where security boundaries are located and where hierarchy occurs through traffic flow aggregation. Often different security, performance, and routing mechanisms are applied to either side of such interfaces. Recall from your flow analysis that network backbones usually provide transport only to transient traffic flows, whereas networks that connect to and are interconnected by a backbone originate and terminate traffic flows. Using this definition we can apply different mechanisms to transient and non-transient traffic flows. For example, we may choose to apply differentiated services as the IP QoS mechanism in the backbone, where we can map traffic classes to aggregates of transient traffic flows. However, as traffic flows get closer to their originations and destinations, we want to be able to apply QoS on a more granular basis, possibly per IP address, per port, or per traffic flow. Interfaces at the network backbone are logical locations for such duality of function, and this also makes them strategic from a topological perspective.

From a planning perspective, locations that incorporate several of the above examples are strategic in that they are key places for future growth of your system. Since strategic locations have some or all of the functions of security, performance, monitoring, routing, and others, they are excellent places for services that can take advantage of co-location with these functions. VoIP, IP video, messaging, and a variety of distributed applications are examples.

Because strategic locations house a number of important network devices, you want to ensure that their physical environments provide appropriate support. Such locations should provide a relatively high degree of physical security, electrical conditioning, and HVAC. You may need to improve the physical environment of wiring closets, communications rooms, computing rooms, and the like as part of your network deployment when they are identified as strategic locations in your network.

Example 10.4.

On visiting a customer to perform a site review of its network infrastructure, I was amazed to find a strategic network location where critical equipment (routers and security devices) were sitting on tables, in the middle of an open room, in 2 to 3 feet of standing water. There was no restricted access (the doors were wide open), no wiring closet (in fact, the wiring was hanging from the ceiling), and no special HVAC considerations. Needless to say, the renovation of this location was of primary importance in the new network design.

It is possible that there are no obvious strategic locations in your network. If, during the requirements and architecture processes, you cannot identify any of the possible strategic locations listed earlier, you may be developing a structurally and topologically homogeneous network. This is rare, however, and care must be taken to ensure that you have not missed potential locations.

Applying Topology Selections

Your choices of strategic locations should map to your selected topology for the network. Topologies imply hierarchical interfaces, which indicate traffic flow aggregation and the potential to identify strategic locations.

Your topology choice describes the high-level structure of your network and consists of the major locations that support this structure and the interconnectivity between these locations. The term *location* is used here, as there can be much flexibility in describing what is connected in a topology. Each location in a topology may be as large as a network or as small as a single device. Typically, a topology consists of network devices (routers and/or switches), possibly co-located with security, monitoring, and/or performance devices and servers. The sets of (network, support, server) devices at each site that are interconnected by the topology are what I refer to as locations, and are shown in Figure 10.15.

Interconnectivity describes how the locations are connected. This may be as basic as describing the physical paths, or may include the cable plant as well as the technologies used at one or more layers in the network. Depending on your design, you may be able to fully describe the connections at this point or may need to wait until after the topology is applied to the design.

Consider, for example, a ring topology. This topology consists of a ring of locations, where each location is interconnected to two neighboring locations. As shown in Figure 10.16, these are often the two neighbors closest in distance.

Each location implies a hierarchical connection to another portion of the network. For example, if a ring topology is applied to a WAN, then each location

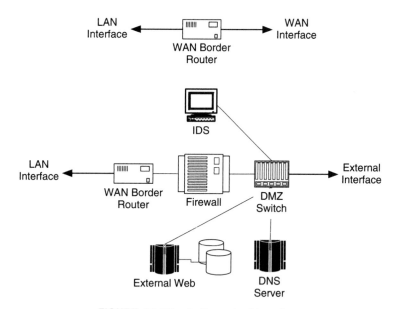

FIGURE 10.15   An Example of Locations

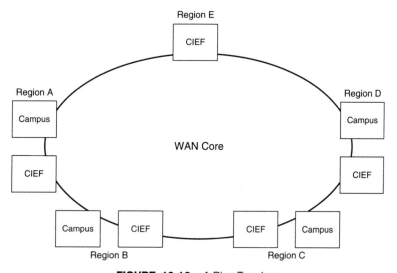

FIGURE 10.16   A Ring Topology

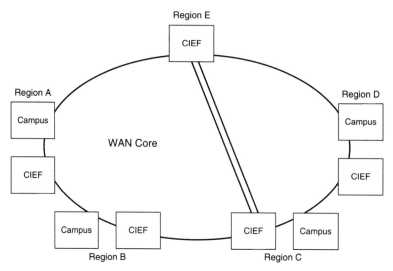

FIGURE 10.17   A Dual- or Split-Ring Topology

can be an interface to one or more regional MANs or LANs connecting to this WAN. If a ring is applied to a LAN, then this implies a LAN backbone, where each location can be an interface to access (edge) or distribution networks in different parts of a building or campus.

A ring topology can be modified into a dual-ring topology (also known as a split-ring or bifurcated-ring topology) by adding a connection between selected locations. Doing so not only modifies the topology, but also changes the traffic flow patterns for the network, adding route diversity. This increases the importance of those locations selected for the additional connection.

In Figure 10.17 additional connections are added between the CIEFs in Regions C and E, splitting the ring and adding diversity across the WAN core.

Other examples are mesh and partial-mesh topologies (a partial-mesh is shown in Figure 10.18). Like the ring or dual-ring topologies, these topologies also show locations and their interconnectivity. The relative importance of each location in these topologies is dependent on the requirements and traffic flows of the network, both of which are expressed to some degree by the choice of technology used for each connection.

The importance of the locations in a topology indicates that they may be strategic locations in the network. Having identified such locations, your selected topology is applied to them. Since strategic locations are closely coupled to topology, typically the full set of locations is used when applied to your topology choice. However, you may apply all or part of your set of strategic locations to your topology.

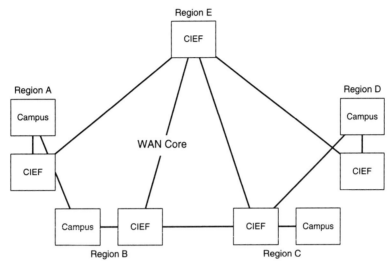

FIGURE 10.18   A Partial-Mesh Topology

A topology provides a start toward developing the design; however, it will not describe every location in your network. It is usually best to begin at the top of your network hierarchy (WAN or LAN backbones) and work your way down. You may apply a topology iteratively, several times throughout your network, or change topologies as you move down the hierarchy.

Applying Technology Selections

At this point you should be able to apply your technology choices from the architecture process. This consists of fully describing the technologies used for your network, and how devices will be interconnected.

In the previous section we described how locations in the topology are interconnected, in terms of physical paths and cable plant. Now we want to apply technology choices across the topology, working from the highest level of hierarchy down to the edges of the network.

For our WAN backbone with a dual-ring topology, we would start at a strategic location (probably one of the locations where the dual rings intersect), describe the technology choices within that location (between devices at that location), as well as technology choices between that location and the other three that it connects with. We would then describe the other location at the intersection of the rings, and then walk the ring, describing each of the locations making up the rings. The result would look something like Figure 10.19. This may be done in conjunction with applying equipment selections, discussed next.

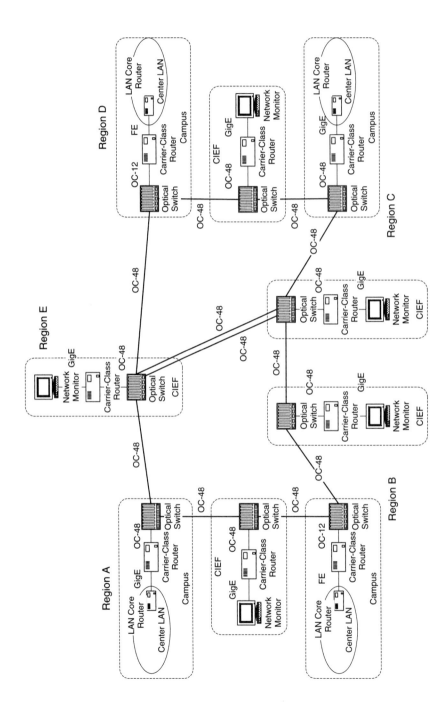

FIGURE 10.19 A Dual-Ring Topology with Technology Choices Added

Applying Equipment Selections

If you have made your vendor and equipment choices by this point, you can apply them to the design. If not, you can use the equipment type and class choices made during the architecture process. Here you should specify some or all of the following for each device:

- Equipment vendor
- Equipment type/class
- Device ID
- Interface types and rates
- Device hardware configuration
- Device OS level/revision
- Degrees of connection, power, internal (card, board, engine) diversity
- Any appropriate vendor-specific information
- Routing protocols used

In order to save space and make the drawings cleaner you can group devices with the same information into specific classifications and provide the information for each classification once on the diagram or in a companion diagram or document. This adds the final detail to the description of your blueprints.

Each location in your network now provides topology information, technology information, and details regarding the equipment to be placed at that location. This can take up a lot of space in your blueprints, and it may be at this point that you decide to develop a separate set of blueprints that separate the network and allow you to provide more information per location. Figure 10.20 below shows a portion of our WAN ring with some equipment information added.

10.5.3   Component Plans

During the network architecture process you should have decided whether or not you were going to provide detailed component plans for specific functions of your network. Component plans build upon information you gathered in developing the network architecture (i.e., mechanisms of each function, interactions among these mechanisms, and interactions among functions) and include diagrams for each function.

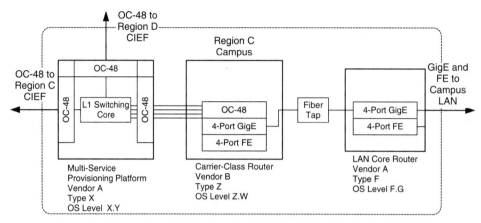

FIGURE 10.20   Region C Campus with Equipment Information Added

Each component plan is similar to a network diagram or blueprint but focuses on a specific function. You need not have a component plan for each function of your network, but rather only for those functions that you choose to focus on.

A common component plan focuses on security, showing which security mechanisms you will deploy and where they will be located. Such a plan can even focus on specific mechanisms. An example of this is describing a VPN architecture as part of a security component plan. A VPN architecture can be complex enough to warrant its own diagrams, as a subset of the overall security diagrams.

Another common component plan is for routing and addressing. This component plan shows where each type of routing protocol is applied, route-specific information, AS information, and where peering and route aggregation occur.

Such plans are especially useful when developed as overlays, so that you can see how each function contributes to the overall design. For example, the component plan for security can overlap with plans for routing, addressing, network management, performance, and others, showing where security devices are co-located and interconnected with devices from other plans.

The purpose of having diagrams, blueprints, and component plans is to provide both a complete set of design data and sets that focus on network specifics. Thus, while blueprints are useful to quickly get the big picture of the network, diagrams are helpful in understanding logical connectivity, while component plans let you focus on routing, security, or other network functions.

In addition, having additional sets of diagrams and plans can actually simplify your views of the network. Network blueprints can become unwieldy, packing so much information into the drawings that they become difficult to read, understand, and use, particularly when trying to trace interactions among various devices, whereas diagrams and component plans are tailored to tracing interactions.

Blueprints and component plans are meant to be complementary. When both blueprints and component plans are developed, the network blueprint describes physical infrastructure, including the cable plant, physical security, and HVAC; while component plans provide detail in each of the network functions. Typically, routing, switching, and addressing are included in the blueprint as well as in a component plan, as they are the most basic network functions.

It is useful to have component plans developed as overlays, where you can place one diagram on top of another, in order to see how and where the functions are applied within the network, and where they overlap (Figure 10.21). As such,

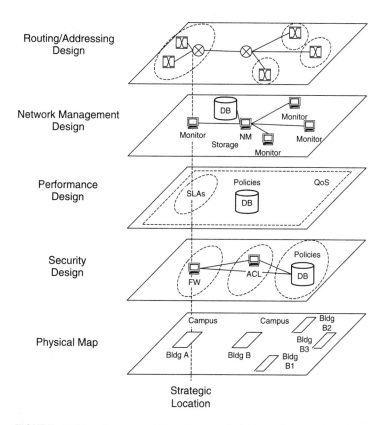

FIGURE 10.21   Component Plan Overlays Line Up at Strategic Locations

they need to line up structurally, so that each location in the network is shown at the same place in each component plan.

However, in developing your network design you may decide to have the traditional set of blueprints that describes all aspects of your design. For small-scale networks you may be able to describe all appropriate information in a single blueprint or set of blueprints. If you choose to do this, information in this section on developing component plans would simply be applied to developing a set of blueprints.

10.6 Design Traceability

Each decision made regarding your network design should be traceable to one or more architecture decisions and thus to requirements and problem statements. This completes the traceability of your decisions, a critical part of the analysis, architecture, and design processes.

The ability to trace each design decision all the way back to how it addresses the project's architecture, requirements, and problem statements is a powerful capability. Figure 10.22 illustrates this traceability. Each design decision maps to one or more architecture decisions, which then map to requirements, which map to problem statements. This allows you to demonstrate how each and every design decision addresses your project's requirements and problems.

Without traceability you may not know that some of your project's problems and requirements are not being met, that there are architecture and design decisions that do not address project requirements, or that your design may be heavily weighted toward particular requirements and problems. Traceability demonstrates how well your network design addresses project requirements and problem statements.

An example of traceability is shown in Figure 10.23. This example is for a project to define and implement a network security perimeter as part of a defense-in-depth strategy. The design decisions regarding vendor and equipment selections, and standards development, trace to the architecture decisions each one addresses, which map to their respective requirements, and finally to the problem statement. With this technique you can clearly see how decisions made during the analysis, architecture, and design processes apply to solving the project's stated problems.

I have found traceability useful in a variety of situations, including those described here.

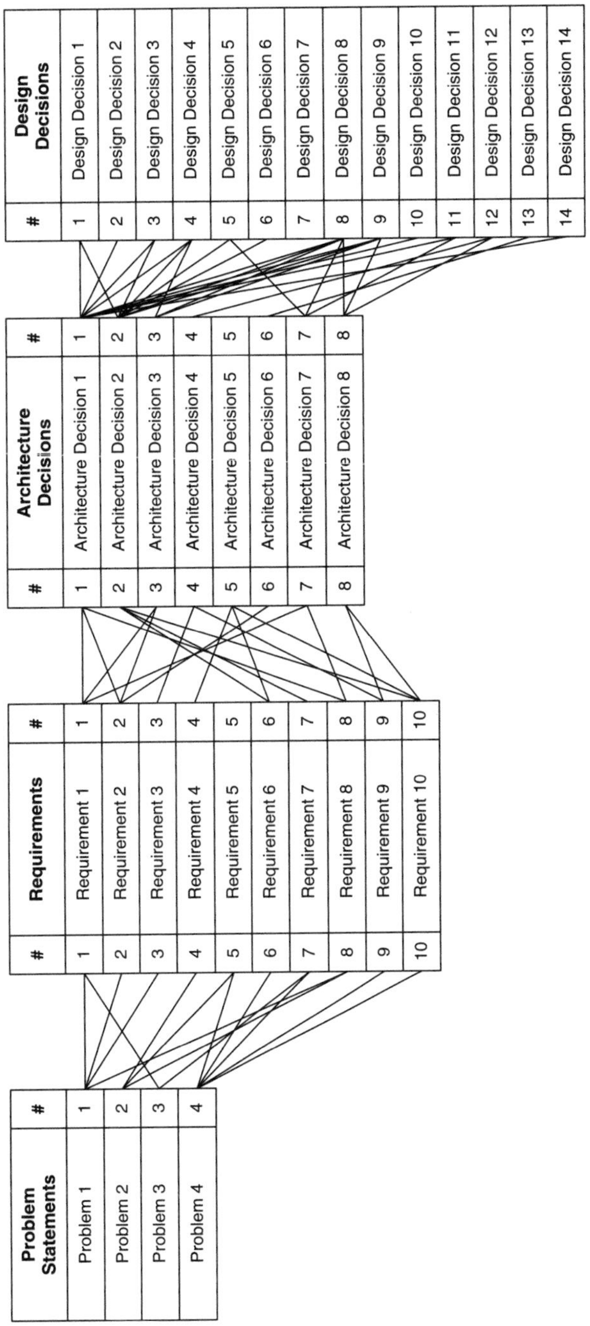

FIGURE 10.22   Design Decisions Trace to Architecture Decisions, Requirements, and Problem Statements

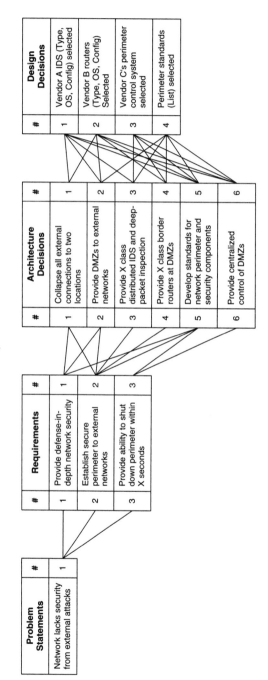

FIGURE 10.23 An Example of Traceability for a Network Security Perimeter Project

Addressing challenges to the network design. For a variety of reasons someone may challenge all or part of your network design. Such challenges may be reasonable and expected, as when new network engineers are added to the design team, or when engineers outside of the project see the design for the first time. With this process such challenges should be rare, however, as network engineers within your organization should have early and frequent access to project information as it evolves through the analysis, architecture, and design processes.

At times these challenges may be more political than technical. This is an unfortunate aspect of projects, one that we must be prepared to address. Fortunately, there will be a wealth of information by the time you get to the design, all of which can be used to address challenges, regardless of whether they are genuinely technical or merely political in nature.

Before applying the discipline described in this book, my experiences were often that network designs would get challenged late in the design process, sometimes in competition for funding, other times over differing opinions regarding design choices. When such challenges were made, there inevitably followed long periods of discussion, wrangling, arguing over competing designs. What I discovered was that, without a well-documented set of problem statements, requirements, architecture and design decisions, it was difficult to address competing design choices (technologies, vendors, equipment). Arguments often came down to differences in personal choices or desires, or at times simply what felt most comfortable—not a particularly strong position from which to drive a project to completion.

However, after applying the analysis, architecture, and design processes, my experiences have been surprisingly (or maybe not so surprisingly) consistent. Armed with well-documented problem statements, requirements, and architecture and design decisions, I have been (and continue to be) consistently able to address any and all challenges to my projects. In fact, when such challenges arise, all arguments quickly dry up as soon as I describe the traceability from decisions to their requirements and problem statements. As you will see for yourself, this is a testament to the power of this process.

Addressing budget, schedule, and resource questions. Another type of challenge to the network design is to justify your budget, schedule, and resource expenditures. Questions such as "Why are we spending X$ for this project?," "What are we getting for this money?," "Why will it take this project so long to complete?" may need to be addressed. In addition, you may need to request more time or funding to complete your project and will have to make the necessary arguments. The background information provided by the processes in this book can be extremely helpful in arguing your case.

Bringing newcomers up to date on how the design evolved. The documentation that you have developed throughout the project can be quite useful in helping others follow the evolution of your design. For example, I have found that those unfamiliar with the design (e.g., newly hired engineers) often have questions regarding why and how particular choices were made. Having to explain the design to such folks can be avoided by providing the project documentation. In this regard, it can be handy to develop a project folder that contains the relevant analysis, architecture, and design information. Keeping the proper documentation available is useful, not only to bring newcomers up to date, but also to bring to meetings and discussions when you might be called upon to provide such background information.

You can describe traceability either textually or via diagrams, or with a combination of these. I prefer to use diagrams, because they make it easier to see the connections between problem statements, requirements, architecture decisions, and design decisions. However, I also use text (spreadsheets) to describe traceability, usually as part of the documentation I deliver as products of the project.

From the designer's perspective, showing how design decisions trace back to architecture decisions provides two important sanity checks. First, if you have design decisions that do not map to any architecture decisions (and thus do not map to any requirements or problem statements), then either your design decisions are not appropriate for the project or your set of architecture decisions is not complete. Second, if the mapping between design decisions and architecture decisions is heavily weighted toward a few architecture decisions, then those architecture decisions may be too broad in scope. While the second case is not as critical as the first, it still may indicate a need for a reexamination of the architecture decisions.

In Figure 10.24 there are design decisions that do not map to any architecture decisions and thus do not map to any requirements or problem statements. This demonstrates either that these design decisions (numbers 2, 6, 7, and 14) are important to the project, but we are lacking the proper architecture decisions (and possibly requirements and problem statements); or that these design decisions are not important for our project. Using traceability you can clearly see when this occurs. Without it, you could end up with design decisions that are inappropriate and costly for your project.

In the same figure we also have the opposite problem: There is an architecture decision that has no design decisions mapping to it (number 5). This demonstrates

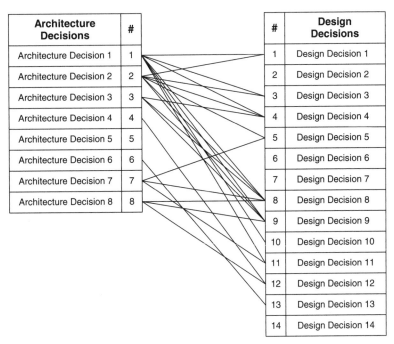

FIGURE 10.24 Traceability Shows Incomplete Mapping between Design and Architecture Decisions

either that we have not done a complete job of developing our design decisions, so that there are some that address Architecture Decision 5; or that this architecture decision is not important to our project. If it is not important, it should be removed and its mapping to requirements reexamined.

In Figure 10.25 we have a complete mapping between architecture and design decisions; however, the mapping is heavily skewed toward a few architecture decisions (numbers 1 and 2). This may not be a problem; in fact, it may demonstrate that these decisions are more significant than the others. Your development of problem statements and requirements may have even indicated that these architecture decisions would be more important than the others. However, it may also indicate that these architecture decisions are too broad, that they could be separated into more focused decisions. When you see such skewing in traceability, it indicates that you should reexamine your architecture decisions to make sure they are what you really want.

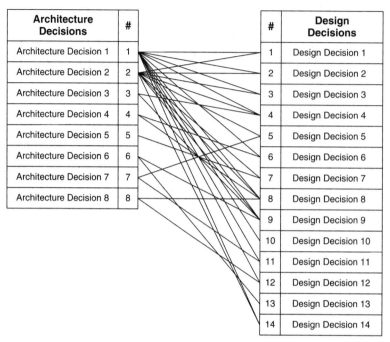

FIGURE 10.25   Traceability Shows Mapping between Design and Architecture Decisions Heavily Skewed toward Architecture Decisions 1 and 2

10.7   Design Metrics

Recall that a necessary part of each validated requirement is that it have one or more metrics associated with it, and that these metrics are used to determine your success in meeting each requirement. Coupling metrics to network requirements is an important commitment that you make to ensure project success. The metrics associated with requirements should also be coupled to metrics you have developed for the design.

Like metrics associated with requirements, design metrics describe how you measure the success of your design decisions. Common examples of design metrics include the ability to achieve a desired diversity level in the network, via routing, topology, equipment redundancy, provider redundancy, and the like, often associated with metrics for performance requirements such as network availability and reliability, or service delivery requirements such as SLAs; the ability to bound end-to-end or round-trip delay in the network, often in support of real-time or interactive applications, again associated with metrics for performance and service delivery requirements; or the ability to deliver desired capacity or throughput levels (either throughout the network or to specified applications and/or devices), also associated with metrics for performance and service delivery requirements.

As you might expect, an additional component of traceability is the ability to trace metrics from the design back to its requirements. It is desirable to do this whenever possible, as it provides direct evidence for satisfying requirements with the delivered design. In the previous examples where design metrics are associated with (and thus traceable to) requirements metrics, demonstrating performance and service delivery in the network satisfies both requirements metrics and design metrics.

In this sense design metrics are useful in validating your design. Figure 10.26 shows an example of this. Using the security perimeter traceability matrix shown earlier, a metric is provided for Requirement 3: Demonstrate that the security perimeter can be shut down within X seconds, where X is to be determined. This metric is supported by two of the architecture decisions—to develop standards for network perimeter and security components, and to provide centralized control of DMZs—by adding the shut-down time (X) as one of the standards to be developed, and by making X one of the criteria by which vendors and products will be evaluated.

Design decisions regarding vendor and service-provider evaluations are influenced by X, which is determined during standards development. One metric for Design Decision 4 is the successful development of X, which can then be used to successfully demonstrate shut down of the perimeter within X seconds, and satisfy the metrics for Design Decision 3 and Requirement 3.

Note that the value of X is critical to the resulting network design and success of the perimeter. Thirty minutes versus thirty seconds for X makes the difference between having a fully automated perimeter and being able to have humans in the loop. It also can make the difference in keeping a security attack from reaching beyond your perimeter.

10.8   Conclusions

The network design is the ultimate product of the analysis, architecture, and design processes. The design is where your architectural decisions regarding network topology and technologies come together with selections for equipment, vendors, and service providers to provide detailed diagrams, blueprints, and component plans for your network.

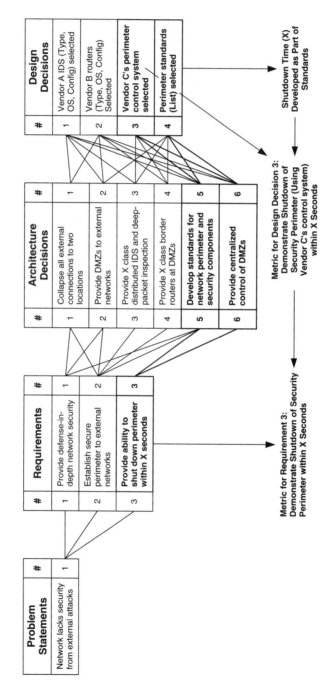

FIGURE 10.26 Metrics for Design Can Be Coupled with Metrics for Requirements

By using the processes described in this chapter, as well as throughout this book, you will be able to develop better network designs.

10.9   Exercises

1. What are ad hoc design decisions? How do such decisions reduce the quality of the resulting design? Give an example of an ad hoc design decision.

2. If we have followed the analysis and architecture processes, what products from those processes are used as input to the design?

3. What are the primary differences between first-order, second-order, and third-order design products?

4. What are network blueprints, network diagrams, and component plans? Why would a network design have sets of each of these?

5. What are the major components of the evaluation process for vendors, service providers, and equipment?

6. In evaluating vendors, service providers, or equipment for a network design, why would you seed the evaluation process?

7. Which of the following evaluation criteria most likely apply to equipment evaluations, which ones apply to service-provider evaluations, and which apply to both?
    - Available service-level agreements (SLAs)
    - Standards compliance (IETF)
    - Mean time between failure (MTBF)
    - Mean time between service outage (MTBSO)
    - Hardware scalability

8. In the evaluations matrix in Figure 10.10, how would the ratings have changed if:
    a. The relative weights were all changed to be 1 (i.e., there were no relative weights)?
    b. The last three criteria (available services, operations, scalability) were each given a weight of 1.0, while the others remained unchanged?
    c. Each relative weight was multiplied by 10 (i.e., the scale changes from 0–1 to 0–10)?

9. The results of a service-provider evaluation are as follows: Service Provider A: 28.7 points; Service Provider B: 28.5 points; Service Provider C: 29.0 points; Service Provider D: 27.5 points; Service Provider E: 21.9 points; Service Provider F: 27.6 points. How would you modify this set of service-provider candidates?

Glossary of Terms

80/20 rule A rule of thumb by which 80% of a network's traffic is local and 20% is remote.

Adaptability A user requirement for the system to be able to adapt to users' changing needs.

Address For IP, a 32-bit number that identifies a device at the network layer.

Addressing Applying identifiers (addresses) to devices at various protocol layers (e.g., data-link and network).

Address mask For IP, a 32-bit number that identifies which bits in the address are considered part of the network and (by default) which bits are considered part of the device.

Address prefix When an address mask is noted by its length (N) in bits, as $/N$.

Addressing Assigning local or global, private or public, temporary or persistent identifiers to devices.

Affordability A user requirement for what users or management can afford to purchase for the network.

Alarm A network management event that triggers a real-time notification to network personnel. See also *Event*.

Application requirements Requirements that are determined from application information, experience, or testing and are what are needed by applications to successfully operate on the system.

Architectural components These are functional areas of the network, whose relationships define the network architecture. Examples of architectural components include IP services, security and privacy, network management, and addressing and routing.

Areas Segments of a network design that are the result of sizing the network.

Asynchronous applications Applications that are relatively insensitive to time, either assuming no timing relationship between source and destination or that the timing relationship is outside the bounds of the applications session.

Audit trail The set of documents, data, and decisions for the architecture and design.

Autonomous system (AS) A collection of networks that is under the same management control.

Availability The relationship between the frequency of mission-critical failures and the time to restore service. This is also known as operational availability.

Bandwidth The theoretical capacity of one or more network elements in the system.

Bandwidth*delay product An estimate of the maximum amount of information that may be in transit across a particular technology at any given time.

Best-effort service Network service in which there is no control over how the network will satisfy the service request and there are no guarantees associated with this service. Service will be both unpredictable and unreliable, with variable performance across a range of values (from the network being unavailable [0 performance] to the lowest common denominator of performance across all of the technologies in the end-to-end path).

BGPv4 A path-vector–based External Gateway Protocol.

Blocking When computing devices halt their computations, waiting for information from other computing devices.

Broadcast domain A group of network-addressable devices where all of the devices in that group can be reached by a single network address, the broadcast address.

Broadcast technologies Network technologies that support the ability of a device to communicate simultaneously with all other devices on their network or subnet, through using a well-known broadcast address specific to the network technology.

Call admission control A mechanism to limit the number of calls on a network and thus control the allocation of resources.

Capacity A measure of the system's ability to transfer information (voice, data, video, combinations of these).

Capacity plan A written description of network performance (capacity) required for the flows that are described in the flowspec.

Capacity planning Over-engineering bandwidth in the network to accommodate most short- and long-term traffic fluctuations. Also known as traffic engineering.

Centralized management When all management data (e.g., *pings*, SNMP polls/ responses, *traceroutes*) radiate from a single (typically large) management system.

Characterizing behavior Representing how users and applications use the network to develop and understand their requirements.

Checks and balances Methods to duplicate measurements to verify and validate network management data.

CIDR block A group of network addresses that are represented by a classless interdomain routing (CIDR) advertisement of the form (network address, mask length).

Classful addressing Applying predetermined mask lengths to addresses to support a range of network sizes. The result is a set of classes of addresses (A, B, C, D, and E), each of which supports a different maximum network size.

Classification The ability to identify traffic flows as part of traffic conditioning.

Classless interdomain routing The absence of class boundaries in network routing.

Client–server architectural model An architectural model that follows the client–server flow model. In this case there are obvious locations for architectural features, in particular where flows combine.

Client–server flow model A flow model in which the flows are asymmetric and hierarchically focused toward the client.

Closely coupled In the distributed-computing flow model, when there are frequent transfers of information between computing devices.

Coarse granularity In the distributed-computing flow model, when each task is dedicated to a single computing device.

Component characteristics The characteristics between architectural components (IP services, network management, security and privacy, and addressing and routing) that describe the relationships between these components. These characteristics are operation, interactions, dependencies, trade-offs, and constraints.

Component constraints Restrictions within a component architecture or between component architectures; can even be across the entire (reference) architecture.

Component dependencies Requirements that one component has on one or more other components in order to function.

Component interactions The requirements that each component has to communicate with other components.

Component operation Determining the mechanisms that make up each component, how each mechanism works, and how that component works as a whole.

Component trade-offs Decision points in the development of an architecture to prioritize and choose between features and functions of each component and thereby optimize the overall (reference) architecture.

Composite flow A combination of requirements from multiple applications, or of individual flows, that share a common link, path, or network.

Confidence A measure of the ability of the network to deliver data without error or loss at the design throughput.

Configuration For network management, the setting of parameters in a network element for operation and control of that element.

Conforming traffic Traffic that is within performance boundaries as determined by metering (traffic conditioning).

Connection support When a connection is established by the technology whenever information is transferred across the network.

Content delivery network A network that bypassed the core of the Internet to provide better performance in delivering information to its users.

Critical flows Flows that are considered more important than others in that they are higher in performance, have strict requirements, or serve more important users, applications, and devices.

Data flows See *Flows*.

Data sink A device that collects or terminates data on a network.

Data source A device that produces data on a network.

De facto standard A standard that is generally accepted through being widely implemented and used.

Default route The route used when there is no other route for that destination. It is the route of last resort.

Default route propagation The technique used to inform the network (or subnets or functional areas) of the default route.

Delay A measure of the time difference in the transmission of information across the system.

Differentiated services A quality-of-service mechanism that defines a set of values (termed differentiated services code points [DSCPs]) for classes of traffic flows to be used by resource control mechanisms.

Directionality The preference of a flow to have more requirements in one direction than in another.

Distributed–computing architectural model An architectural model that follows the distributed-computing flow model and in which the data sources and sinks are obvious locations for architectural features.

Distributed–computing flow model A flow model that either has the inverse of the characteristics of the client–server flow model or is a hybrid of peer-to-peer and client–server flow models.

Distributed management When there are multiple separate components to the management system and these components are strategically placed across the network, localizing network management traffic and distributing management domains.

Downstream Traffic flowing in the direction from the source to the destination.

Dropping In traffic conditioning, discarding nonconforming traffic.

Encryption A security mechanism in which cipher algorithms are applied together with a secret key to encrypt data so that they are unreadable if intercepted.

End-to-end architectural model Architectural model that focuses on all components in the end-to-end path of a traffic flow.

End-to-end (network element) characteristics Characteristics that can be measured across multiple network elements in the path of one or more traffic flows and may extend across the entire network or between devices.

Environment-specific thresholds Performance thresholds that are determined for the environment of the current network project on which you are working.

Event Something that occurs in the network that is worthy of noting, whether informational, as a problem, or as an alarm.

Exterior Gateway Protocols Routing protocols that communicate routing information (reachability and metrics) primarily between ASs.

External interfaces The network interfaces between your network and other, outside (external) networks.

Features Network functions and performance that are desired but are not necessary for the network to successfully support its users, applications, and devices.

Fine granularity In the distributed-computing flow model, in which a task is subdivided between several devices and the computing is done concurrently.

Firewalls Combinations of one or more security mechanisms, implemented in devices or network elements (routers), which are placed at strategic locations within a network.

Flow analysis The process of characterizing traffic flows for a network, where they are likely to occur, and what levels of performance they will require.

Flows Sets of network traffic (application, protocol, and control information) that have some common attributes, such as source/destination address, information type, routing, or other end-to-end information. Flows also have directionality. Also known as traffic flows or data flows.

Flow-based architectural models Models that take particular advantage of traffic flows from the flow specification.

Flow models Groups of flows that exhibit specific, consistent behavior characteristics. Flow models are characterized primarily by their directionality, hierarchy, and interconnectivity.

Flow prioritization Ranking flows based on their importance (e.g., number or users, applications, or devices supported).

Flow specification A listing of the flows for a network, along with their performance requirements and priority levels (if any). Also known as a flowspec.

Flowspec See *Flow specification*.

Flowspec algorithm A mechanism to combine the performance requirements (capacity, delay, and reliability) for flows in such a way that describes the optimal composite performance for that flow or group of flows.

Function A major capability of a network.

Functional architectural models Models that focus on one or more functions or features planned for in the network.

Functional areas Groups within the system that share a similar function. Groups may be of users (workgroups), applications, devices, or combinations of these, and they may share similar jobs/tasks, physical locations, or functions within the network (e.g., backbone routing).

General access Common access of users to applications, computing, and storage resources across a network.

General-performance network A network that does not have a distinctive set of applications, users, or hosts that would be the performance driver for that network.

General thresholds Performance thresholds that apply to most or all networks.

Generic computing devices Common desktop and laptop computers that most users have.

Guaranteed service Network service that is predictable and reliable to such a degree that, when service is not available, the system is in some way held accountable.

Hard boundary A routing boundary in which Exterior Gateway Protocols are predominantly used to pass routing information.

Hard state Determining and persistently maintaining connection information along the path of a connection, between source and destination.

Hierarchical client–server architectural model An architectural model based on the hierarchical client–server flow model. In addition to the functions, features, and services being focused at server locations and client–server flows, they are also focused at the server–server flows.

Hierarchical client–server flow model A flow model that has the characteristics of a client–server flow model but that also has multiple layers, or tiers, between servers.

Hierarchical management When the management functions (monitoring, display, storage, and processing) are separated and placed on separate devices.

Hierarchy The degree of concentration of networks or traffic flows at interconnection points within the network, as well as the number of tiers of interconnection points within the network.

High performance An indicator that the service request or requirement's performance characteristics are greater than a performance threshold determined for that network.

High-performance network A network that typically has one or a few applications, users/groups, and/or devices whose performance requirements are significantly greater than other performance requirements for that network.

High-performance/general-performance architectural model Model that focuses on identifying networks or parts of a network as general performance, as high performance, or as having components of both.

Human response time An estimate of the time threshold when users begin to perceive delay in the system.

In-band management When the data flows for network management follow the same network paths as the traffic flows for users and their applications.

Individual flow The flow associated with a single session of an application.

Initial conditions Initial input to the requirements analysis process, consisting of the type of network project, scope of the architecture and design, initial architecture/design goals, and any outside forces acting on the network.

Instrumentation For network management, the set of tools and utilities needed to monitor and probe the network for management data.

Interconnection mechanisms Mechanisms that interconnect network technologies, including shared media, switching, bridging, and routing.

Integrated services A quality-of-service mechanism that defines values and mechanisms for allocating resources to flows across the end-to-end path of the flow.

Interactive applications Applications that assume some timing relationship between source and destination while the application session is active, however, the timing relationship is not as strict as it is in real time.

Interactive bulk applications Applications in which the end-to-end or round-trip network delays are not the predominant delay for that application, but processing at the device or application component is the predominant delay.

Interactive burst applications Applications in which the end-to-end or round-trip network delays are the predominant delay for that application.

Interactivity A user requirement for a response time from the system (as well as the network) that is on the order of the response times of users.

Interconnectivity A balance to hierarchy in a network, interconnectivity is the degree of connections within the network at different levels in the design, to provide greater performance through parts of the network.

Interior Gateway Protocols (IGPs) Routing protocols that communicate routing information primarily within an AS.

Intranet/extranet architectural model Architectural model that focuses on security and privacy, including the separation of users, devices, and applications based on secure access.

IPSec A protocol for providing authentication and encryption between devices at the network layer.

IP services A set of mechanisms to configure, operate, manage, provision, and account for resources in the network that allocate performance to users, applications, and devices.

Latency System or component response time, a measure of delay that incorporates device and application processing, taking into account the time to complete a task.

Limit A boundary between conforming and non-conforming regions; is taken as an upper or lower limit for a performance characteristic.

Loosely coupled In the distributed-computing flow model, when there may be little to no transfer of information between computing devices.

Low performance An indicator that the service request or requirement's performance characteristics are less than a performance threshold determined for that network.

Maintainability A statistical measure of the time to restore the system to fully operational status after it has experienced a fault.

Marking Tagging an IP packet with a priority level, as part of traffic conditioning.

Mechanisms Hardware and software that help a network to achieve each function.

Metadata Additional information about the collected data, such as references to the data types, time stamps of when the data were generated, and any indications that these data reference any other data.

Metering Measuring the temporal performance characteristics of a traffic flow, as part of traffic conditioning.

MIB selection Determining which SNMP MIBs to use and apply, as well as which variables in each MIB are appropriate, for your network.

Mission-critical applications Applications that require predictable or high reliability.

Monitoring Obtaining values for end-to-end, per-link, and per-element network management characteristics.

Multipart flowspec A flow specification that describes flows that have guaranteed requirements; may include flows that have stochastic and/or best-effort requirements.

Natural mask The IP address mask that coincides with a class boundary.

Network address translation The mapping of IP addresses from one realm to another. Typically this is between public and private address space.

Network analysis Studying network components, its inputs and outputs, to understand network behavior under variable situations.

Network architecture Developing a high-level end-to-end structure for the network. This includes the relationships between major architectural components of the network, such as security, network management, addressing, and routing.

Network design Details (physically) the reference network architecture, evaluating and choosing technologies for each area of the network, as well as developing strategies to connect these technologies across the network.

Network element An individual component of the network that participates at one or more of the protocol layers.

Network environment Everything that is external to the network, such as the physical or business environments. Can also include users, applications, and devices, although they are usually considered with the network to be part of the system.

Network management Providing functions to control, plan, allocate, deploy, coordinate, and monitor network resources.

Network perimeter security Protecting the external interfaces between your network and external networks.

Network propagation delay An estimate of how long it takes for a signal to cross a physical medium or link.

Network privacy A subset of network security, focusing on protection of networks and their services from unauthorized access or disclosure.

Network requirements Requests for capabilities in the network, usually in terms of performance and function, that are necessary for the success of that network.

Network security The protection of networks and their services from unauthorized access, modification, destruction, or disclosure. It provides assurance that the network performs its critical functions correctly and that there are no harmful side effects.

Network services Levels of performance and function in the network.

Non-broadcast multiple-access technologies Network technologies that do not inherently have broadcast support. See also *Broadcast technologies*.

Non-conforming traffic Traffic that is outside of performance boundaries, as determined by metering (traffic conditioning).

Non-real-time applications Applications with various end-to-end delay requirements, at times more stringent (in terms of the amount of delay) than real-time applications, but the destination will wait (within reason) until the information is received.

Northbound interface A management interface that is oriented toward higher-level (thus up or northbound) management functions. This term is commonly used for the interface from network management to service or business management.

One-part flowspec A flow specification that describes flows that have only best-effort requirements. Also known as a unitary flowspec.

Operational suitability A measure of how well our network design can be configured, monitored, and adjusted by the customer's operators.

OSPF An IGP that is based on a link-state algorithm.

Out-of-band management When different paths are provided for network management data flows and user traffic flows.

Packet filtering A mechanism in network elements to explicitly deny or pass packets at strategic points within the network.

Peers Users, applications, devices, networks, or ASs that act at the same level in their hierarchy. For example, in a hierarchical client–server model, servers that act at the same level (e.g., directly above their clients) are considered peers. ASs that form a peering arrangement (using BGP4 and policies) are considered peers.

Peer-to-peer architectural model Based on the peer-to-peer flow model, the important characteristics of this model are that there are no obvious locations for architectural features; functions, features, and services toward the edge of the network, close to users and their devices; and flows are end-to-end between users and their devices.

Peer-to-peer flow model A flow model in which the users and applications are fairly consistent throughout the network in their flow behaviors.

Performance The set of levels for capacity, delay, and reliability in a network.

Per-link and per-element (network element) characteristics Characteristics that are specific to the type of element or connection between elements being monitored.

Physical security The protection of devices from physical access, damage, and theft.

Planned hierarchy Integrating into the network design methods to isolate and hide networks and their traffic from one another.

Policies (1) Sets (formal or informal) of high-level statements about how network resources are to be allocated among users. (2) High-level statements about relationships between networks or ASs, as with peering arrangements. A policy may take an action (e.g., drop, accept, modify) on traffic that matches one or more AS parameters (e.g., AS number or list of AS numbers and metrics).

Polling Actively probing the network and network elements for management data.

Polling interval Time period between polls. See also *Polling*.

Primary storage Storage locations where data are staged for short periods (e.g., hours).

Privacy A requirement to protect the sanctity of user, application, device, and network information.

Private IP addresses IP addresses that cannot be advertised and forwarded by network elements and devices in the public domain (i.e., the Internet).

Public IP addresses IP addresses that can be advertised and forwarded by network elements and devices in the public domain (i.e., the Internet).

Public key infrastructure A security infrastructure that combines security mechanisms, policies, and directives into a system that is targeted for use across unsecured public networks (e.g., the Internet), where information is encrypted through the use of a public and a private cryptographic key pair that is obtained and shared through a trusted authority.

Quality In requirements analysis, refers to the user requirement for quality of the presentation to the user.

Quality of service Also known as QoS; determining, setting, and acting on priority levels for traffic flows.

Rate-critical applications Applications that require a predictable, bounded, or high degree of capacity.

Real-time analysis Setting and monitoring of thresholds or boundaries for end-to-end, per-link, or per-element characteristics for short-term or immediate notification of events and transients.

Real-time applications Applications that have a strict timing relationship between source and destination, with one or more timers set for the receipt of information at the destination.

Reference network architecture A description of the complete architecture, considering all of its components. It is a compilation of the relationships developed during the network architecture process.

Reliability (1) A statistical indicator of the frequency of failure of the network and its components and represents the unscheduled outages of service. (2) In requirements analysis, reliability is a user requirement for consistently available service.

Remote access Network access based on traditional dial-in, point-to-point sessions, and virtual private network connections.

Requirements Descriptions of network functions and performance that are needed for the network to successfully support its users, applications, and devices.

Requirements analysis Gathering and deriving requirements in order to understand system and network behaviors.

Requirements map A diagram that shows the location dependencies between applications and devices, which will be used for flow analysis.

Requirements specification A document that lists and prioritizes the requirements gathered for your architecture and design.

Resource control Mechanisms that will allocate, control, and manage network resources for traffic.

RIP and RIPv2 IGPs that are based on a distance-vector routing algorithm.

Route aggregation The technique exchanging of routing information between ASs, usually between service providers with transit networks, and between large customer networks.

Route filter A statement, configured in one or more routers, that identifies one or more IP parameters (e.g., an IP source or destination address) and an action (e.g., drop or forward) to be taken when traffic matches these parameters.

Route filtering The technique of applying filters to hide networks from the rest of an AS or to add, delete, or modify routes in the routing table.

Routing Learning about the connectivity within and between networks and applying this connectivity information to forward IP packets toward their destinations.

Routing boundaries Physical or logical separations of a network based on requirements for or administration of that network.

Routing flows Flows of routing information, passed between functional areas and between ASs.

Scheduling Determining the order in which traffic is processed for transmission onto a network.

Secondary storage Storage sites that aggregate management data from multiple primary storage sites.

Secure sockets library A security mechanism that uses RSA-based authentication to recognize a party's digital identity and RC4 to encrypt and decrypt the accompanying transaction or communication.

Security A requirement to guarantee the integrity (accuracy and authenticity) of a user's information and physical resources, as well as access to the user's and system's resources.

Security awareness Getting users educated and involved with the day-to-day aspects of security in their network and helping them understand the potential risks of violating security policies and procedures.

Security cell In the network architecture, when security constrains performance to operate within a security perimeter, or cell.

Security policies and procedures Formal statements on rules for system, network, and information access and use designed to minimize exposure to security threats.

Server Computing device that provides a service to one or more users (i.e., clients).

Service See *Network service.*

Service characteristics Individual network performance and functional parameters that are used to describe services.

Service levels A group or set of characteristics that form a higher-level representation of services.

Service metrics Measurements of service characteristics in the network to monitor, verify, and manage services.

Service-level agreement Also known as an SLA, an informal or formal contract between a provider and user that defines the terms of the provider's responsibility to the user and the type and extent of accountability if those responsibilities are not met.

Service offering Services offered by the network to the rest of the system.

Service plan A written description of the network performance (capacity, delay, and reliability) required for the flows that are described in the flowspec.

Service request Network services that are requested by users, applications, or devices.

Service-provider architectural model Architectural model based on service-provider functions, focusing on privacy and security, service delivery to customers (users), and billing.

Service switching Switching based on flow or end-to-end information, dependent on the type of service required.

Session An instance of one or more concurrent applications, resulting in one or more traffic flows.

Shaping In traffic conditioning, delaying traffic to change a performance characteristic.

Shared-medium mechanism When all devices on the network (or subnetwork) share the same physical medium.

Soft boundary A routing boundary in which IGPs are predominantly used to pass routing information.

Soft state Determining and maintaining state until the connection is established or for a short period after the connection is established.

Specialized devices Devices that provide specific functions to their users.

Specific As used with security, refers to well-defined rules about who, what, and where security is applied.

State Information (typically local or end-to-end addresses) associated with connections in a technology.

Stateful Determining and maintaining state information for connections between source and destination.

Stateless Not determining or maintaining any state information between source and destination for connections.

Static routes Routes that are configured manually, by network personnel or scripts, in network elements and that do not change until manually deleted or modified.

Stochastic service Service that requires some degree of predictability (probability), more than best effort, yet does not require the accountability of a guaranteed service.

Storage archives Secondary and tertiary storage sites for network management data.

Stub network A network with only one path into or out of it.

Subnet A segment of a network, created as an additional level of hierarchy imposed on a network, through changing its address mask.

Subnet mask An address mask that has been changed from its natural (classful) mask to add an additional level of hierarchy.

Subnetting Using part of the device (host) address space to create another layer of hierarchy. This is done by changing the address mask.

Supernet mask The address mask created when supernetting—that is, reducing the mask size to aggregate network addresses.

Supernetting Aggregating network addresses by changing the address mask to decrease the number of bits allocated to the network.

Supportability A measure of how well the customer can keep the system performing, as designed, over the entire life of the system.

Switching Forwarding information (e.g., cells, frames, packets) between segments of a network or subnetwork. This is usually done at the link or network layers but may occur at any layer.

System A set of components that work together to support or provide connectivity, communications, and services to users of the system.

Systems architecture Developing a high-level end-to-end structure for the system, which consists of users, applications, devices, and networks. This includes the relationships between each of these components.

Systems methodology Viewing the network that you are architecting and designing, along with a subset of its environment (everything that the network interacts with or impacts), as a system.

Tele*services The set of multimedia applications, such as teleseminars, telelearning, teleconferencing, and so on.

Tertiary storage Storage sites where management data are secure and persistent (permanent or semi-permanent).

Threat analysis A process used to determine which components of the system need to be protected and the types of security risks from which they should be protected.

Threshold A value for a performance characteristic that is a boundary between two regions of conformance and, when crossed in one or both directions, will generate an action.

Throughput The realizable capacity of the system or its network elements.

Topological architectural models Models based on a geographical or topological arrangement; often used as starting points in the development of the network architecture.

Traffic engineering Over-engineering bandwidth in the network to accommodate most short- and long-term traffic fluctuations. Also known as capacity planning.

Traffic flows See *Flows*.

Transients Short-lived events or changes in the behavior of the network.

Trap A user-configurable threshold for a parameter. Used in network management.

Trend analysis Using network management data to determine long-term network behaviors, or trends.

Timeliness A user requirement to be able to access, transfer, or modify information within a tolerable time frame.

Tunneling Encapsulating information within protocol headers for the purpose of isolating and protecting that information.

Two-part flowspec A flow specification that describes flows that have stochastic requirements and may include flows that have best-effort requirements.

Unitary flowspec A flow specification that describes flows that have only best-effort requirements. Also known as a one-part flowspec.

Upstream Traffic flowing in the direction from the destination to the source.

User requirements The set of requirements gathered or derived from user input; what is needed by users to successfully accomplish their tasks on the system.

Variable-length subnetting Subnetting in which multiple subnet masks are used, creating subnets of different sizes.

Virtual private networks Applying tunneling to create multiple isolated networks across a common infrastructure.

Workgroups Groups of users who have common locations, applications, and requirements or who belong to the same organization.

xDSL A variety of DSL options, such as asymmetric DSL, symmetric DSL, highspeed DSL, and ISDN DSL.

Glossary of Acronyms

AAAA	authentication, authorization, accounting, and allocation
ABR	available bit rate
ACL	access control list
AF	assured forwarding
AH	authentication header
API	application programming interface
AR	acceptance review
ARCP	asynchronous remote copy
ARP	Address Resolution Protocol
AS	autonomous system
ATM	asynchronous transfer mode
AToM	ATM monitoring
BE	best effort
BER	bit error rate
BGPv4	Border Gateway Protocol version 4
BSD	Berkeley Software Distribution
BUS	broadcast/multicast server
CA	certificate authority
CAC	call admission control
CAD	computer-aided design/computer-aided drawing
CBC	cipher block chaining
CBQ	class-based queuing

CBR	constant bit rate
CD	compact disk
CDN	content-delivery network
CDR	critical design review
CF	composite flow
CHAP	Challenge-Response Authentication Protocol
CIDR	classless interdomain routing
CIR	committed information rate
CLI	command line interface
CLR	cell loss ratio
CMIP	Common Management Information Protocol
CMOT	CMIP over TCP/IP
CMR	cell misinsertion ratio
COPS	common open policy services
CORBA	common object request broker architecture
CoS	class of service
COTS	commercial off the shelf
CPU	central processing unit
CRM	customer relationship management
CT	computed tomography
DES	data-encryption standard
DET	deterministic
DHCP	Dynamic Host Configuration Protocol
DiffServ	differentiated services
DMZ	demilitarized zone
DNS	domain name system
DR	default route

DSCP	differentiated services code point
DSL	digital subscriber loop
DSx	digital signal ($x = 1, 3$)
DSU	data service unit
dWDM	dense wavelength division multiplexing
EBGP	external BGP
ECS	engineering compute server
EF	expedited forwarding
EGP	External Gateway Protocol
EMS	element management system
ENET	Ethernet
EOC	extended operational capability
ERP	enterprise resource planning
ESP	encapsulating security payload
f	flow
FA	functional area
FAA	Federal Aviation Administration
FB	flow boundary
FCAPS	fault, configuration, accounting, performance, and security
FCIP	fiber channel over IP
FDDI	fiber distributed data interface
FE	Fast Ethernet
FIFO	first in first out
FMECA	failure modes, effects, and criticality analysis
FTE	full-time equivalent/full-time employee
FTP	File Transfer Protocol
FY	fiscal year

Gb/s	gigabits per second
GigE	Gigabit Ethernet
HDLC	high-level data link control
HiPPI	high-performance parallel interface
HMAC	hash-function message authentication code
HRT	human response time
HTTP	HyperText Transfer Protocol
HVAC	heating, vacuum, air conditioning
HW or H/W	hardware
IBGP	internal BGP
ICD	interface control description
ICMP	Internet Control Message Protocol
ID	identifier
IETF	Internet Engineering Task Force
iFCP	Internet Fiber Channel Protocol
IGP	Interior Gateway Protocol
iLAN	isolation LAN
INTD	interaction delay
IntServ	integrated services
I/O	input/output
IOC	initial operational capability
IP	Internet Protocol
IPSec	IP security
ISP	Internet service provider
IT	information technology
IXC	interexchange carrier

Kb/s	kilobits per second
KB/s	kilobytes per second
L	link
L2F	layer 2 forwarding
L2TP	layer 2 Tunneling Protocol
LAN	local area network
LANE	LAN emulation
LDAP	Lightweight Directory Access Protocol
LEC	LAN emulation client
LECS	LAN emulation connection server
LES	LAN emulation server
LIS	logical IP subnet
LLNL	Lawrence Livermore National Lab
LOH	line overhead
LRU	local repair unit
MAN	metropolitan-area network
Mb/s	megabits per second
MB/s	megabytes per second
MC	mission-critical
MD	message digest
MDR	minimum data rate
MFTP	multiple FTP
MIB	management information base
MIS	management information systems
MPC	MPOA client
MPS	MPOA server
MPLS	multi-protocol label switching

MPOA	multi-protocol over ATM
MRI	magnetic resonance imaging
ms	milliseconds
MTBF	mean-time-between-failures
MTBCF	mean time between mission-critical failures
MTBSO	mean time between service outage
MTTR	mean time to repair
NA or N/A	not available
NAP	network access point
NAPT	network address port translation
NAS	network access server
NAT	network address translation
NBMA	non-broadcast multiple access
NFS	network file server
NHRP	Next-Hop Resolution Protocol
NIC	network interface card
NM	network management
NMS	network management system
NOC	network operations center
NOS	network operating system
NR	network requirement
OAM	operations, administration, and maintenance
OAM&P	OAM and provisioning
OCx	optical carrier ($x = 1, 3, 12, 24, 48, 192$)
OLTP	online transaction processing
ORR	operational readiness review
OS	operating system

OSPF	Open Shortest Path First routing protocol
OSI	open systems interconnect
OSS	operations support system
P	peering
PADI	PPPoE active discovery initiation
PADO	PPPoE active discovery offer
PADR	PPPoE active discovery request
PADS	PPPoE active discovery session
PAP	Password Authentication Protocol
PC	personal computer
PDA	personal digital assistant
PDP	policy decision point
PDR	peak data rate; preliminary design review
PEP	policy enforcement point
PING	packet Internet groper
PKI	public key infrastructure
PM	program management
POH	path overhead
PoP	point of presence
PoS	packet over SONET; point of sale
POTS	plain-old telephone service
PP	patch panel
PPP	Point-to-Point Protocol
PPPoE	PPP over Ethernet
PPTP	Point-to-Point Tunneling Protocol
QoS	quality of service

R&D	research and development
RA	route aggregation
RADIUS	remote access dial-in user service
RBD	reliability block diagram
RC	rate critical
RED	random early detect
RF	route filter
RFC	request for comments
RFI	request for information
RFP	request for proposal
RFQ	request for quote
RIP	Routing Information Protocol
RMA	reliability, maintainability, and availability
RMON	remote monitoring
RO	read only
RPV	remotely piloted vehicle
RSA	Rivest-Shamir-Adleman
RSVP	Resource Reservation Protocol
RT	real time
RW	read/write
s	seconds
SA	systems administrator
SAN	storage area network
SAR	segmentation and reassembly
SCM	supply chain management
SCSI	small computer system interface
SDR	sustained data rate

SHA	secure hash algorithm
SIP	Session Initiation Protocol
SLA	service-level agreement
SLAPM	SLA performance metrics
SMDS	switched multimegabit data service
SMON	switch monitoring
SMS	special multicast server, subscriber management system
SNMP	Simple Network Management Protocol
SOH	section overhead
SONET	synchronous optical network
SPE	SONET payload envelope
SSH	secure shell
SSL	secure sockets library
ST	stochastic
SW or S/W	software
TCP	Transmission Control Protocol
T&I	test and integration
TFTP	Trivial File Transfer Protocol
ToS	type of service
UBR	unspecified bit rate
UI	user interface
UID	user ID
UPS	uninterruptible power supply
USM	user-based security model
VBR	variable bit rate
VLAN	virtual LAN

VLSM	variable-length subnet mask
VoIP	voice over IP
VPN	virtual private network
VRML	Virtual Reality Markup Language
WAN	wide area network
WDM	wavelength division multiplexing
WFQ	weighted fair queuing
WG	workgroup
WRED	weighted random early detect
xSP	(various) service provider

Index

Page numbers followed by "f" denote figures